THE LIMITS OF LAW

The Amherst Series in Law, Jurisprudence, and Social Thought

EDITED BY
Austin Sarat, Lawrence Douglas, and Martha Merrill Umphrey

The Limits of Law

Edited by

AUSTIN SARAT

LAWRENCE DOUGLAS

MARTHA MERRILL UMPHREY

STANFORD UNIVERSITY PRESS

Stanford, California, 2005

58604862

Stanford University Press
Stanford, California
© 2005 by the Board of Trustees of the
Leland Stanford Junior University

Library of Congress Cataloging-in-Publication Data

The limits of law / Edited by Austin Sarat, Lawrence Douglas, Martha Merrill Umphrey.
    p.   cm. — (Amherst series in law, jurisprudence, and social thought)
    Includes bibliographical references and index.
    ISBN 0-8047-5235-4 (alk. paper)
    1. Justice. 1. Justice and politics. 3. Restorative justice. I. Sarat, Austin. II. Douglas, Lawrence. III. Umphrey, Martha Merrill. IV. Series.
    K238.L56   2005
    340'.11—dc22   2005007944

This book is printed on acid-free, archival-quality paper

Original printing 2005

Last figure below indicates year of this printing:
14   13   12   11   10   09   08   07   06   05

Designed and typeset at Stanford University Press in 10/14.5 Minion

To Benjamin (AS)
For Jacob and Milo (LD)

Acknowledgments

We are grateful to our colleagues David Delaney, Nasser Hussain, and Thomas R. Kearns for helping us think about the limits of law and for their help in shaping the ideas that inform this book. We thank our students in Amherst College's Department of Law, Jurisprudence, and Social Thought for their interest in the issues addressed in *The Limits of Law*. Finally, we would like to express special appreciation to the Amherst College Faculty Lecture Committee for its generous financial support.

Contents

Contributors

LAURA DICKINSON is Associate Professor at the University of Connecticut School of Law

LAWRENCE DOUGLAS is Professor of Law, Jurisprudence, and Social Thought at Amherst College

DAVID DYZENHAUS is Professor of Law and Professor of Philosophy at the University of Toronto

BONNIE HONIG is Professor of Political Science at Northwestern University and Senior Research Fellow at the American Bar Foundation

AUSTIN SARAT is the William Nelson Cromwell Professor of Jurisprudence and Political Science and Professor of Law, Jurisprudence, and Social Thought at Amherst College

ADAM SITZE is Assistant Professor of Law, Jurisprudence, and Social Thought at Amherst College

JOHN TORPEY is Professor of Sociology at the CUNY Graduate Center

MARTHA MERRILL UMPHREY is Associate Professor of Law, Jurisprudence, and Social Thought at Amherst College

ROBIN WAGNER-PACIFICI is Professor of Sociology at Swarthmore College

THE LIMITS OF LAW

At the Limits of Law:
An Introduction

LAWRENCE DOUGLAS

AUSTIN SARAT

MARTHA MERRILL UMPHREY

To speak of limits is to conjure images of edges, boundaries, borders—spectral areas at the periphery, the margin, the extremity. It seems paradoxical, then, that the study of law's limits has always occupied a spot close to the heart of legal scholarship. Other disciplines—religious studies, economics, literary analysis—betray no such deep preoccupation with boundary questions. How, then, can we explain what looks like an anomaly, if not a morbidity of legal scholarship: its fixation on the question of limits, a subject of inquiry which, as the essays gathered in the volume make clear, remains the source of urgent, vital, and creative work?

To answer this question, we need to identify the different meanings of the concept of limits as it applies to theories of law. If, as Lon Fuller puts it, law is the "enterprise of subjecting human conduct to the governance of rules," the subject before us seeks to characterize and theorize the limits to this rules-based control of human actions.[1] That such limits exist cannot be denied; the case of prohibition remains a famous failure to regulate human behavior by law. Moreover, it is commonplace to assert that law can only concern itself with external conduct, not inner feeling.[2] The only time motive, intentions, and feelings are of concern to the law is when they manifest themselves in some course of visible conduct or behavior; otherwise, people are free to feel and think what they please. Scholars often confuse this position with the notion of liberal tolerance or with some variety of Mill's canonical harm principle, though, in fact, it is simply a statement of law's practical limits.[3] The law does not concern itself with internal states for the simple reason that it cannot—such states remain beyond its grasp. Some legal systems might choose to punish mental states when they manifest themselves in the intention to commit a violent act; others might choose to punish them when they express themselves in a lyric poem. Pure "thought crimes," however, remain an Orwellian fantasy—not because it's impossible to imagine a legal system that would like to punish thoughts, but because thoughts remain beyond the limits of legal control.

Just as thoughts have been considered to lie beyond law's control, so too have impersonal systems. Classical Marxist critiques branded law as a mere epiphenomenon, a superstructural artifice capable of rationalizing class interests, but incapable of stabilizing the contradictions inherent in the capitalist mode of production.[4] This critique, which has found new life in some of the more strident jeremiads against globalization, received a more satisfying elaboration in the work of neo-Marxists, who treated law as an ideological apparatus capable of operating semiautonomously from the classes on whose behalf—and at whose behest—it was thought to function.[5] The neo-Marxist critique of law, in turn, exerted a powerful influence upon a broad range of legal scholars—liberals, feminists, scholars of Critical Legal Studies—concerned with exploring the limits of law as a tool of social change.[6]

This concern, as of late, has been the particular focus of scholars of transitional justice.[7] The collapse of the Soviet empire; the dismantling of the apartheid regime in South Africa; the creation of fledgling democratic states in South America; the acceptance of the free market by China—all these developments explain why transitional justice has emerged as a vital subject of inquiry among legal scholars today, particularly those concerned with exploring law's limits. It is no surprise, then, that the contributors to this volume are all concerned with issues of transition—the moment when combat ceases in the gesture of surrender; the act of conferring amnesty upon a former adversary; the process of protecting rights during states of emergency, *inter alia*. And they share a common focus in examining what happens to law in these moments: how law is stretched and frayed, but also reconstituted and reinvigorated by contact with its own limiting conditions.

Descriptive and Empirical Limits

To say that law cannot control the thoughts of humans; that it cannot overcome market contradictions; that legislation cannot eliminate racism; or that a constitution cannot, by itself, remake a political culture—this is to speak of the practical or empirical limits of law. A discussion of these descriptive limits is the most common focus of studies of law's limits, a subject that—as the essays collected in this volume make clear—has been importantly reinvigorated in the wake of the events of 9/11. Much of this recent work has focused on procedure and prevention, as scholars, legal officials, and government actors have debated whether the law is capable of shielding us from the threats posed by terrorists. Can we afford to provide terrorists with the kind of procedural protections that our Constitution extends to the ordinary defendant in a criminal proceeding, or must these protections be relaxed—or abandoned altogether—when dealing with those accused of plotting or perpetrating spectacular crimes? Must the rules that limit the government's power to intrude on personal space and property be modified or ignored to facilitate the kind of fact-finding and evidence-gathering needed to confront the terrorist threat? Are even the most foundational limits on the power of government—such as the person's right to be free of bodily torture—luxuries that need to be curtailed in an age of "holy terror"?

These questions have unleashed a fierce debate within the legal community. Some insist that present procedures are more than sufficient to respond to terrorist threats and thus require no fine-tuning.[8] Alan Dershowitz, by contrast, has argued in favor of relaxing bars against torture, and for placing its use under judicial oversight in order to check the occasions and scope of its use (better that, he argues, than leaving it entirely to the whimsy of, say, special military interrogators).[9] Others still, such as Ruth Wedgwood, believe that the successful fight against terrorism must be waged on a terrain beyond law's conventional application. The attempt to bring the fight against terrorism within law's vigilant oversight, will, Wedgwood argues, yield marginal benefits in terms of fighting terrorism, yet will erode the guarantees that protect ordinary citizens.[10] Finally, there are those, like Michael Ignatieff and Michael Glennon, who believe that both civil libertarians and national security defenders must embrace a more realistic understanding of the inevitable costs of their respective positions and thus seek out fair-minded and balanced compromises.[11]

Notwithstanding the differences between these various viewpoints, they all share certain family resemblances. First, they all work from the assumption that law does have certain limits; that these limits are capable of being identified and described; and that these limits are, in certain critical respects, flexible. Finally, for the purposes of bringing the fight to global terrorism, the relevant limits of law are procedural or means-oriented—they describe the outer bounds of the power of states to surveil, detain, and prosecute terrorists.

Another set of descriptive limits—also mentioned in connection with the global fight against terrorism and of relevance to Laura Dickinson's essay in this book—can be described as more foundational or structural in nature. Sixty years ago, at the time of the Nuremberg trial before the International Military Tribunal, Hannah Arendt observed:

> The Nazi crimes, it seems to me, explode the limits of law; and that is precisely what constitutes their monstrousness. For these crimes, no punishment is severe enough. It may well be essential to hang Göring, but it is totally inadequate. That is, this guilt, in contrast to all criminal guilt, oversteps and shatters any and all legal systems. That is the reason why the Nazis in Nuremberg are so smug. . . . We are simply not equipped to deal, on a human, political level, with a guilt that is beyond crime.[12]

Although Arendt's claim remains somewhat opaque—she never specifies exactly *how* Nazi crimes "explode the limits of law"—it has been widely cited as giving voice to a critical insight regarding the limited capacity of law to respond to horrific crimes, specifically when it comes to the question of shaping an adequate punishment. The two most common justifications for punishing criminals—deterrence and retribution—seem oddly weak if not irrelevant when it comes to dealing with mass crimes. It is hard to imagine any architect of genocide or would-be suicide bomber being deterred by any legal sanction, even the most extreme. Likewise, if the notion of retribution contemplates a legal evening of the scales, it seems that no amount of juridically authorized violence could ever balance out the burden of genocide or mass atrocities. Legal responses to mass crimes are, then, at best symbolic gestures—and, if we accept Arendt's observation, they symbolize little besides their own impotence.

Robert Jackson, who took an unprecedented leave from his post on the Supreme Court to head the prosecution at Nuremberg, was likewise sensitive to the question of law's structural limits as they apply to mass crimes. At the beginning of his address to the International Military Tribunal, Jackson observed: "The commonsense of mankind demands that law shall not stop with the punishment of petty crimes by little people. It must also reach men who possess themselves of great power and make deliberate and concerted use of it to set in motion evils which leave no home in the world untouched."[13] Jackson returned to this theme at the conclusion of his opening statement: "Civilization asks whether law is so laggard as to be utterly helpless to deal with crimes of this magnitude by criminals of this order of importance."[14] It would be grotesque, Jackson suggests, to hold that law is adequate to the task of condemning the isolated killer but powerless to respond to the perpetrator of genocide. Such atrocities *must* avail themselves of legal response; to think otherwise is to make a travesty of the idea of submitting human conduct to the rule of law.

For our purposes, it is not critical to take sides in the debate between Arendt and Jackson. Rather, it suffices to note that both agree that mass atrocities—such as genocide, crimes against humanity, or acts of global terrorism—pose unique challenges to the rule of law and usher law toward the frontier of its substantive efficacy.

This debate about the structural limits of law in dealing with macro phenomema finds an interesting corollary in debates about law's control of micro relationships. Scholars such as Robert Ellickson, Peter Yeager, and Neil Komesar have argued that when it comes to regulating small phenomena— say, the behavior of neighbors arguing over a nuisance, or land rights, or the allocation of resources—the law serves as a particularly inefficient tool of control.[15] Here it is argued that private parties left to their own devices will arrive at more efficient and equitable solutions to debates over property use than can be achieved through legal means. This, of course, suggests a somewhat different notion of limits; for these scholars, the question is less whether such behavior can be controlled by law at all, than whether it can be controlled *efficiently*. Yet if some scholars contend that the underlying goal of law *is* efficiency, then the difference really is quite minimal. Moreover, if we combine the challenges that macro and micro phenomena pose to rule-ordered legality, we are left with a distinctly Newtonian vision of the mechanics of law: more than capable of controlling the "medium range" of human conduct, but frayed by its contact with extraordinarily large and exceedingly small challenges to rule-bound existence.

Prescriptive, Normative, Moral Limits

The analogy between the laws controlling human conduct and those describing the natural world has, however, its own limits. This is because the latter are descriptive and explanatory, while the laws that govern human conduct are ineluctably prescriptive and normative. The prescriptive nature of law thus raises its own specialized questions—are there distinctly normative limits to the laws that govern human conduct?

This inquiry raises certain immediate complications. First, it is often difficult conceptually to distinguish between descriptive and prescriptive limits. Recall our brief review of the debates concerning the efficacy of law as a tool for fighting global terrorism. There we encountered the argument that law is of limited utility inasmuch as it places undue restrictions upon the government's power to surveil and detain. But how do we characterize the limitations that, for example, the Constitution places on the government? Are these descriptive limits or normative ones? Obviously constitutional principles are prescriptive—they are based upon a vision of how the government should act and of the appropriate reaches of government action. And yet these principles are not simply expressive or declarative. Grounded in doctrine and enforced by executive power, these principles describe the real-world boundaries of the power of the state. The state *cannot* overstep these bounds because, as a polity, we have decided that it *should not*. The fact that they can be changed or modified does not alter the reality of their descriptive force. And so questions of descriptive and normative limits find themselves inextricably tied.

A study of law's prescriptive limits is further, and perhaps ruinously, complicated by the fact that one's position on the question depends crucially on one's very definition of law itself. Classical natural law theory, for example, is predicated upon the idea that law has normative limits.[16] When Locke writes in *Two Treatises of Government* that "the Legislative, or Surpream [*sic*] Authority, cannot assume to its self a power to Rule by extemporary Arbitrary Decrees," he means this quite literally—that such arbitrary rule can no longer claim to be lawful.[17] Morality thus places limits upon legality; commands—even those which issue from the somewhat paradoxically named "supreme authority"—are not law if they violate fundamental moral principles.

This, of course, is the position that John Austin famously described as "stark nonsense."[18] "The most pernicious laws," Austin observed, "and therefore those which are most opposed to the will of good, have been and are continually enforced as laws by judicial tribunals."[19] For legal positivists—at least those subscribing to Austin's strict and influential adumbration—it makes no sense to speak of prescriptive limits to law. Morality may provide a guide to lawmakers. It may provide a set of limits that most citizens would like lawmakers to respect. To insist, however, that the *validity* of a law can be measured by its conformance to moral principle makes no sense. Put another way, the legal positivist insists that the only meaningful limits upon law are descriptive or empirical.

Austin's attack on the natural law tradition found its corollary in the famous debate between H. L. A. Hart and Lon Fuller that appeared in the pages of the *Harvard Law Review* in 1958 (and the subject of David Dyzenhaus's contribution to the this volume). Though Hart launched a devastating critique of Austin's brand of positivism in *The Concept of Law*,[20] he also vigorously defended the "separation thesis"—the idea that there is no *necessary* connection between law and morality.[21] Fuller, of course, disagreed, insisting that law's inner morality, regardless of its positive content, established limits on what could count as law.[22] Though the terms of this debate remain well known, largely overlooked is the fact that, as in the case of Arendt and Jackson, Fuller's and Hart's understandings of law's limits were shaped by the extraordinary challenge that Nazi crimes posed to principles of liberal legality. The specific issue that gave rise to the famous debate involved the case of the so-called Nazi grudge informer. A soldier in the German Wehrmacht during World War II had complained about the Nazi regime to his wife. The wife—who apparently was involved in a clandestine affair—denounced her husband to the authorities. The husband was then arrested, tried, and convicted under a Nazi law that criminalized such utterances. After the war, the man initiated an "unlawful deprivation of liberty" prosecution against his former wife. The *Landesgericht* (the state appellate court) concluded that the controlling Nazi statutes were "highly iniquitous laws . . . considered to be terror laws by the great majority of the German people," and that the wife should have known that informing against her own spouse "was contrary to the sound conscience and sense of justice of all decent human beings."[23] As a consequence, the court reversed her original acquittal.

Hart famously criticized the ruling of the German appellate court.[24] While acknowledging the odiousness of the wife's behavior, Hart insisted that her conduct was entirely lawful under the reigning Nazi legal system. The only way to criminalize her conduct after the fact, according to Hart, would have been to do so legislatively through the passage of an ex post facto law. Despite the obvious moral problems raised by retrospective law, Hart insists that passing such a statute would have been far preferable to the actual outcome in which a court essentially denied the status of law to a duly enacted, if admittedly perverse, statute.[25]

Fuller also defended the appropriateness of ex post facto law in this case—though for very different reasons. For Fuller, a retrospective law was not needed in order to make "unlawful what was once law"—as it was for Hart. Contra Hart, Fuller was less convinced that the original Nazi statute ever properly constituted law. Thus Fuller insists: "it becomes impossible to dismiss the problems presented by the Nazi regime with a simple assertion: 'Under the Nazis there was law, even if it was bad law.' We have instead to inquire how much of a legal system survived the general debasement and perversion of all forms of social order that occurred under the Nazi rule."[26] Fuller consequently defended the application of a retroactive statute as a means of serving the interests of transitional justice; it would function "as a way of symbolizing a sharp break with the past."[27] It was not, however, necessitated by the logic of ordered legality.

Again, for our purposes it is not necessary to take sides in the famous Hart-Fuller debate—although, as we shall see, David Dyzenhaus convincingly defends Fuller's position. What is clear, however, is that our position concerning the controversy—whether the Nazi statute under which the husband was originally convicted constituted valid law—will depend entirely on our concept of law. Our understanding of law's normative limits is inseparable from our very definition of the law.

Constitutive Limits

Which brings us to the third critical notion of limits as it applies to a study of law—the constitutive. From this perspective, law is constituted by the very idea of limits. At first blush, this claim seems merely to repeat the idea introduced in our quick sketch of the natural law tradition—that is, that human law is constituted by the limitations placed upon it by the laws of nature. All law-bound governance is by its very nature limited, a proposition made famous by natural law and social contract theorists.

On closer examination, however, the claim that law is constituted by limits does not resolve itself into a restatement of natural law thinking. On the contrary, it repudiates this thinking and demands that we understand the law as a subject defined by limitations that law *defines for itself*. Consider for example the opening lines of an oft-cited essay by Stanley Fish:

> The law wishes to have a formal existence. That means, first of all, that the law does not wish to be absorbed by, or declared subordinate to, some other—nonlegal—structure of concern; the law wishes, in a word, to be distinct, not something else. And second, the law wishes in its distinctness to be perspicuous; that is, it desires that the components of its autonomous existence be self-declaring.[28]

One might rightly object to Fish's reification of the law, and his failure to specify why the law "wishes" to have a formal existence. Still, his point is valuable, as it reminds us that law, as a discourse and system of rules, defines itself in terms of its formal separation from other fields and systems, such as politics, economics, and philosophy. Far from being imperial, law aspires to insularity, to closing itself off, to establishing boundaries, delineations, and hermetic enclosures. These limits are not simply means of consolidating legal authority; rather, as Fish suggests, they are the *basis* of law's power.

Some of these rules of self-limitation are familiar, such as laws of jurisdiction. Fashioned internally by the law itself, laws of jurisdiction establish the limits beyond which legal authority cannot extend.[29] Yet at the same time that these laws delimit, they also empower and legitimate. For within the

lines drawn by rules of jurisdiction, a court's authority may be all but ple-
nary. Laws of jurisdiction provide, then, but one example of how law constitutes itself qua law through practices and rituals of self-limitation. Norms
that control the behavior of judges, such as principles of recusal, provide another instance. Judicial review, as exercised by the U.S. Supreme Court, provides a powerful example of a specialized legal practice that legitimates itself
through gestures of self-limitation.[30] More generally, Hart's secondary
rules—the rules at the center of his theory of law—can be understood as
rules created internal to the system that define, limit, and constitute the system.[31]

If we accept that law constitutes and empowers itself through rules of self-
limitation, we begin to realize the inadequacy of characterizing law's limits,
as many scholars have, as simply empirical and/or normative.[32] Consider,
again, laws of jurisdiction: one might be tempted to say that such rules simply provide another example of law's empirical limits. But this formulation is
hardly satisfactory, inasmuch as these "empirical" limits are entirely self-
fashioned by the law. They are "real" limits only to the extent that the law
has made them so. Likewise, it makes little sense to say that such rules are, in
essence, prescriptive or normative. While it is true that they describe how
courts should act, this concept of "shouldness" has been generated entirely
within the system of ordered legality and thus derives its normative force
simply from its status as a legal decree. Not only do these norms have nothing to do with an external system of morality, they aim, as Fish reminds, to
insulate and cabin law from the moral. Morality, at least from the ascendant
positivist model, challenges law's autonomy by threatening to turn law into a
subspecies of ethics. Law resists this challenge through its attempt to constitute itself as a formal, sealed, and delimited system. Morality, obviously, is
not banished from this system. But it also does not control law—it is drawn
in and appropriated according to the formal requirements of law itself.

This observation helps us, then, to answer the question posed at the outset of this introduction, why the question of limits lies at the heart of so
much legal scholarship. The ultimate answer is that law is constituted
through limits. These limits are neither empirical nor prescriptive in nature;
rather, they are the practices that create and effectuate the rule of law
through the peculiar artifice of establishing boundaries and policing borders.

Law confers authority upon itself through these practices. They constitute law, in its own self-understanding, as something other than the naked exercise of power. By staying its power, by limiting its reach and domain, law creates its integrity and efficacy as a system of rules.

The Essays

The essays in this volume examine the different meanings of the limits of law—the descriptive, the normative, and the constitutive. And they do so, as mentioned earlier, by taking as their focus law's relationship to transitional moments and spectral spaces.

Laura Dickinson's contribution, "Terrorism and the Limits of Law: A View from Transitional Justice," examines legal responses to the events of 9/11. Specifically, she challenges the belief, voiced in many circles these days, that law is "inadequate to cope with the current threat." This belief, as we have seen, is anchored in an assessment of law's empirical limits as a tool for fighting terrorism. Dickinson's response can also be seen as descriptive—she insists that by failing "to give sufficient emphasis to the expressive and discursive potential of law," these critics offer an unduly crabbed and pessimistic view of what law can do.

In making this claim, Dickinson turns to recent work on transitional justice, the field that studies law's role as an agent of regime change following episodes of mass atrocity or great social upheaval. Notwithstanding its breadth and diversity, transitional justice scholarship has challenged many received shibboleths concerning the limits of law as a tool for redressing vast systemic injustices. The core claims of this scholarship, in Dickinson's elaboration, include the following insights:

> (1) that transitional justice mechanisms provide a forum for uncovering and airing various conceptions of truth and experience that exist following mass atrocities; (2) that law can help to provide relief to individual victims; (3) that law and legal process fosters the future development of norms even though it may not specifically deter all violations of those norms; (4) that legal processes to address past atrocities support the development of the capacity of the local justice sector; and (5) that justice in these settings may consist of a dialogue among multiple groups.

Of these various "transitional justice mechanisms," the one of greatest interest to Dickinson is the "hybrid tribunal"—an institution that serves as a blend of an international tribunal and a domestic court. Such tribunals, Dickinson argues, are well designed to promote the twin goals of transitional justice—retribution and restoration. More trenchantly, she claims that this device, used successfully in transitional societies such as East Timor and Sierra Leone, could also be employed as a tool for trying terrorists. She convincingly argues that the hybrid tribunal could serve the interests of creating an adequate legal infrastructure in war-ravaged Afghanistan, and could even help promote the perceived justice of convictions if used in the United States. Thus, far from accepting arguments that fret over the limits of law as a tool for responding to terrorism, Dickinson reminds us that in its creative labors, law provides a powerful mechanism for responding to profound social trauma and foundational challenges to social order.

Like Dickinson, John Torpey, in his essay "Legalism and Its Discontents: The Case of Reparations for Black Americans," also examines the uses of the law as a tool for responding to collective trauma. But his focus is not on unfolding traumas in the present; instead, he examines the wisdom and efficacy of employing the law to address historical grievances and wrongs that may be centuries old. In exploring the various controversies swirling around the issue of slave reparations, Torpey's essay situates itself in the larger debate on law's limits in a provocative fashion. For as Torpey points out, the reparations movement can be seen as part of a larger trend toward the juridification of politics—the tendency to turn all political questions into questions of law. Far from speaking to the limits of law, this trend seems to speak to the limits of politics. When politics fail—when political vision is absent and groups are unable to achieve their aims through majoritarian institutions of governance—the law is employed *faute de mieux*. As Torpey points out, this mode of carrying on disputes "privileges lawyers over citizens and courtrooms over more widely accessible sites of debate and deliberation."

Despite the critical tone of this observation, much of Torpey's essay considers the prospects for success of the reparations movement; he examines the various legal strategies and goals of the movement as they might affect the chance of prevailing. Ultimately, however, Torpey's essay raises questions that pertain to matters weightier than the merely tactical or predictive; in the final analysis, the reparations movement—and the larger juridification of politics—poses crucial normative questions about the appropriate uses of law as a tool of redressing past injustices. Are there moral, rather than practical, limits to using the law as a tool for addressing past injustices?

This is the question directly addressed by David Dyzenhaus in his essay "The Dilemma of Legality and the Moral Limits of Law." Like Dickinson, Dyzenhaus is concerned with the topic of transitional justice—"how a country seeking to escape from an unjust past should use law in the attempt both to come to terms with the past and to promote a better future." And like Torpey, Dyzenhaus is, as the title of his essay suggests, ultimately devoted to the question of the normative.

The particular "dilemma of legality" that Dyzenhaus examines is the problem of retroactive law. As Dyzenhaus rightly points out, this problem tends to plague nations in the throes of transitional justice. In cases in which a new, democratic state replaces an authoritarian regime that perpetrated widespread human rights abuses, the question of how the new state should treat the laws of the earlier regime invariably arises. Is it right, for example, to try border guards of the former East Germany for the killing of "wall jumpers" when such shootings were authorized under East German law?[33] Must the democratic state accord full legal effect to the laws of its authoritarian predecessor? Or may the new state deny the status of law—after the fact—to statutes enacted and enforced by its earlier incarnation?

As Dyzenhaus demonstrates, these vexing questions of retroactivity arise in nations other than those commonly identified as transitional. In fact, Dyzenhaus challenges the conventional wisdom that a neat, analytic divide separates transitional nations from more stable societies. As the American experience during the civil rights movement makes clear, all nations, to a greater or lesser degree, can be seen as in the throes of transitional justice. And so to illustrate the problem of retroactivity in transitional societies, Dyzenhaus picks the unlikely example of Canada and the recent legal controversies involving the Chinese Immigration Act. Passed in 1885 and not repealed until 1947, the law required Chinese immigrants to pay a head tax imposed on no other immigrant groups. Recently Chinese Canadians have sued the state to get back the taxes collected under the transparently racist law. These efforts have failed, however, as courts have concluded that the statute constituted "a valid juristic reason" for the collection.

By way of critiquing the courts' decisions, Dyzenhaus returns to the Hart-Fuller debate. As we recall, this debate focused on whether properly enacted commands must be considered law if they violate fundamental principles of morality. Here Dyzenhaus attacks Hart's position, which admits no middle ground between validity or invalidity—statutes "have either all their force or none." Against this position, Dyzenhaus subtly defends the Fullerian position that "a statute should always be understood in terms of the principles constitutive of the authority of law, even if the majority of judges at the time rejected those principles."[40] Like Fuller, then, Dyzenhaus insists that there is "a limit to which legal institutions can be used as the instrument of substantive injustice without a very severe strain on their claim to be legal." Yet in defending the idea of law's normative limits, Dyzenhaus also recognizes that law *itself* sets limits to what can be done in its name. Here the idea of the normative nudges up against the idea of the constitutive.

Robin Wagner-Pacifici's essay, "The Conditions of Surrender: Reconstituting the Limits at Conflict's End," likewise ushers us toward a consideration of law's constitutive limits. At first blush, Wagner-Pacifici's project seems, like Laura Dickinson's, to be devoted to a study of law's empirical limits. Focusing on one emblematic moment of transition—the act of surrender, the cessation of hostilities between warring nations, groups, or factions—Wagner-Pacifici asks, "Where do the fixed rules, the recognized bodies and institutions of law enter the acts of surrender?" In asking this, she wants to learn "where and how" the violence of war passes "the baton to the conventions of law."

Surrender, according to this analysis, is conceptualized as a gap, a void, a space that law cannot enter or control. In its most extreme manifestation, the unconditional surrender, the gesture reveals its paradoxical nature, as the unconditional nature of the terms contemplates the dissolution or "*absence* of any sovereign authority with which it would be possible to negotiate." If the paradox of surrender cannot be solved on its own terms, it can be managed and controlled, and through a fascinating analysis of the ceremonies and exchanges of surrender, Wagner-Pacifici reveals how the way is paved to the reimposition of lawful relations between previously warring parties. These ceremonies and rituals—which commonly enact and demonstrate attitudes of submission, degradation, and recognition—thus serve as powerful examples of the semiotics of politics. As highly staged acts of political theater, rituals of surrender, however, are more than merely symbolic acts. They are complex processes, which, as Wagner-Pacifici reminds us, make possible "the cauterization of violence and the reimposition of lawful relations."

Thus, if Wagner-Pacifici begins her essay by portraying surrender as a space of emptiness and evacuation, by the end she has shown it to be richly and densely furnished with rituals and ceremonies of transaction. More to the point, she has, for our purposes, told a story about something other than law's descriptive limits. Though surrender is, for Wagner-Pacifici, a practice beyond law's control, it is also a ritual through which law is renewed and reconstituted. Following in the tradition of Weber, Benjamin, Derrida, and others who have explored the "aporia of founding,"[34] Wagner-Pacifici ultimately tells a story of jurisgenesis—how legal force is forged out of the crucible of lawless violence. An analysis of an exemplary case of law's limits thus resolves itself into a story of the provocative constitution of the legal.

Similarly, Bonnie Honig's essay, "Bound by Law? Alien Rights, Administrative Discretion and the Politics of Technicality: Lessons from Louis Post and the First Red Scare," also challenges the stability of the distinction between law's descriptive and constitutive limits. Like Dickinson, Dyzenhaus, and Wagner-Pacifici, Honig is concerned with a moment of constitutional extremis—the state of emergency. The state of emergency stands, for many political and legal theorists, as the archetypical instance of the exceptional—the condition "in which ordinary law is legally suspended and sovereign power operates unfettered, by way of decision." On the most obvious level, the state of emergency appears to describe an empirical limit of law, though here the distinction between the empirical and definitional blurs. In Schmitt's writing, for example, the state of emergency does not simply provide an occasion for sovereign "decisionism"; rather, it is defined as such by the exercise of unbridled sovereign prerogative.

But the idea of normative limits also plays a role in Honig's essay. For she points out that the exercise of discretionary executive power is never uncontroversial as legal actors and civil libertarians struggle to "rejudicialize the terrain in question," a process very much in evidence in recent court challenges to the detaining of alleged enemy combatants in Guantanamo Bay. Classically, then, the struggle over emergency powers has been conceptualized as a struggle over extra-legal executive decisionism versus rule-bound judicial authority.

Unlike Dickinson, however, Honig examines the terms of this struggle not by looking at the ongoing war against terrorism, but by turning back to the First Red Scare that followed close on the heels of the armistice that ended the First World War. In 1919, a wave of terrorist bombings spread panic through the United States; as a result, the Justice Department sought to deport thousands of immigrants without any legal process. Honig focuses on the experience of one government official, Louis Post, who was at the time the assistant secretary of labor and resisted the Justice Department's arbitrary actions. Honig shows how Post worked to "whittle away at the category of deportability" by proceduralizing the act of deportation and submitting it to constitutional scrutiny.[48] What is fascinating in Honig's discussion, however, is her claim that Post was *not* constitutionally or legally bound to apply these processes and norms. On the contrary, Honig insists that Post's actions were themselves somewhat arbitrary. Hardly compelled by the rule of law, Post strategically exercised administrative discretion. In this case, Post's discretionary action was to submit to the rule of law; still, inasmuch as this submission was willfully chosen and not legally compelled, Post essentially engaged in the very decisionistic practices that aroused the ire of civil libertarians like himself.

Honig's fascinating discussion thus reveals the insufficiencies of characterizing the clash over emergency powers as one between executive discretion and rule-bound authority. As in the case of surrender, the exercise of emergency powers cannot simply be tamed by the reimposition of law. Rather, as the case of Post makes clear, in the spectral space of emergency, law is complexly reconstituted by the decision of the executive actor to bind his own authority. Post did not submit to the rule of law; he reconstituted it through his own discretionary act.

The final essay in the collection, Adam Sitze's "At the Mercy Of," is likewise devoted to exploring law's constitutive limits. For Sitze, however, the outer empirical and definitional limits of the law are not defined, as they are for Honig, by the exercise of emergency powers. Rather, for Sitze, "the exemplary form of the sovereign exception" is the power to pardon and grant amnesty; law's limits are defined by the act of granting forgiveness. (And here we are reminded of the remarkable scene in Steven Spielberg's *Schindler's List* in which Oskar Schindler attempts to convince Amon Goeth, the sociopathic commandant of the Plaszow labor camp, that mercy is the surest expression of power.)

Like Dyzenhaus's, Sitze's essay operates on the register of theory, though his methodology is strictly interpretive. Through a close reading of Kierkegaard's notion of forgiveness, he circles back to the idea of amnesty, examining it as the limit where the law becomes itself by becoming other than itself. Thus echoing Wagner-Pacifici's study of surrender and Honig's discussion of exception, Sitze understands amnesty as a practice that at once stands exterior to, yet is constitutive of, law. Here Sitze reads Arendt through the filter of his earlier treatment of Kierkegaard. As the exemplary form of sovereign exception, the power of forgiveness can be seen as the "ground of totalitarian power." Consequently, for Arendt, forgiveness cannot be forgiven; it stands as the ultimate repudiation of judgment, law, and memory. Yet forgiveness is also, for Arendt, a "mode of natality," *the* act that "enables human beings to dismiss the irreversible effects of past deeds," and so to constitute new law.[51] At the heart of the aporia of founding thus lurks the paradox of forgiveness—at once beyond law, yet making possible the conditions of its natality.

Acts of terror, states of emergency, gestures of surrender, payments of reparations, offers of amnesty, and invocations of retroactivity—these are the limiting conditions explored in the essays in this volume. As befits a collection devoted to exploring law's limits, the essays are concerned with states of exception and moments of transition. But the stories they tell are not simply about law's exhaustion, impotence, or failure. Instead, these essays ultimately are studies of complex renewal and regeneration. They tell how law is challenged, frayed, and constituted out of contact with conditions that lie at the farthest reaches of its empirical and normative force.

Notes

1. Lon L. Fuller, *The Morality of Law* (New Haven, CT: Yale University Press, 1964), 74.

2. See, for example, Hermann Kantorowicz, *The Definition of Law* (Cambridge: Cambridge University Press), 41–51.

3. Kantorowicz, *The Definition of Law*, 49.

4. See, for example, Hugh Collins, *Marxism and Law* (Oxford: Oxford University Press, 1982).

5. See, for example, E. P. Thompson, *Whigs and Hunters: Origins of the Black Act* (New York: Penguin Books, 1977); and Roberto Mangabeira Unger, *Law in Modern Society: Toward a Criticism of Social Theory* (New York: The Free Press, 1976).

6. See, for example, Roberto Mangabeira Unger, *The Critical Legal Studies Movement* (Cambridge: Harvard University Press, 1986); and Mark Kelman, *A Guide to Critical Legal Studies* (Cambridge: Harvard University Press, 1987).

7. See, for example, Martha Minow, *Between Vengeance and Forgiveness: Facing History after Genocide and Mass Violence* (Boston: Beacon Press, 1998); Ruti Teitel, *Transitional Justice* (New York: Oxford University Press, 2000); and Steven R. Ratner and Jason S. Abrams, *Accountability for Human Rights Atrocities in International Law* (Oxford: Oxford University Press, 2001).

8. Kenneth Roth, "The Law of War in the War on Terror," *Foreign Affairs* 83, no. 1 (January/February 2004).

9. Alan M. Dershowitz, *Why Terrorism Works: Understanding the Threat, Responding to the Challenge* (New Haven, CT: Yale University Press, 2002), 131–63.

10. Ruth Wedgwood, "Al Qaeda, Terrorism and Military Commissions," *American Journal of International Law* 96, no 2 (April 2002): 328–37; "The Law's Response to September 11," *Ethics and Foreign Affairs* 16, no. 1 (April 2002): 8–15.

11. Michael Ignatieff, *The Lesser Evil: Political Ethics in an Age of Terror* (Edinburgh: University of Edinburgh Press, 2003); Michael J. Glennon, "Terrorism and the Limits of Law," *Wilson Quarterly* (Spring 2002): 12–19.

12. *Hannah Arendt-Karl Jaspers Correspondence 1926–1969*, ed. Lotte Kohler and Hans Saner, trans. Robert Kimber and Rita Kimber (New York: Harcourt Brace and Jovanovich, 1992), 54 (footnote omitted).

13. *Trial of the Major War Criminals before the International Military Tribunal* (hereafter *IMT*) (Nuremberg: International Military Tribunal, 1947), v. I, 98.

14. *IMT* v. I, 155.

15. Robert C. Ellickson, *Order Without Law: How Neighbors Settle Disputes* (Cambridge: Harvard University Press, 1991); Peter Yeager, *The Limits of Law: The Public Regulation of Private Pollution* (Cambridge: Cambridge University Press, 1991); and

Neil K. Komesar, *Law's Limits: The Rule of Law and the Supply and Demand of Rights* (Cambridge: Cambridge University Press, 2001).

16. See, for example, John Finnis, *Natural Law and Natural Rights* (Oxford: Clarendon Press, 1980).

17. John Locke, *Two Treatises of Government* (Cambridge: Cambridge University Press, 1988), 358.

18. John Austin, *The Province of Jurisprudence Determined* (Cambridge: Cambridge University Press, 1995), 77.

19. Ibid.

20. H. L. A. Hart, *The Concept of Law* (Oxford: Clarendon Press, 1988), 18–25.

21. H. L. A. Hart, "Positivism and the Separation of Law and Morals," reproduced in H. L. A. Hart, *Essays in Jurisprudence and Philosophy* (Oxford: Clarendon Press, 1983).

22. Fuller, *The Morality of Law*, 33–94.

23. Quoted in H. O. Pappe, "On the Validity of Judicial Decisions in the Nazi Era," 23 *Modern Law Review* 260 (1960): 263.

24. Both Hart and Fuller relied on an account of the case presented in volume 64 of the *Harvard Law Review*. This account suggested that the *Landesgericht* had held that the Nazi statutes could not be truly considered law. As Pappe, however, has shown, this was a misstatement of the ruling of the *Landesgericht*. See Pappe, "On the Validity of Judicial Decisions in the Nazi Era," and Ian McLeod, *Legal Theory* (London: Palgrave Macmillan, 2003), 25.

25. Hart, "Positivism and the Separation of Morals," 76.

26. Lon L. Fuller, "Positivism and Fidelity to Law: A Reply to Professor Hart," 71 *Harvard Law Review* 630 (1958): 646.

27. Fuller, 71 *Harvard Law Review* 630, at 661.

28. Stanley Fish, "The Law Wishes to Have a Formal Existence," in *The Fate of Law*, ed. Austin Sarat and Thomas R. Kearns (Ann Arbor: University of Michigan Press, 1991). Fish's hermeneutic-interpretive description of law as a self-defining system finds elaboration in the work of systems theorists. See, for example, Gunther Teubner, *Law as an Autopoietic System,* Anne Bankowska and Ruth Adler, trans. (Oxford: Blackwell 1993); and Niklas Luhmann, *Law as Social System*, ed. Richard Nobles et al. (Oxford: Oxford University Press, 2004).

29. See, for example, Luc Reydams, *Universal Jurisdiction: International and Municipal Legal Perspectives* (Oxford: Oxford University Press, 2003).

30. See, for example, Lawrence Douglas, "Constitutional Discourse and Its Discontents," in *The Rhetoric of Law*, ed. Austin Sarat and Thomas R. Kearns (Ann Arbor: University of Michigan Press, 1994).

31. Hart, *The Concept of Law*, particularly 77–96.

32. This is the case, for the essays collected in J. Roland Pennock and John W. Chapman, eds. *The Limits of Law* (New York: Lieber-Atherton, 1974).

33. See, for example, Rudolf Geiger, "The German Border Guard Cases and International Human Rights," 9 *European Journal of International Law* (1998): 540–49.

34. See, for example, Jacques Derrida, "Force of Law: The 'Mystical Foundation of Authority,'" in *Deconstruction and the Possibility of Justice*, ed. Drucilla Cornell, Michael Rosenfeld, and David Gray Carlson (New York: Routledge, 1992).

Terrorism and the Limits of Law:
A View from Transitional Justice

LAURA DICKINSON

The attacks on the World Trade Center and Pentagon on September 11, 2001, have ignited a debate about the role of law and its limits in combating terrorism. Although questions about law's efficacy in times of crisis have often served as a source of discussion, the sheer magnitude of the attacks and the enormous scope of the devastation they wrought have changed the tone of the debate and given it a new urgency. Policymakers and scholars alike have charged that existing laws and institutions, both domestic and international, are inadequate to cope with the current threat.

Amid the tumult of debate, at least three distinct "limits of law" arguments can be discerned. These arguments are not mutually exclusive, and sometimes one person might take two or all three of these perspectives. Yet, by identifying the types of argument, we may be able to see how best to frame a response.

The first, which might be described as the neo-Hobbesian or neo-realist view, emphasizes a minimalist understanding of law as only that which is linked to the sovereign power necessary for ensuring safety. According to this view, in times of crisis obedience to rules of fair procedure or international human rights must be limited because such rules impede efforts to track down, capture, and punish terrorists. Moreover, even if law rooted in sovereign power is unlimited *within* the state, a war of all against all with few (if any) legal restraints ought to apply in the international sphere. Thus, this view reflects a resurgence of what is often called an international relations realist approach to international law: according to this approach, power politics, rather than international law, guides and constrains the behavior of states.[1]

Many in the George W. Bush administration and in Congress appear to have adopted this view, which is reflected in the administration's rejection of numerous international treaty regimes such as the Anti-Ballistic Missile Treaty, the Kyoto Accord, and the International Criminal Court, as well as the promotion of a national security policy, powered by American military muscle, that advocates pre-emptive strikes outside the existing U.N. peace and security framework, contemplates the pre-emptive use of nuclear, biological, and chemical weapons, and asserts that neither domestic constitutional principles nor international human rights and humanitarian standards ought to limit efforts to capture and interrogate terrorists overseas. For example, despite the fact that the United States has ratified the Convention Against Torture, some administration officials have taken the position that terrorism suspects apprehended overseas could be subjected to treatment by U.S. actors that might qualify as torture, or turned over to countries known to practice torture.[2] Those advocating this approach have justified it as necessary to promote security. Law must bend or fall or change in order to eliminate the terrorist threat.

The neo-Hobbesian view has not been confined to the international sphere, however. The administration and its allies in Congress have enacted sweeping new limits on civil liberties[3] and the creation of the vast new Homeland Security Department, part of the largest government reorganization since World War II, to expand and improve executive authority to fight terrorism. Moreover, some have gone beyond advocacy of legislative reform and have taken the view that the Constitution should be interpreted flexibly to allow for greater limitations in times of severe threats to national security. For example, some administration lawyers have contended that as commander-in-chief, the president has the inherent constitutional authority to allow torture of enemy combatants during wartime, even if interrogation tactics clearly violate domestic legislation implementing the Convention Against Torture.[4] Similarly, Alan Dershowitz has argued that authorities should be allowed to torture terrorism suspects—even those within the United States—to obtain information that might thwart future attacks.[5]

Some might argue that this jettisoning of domestic civil liberties is not truly a "limits of law" view because it still relies upon statutes and interpretations of the Constitution. Thus, this might be a view not about the limits of *law* but the limits of *civil liberties.* Nevertheless, the extent of the refashioning of previously accepted legal rules is so sweeping that it borders on an abandonment of legal process altogether for certain categories of persons and certain categories of offenses. For example, the administration has argued that even a U.S. citizen cannot claim minimal constitutional rights such as the right to counsel, the right to be charged with an offense, the right to be brought before a judge promptly upon being detained, or the right even to be tried at all, once the executive branch has determined that the citizen is an "enemy combatant."[6] Indeed, the administration has gone so far as to argue that U.S. courts must essentially defer to the administration's determinations regarding who qualifies as an enemy combatant.[7] Despite the fact that the U.S. Supreme Court has now rejected this view,[8] many such persons have been held for years as of the writing of this essay, and the administration still has offered no timeframe for their trial or release.[9] The administration's position therefore seems to imply that the American tradition of legal process itself must be limited in times of crisis and replaced with a greater deference to the prerogatives of executive power.

A second argument focusing on the limits of law might be termed the neo-moralist view. This perspective, which has many adherents both inside and outside the Bush administration, urges the suspension of existing legal frameworks in order to fight terrorism not merely because terrorists threaten peace and security, but because there is a moral urgency to the project of ridding the world of them. President Bush has made many assertions along these lines, presenting the fight against terrorism as a moral, and perhaps even a religious, crusade.[10] Even some liberal critics of the administration have made similar arguments, suggesting that combating terrorism is a morally grounded human rights imperative.[11]

This neo-moralist view sees certain existing laws as impeding the prosecution of a morally just war on terrorism and implies that, to the extent that such laws stand in the way, morality requires them to fall. Moreover, while one could imagine such a critique being grounded in a vision of a transcendent legal framework, such as natural law, the neo-moralist vision I describe seems rarely to use the framework of law at all. For example, in the discussion about military intervention in Iraq, the administration eschewed even the justifications offered by the British: that an emerging norm of international law justified "humanitarian intervention" in Iraq, as it did in Kosovo, even without U.N. Security Council approval, because Saddam Hussein had committed such widespread atrocities.[12] Instead the United States argued that the war was justified despite Security Council inaction because morality demands action, regardless of the strictures of the U.N. peace and security framework (which generally requires Security Council authorization before a state may attack another). To be sure, this argument was framed in terms of security: military action was justified, many argued, because Hussein's regime posed a serious security threat. Yet this argument had a moralistic overlay, and the security concerns may have been largely pretextual and built on unreliable or forged evidence.[13] In short, the primary justification for the military intervention was the "evil" nature of Hussein and his regime.

A third perspective, which we might call the neo-Arendtian view, contends that the categories and institutions of law simply cannot cope with atrocities of a certain magnitude. This view finds its roots in a comment Hannah Arendt made to Karl Jaspers about the Nazi trials at Nuremberg, that for Nazi crimes "no punishment is severe enough" because such crimes "explode the limits of the law."[14] Years later, Arendt called this the problem of "radical evil."[15] Since then, many have critiqued legal means to combat atrocity on these grounds.[16] For example, some have argued that the international criminal tribunals for the former Yugoslavia and Rwanda represent impossible and misguided attempts to cabin unimaginable horrors into seemingly manageable legal categories, leading to absurd results and perhaps even a false sense of accomplishment, a naïve triumphalism about the power of the "rule of law" that has impeded more direct and overt efforts to halt atrocity.[17] Similar beliefs may animate attitudes toward those captured in Afghanistan and the United States after the terrorist attacks of September 11, 2001. Such attacks, so the thinking goes, are sufficiently immense that legal process is simply not the appropriate response.[18] Using the language of law and of criminal trials to address these crimes may not do justice to the magnitude of such crimes and may give a false sense that the law can contain them, either retrospectively or prospectively.

It seems to me that these three perspectives have an unduly limited vision of law's potential. The first two emphasize only law's immediate instrumental role. To the neo-Hobbesian, law stands largely in the way of getting the job done. If the goal is to catch terrorists and prevent future terrorist acts, existing law serves as an impediment and must be reformed to better promote that goal. Legal restraints hinder executive action to track down and punish terrorists. Legal sanctions for terrorists—in the form of criminal trials and punishments—appear puny and insufficient, and therefore cannot be an important mechanism to deter terrorists. The neo-moralists, though framing their ultimate rationale in different terms, similarly see law as an impediment when a serious need occurs and important results are sought. The neo-Arendtian critique does not see law solely in instrumental terms, but it focuses on the inability of law to provide a commensurate response to atrocity, thereby limiting law's ability to prevent future evil.

All of these approaches, however, fail to give sufficient emphasis to the expressive and discursive potential of law over time. This may be because all three views also take an unduly limited view of terrorism, seeing it either as an act of war or an act of evil. But terrorism is also an expressive act.[19] Indeed, terrorism gains its power through representation. Terrorists seek to instill fear and gain notoriety through the symbolic power of their actions, discussed and displayed in the popular press and media. They attempt to tap into symbols and signs in order to give their acts meaning and power.

Thus, we need to focus on legal rules and institutions not merely as the facilitators or impediments to immediate action, but as important sites for societal discourse. Law both reflects and creates social meanings. As sociolegal scholars have long noted, legal discourse is a forum for the creation of such meaning. Accordingly, there is now a large body of scholarship emphasizing the meaning-producing function of law—the role that trials and other forms of legal discourse have in shaping social norms and collective understandings—and providing a forum for debate.[20] A complete review of that literature is beyond the scope of this essay. Instead, I wish to focus on these insights as they have been deployed in a new field of scholarship that specifically analyzes various legal responses to mass atrocity: the field known as transitional justice.

The transitional justice literature examines an emerging array of legal mechanisms—from criminal trials, to civil compensation schemes, to lustration, to truth commissions—designed to address large-scale human rights abuses.[21] Significantly, scholars have assessed the way in which law and legal solutions can produce meaning that addresses not only the past but also the future. Although the ultimate goal may be instrumental—promotion of the "rule of law"—it is a broad one, focusing on long-term norm development rather than on the possibility of deterring a specific set of crimes.

This essay will explore ways in which this transitional justice literature, though it is still undeveloped in significant respects, provides useful insights for thinking about responses to terrorist acts such as those committed on September 11. First, I will look at several core insights from this literature: (1) that transitional justice mechanisms provide a forum for uncovering and airing various conceptions of truth and experience that exist following mass atrocities; (2) that law can help to provide relief to individual victims; (3) that law and legal process fosters the future development of norms even though it may not specifically deter all violations of those norms; (4) that legal processes to address past atrocities support the development of the capacity of the local justice sector; and (5) that justice in these settings may consist of a dialogue among multiple groups. Second, I will explore the central distinctions between acts of terrorism and the kinds of atrocities and transitions this literature normally addresses: (1) the paradigmatic transitional justice case involves atrocities committed during a civil war within one country; (2) the atrocities generally are in the past and the commitment to move forward has already been made; and (3) the actors involved are often state actors, and when they are nonstate actors, they belong to defined rebel groups. Nevertheless, I argue that these differences do not significantly detract from the potential usefulness of transitional justice insights in the context of terrorism. Third, I examine one particular emerging form of transitional justice, the hybrid domestic-international tribunal, and consider the potential benefits of such a model. Finally, I suggest how hybrid tribunals could be used to prosecute those accused of terrorism in relation to the September 11 attacks. The discussion of hybrid tribunals provides one site for exploring the ways in which the insights from transitional justice can broaden our understanding of law's role in responding to terrorism. Such a broader understanding may provide a battery of responses to those who see only law's limits in the face of terrorism and not law's possibilities.

Of course, the ambitious goals of transitional justice sometimes conflict both with each other and with the narrower goals often described as the focus of conventional criminal justice. For example, the goal of airing the truth about a set of atrocities may be best served in a particular setting by offering perpetrators the incentive of amnesty in exchange for public acknowledgment and testimony—the arrangement adopted by the South African Truth and Reconciliation Commission—which may anger some victims or their families who want the potent redress of criminal prosecution. Similarly, rights accorded to criminal defendants, such as the privilege against self-incrimination, may in some cases impede efforts to establish a historical record. On the flip side, efforts to establish a historical record of atrocities may interfere with the fair trial of individuals. For example, in the various international criminal tribunals, the broad use of theories of collective responsibility in order to demonstrate the widespread societal nature of the harms in question may taint trials by infringing on defendants' rights.[22]

Some might also argue that transitional justice is the wrong rubric for analyzing responses to the September 11 attacks because the United States is not a country undergoing a shift from dictatorship to democracy, as are many of the countries that serve as models for transitional justice. Moreover, it is certainly the case that transitional justice mechanisms do not always "work." That is, they may not be able to achieve the goals of either long-term societal reconciliation or individual accountability (though given the fact that the goals of transitional justice are so long term, we may not know for several generations just how effective the various mechanisms might be).

Yet, though the ideas suggested by the transitional justice literature surely are not a panacea in the fight against terrorism (and are, in any event, not the only response to be taken to combat terrorist violence), they still provide important ammunition to respond to those who believe that law is necessarily powerless in the face of random, chaotic violence. Indeed, even when we are not talking about a political transition to democracy, this literature suggests ways in which law can respond to traumatic acts of abuse in a society. Thus, I believe that speaking of transitional justice can be useful to help combat arguments about the inherent limitations of law in responding to terrorism.

I. Insights from the Transitional Justice Literature

The emerging field of transitional justice has offered a diverse array of approaches and analyses regarding the way in which societies can cope with and move beyond mass atrocities. The literature grows out of concrete, on-the-ground experiences of a variety of actors in different societies as they have constructed institutions and processes to confront the past. Although there are few formal empirical studies in the literature to date (and much more empirical work of this kind is needed), the transitional justice literature is empirically grounded in the sense that many of the authors in this area are scholars, lawyers, and policymakers who have participated in the design and implementation of these institutions and therefore have direct, first-hand experiences of the transitional justice processes they are analyzing.

The sheer number and variety of institutional mechanisms for promoting accountability and reconciliation suggest that questions of how people address gross human rights abuses and move forward into the future will continue to be a source of international interest as well as a site for innovation and creative adaptation. Four types of transitional justice mechanisms in particular have proven to be both significant and controversial. First, scholars and policymakers have focused on the multiple forms of criminal justice available in response to past atrocities. The promise and pitfalls of international criminal justice bodies—such as the International Tribunal for the Former Yugoslavia (ICTY) and the International Criminal Tribunal for Rwanda (ICTR)—have taken on increased importance with the establishment of the International Criminal Court (ICC). The use of domestic courts to try the perpetrators of mass atrocities, such as Israel's trial of Adolf Eichmann, France's trial of Klaus Barbie, and Argentina's recent efforts to try military officials involved in the "dirty war" of the 1970s, has also proven to be an option in some, if not many, circumstances. And transnational criminal accountability efforts—such as Spain's attempt to extradite Augusto Pinochet to stand trial for torture and other human rights abuses committed in Chile, or Belgium's application of its relatively recent, and now dramatically limited, universal jurisdiction law—have sparked vigorous debate. Second, the growing use of truth commissions, pioneered in Latin America, developed famously in South Africa, and now being used around the globe from

East Timor to Nigeria to Peru, has elicited enormous interest within policy, advocacy, and scholarly communities. Third, lustration or purging of government officials involved in a regime that has committed widespread human rights abuses, such as the de-Nazification programs after World War II and purges following the fall of the communist regimes in Eastern Europe in the early 1990s, has received less attention than other transitional justice mechanisms, but remains an important option. Finally, the use of civil compensation schemes, either through tort claims in court or through government-sponsored relief programs such as Chile's and South Korea's programs to compensate human rights abuse victims, have generated growing interest. These compensation efforts sometimes take on a transnational character, as when Holocaust survivors bring suit in the United States against German and other European companies that profited from Jewish slave labor, or when victims of human rights abuses overseas sue in U.S. courts for compensation under the Alien Tort Claims Act.

The literature's view of these institutions is far from monolithic. Transitional justice scholars are divided on many questions, both pragmatic and theoretical. One of the biggest fault lines in the literature to date runs between those who advocate formal legal processes such as criminal trials and those who promote less formal, quasi-legal processes such as truth commissions. This divide has sometimes been termed a choice between "truth" and "justice."[23] Others have defined this debate as one between restorative justice, represented by truth commissions and the reconciliation and forgiveness they are said to promote, on the one hand, and retributive justice, represented by the stiff penalties and a sense of retribution they are said to accord to victims and their families, on the other.[24]

In my own view, the organization of much of the literature around this divide is unfortunate, because many of the values promoted by truth commissions are also promoted by criminal trials—both seek truth *and* justice. Even if the form in which they do so may differ, these differences should not overshadow the overlapping goals and values that each institution seeks to promote. Thus, for the purposes of this essay, I will group the insights of the transitional justice literature as a whole together, while recognizing that there are disputes about the extent to which particular transitional justice mechanisms further specific goals. From this literature, I think we can draw a number of useful insights to help expand our vision as we attempt to understand the role of law in responding to terrorism.

Of course, speaking of transitional justice in the U.S. context is somewhat anomalous because the United States is not undergoing a political transition from an authoritarian regime to a democracy, as in most transitional justice scenarios. Yet the concept of a transition is broader than that. The idea behind transitional justice mechanisms is that they help with a societal psychic transition after a traumatic event. For example, Israel in 1961 was not in the midst of a political transition, but the Eichmann trial may have provided an important symbolic transition. Thus, given that the attack on the World Trade Center and Pentagon was one of the most traumatic atrocities perpetrated on U.S. soil, and the very purpose of transitional justice as a field is to study the ways in which law can respond to trauma, it seems useful to consider the transitional justice literature. This literature suggests possible roles law and legal mechanisms might play in the aftermath of trauma. And while such mechanisms have surely not always fulfilled their lofty goals, as discussed below, simply describing these goals at the very least challenges the assumption that law is necessarily a straitjacket in the response to terrorism. Whether such responses can ever be sufficient or not, the transitional justice literature at least provides a more nuanced perspective from which we might respond to arguments about the limits of law.

A. Transitional Justice Mechanisms Help to Uncover the Truth

One core insight from the field of transitional justice is that transitional justice mechanisms can bring truths to light in the wake of mass atrocity, and that this is an important goal in such circumstances. In many settings in which widespread human rights abuses have taken place, those abuses were often accompanied by vigorous official denials in some quarters. For example, Latin American dictatorships vigorously denied their policies of summary execution, torture, and disappearance. Although human rights organizations and the press often reported that such abuses were taking place, many segments of the population refused to acknowledge that these practices were occurring, and there was little knowledge about the particular individuals and particular acts involved. Similarly, in South Africa under the apartheid regime, while the institutionalized racism was widely known, the extent and nature of abuses committed by government actors against the black population were unacknowledged. And, to use another well-known example, not all Germans acknowledged the horrors of the Holocaust. In each case, transitional justice mechanisms—truth commissions in Latin America and South Africa, and the war crimes trials at Nuremberg—brought to light the extent and nature of the abuses, establishing a record that made it virtually impossible to ignore or refute.

Of course, "truth" is an elusive term, and many have argued that speaking about uncovering the truth is unduly simplistic because it conflates different types of truth and ignores the fact that some forms of truth can never be found. To address these concerns, scholars have described transitional justice processes as uncovering layers of truth. For example, in Albie Sachs's schema, forensic truth—the facts about individual guilt or innocence of particular crimes in particular cases—is only one type of truth. Other forms of truth, such as logical truth or experiential truth, can also emerge.[25] Sachs defines experiential truth as a continuing dialogic process for participants in a proceeding or event. Other scholars have written about the way in which transitional justice processes promote not only truth at an individual, interpersonal level, but also at the societal level, a kind of social self-inquiry.[26] Such truth-seeking attempts to determine not only the facts of particular cases but also the broader societal causes of events.

To be sure, there is a good deal of debate within the literature about which types of transitional justice mechanisms do the best job of uncovering these various truths. Some argue that truth commissions, with their more flexible evidentiary rules, their ability to consider testimony from large numbers of individuals—including many who might be considered bystanders to a normal criminal proceeding—and their mandate, in most circumstances, to write a broad-ranging report, offer the best venue for exploring the multiple layers of truth. Martha Minow, for example, has compared truth commissions favorably to criminal trials, which she describes as taking a much narrower approach.[27] Because criminal trials must necessarily focus on an individual defendant's guilt or innocence, much information relevant even to forensic truth in Sachs's schema—what actually happened in a particular circumstance—as well as to broader forms of truth such as widespread institutional involvement in the atrocities and their social causes, is excluded. This reading of criminal trials may be too narrow, however, particularly in cases involving mass human rights abuses where the elements of the crimes to be proved require a showing, that, for example, atrocities were widespread or systematic.[28] Indeed, one might argue that the more rigid evidentiary standards in criminal trials enhance the value of the facts found in such circumstances, leaving less room for debate. Similar arguments might be made for civil tort suits for compensation or even for administrative proceedings to determine whether particular bureaucrats should be purged from the government. Thus, regardless of differences among the transitional justice mechanisms, they all do have the potential to help uncover truths about atrocities that were committed, to provide a record of what occurred.

B. Transitional Justice Processes Help to Provide Relief to Individual Victims of Mass Atrocity

Like the scholarship on criminal justice in ordinary cases, the transitional justice literature emphasizes that one value served by criminal trials of those suspected of committing mass atrocities is to establish the accountability of perpetrators and assure a form of retributive justice for victims. The determination of the offender's guilt and his or her punishment provides a kind of relief to victims and a sense that justice has been done, a particularly important goal in the wake of long periods in which the commission of massive atrocities has gone unacknowledged and unpunished.

As with the goal of promoting truth, a debate runs through the transitional justice literature both about the relative importance of this type of retributive justice and about the extent to which different transitional justice mechanisms achieve such justice. On the one hand, there are those who argue that retributive justice is the most important value to be served and that only criminal trials can deliver this type of justice adequately. They argue that truth commissions, for example, which often are accompanied by amnesties and sometimes do not even name individual perpetrators, are a poor substitute for criminal trials. In East Timor, in the aftermath of the widespread violence committed by Indonesian-backed militias after the Timorese population voted overwhelmingly for independence in a 1999 referendum, Timorese Bishop Carlos Belo, winner of the Nobel Peace Prize, sought criminal trials of the perpetrators and rejected calls for a truth commission, amnesties, and "reconciliation."[29] In South Africa, many have criticized the South African Truth and Reconciliation Commission—which did bring to light the names of individual perpetrators of apartheid-era crimes but awarded them amnesty in exchange for their willingness to give a full public account of their role in the atrocities—for robbing victims of their right to see perpetrators put in jail.[30] Lustration and civil compensation schemes, according to this view, similarly fail to promote retributive justice because they do not ensure that perpetrators will be placed behind bars. Indeed, it is possible to view all such transitional justice processes as mere second-best alternatives, useful only when political and resource constraints make criminal trials impossible.

On the other hand, there are those who argue that the value of retributive justice may not be the most important value in the aftermath of mass atrocities, particularly because it is so difficult to achieve. For example, in East Timor Xanana Gusmao, the leader of the opposition to Indonesian rule for many years and now the first president of East Timor, has advocated reconciliation and forgiveness in response to the atrocities committed by the Indonesian-backed militias.[31] In South Africa, many have contended that the Truth and Reconciliation Commission promoted a societal healing process that trials never could have achieved. Moreover, they emphasize that trials would not have been successful in any event because it would have been very difficult to gather the evidence necessary to secure convictions. As Martha Minow points out, because political and resource constraints make trials so difficult in such circumstances—even where trials are possible only a small number of persons can in the end be tried—the importance of values beyond retributive justice should be emphasized.[32]

Moreover, the classic mechanism of criminal trials, with their robust protections of the rights of the accused, may sometimes appear to conflict with the demands of other forms of transitional justice. Thus, as Allison Danner and Jenny Martinez have argued, the use of theories of collective responsibility such as the command responsibility doctrine and the joint criminal enterprise doctrine in criminal proceedings threaten to undermine the fairness of those proceedings. Prosecutors may adopt these doctrines in part to further goals that extend beyond imposing individual criminal accountability—for example, to promote truth-telling and societal healing by establishing a record of the widespread nature of the atrocities at issue rather than focusing on the narrow role of one individual. But pursuing those goals can infringe upon the rights of individual defendants and compromise the integrity of criminal proceedings.[33]

Yet again, despite the relatively stark contrast drawn in the literature (and replayed to some extent in actual debates within societies seeking to confront past atrocities), the different transitional justice mechanisms should be seen not as stark opposites, but as complementary points on a continuum. Thus, while criminal trials may lead to the most robust form of retributive justice, other transitional justice processes can be seen as serving this value to some extent. For example, if truth commissions bring the identity of individual perpetrators to light, that can lead to a kind of punishment. As Dumisa Ntsebeza has observed in the South African context, when perpetrators came forward to admit their role in atrocities, they may have received amnesty from criminal punishment, but they were nonetheless punished in innumerable, more subtle, ways.[34] Many were forced to endure shame among their friends and in their families, were essentially pushed out of their jobs, and had to live with a kind of ongoing stigma. Similarly, lustration subjects perpetrators to public humiliation and, of course, deprives such perpetrators of their positions in the government, which is itself a form of punishment. Civil compensation, if paid directly by perpetrators, is also a form of punishment, and if paid by the state, may function as a form of recompense for victims.

Moreover, none of these transitional justice processes necessarily must be used to the exclusion of any other. In Chile, the truth commission did not name the individual perpetrators and was accompanied by an amnesty, but a government compensation scheme was also instituted. And truth commissions need not be accompanied by amnesties. In Sierra Leone, for example, those who came before the truth commission did not necessarily receive amnesty, and in East Timor, they received immunity from prosecution only if they had not committed a serious human rights crime and agreed to submit to community reconciliation processes, rooted in indigenous customary practices. Even if truth commissions provide amnesties, such amnesties are only effective if there is a credible threat of criminal prosecution for perpetrators who do not come forward voluntarily. Lustration and civil compensation likewise can be pursued in tandem with criminal prosecutions and/or truth commissions. Thus, the variety of transitional justice processes can, to a degree, be viewed as serving the retributive justice value.

C. Transitional Justice Processes Help to Foster Future Development of Norms

A third, and related, insight emerging from the transitional justice literature is the role of transitional justice processes in fostering the future development of norms. This goal takes seriously the fact that law is not merely backward-looking and corrective or retributive, but is also forward-looking and norm-generating. Moreover, the rule of law is not simply about justice in the individual case, but also about the role of justice, courts, and other legal institutions more broadly in society. Thus, it is necessary to develop discourse and establish norms for the future, rather than merely assign individual guilt and responsibility.

This view of law goes beyond what Arendt believed to be the sole purpose of a trial: "to render justice and nothing else; even the noblest of ulterior purposes, the making of a record of the Hitler regime which would withstand the rest of history can only detract from the law's main business: to weigh the charges brought against the accused, to render judgment, and to mete out due punishment."[35] As Lawrence Douglas has argued, Arendt's narrow, crabbed view of the criminal trial—and of legal processes more broadly— ignores the important role that they play in establishing history and creating a societal narrative about the past.[36] Douglas contends that the major trials of the Nazis, from the Nuremberg trials to the Eichmann trial to the Barbie trial, have all had as a goal the desire to establish a societal record of the atrocities that were committed and thereby inculcate norms for the future.[37] Indeed, all of these trials "were staged with an eye toward satisfying the requirements of both principled judgment and historical tutelage."[38] To be sure, they also sought to establish individual criminal responsibility. But this broader record-making role was no less important than the individual justice role. Douglas criticizes those such as Arendt who suggest that a trial cannot do both: "the notion that a trial can succeed as pedagogy yet fail to do justice is crucially flawed. To succeed as didactic spectacle in a democracy, a trial must be justly conducted insofar as one of the principal pedagogic aims of such a proceeding must be to make visible and public the sober authority of the rule of law."[39]

Not only criminal trials for mass atrocities, but other transitional justice processes can serve this value as well. Truth commissions are organized around uncovering the truth of certain categories of widespread human rights abuses that are defined under international law. Thus, they serve in part to implement and inculcate those norms. To the extent that a lustration program proceeds according to criteria established by such international norms, it can fulfill the same function. And civil trials or civil compensation schemes also help to demonstrate the importance of international law's categories for human rights.

Transitional justice processes can promote the development of norms on a variety of levels. First, such proceedings themselves may generate interpretive norms. The extent of this interpretive function is most apparent in court cases. For example, the decisions of the International Tribunals for the former Yugoslavia and Rwanda have created a body of important legal interpretations of international criminal law, the law of armed conflict, and human rights law. Those interpretations have helped to resolve long-debated aspects of the law in this area. As Sean Murphy has noted:

> [T]he ICTY is developing an unprecedented jurisprudence of international humanitarian law. Prior to its creation, the principal sources of international judicial precedent remained the fifty-year-old decisions of the Nuremberg and Tokyo Tribunals. Now there is a further substantial and growing corpus of international judicial decisions that will ultimately affect international humanitarian law in a variety of areas, comprising (to name just a few) . . . the attribution of crimes to superiors pursuant to theories of "command responsibility"; the permissibility of defense to such crimes, such as those based on reprisal or duress; . . . the rights of suspects to counsel, cross-examination of witnesses, and exculpatory evidence; and the treatment of victims and witnesses.[40]

Domestic trials, whether civil or criminal, serve a similar function. And truth commissions and lustration schemes can also generate interpretive norms because their work is organized around the legal categories of international human rights law.

Second, the establishment of these transitional justice processes has contributed to the development of networks: cadres of lawyers, judges, and others who are familiar with, and committed to, the implementation of these norms.[41] Such governmental officials and members of civil society can form both formal and informal relationships that may help develop the local human rights movements. Moreover, because these individuals come from a diverse array of countries and backgrounds, they can draw on their experience and help to generate increased support within their own countries for international human rights norms.

Third, and perhaps most important, transitional justice processes have the capacity to act as a catalyst in a much larger sense for the development of norms. They can promote broad public support for and acknowledgment of such norms, both domestically and internationally. The Nuremberg trials themselves are a good example of this phenomenon. Consider that, at the time of their creation, although almost nobody seriously argued that the perpetrators should go unpunished,[42] there was considerable disagreement about whether it was appropriate to create a legal proceeding.[43] Charles Wyzanski, for example, contended that punishing those captured in war was not a legal but a political act.[44] And some, including British officials and the U.S. Secretary of the Treasury, argued that the Nazi war criminals should simply be summarily executed.[45]

One of the great achievements of Nuremberg, therefore, was its "capacity ... to project a new legal meaning into the future."[46] As Wyzanski himself later acknowledged, "the outstanding accomplishment of the trial, which could never have been achieved by any more summary executive action, is that it has crystallized the concept that there already is inherent in the international community a machinery both of the expression of international criminal law and for its enforcement."[47] Significantly, Wyzanski's statement reveals that he came to believe not only that the tribunals were legitimate, but also that they served a norm-creating function that went beyond the realm of political or military power and that could not have been achieved through the use of such power. Robert Jackson, chief prosecutor at Nuremberg, has made a similar argument:

> We have also incorporated [the trial's] principles into a judicial precedent. "The power of the precedent," Mr. Justice Cardozo said, "is the power of the beaten path." One of the chief obstacles to this trial was the lack of a beaten path. A judgment such as has been rendered shifts the power of the precedent to the sup-

port of these rules of law. No one can hereafter deny or fail to know that the principles on which the Nazi leaders are adjudged to forfeit their lives constitute law—and law with a sanction.[48]

Thus, transitional justice processes may help to inculcate norms for the future. By drawing the attention of the world to an international proceeding, the Nuremberg trials created a significant moment that spawned sixty years of development of international human rights and humanitarian law, including new international tribunals in the former Yugoslavia and Rwanda, the creation of a permanent International Criminal Court, and a host of other international human rights treaties and transitional justice mechanisms.

D. Legal Processes Can Help Build the Capacity of Local Legal Institutions

The transitional justice literature also teaches that transitional justice processes seeking accountability and reconciliation for mass atrocities can help build local capacity within the legal systems of societies emerging from those atrocities. Societies in which mass atrocities have taken place typically have suffered widespread devastation in all sectors, but particularly in the justice sector. To the extent that the justice system ever functioned well in these societies, it was often racked by corruption. Moreover, the period of atrocities is often associated with civil war and conflict that taints the justice system and destroys the physical infrastructure of the country. Accordingly, in the transitional period, many countries lack the resources, both human and physical, to run a justice system.

In East Timor, for example, Indonesians had occupied the territory beginning in 1975, and, in the course of their repressive rule, had virtually excluded East Timorese from serving within the civil administration. In 1999, after the East Timorese population voted overwhelmingly for independence in a U.N.-backed referendum, the Indonesian military and police officials supported local militias in a rampage of mass killings, rapes, forced deportations, and widespread destruction of property. The Indonesians departed when the United Nations sent in an Australian-led multilateral peacekeeping force, but they looted and destroyed the territory as they left. Many governmental buildings and equipment, including prisons and courthouses, were completely demolished. Moreover, due to the repression in the region for years, few East Timorese were trained as lawyers, and there was thus little local expertise available to rebuild the justice system.[49]

Similarly in Kosovo, Serbs had engaged in repressive, discriminatory rule for years. Decades of persecution erupted into mass killings, deportations, and ethnic cleansing in 1999. After the NATO airstrikes helped to end the atrocities, and the United Nations set up a transitional authority in the region, the physical and human devastation was immense. Buildings and equipment had been destroyed in the conflict. Moreover, although many Serbs and Kosovar Albanians were trained as lawyers, the Albanians had little experience due to their exclusion from the predominantly Serb regime, and the Serbs were wary of serving alongside the Albanians. As a result the justice system was in shambles.[50]

One of the central insights from the transitional justice literature, then, is that legal processes to address mass atrocities can play a role in helping to build the infrastructure necessary to reestablish and reconstitute the legal system more broadly. These legal processes often garner international or domestic aid, which can translate into support for longer-term justice institutions. Moreover, this support is not merely the symbolic credibility that the justice institutions can gain when they bring perpetrators of these mass atrocities to justice. Rather, it consists of support for physical equipment and buildings as well as technical assistance and human resources—in short, support for the building blocks of a justice system.

In some cases, this type of support is more direct than others. In East Timor and Kosovo, for example, where civil conflict and mass atrocities had wrought devastating destruction to the local justice systems and the United Nations had established a transitional administration, international support for the justice sector was direct and extensive. In addition, the establishment of hybrid domestic-international tribunals within the domestic justice system made it possible for international actors to be appointed as judges and lawyers and therefore to work alongside their domestic counterparts in trying mass atrocity cases.[51] In other postconflict settings, international support for local justice has been less extensive. Rather than broad multilateral programs, such support has taken the form of bilateral assistance—as in Indonesia where experts from various countries were dispatched to assist the attorney general—or simply aid grants to nongovernmental organizations (NGOs) charged with monitoring the justice sector. And in some cases the support comes from within the country in question or from NGOs and other private sources. This funding is often inadequate and less well coordinated than it might be (and many criticize it on those grounds), but obviously it is better than no help at all.

It should also be noted that different transitional justice mechanisms are linked to different kinds of support. Truth commissions do not garner direct support for a country's legal system, but resources dedicated to a truth commission's work, as in the cases of Chile and South Africa, can aid in the training of lawyers and others who then play a role in the development the country's legal system. An international tribunal located far from the country in question or a "transnational" proceeding in a third country not only fails to channel aid directly to a country's justice system, but may even divert resources away from it. Yet, even in such cases, the legal proceedings abroad can catalyze domestic developments. In the case of the Pinochet prosecution, for example, the Spanish judge's efforts jumpstarted a movement within Chile and elsewhere that had lain dormant for many years to try Pinochet and others involved in the Pinochet regime.[52] The important point is that a focus on accountability and reconciliation for mass atrocities can be linked to support for the justice system more broadly.

E. Transitional Justice Processes Can Provide a Discursive Forum for Multiple Populations

Finally, scholars note that transitional justice processes provide a forum for multiple competing groups within a society to engage in a dialogue about the past and the future. This dialogue occurs both within the courtroom or the truth commission hearings and in the public discussion that surrounds the events taking place in those formal legal spaces. The existence of such dialogue potentially has long-term consequences for the promotion and acceptance of shared norms and understandings within the society more broadly.

The debate about the extent to which trials as compared to truth commissions and other transitional justice processes promote this kind of dialogue is similar to the debate about the relative abilities of each of the transitional justice processes to uncover truths about atrocities. Many argue that quasi-legal fora, such as truth commissions, are better suited to the task of promoting dialogue than courts because they can allow for relaxed evidentiary standards, offer a site for encounters between victims and perpetrators, provide a role for bystanders, and explicitly seek to establish a historical record to provide some form of social understanding about why the atrocities took place and how best to prevent them in the future.[53] Courts, by contrast have a narrower and less flexible mandate. In establishing the guilt or innocence of individual defendants, criminal trials cannot directly explore more systemic questions concerning causes of mass atrocities or methods of future prevention.[54] As a result, they are less likely to stimulate a debate among different groups in society about the underlying causes of the mass atrocities and the means of preventing them in the future.

Yet, once more, these distinctions are often overstated. To begin with, the types of crimes at issue, such as genocide, crimes against humanity, and war crimes, actually require proof of systemic violence. Thus, the question of the broader society's role in the atrocities is explicitly part of the case in question, and evidence of systemic oppression must be discovered and admitted in order to prove the elements of the crimes. Addressing such systemic questions inevitably makes the courtroom into a forum for debating competing perspectives on the atrocities. Moreover, the debate extends beyond the courtroom. The trials trigger broader discussion of these issues in the popular press. Even those who see the truth commission as a better forum for debate recognize the significance of criminal trials in this respect.[55]

The existence of a forum for debate—whether through the vehicle of a criminal trial or a truth commission or indeed a legislative session—does not, of course, ensure that a clearly resolved unipolar meaning will emerge, or that different groups in society will adopt shared norms and values as a result of the process. In many cases, no document is produced that gives an officially sanctioned version of events. Even where such a document does result—in the form of a criminal verdict or a truth commission report or a legislative resolution—societal debate about it continues. Many discuss its omissions and its failures and dispute its approaches and findings. Yet, despite continuing disagreements, these reports often point the way toward, if not societal consensus about the meaning of certain events, at least shared understandings about where the points of disagreement remain and where they do not. After the truth commissions' work in Chile and South Africa, for example, few could dispute that governmental actors participated in widespread torture, extrajudicial killings, and other mass atrocities, even if disagreement still persists about the motivations for such actions and the broad historical causes of them.[56] Similarly, after the Nazi trials at Nuremberg, no one could seriously dispute the evidence of the concentration camps and the war crimes committed by the accused, even if debates remain about retroactive punishment and victors' justice.[57] In contrast, as Atom Egoyan's recent film *Ararat* painfully shows, the trauma of the Armenian genocide at the hands of the Turks in 1915 continues to haunt Armenians today in part because no official investigation or acknowledgment has ever been undertaken.[58] Even generations later, the lack of an official process means there is no established forum for memory and understanding of a past trauma.

Thus, trials and other proceedings can provide fora and material for such debate and the development of new political and social communities. The existence of such fora stands in marked contrast to the period of atrocities when, typically, no public space existed for such inquiries. Accordingly, to the extent that a dialogue took place, it usually occurred in the language of violence. Transitional justice fora, therefore, provide a language within which an ongoing dialogue about past atrocities can take place, and new meanings can emerge.

Needless to say, these lofty goals of transitional justice are often thwarted by a lack of funding, failure of political will, or the sheer magnitude of the problems faced. Moreover, progress toward achieving these goals can be extraordinarily difficult to measure (particularly those seeking long-term psychological shifts in a political community). Accordingly, commentators sometimes appear to take it on faith that transitional justice mechanisms will have certain long-term effects even in the absence of empirical data.

Nevertheless, the purpose of thinking about the various aims of transitional justice is not to assume (much less prove) that they "work" in all circumstances. Instead, the important point is that this literature reveals some potential effects of law and legal processes that are generally ignored by those who argue that law is ineffective in the face of terrorism. Certainly, before we accept arguments about the limits of law, we must at least consider law's potential benefits.

II. Transitional Justice and the "War on Terrorism"

The central purpose of this essay is to suggest that the core insights from the transitional justice literature that I surveyed in Part I are relevant to efforts to combat terrorism, and that these insights offer a response to those who argue that law is limited in its ability to address terrorism. There are, of course, important differences between the paradigmatic transitional justice setting and the current "war on terrorism." These differences do not, however, deprive the central transitional justice insights of their relevance to the debate about the role of legal process in combating terrorism. Here, I will discuss these differences and explain why the lessons from transitional justice remain important in spite of them.

First, in the paradigmatic transitional justice context, the conditions giving rise to the mass atrocities typically have ceased. Only after the war has ended or the period of repressive rule has drawn to a close does discussion of transitional justice processes begin. For example, the international community did not try Nazi war criminals until after the end of World War II; Eastern Europe began to take legal action against communist officials for their acts of repression only after the fall of the iron curtain; Chile did not begin to investigate the abuses of the Pinochet era in earnest until Pinochet had stepped down; South Africa could only begin its truth and reconciliation process after the fall of apartheid; and so on. Transitional justice is, as its name suggests, transitional: it implies that a movement from repression to more open and tolerant governance has taken, or at least is taking, place.

Certainly much of the transitional justice literature proceeds from this assumption. Ruti Teitel, for example, defines her project as an investigation into the rule of law when political change (from repressive rule toward liberal democratic rule) has taken or is taking place.[59] Neil Kritz describes the goals of transitional justice in similar terms.[60] Though these scholars see the goal of transitional justice processes as forward-looking as well as backward-looking, they take as a given that the process of political transition is well under way.

Yet this assumption is perhaps too neat. In many settings in which transitional justice mechanisms such as tribunals and truth commissions are used, the political transition from the conditions giving rise to the mass atrocities has not yet occurred, or, perhaps more importantly, the transitional justice processes *themselves* are an integral part of the transition. Thus, for example, the United Nations established the International Criminal Tribunal for the former Yugoslavia (ICTY) while the conflict in the Balkans was still raging. Indeed, it may even be that the court's indictment of the Bosnian Serb Slobodan Milosevic for genocide, war crimes, and crimes against humanity played a role in his ultimate ouster from power in Serbia. And while in some cases the political transition precedes the efforts to impose accountability and reconciliation, in many other cases, agreement about the precise nature of the accountability and reconciliation measures to be deployed can actually speed a transition or end a conflict. For example, the South African Truth and Reconciliation Commission can be described as an institution that could come into being only after the apartheid regime had collapsed, but it may also be viewed as an essential element of the compromise that *led* to the end of the regime. Without amnesty, those in power would not have surrendered, but without some form of truth-telling process—making individual amnesties conditional on testifying before the Truth and Reconciliation Commission—the African National Congress would not have consented to the deal.[61] Similarly, in El Salvador, an international truth commission was an important element of the peace agreement that ended the long-running civil conflict there.[62] And even in Chile, where popular support for ousting Pinochet was probably the primary factor in prompting the transition to democracy, some have argued that the movement for change included at least some idea that there must be acknowledgment of, and accountability for, the abuses of the Pinochet era.[63] Former President Patricio Aylwin's truth commission can be seen as an effort to respond to that popular demand.[64]

Accordingly, the paradigm of transitional justice as merely a posttransition accountability and reconciliation process is too rigid. In many cases the transitional justice mechanisms serve as an important component in making the transition. And in virtually every case, these mechanisms are seen as a way, if not to win the war, then at least to help keep the peace. The hope is that they will function as part of the bulwark against repeat outbreaks of atrocities in the future.

A second distinction that might be drawn between the transitional justice paradigm and the "war on terrorism" concerns both the types of atrocities at issue and whether or not those atrocities were committed by state actors. Thus, one might argue that transitional justice mechanisms are addressed primarily to specific legal categories of gross human rights violations and violations of international humanitarian law: genocide, war crimes, and crimes against humanity, including widespread rape, torture, summary execution, and disappearances. Moreover, the atrocities addressed in these settings typically involve circumstances in which state actors are the ones engaging in radical evil. In contrast, terrorist crimes, to the extent that there is international agreement about their scope, tend to sweep more broadly than the categories of human rights and humanitarian law violations that are typically the subject of transitional justice processes. And terrorist acts, of course, are often committed by nonstate actors.

This distinction too is overstated. Indeed, to a large degree, terrorist crimes overlap with the gross human rights abuses and international humanitarian law violations described above. For example, a strong argument can be made that the September 11, 2001, attacks constituted crimes against humanity, which are defined as systemic and widespread attacks on a civilian population by an organization or group with knowledge of the attack, involving acts of murder, torture, or other abuses.[65] To some extent, of course, terrorism does include a broader swath of crimes than just crimes against humanity, genocide, or war crimes. International treaties define certain acts as terrorist—such as hijacking airplanes and taking hostages or using bombs in certain circumstances—that might not in each instance constitute a crime against humanity if the act did not rise to the level of a "widespread or systematic attack" by an "organization or group" involving numerous acts of murder, torture, or other underlying offenses.[66] Yet these offenses are relatively specific, and for transitional justice mechanisms to expand their scope to include offenses beyond the above list (war crimes, genocide, and crimes against humanity) is not unprecedented. For example, in East Timor, special courts to address past atrocities have jurisdiction to consider not only genocide, war crimes, and crimes against humanity, but individual instances of rape and murder associated with the violence in the aftermath of the referendum.[67] In Sierra Leone, the forced recruitment of child soldiers is included in the offenses to be considered by the Special Court there.[68] And in South Africa, the Truth and Reconciliation Commission considered single instances of murder and other crimes if committed with a political motive.[69] A greater difficulty is posed by the fact that some individual states, such as the United States, have such a broad definition of terrorism that terrorist crimes could under some definitions be deemed to include almost any crime. If transitional justice processes were used to address terrorism construed this broadly, there would be little difference between transitional justice and ordinary justice, at least in terms of the scope of applicable crimes and offenses. Nevertheless, although there is no clear consensus on the outer boundaries of what constitutes terrorism, there is widespread agreement about certain specific acts as constituting terrorist crimes, and if one were to stick to these definitions, terrorism could be accommodated within the transitional justice paradigm.

It is also certainly true that, in most transitional justice settings, state actors are the ones who have committed the atrocities, while terrorist acts are most commonly committed by nonstate actors. For example, the Nazis' acts of genocide and other crimes against humanity, the Communists' brutal repression in the former Soviet Republic and the Eastern Bloc, the Latin American dictators' policies of disappearance, torture, and summary execution, and the South African regime's institutionalized racism and apartheid were principally perpetrated by state actors. Yet just as often, nonstate actors also played some role, albeit usually a lesser one. In South Africa, for example, the African National Congress used violence during the struggle to end apartheid, and in so doing harmed civilians and others. The South African Truth and Reconciliation Commission accordingly examined not only acts committed by the apartheid regime, but also by these nonstate actors.[70] Similarly, in Latin America, rebel groups fighting against repressive regimes committed atrocities. In most cases, human rights abuses by state actors far outweighed and outnumbered those committed by nonstate actors.[71] Nevertheless, nonstate actors have committed atrocities in many of these settings, and transitional justice mechanisms have been used to hold these nonstate actors accountable. Indeed, it is significant that many violations of international human rights and humanitarian law, including genocide,[72] crimes against humanity,[73] and violations of Common Article 3 of the Geneva Conventions,[74] can be committed by nonstate actors.

A third distinction that might be drawn between the paradigmatic transitional justice setting and the aftermath of international terrorist incidents is that terrorism often involves transborder acts, whereas most crimes within the jurisdiction of transitional justice mechanisms are committed within one state. Thus, not only are the perpetrators of terrorism usually nonstate actors, but they may be nonstate actors from countries other than the site of the attacks. Like the other two distinctions discussed above, however, this one also is less important than it might first appear.

Certainly many transitional justice case studies have involved atrocities committed within states by actors from those states. For example, in South Africa, the regime committed widespread abuses against its own citizens, and even those abuses committed by opposition groups seeking to end the regime occurred primarily within the country.[75] Similarly, in Argentina, Uruguay, Chile, and elsewhere in Latin America, atrocities were committed primarily as part of intrastate conflict (or perceived intrastate conflict).[76] And in Sierra Leone, the rebel groups seeking to oust the government recruited Sierra Leoneans to commit brutal acts against Sierra Leonean civilians.[77] Thus, it is indeed often the case that transitional justice mechanisms address atrocities committed as part of primarily intrastate disputes.

Yet that is not always the case, and many of the conflicts leading to the use of transitional justice mechanisms have been international or regional in nature. World War II was, of course, a far-reaching international conflict. So too was the war in the Balkans.[78] The conflict over East Timor might also be said to be international in nature because, even though Indonesia had claimed sovereignty over the territory, the international community had never recognized Indonesia's claim.[79]

Moreover, even many of the seemingly intrastate conflicts described above had significant international elements. For example, in El Salvador, U.S. support for the government and other countries' support for the communist rebels are well known.[80] The United States also supported the coup in Chile that ousted and killed Salvador Allende and resulted in widespread disappearances, summary executions, and torture.[81] In South Africa, many countries sheltered and supported antiapartheid activists and imposed sanctions on the South African government, while other governments supported the apartheid regime. In Rwanda, Hutus engaging in genocide were aided by ethnic Hutus across the border in Burundi.[82] And the international community's tragic withdrawal of peacekeepers from Rwanda, along with its failure to bring in more, allowed the genocide there to continue. The killing fields in Cambodia likewise cannot be seen outside the context of U.S. involvement in the war in Vietnam and Cambodia. Indeed, in this globalized world, with so many transborder contacts among government officials, nongovernmental organizations, international criminal and terrorist organizations, multinational corporations, academic and professional associations, refugees, and other groups, it is difficult to argue that *any* conflict truly takes place within the territory of a single state anymore.

Thus, there is no inherent reason to believe that the insights from the transitional justice literature are necessarily inapplicable to the question of how law can best respond to the September 11 attacks. Although the context is superficially different from the paradigmatic transitional justice situation, the lessons from the field of transitional justice need not be so cabined. Instead, the variety of creative legal responses to mass atrocities found in transitional justice settings provides a set of possibilities that can help us think about the potential benefits of legal process even in a time of terrorism.

III. Hybrid Tribunals, Terrorism, and the Limits of Law

Because terrorism can be conceived as a form of mass atrocity, the insights from the transitional justice literature have relevance for the debate about the limits of law and the appropriate responses to terrorism. Grounded in the experiences of multiple societies facing widespread human rights abuses, transitional justice scholarship suggests that transitional justice processes at least hold the potential to help societies respond to the trauma that inevitably accompanies mass atrocities, build a better system of justice for the future, and perhaps even address some of the root causes of the atrocities.

In this last section, I suggest that these benefits are no less relevant when considering how to respond to terrorism. And though we cannot know for sure how effective such legal responses might be, the long-term consequences of *nonlaw* responses to terrorism are no more certain. At the very least, we must consider the possible advantages of legal responses before simply assuming that law is necessarily limited in a time of terrorism. Of course, there are many transitional justice mechanisms that might be used in response to the attacks of September 11 and other related terrorist incidents, and it is beyond the scope of this essay to survey all of them. Instead, I will focus on one particular type of legal response—criminal accountability— and one particular accountability mechanism—the hybrid domestic-international tribunal—to investigate more closely the implications of transitional justice insights for efforts to combat terrorism.

Comparatively little scholarly attention has been paid to the idea of hybrid domestic-international courts. Such courts are "hybrid" because both the institutional apparatus and the applicable law consist of a blend of the international and the domestic. Foreign judges sit alongside their domestic counterparts to try cases prosecuted and defended by teams of local lawyers working with those from other countries. At the same time, the judges apply both domestic and international law. The substantive offenses in question thus usually consist of the core mass atrocities addressed by transitional justice mechanisms and defined in international law—war crimes, crimes against humanity, and genocide—supplemented by other international law offenses such as summary execution and torture. The courts sometimes have jurisdiction over these offenses because domestic law directly incorporates the international law offenses. In other instances, the court has jurisdiction to consider offenses directly under international law, as well as jurisdiction to consider a limited number of serious domestic crimes. The hybrid model has developed in a range of settings, generally postconflict situations where no politically viable full-fledged international tribunal exists, as in East Timor or Sierra Leone, or where an international tribunal exists but cannot cope with the sheer number of cases, as in Kosovo. Frequently, such courts have been conceived in an ad hoc way, the product of on-the-ground innovation rather than grand institutional design. As a result, hybrid courts have not yet been the subject of sustained analysis, even among scholars and policymakers who focus on transitional justice issues.

This neglect is unfortunate, because such courts can potentially address some of the limitations of both purely domestic and purely international approaches. Indeed, as I have written elsewhere,[83] hybrid tribunals have particular advantages, as compared to domestic trials or international tribunals, with respect to two of the transitional justice insights discussed above: norm development and capacity building. They also serve the other values described above of promoting truth, providing a measure of justice, and establishing a forum for discourse among competing groups within society. And, they may be more likely to gain acceptance among multiple populations, who might otherwise distrust a legal process that appears to be overly controlled by one group or another. Given the potential benefits of such courts, we should expect to see them used in future postconflict situations. Indeed, an agreement has now been reached to establish a new hybrid court in Cambodia to try atrocities connected with the Khmer Rouge regime.[84]

Rather than focusing on the general attributes of hybrid courts, however, I am here going to look at how they might be used to address terrorism specifically, and to suggest ways in which their use might provide a response to those who argue that law can play only a limited role in responding to terrorist violence. Considering hybrid tribunals allows us to see ways in which legal processes can be creatively adapted to respond to the threat of terrorism in order to achieve concrete, pragmatic ends that might not be achievable through other means.

A. Hybrid Courts in Afghanistan (and Iraq)

In Afghanistan, as in Kosovo and East Timor, the international community intervened to help a country make a transition to democracy after a period of oppression and widespread human rights abuses. Of course, in Afghanistan, the primary motivation for the international intervention was to halt the terrorist activities of the Al Qaeda network, which was extensively supported by the Taliban regime. Although the Taliban had committed human rights abuses on a grand scale for many years, it was only after the attacks of September 11 that a U.S.-led multilateral military force intervened in the country, putting an end to the regime. Moreover, the ongoing commitment of the United States to nation-building in Afghanistan in the wake of the military intervention, remains unclear.[85] Nonetheless, U.S. officials, as

well as those from other governments who participated in the military intervention and the international community more broadly, have supported efforts to promote peace and build democratic institutions in Afghanistan,
goals similar to those articulated in Kosovo and East Timor.[86] If for no other
reason, there is a widespread consensus that building the rule of law in Afghanistan will make the region less likely to produce future generations of
terrorists.[87]

As in Kosovo and East Timor, the success of these rule-of-law efforts depends on the establishment and development of a functioning judicial system. While the international community is not itself taking temporary
charge of the civil administration, international support for the local justice
system will be essential to ensure its effectiveness. An important task for Afghan courts will be to hold those on all sides accountable for violations of
the laws of armed conflict, as well as to try those responsible for serious
crimes and human rights violations committed under the Taliban regime.
Meaningful accountability and fair proceedings will not be possible without
a significant contribution of funding and expertise by the international
community. As part of that effort, a hybrid court, with domestic Afghan
judges sitting alongside judges from other countries, could be established to
try those accused of human rights crimes and violations of the laws of armed
conflict. A hybrid process is likely to be particularly important in a setting
such as Afghanistan, where external solutions are often greeted with suspi-
cion, but internal solutions are not workable.[88] Indeed, a hybrid institution is
likely to be necessary in order to gain even grudging acceptance for an accountability process. In this respect, Afghanistan is similar to Kosovo, where
a purely domestic process was unacceptable because it was subject to capture
by one ethnic group or another and a purely international process was perceived as a distant and possibly even illegitimate imposition of outside conceptions of justice.[89] In such settings hybrid courts offer a viable alternative.

Moreover, as in Kosovo and East Timor, there is a growing accountability
crisis in Afghanistan, with thousands of suspects imprisoned around the
country in makeshift jails in poor conditions.[90] The United States has taken
several hundred of these suspects into custody and brought them to Guantanamo naval base, but it is estimated that many more remain detained in
Afghanistan.[91] Their ongoing detention will undoubtedly continue to con-

tribute to instability and unrest within Afghanistan, and it is unclear to what extent there are reasonable grounds to believe the detainees actually engaged in violations of international humanitarian law, committed human rights crimes, or were involved in terrorist acts, and to what extent they simply were captured as Taliban fighters. Yet the release of the suspects, without investigation or trial, could lead to even greater unrest.

Hybrid courts also could aid in capacity-building. Currently, there is no centralized Afghan justice system. Justice in Afghanistan has been predominantly local, religious, and tribal, in large part because the central state has been weak and the country has been in a virtually perpetual state of conflict for decades.[92] In addition, as in Kosovo and East Timor, the physical infrastructure of the court system has been decimated by conflict.[93] And during the Taliban regime, as in the regimes in Kosovo and East Timor prior to international intervention, large segments of the population were excluded from the legal system.[94] As a result, the courts are extremely weak, and there is little prospect for trial of these suspects before state-run tribunals.[95]

Accordingly, an international-domestic hybrid court would be useful if only to process the sheer number of people awaiting trial. Moreover, as the Kosovo and East Timor experiences have made clear, support for the establishment of a strong judiciary is an essential foundation for lasting peace.[96] A hybrid domestic-international structure for some courts and for some prosecution efforts helps to provide both a vehicle for training of, and consultation with, the local population and helps to establish a degree of independence in cases involving intense ethnic conflicts and rivalries. Such a model may well be highly useful in Afghanistan. Moreover, while the United States might be unlikely to accept such a process for trying Taliban or Al Qaeda leaders, it might be willing to accept and support such trials for low-level Taliban or Al Qaeda operatives.

I should note that I am not suggesting that hybrid domestic-international tribunals could be, or should be, the *only* forum in which to hold suspected terrorists accountable for their actions. If a hybrid court in Afghanistan were established, it would probably be best suited for trying lower-level Al Qaeda and Taliban operatives for crimes committed on Afghan soil (or with at least a link to Afghanistan). Based on the types of crimes committed, cases could be assigned either to a hybrid court in Afghanistan or other Afghani courts.

Relevant crimes might include crimes against humanity, violations of the laws of armed conflict, and perhaps crimes of international terrorism as defined under the existing terrorism conventions. Finally, because the hybrid court could also serve the goal of ensuring more general accountability for serious human rights abuses committed before or during the Taliban regime, as well as abuses associated with the Northern Alliance insurgency itself, the court should have a relatively broad mandate to hear other Afghanistan-based human rights crimes.

One might make a similar argument in favor of establishing a hybrid court to try terrorism suspects in Iraq following the U.S.-led military intervention. Unlike the Taliban regime in Afghanistan, however, the Iraqi government had no links to the September 11 terrorist attacks on the United States and only the most minimal ties, if any, to Al Qaeda—despite assertions by some administration officials to the contrary.[97] There is therefore little reason to create a hybrid court in Iraq to try those involved in the September 11 terrorist attacks. On the other hand, in the wake of the U.S.-led military intervention—perhaps partly in response to the intervention itself—terrorist attacks within Iraq have become widespread. Thus, a hybrid court might be established to try those suspected of committing such attacks. In any event, Iraq would do well to establish a hybrid court to address the widespread human rights abuses committed during the regime of Saddam Hussein. Yet the current tribunal convened to try Saddam Hussein and others from his regime is essentially a domestic court,[98] though it could be converted into a hybrid court if international judges were ultimately invited to serve alongside domestic judges.

B. Hybrid Courts in the United States

Hybrid courts to address terrorism might be used within the United States as well. The Bush administration has thus far opted to keep most terrorism suspects outside of any legal system altogether. Hundreds have been detained for years at Guantanamo naval base.[99] Moreover, the administration argued that U.S. courts lacked jurisdiction even to consider any claims the detainees might have.[100] Even though the U.S. Supreme Court has now rejected this argument,[101] most of those who were sent to Guantanamo remain in detention and have not been tried. Moreover, many other suspects are being detained at undisclosed locations around the world.[102] And the administration continues to claim that noncitizen detainees designated as "enemy combatants" need not be accorded any rights that can be protected in court.[103] The only legal process that the administration has proposed to assess the individual accountability of terrorism suspects is a truncated trial before military commissions.[104] And, to date, no such trials have begun.[105]

The United States might profitably use hybrid courts to try these terrorism suspects. For example, the United States could establish a special civilian court, with slots for judges from other countries, to try the suspects. Or, perhaps slightly more plausibly, the United States could allow judges from other countries to serve on the proposed military commissions, and allow prosecutors and defense attorneys from other countries to work alongside U.S. prosecutors and defense attorneys. The hybrid nature of this arrangement might help promote the transitional justice values identified previously.

First, the use of hybrid tribunals would help to create a historical record of the attacks and responsibility for them. Some might argue that there is little need to create such a record, when it seems clear enough both what the Al Qaeda operatives did and the horrifying consequences of their actions. Yet, even if there is consensus within the United States about Al Qaeda responsibility for the attacks, there remains a disturbing doubt in some quarters about whether Al Qaeda really is responsible. A trial of key Al Qaeda operatives could put those doubts largely to rest. Moreover, a trial could lay bare the nature of the Al Qaeda organization, its aims, goals, and structure. While certain facts about the attacks are known, much remains a mystery.

Although a purely domestic proceeding could also serve this goal, a hybrid tribunal would be likely to do an even better job in this respect because the participation of judges and other actors from outside the United States would likely enhance respect for the tribunal's findings overseas, where the doubts are most likely to fester. To be sure, if the proceedings were held in secret, which is permitted under the regulations for the proposed military commissions,[106] even a hybrid court could do little to lay out the facts surrounding the attacks in a form for the world to see. Yet, despite this significant failing, if judges and lawyers from other countries were at least able to participate in the secret proceeding, it would do more to establish some kind of record than a purely unilateral process. For example, the fact that judges from other countries agreed to a guilty verdict would at least establish that individuals who would be perceived as more independent than members of the U.S. military had concurred in the result.

Second, hybrid tribunals would establish retributive justice by holding the perpetrators accountable for their actions and punishing them. One might argue that the approaches adopted by many of those who take the various "limits of law" positions would also serve this retributive justice value. For example, it could be argued that military commissions, indefinite military detention of suspects, or indeed summary executions (as some advocated for the Nazi war crimes suspects in the aftermath of World War II) would provide retribution. Yet without a proceeding that follows minimal evidentiary and procedural rules, it would be difficult to establish that the individuals being punished were indeed the individuals who committed the atrocities in question. Thus, even with respect to this goal of transitional justice, the actions flowing from the "limits of law" positions fall far short. A trial or proceeding of any kind, as long as it followed minimal procedural standards, would serve this goal. But a hybrid proceeding would have particular advantages because the inclusion of judges from other countries on the tribunal would enhance the credibility of the proceedings, both in the United States and abroad. Indeed, if the United States were to pursue military trials, a hybrid process would be particularly important for precisely this reason. Even with measures in place to ensure procedural fairness, a purely unilateral military trial would be far less likely to garner broad acceptance because of the lack of independence of the judges, who would be drawn from within the military hierarchy. The participation of judges from other countries would add an important check.

Third, hybrid tribunals could promote the development of norms and procedures for addressing terrorism. Here I do not mean only that legal proceedings result in decisions that establish specific precedents, although certainly that is the case. For example, legal proceedings to try terrorists would likely lead to the further development of laws and norms related to terrorism, both through the precedential weight of judicial decisions themselves and through the catalyzing effect such proceedings would have on efforts around the world to enact new statutes and draft new treaties, based on understandings that would emerge from the trial process. In addition to norm development in this narrow sense, however, we might also think that legal proceedings themselves have an educative effect on the broader population as a whole, creating a space for the engagement with and acceptance of norms. Of course, the meaning of such proceedings is never unipolar; different constituencies will find different meanings in the same legal outcome. Yet the proceedings provide a site for the expression of these norms.

Thus, while a unilateral U.S. approach to the problem might also develop norms, those norms would be less likely to be shared across countries and cultures. The participation of foreign judges in the enterprise would help build joint commitments to eradicate terrorism, as well as standards for measuring acts of terrorism that fall beyond the pale of the acceptable. Moreover, if the court were hybrid in the sense of applying both domestic U.S. as well as international law, the court would do a much better job of broad norm development as well.

Fourth, a hybrid court could help build the capacity of local justice systems around the world and create a framework for transnational antiterrorism activities. The multilateral nature of the tribunal would help form networks and informal relationships through the interactions of judges and lawyers. These networks could strengthen the hand of participants in these tribunals to help develop the local justice sectors in their home countries. They would return with new insights about international legal norms and processes and might also be better able to secure international aid for their legal systems. In addition, these networks could provide a locus for cooperation regarding intelligence and law-enforcement efforts. Due to the transnational nature of terrorism, information sharing is absolutely essential to combat it effectively. Indeed, in tracking down and locating Al Qaeda suspects, the United States has already relied considerably on intelligence provided by other countries.[107] A hybrid tribunal could help to strengthen the needed intelligence-sharing relationships, while at the same time providing a framework for screening sensitive information that would have greater legitimacy than a purely U.S.-run process.

Finally, and perhaps most importantly, hybrid tribunals would help create a space for dialogue and debate about terrorism, which is the best way to move toward, if not achieve, shared understandings about norms and values, both within the legal forum and in the public debate sure to arise over the court's work. A multilateral tribunal can have tremendous power in projecting norms into the future and in creating a space for those norms to evolve. The Nuremberg trials serve as one powerful example of this process. Of course, multiple meanings can be assigned to any trial, and it would be naïve to suggest that everyone in the world would see the work of such a court in the same way. Some might view its verdicts as unjust or flawed in many respects. Yet a legal proceeding widely viewed as fair would have a much better chance of establishing at least a framework that could be broadly accepted than a denial of legal process altogether.

One of the most potent critiques of using such a hybrid legal proceeding to try those responsible for the September 11 attacks (or indeed other acts of terrorism) is rooted in the concern that the divisions between the United States and the rest of the world, in particular the Arab-Muslim world,[108] run too deep for a hybrid proceeding to work. For example, critics point to the inability of the international community, even after decades of effort, to develop a coherent definition of terrorism. In addition, they note serious differences on other issues that likely would spring to the forefront of any effort to construct a hybrid domestic-international tribunal. For example, some point to the discord that erupted at the recent World Conference on Racism, in which "several Islamic countries sought to use the forum to pursue their political grievances against Israel."[109] One might also think that such deep differences between countries and cultures would render an Arab or Muslim judge incapable of presiding in a fair or impartial manner over the trial of an Arab or Muslim defendant accused of acts of terrorism. And even if such a trial did take place, one might be concerned that, no matter how many procedural protections were provided, there would be little chance that a verdict convicting an Arab or Muslim defendant would be accepted as fair in the Arab-Muslim world.

Nevertheless, although rifts between the United States and the Arab-Muslim world certainly exist, and undeniably run deep, the existence of such rifts does not necessarily make hybrid courts impossible.[110] Indeed, the international realm does not have a monopoly on social conflict and dissension. Serious conflicts exist *within* societies as well, yet such social rifts do not render law and legal process ineffectual. Even if one accepts that greater division exists *among* nation-states than within any one of them, the difference might be better seen as one of degree rather than of kind. Thus, the existence of social divisions should not itself be a bar to efforts to set up an adjudicatory process involving communities on both sides (or multiple sides) of the divide. Otherwise, *no* legal proceedings would be possible or effective.

It is important to emphasize that I am not suggesting that a legal proceeding of any kind, let alone a hybrid domestic-international trial of terrorists, creates a shared narrative or cultural consensus. Indeed, just because one rejects the idea that law has no role to play in responding to terrorism does not commit one to the position that law is a panacea that will magically transform violent disagreement into harmonious shared values. An argument may be made for the rule of law not as a means to deter the most militant terrorists, but rather as a model of justice that may influence more moderate elements throughout the world to accept certain legal norms, thereby dissuading them from supporting terrorism or other extreme positions. Thus, legal proceedings may at least help to forge what we might call provisional compromises, both with respect to certain substantive norms—such as acts that fall so beyond the pale of the acceptable in almost all societies that they can be condemned as criminal—and procedural norms of fairness that allow people to accept outcomes even in the face of political or social disunity.

In the international sphere, the issue of what constitutes fair procedures may be the easiest place to find agreement. Although differences in the views about the precise content of fair procedures might complicate efforts to establish a hybrid domestic-international forum, there is already a broad base of consensus regarding such procedures, and it is unlikely that disagreements would be insurmountable. The International Covenant on Civil and Political Rights, for example, has been widely ratified and establishes a baseline set of procedural norms,[111] as do numerous other treaties. Indeed, some procedures are so widely accepted that they can now be considered a matter of customary international law. Moreover, the existing international criminal tribunals for the former Yugoslavia and Rwanda have forged useful compromises on many procedural issues. Judges from a diverse array of countries sit on these tribunals, including judges from the Arab-Muslim world.[112] Finally, even countries as far apart ideologically as the United States and Libya ultimately have been able to accept as fair the trial of Libyan terrorism suspects in a Scottish court convened in the Netherlands. Ironically, the biggest obstacle to agreement about appropriate procedures for an international proceeding to try terrorism suspects might lie in the reluctance of the United States to adhere to widely accepted standards for just adjudication, rather than the Arab-Muslim world's reluctance to accept "Western" conceptions of fair process.

But in addition to compromises about *procedure*, provisional compromises about *substantive* norms relating to the September 11 attacks may also be possible. Numerous governments, including many Arab-Muslim governments, have strongly condemned the attacks as a violation of international law. One need not delve into contentious issues of how precisely to define terrorism in order to view the attacks as an international crime, because they would very likely qualify as crimes against humanity. Moreover, as noted previously, there is widespread agreement that certain acts, such as the hijacking of airplanes, the commission of acts of violence on airplanes, the taking of diplomatic hostages, and the like easily qualify as criminal. The multiple, widely ratified terrorism conventions reflect this view.[113] And elements of the September 11 attacks would clearly fall within these existing treaties.[114] Thus, although widespread accord on the precise scope of terrorism does not exist—one person's terrorist is still another person's freedom fighter—there is broad-based agreement that certain terrorist acts are so extreme that they qualify as criminal acts in any circumstance. This agreement is almost certainly strong enough to sustain a hybrid trial of the perpetrators of the September 11 attacks.

Furthermore, the purported normative differences between "Western" and "Muslim" interpretations of the Al Qaeda attack may be exaggerated. Indeed, a strong argument can be made that the September 11 attacks and other similar terrorist acts violate Islamic law and Islamic principles. Sohail Hashmi has observed that "the overwhelming consensus of modern scholars is that Islamic ethics endorses international humanitarian law, including the Geneva Conventions, that makes the deliberate targeting of noncombatants and the terrorizing of civilian populations a war crime."[115] Hashmi traces these principles to a verse of the Qur'an that states: "And fight in God's cause against those who wage war against you, but do not transgress limits, for God loves not the transgressors."[116] He notes that, according to authoritative tradition, the Prophet Mohammed always instructed military commanders to "adhere to certain restraints, including giving fair notice of attack and sparing women and children."[117] Successors of the prophet have further developed these rules, clearly establishing the principles of "discrimination [with respect to targets] and proportionality of means."[118] Hashmi also emphasizes that modern Muslim interpreters have continued to develop these principles. For example, the Syrian scholar Wahba al-Zuhayli interprets the verse from the Qur'an quoted above as saying: "Do not fight anyone unless they fight you. Fighting is thus justified if you fight the enemy and the enemy fights you. It is not justified against anyone who does not fight the Muslims."[119] Zuhayli thus "clearly rules out the possibility of collective responsibility, that all citizens belonging to a perceived foe are somehow responsible."[120] Other scholars have made similar arguments. Indeed, an eminent historian of Islam at Harvard University, Roy P. Mottahedeh, recently has launched a project to involve Muslim scholars in drawing up an indictment of Osama Bin Laden under Islamic law.[121] Accordingly, at least on certain topics, there is a very real possibility that compromises and provisional agreements even about substantive norms can be forged.

Thus, we need not idealistically assume that legal process will quell all private violence, heal all social divisions, or forge complete consensus. To the contrary, the insights of transitional justice make clear that deep underlying social conflict will always result in bitter disputes about the interpretation of legal norms and that interpretations of those norms will often be affected or determined by political commitments. Yet a hybrid form of adjudication is one way of ensuring the involvement of multiple actors, creating a forum for dispute among competing narratives, and providing a context for the development of provisional compromises about procedural and substantive norms.

Such a hybrid court would not be difficult to establish. Indeed, as mentioned previously, to the extent that the administration moves forward with military commission trials, one way of achieving some of the benefits of a hybrid proceeding would be simply to internationalize those trials. There is strong historical precedent for such an approach. The International Military Tribunal for the Far East (IMTFE), used after World War II, was essentially a hybridized tribunal that was established by the executive decree of U.S. General Douglas MacArthur, supreme commander for the Allied powers in Japan.[122] Under orders from the U.S. joint chiefs of staff, MacArthur retained absolute authority over the establishment of rules, regulations, and procedures.[123] Accordingly, although modeled on the internationally controlled trials at Nuremberg, the United States effectively set the rules for the IMTFE proceedings. Moreover, the United States appointed the judges.[124] In the end, judges from nine countries sat on the IMTFE, representing Australia, New Zealand, Canada, the Netherlands, France, Britain, the United States, the Soviet Union, and China, along with two colonial territories on the brink of independence, India and the Philippines.[125] Thus, the IMTFE was, in some sense, a "hybrid" court because it was a U.S. created and controlled court with participation from judges from other countries, rather than a full-fledged international court.

If the United States were to "hybridize" the military commission process along the lines of the IMTFE, the administration could retain control over the shape of the proceedings while at least obtaining some of the benefits of a multilateral approach. Nonetheless, the advantages of internationalizing the process would depend in part on how wide a circle of judges the administration would be willing to appoint. Indeed, both the International Military Tribunal at Nuremberg and the IMTFE have been criticized for not opening the circle beyond the Allied powers, thereby imposing victors' justice.[126] Yet even such a limited range of judges would be preferable to the purely unilateral victors' justice that a completely U.S.-run domestic military commission process would offer. Thus, even if the judges on the commission were limited to Western European countries, the administration would still increase the perceived legitimacy of the process. If the administration would further be willing to appoint judges from non-Western countries, particularly Arab or Muslim judges, the credibility of the process would be even greater. The appointment of jurists from countries such as Saudi Arabia, Pakistan, or India might prove to be too difficult for obvious diplomatic reasons; candidates acceptable to the United States might well be found, however, in South Africa or Indonesia, because those countries are democracies with jurists who are well established and recognized both in the West and around the world. Jurists of Arab or Muslim background who are citizens of the United States or Western European countries could also be considered.

⌣

This brief discussion of hybrid domestic-international tribunals illustrates one way in which the growing scholarship on transitional justice may be useful in considering the limits of law in response to terrorism. The assumption underlying the "limits of law" arguments canvassed at the outset of this essay is that legal process is at best ineffectual and at worst an impediment when real interests are threatened and real values are at stake. Legal process is therefore seen as a luxury we cannot afford in the aftermath of an atrocity like the attacks on the World Trade Center and Pentagon.

Yet the whole idea of transitional justice proceeds from the opposite premise. Indeed, the issues of transitional justice *always* arise in the aftermath of trauma and atrocity. Moreover, transitional justice scholars have amassed a body of knowledge concerning the wide variety of mechanisms available and the possibility that such mechanisms will help establish the importance of the rule of law, provide a forum for truth-seeking, offer a measure of retributive justice and relief to victims, develop legal institutions that may gain acceptance among diverse populations, and improve the capacity of justice systems, all while trying to ensure stability and heal trauma in a fragile new order. This is a daunting set of tasks, to be sure, but they must be undertaken if peaceful coexistence is to be rendered possible over the long term. And while there is no guarantee that such mechanisms will be effective in efforts to quell violence, it is equally uncertain whether pure military responses, unchecked by resort to law, will be effective either. Thus, at the very least, arguments about law's limitations must be challenged by alternative narratives.

Although the current context is different in several ways from the paradigmatic transitional justice situation, the insights from this literature are no less important. And while no one is naïve enough to believe that any legal mechanism will ever completely eliminate terrorism, the fact that laws are broken does not mean that we should jettison the idea of law altogether. To the contrary, the insights of transitional justice suggest that law is needed all the more in a period of trauma and instability. Accordingly, as we consider the role of law in the aftermath of the September 11 attacks, the lessons learned elsewhere about forging justice after mass atrocity provide a fertile source of creative innovation and human possibility.

Notes

1. This is, of course, an overly simplified description of a diverse literature on international law and international relations. Indeed, within scholarly circles, the "classical realist" view that "since there is no body to enforce the law, nations will comply with international law only if it is in their interest to do so," Louis Henkin, *How Nations Behave* (New York: Columbia University Press, 1979), 49, no longer holds sway, having been replaced by what might be called a neo-realist, or rational choice model. Nevertheless, even the more nuanced vision of international relations realism leaves little room for understanding the role legal norms and processes might play in the international realm. Rather, neo-realists tend to argue that, "if compliance with international law occurs, it is not because the law is effective, but merely because compliance is coincident with the path dictated by self-interest in a world governed by anarchy and relative state power." Oona A. Hathaway, "Do Human Rights Treaties Make a Difference?," *Yale Law Journal* 111 (2002): 1945–46 (describing the work of Kenneth Walz). Moreover, even if the strong form of classical realism is less embraced in the academy than it once was, it continues to find adherents in policy circles.

2. See, e.g., Office of Legal Counsel, U.S. Department of Justice, "Memo for Alberto R. Gonzales, Counsel to the President Re: Standards of Conduct for Interrogation under 18 U.S.C. §§ 2340–2340A," August 1, 2002, available at http://www.washingtonpost.com/wp-srv/nation/documents/dojinterrogationmemo20020801.pdf, last visited October 7, 2004 [hereinafter DOJ torture memo]; U.S. Department of Defense, "Working Group Report on Detainee Interrogations in the Global War on Terrorism: Assessment of Legal, Historical and Operational Considerations," March 6, 2003, available at http://news.findlaw.com/wp/docs/torture/30603wgrpt3.html, last visited October 7, 2004 [hereinafter DOD torture memo]; Raymond Bonner et al., "Questioning Terror Suspects in a Dark and Surreal World," *New York Times*, March 9, 2003, p. A1; Erik Lichtblau and Adam Liptak, "Questioning to be Legal, Humane, and Aggressive, the White House Says," *New York Times*, March 4, 2003, p. A13; Dana Priest and Barton Gellman, "U.S. Decries Abuse but Defends Interrogations; 'Stress and Duress' Tactics Used on Terrorism Suspects Held in Secret Overseas Facilities," *Washington Post*, December 26, 2002, p. A1.

3. See, e.g., USA Patriot Act of 2001, Pub. L. No. 107–56, 115 Stat. 272, codified as amended in scattered sections of the United States Code.

4. See DOJ torture memo, 31–39.

5. See Alan Dershowitz, *Shouting Fire: Civil Liberties in a Turbulent Age* (Boston: Little, Brown, 2002), 470–76.

6. Brief for Respondents, *Hamdi v. Rumsfeld*, No. 03-6696, 124 S. Ct. 2633 (2004).

7. Ibid.

8. Hamdi v. Rumsfeld, 124 S. Ct. 2633 (2004). Subsequent to the Supreme Court's decision, the administration has asserted that it will release Hamdi from custody and has no plans to try him for any offense. Associated Press, "Supreme Court Will Not Hear Enemy Combatant Case," *Washington Post*, October 5, 2004, sec. A.

9. See Associated Press, "Critics Attack Secret Guantanamo Hearings," *New York Times*, October 5, 2004, sec. A.

10. See, e.g., Sheryl Gay Stolberg, "Mining Purpose Out of Horror," *New York Times*, September 23, 2001, sec. 4, p. 3 (describing concerns arising from Bush's attempts to "cast . . . the fight against global terrorism as a crusade of good against evil").

11. See, e.g., George Packer, "The Liberal Quandary over Iraq," *New York Times*, December 8, 2002, sec. 6, p. 104 (describing variety of liberal views on intervention).

12. Prime Minister Tony Blair has attempted to argue that the use of force would be legal under prior Security Council resolutions, and U.S. Secretary of State Colin Powell has at times made this argument, but it has not been at the foreground of the Bush administration officials' case for war.

13. See, e.g., Walter Pincus, "White House Backs Off Claim on Iraqi Buy," *Washington Post*, July 8, 2003, p. A1 ("The Bush administration acknowledged for the first time yesterday that President Bush should not have alleged in his State of the Union address in January that Iraq had sought to buy uranium in Africa to reconstitute its nuclear weapons program").

14. *Hannah Arendt–Karl Jaspers Correspondence 1926–1969*, ed. Lotte Kohler and Hans Saner (New York: Harcourt Brace Jovanovich, 1992), 54.

15. Hannah Arendt, *The Human Condition* (Chicago: University of Chicago Press, 1958), 241.

16. This view does not necessarily imply opposition to efforts to try and punish the perpetrators of such crimes. Indeed, Arendt supported the Nuremberg trials and argued years later during Israel's trial of Adolf Eichmann that the Israeli trial would have been better if it had more resembled Nuremberg and had been more "legal"— in her conception focusing on the guilt or innocence of the individual rather than on conveying a broader historical message.

17. See, e.g., Payam Akhavan, "Beyond Impunity: Can International Criminal Justice Prevent Future Atrocities?," *American Journal of International Law* 95 (2001): 7 (discussing those who believe that "[t]he pursuit of justice may be dismissed as a well-intentioned, but futile, ritualistic attempt to restore equilibrium to a moral universe overwhelmed by evil"); see also David Kennedy, "When Renewal Repeats: Thinking Against the Box," *New York University Journal of International Law and*

Politics 32 (2000): 335–412 (arguing that the focus on international law norms obscures recognition of and resistance to existing social, political, and economic contexts).

18. See, e.g., Katherine Q. Seelye, "Rumsfeld Lists Outcomes for Detainees Held in Cuba," *New York Times*, February, 27 2002, p. A10 (describing possibility that detainees held at Guantanamo Bay, Cuba, may be held indefinitely without trial because Defense Department priority is to obtain information to prevent attacks, not to punish the prisoners).

19. For an analysis of terrorism as an expressive act, see David E. Apter, "Political Violence in Analytic Perspective," in *The Legitimization of Violence*, ed. David E. Apter (Washington Square, N.Y.: New York University Press, 1997), 1–27.

20. See, e.g., Patricia Ewick and Susan S. Silbey, *The Common Place of Law: Stories from Everyday Life* (Chicago: University of Chicago Press, 1998), 35 (studying the ways in which "legality is experienced and understood by ordinary people as they engage, avoid, or resist the law and legal meanings"); Paul Kahn, *The Cultural Study of Law* (Chicago: University of Chicago Press, 1999), 124 ("We experience the rule of law not just when the policeman stops us on the street or when we consult a lawyer on how to create a corporation. The rule of law shapes our experience of meaning everywhere and at all times. It is not alone in shaping meaning, but it is rarely absent."); Sally Engle Merry, *Getting Justice and Getting Even: Legal Consciousness Among Working-Class Americans* (Chicago: University of Chicago Press, 1990) (studying one court in eastern Massachusetts and observing the way people use the court system to address everyday personal problems); Austin Sarat and Thomas R. Kearns, "Editorial Introduction," in *Law in Everyday Life*, ed. Austin Sarat and Thomas R. Kearns (Ann Arbor: University of Michigan Press, 1993), 1 (collecting essays that "confront law in its dailiness and as a virtually invisible factor in social life"); Austin D. Sarat, "Redirecting Legal Scholarship in Law Schools," *Yale Journal of Law and the Humanities* 12 (2000): 134 (reviewing Paul W. Kahn, *The Cultural Study of Law* [Chicago: University of Chicago Press, 1999]) ("[L]aw shapes society from the inside out by providing the principal categories in terms of which social life is made to seem largely natural, normal, cohesive, and coherent."); Austin Sarat, "'. . . The Law Is All Over': Power, Resistance, and the Legal Consciousness of the Welfare Poor," *Yale Journal of Law and the Humanities* 2 (1990): 343 (interviewing welfare recipients and examining "how people on welfare think about law and use legal ideas as well as how they respond to problems with the welfare bureaucracy"); Susan S. Silbey, "Making a Place for Cultural Analyses of Law," *Law and Social Inquiry* 17 (1992): 41 (The "constitutive perspective . . . argues that law does more than reflect or encode what is otherwise normatively constructed; in the constitutive perspective, law is a part of the cultural processes that actively contribute in the composition of

social relations."); Barbara Yngvesson, *Virtuous Citizens, Disruptive Subjects: Order and Complaint in a New England Court* (New York: Routledge, 1993), 1–14 (observing western Massachusetts county court system to explore how complaints of citizens and responses of courts both reproduce and challenge social hierarchies).

Clifford Geertz perhaps provided a manifesto for this view in 1983:

> [L]aw, rather than a mere technical add-on to a morally (or immorally) finished society, is, along of course with a whole range of other cultural realities . . . an active part of it. . . . Law . . . is, in a word, constructive; in another constitutive; in a third, formational.
>
> Law, with its power to place particular things that happen . . . in a general frame in such a way that rules for the principled management of them seem to arise naturally from the essentials of their character, is rather more than a reflection of received wisdom or a technology of dispute settlement. Clifford Geertz, *Local Knowledge: Further Essays in Interpretive Anthropology* (New York: Basic Books, 1983), 218, 230.

21. See generally Jason Abrams and Steven Ratner, *Accountability for Human Rights Atrocities in International Law: Beyond the Nuremberg Legacy* (New York: Oxford University Press, 2001); Jane Stromseth, ed., *Accountability for Atrocities: National and International Responses* (Ardsley, N.Y.: Transnational Publishers, 2003); Alex Boraine, *A Country Unmasked* (New York: Oxford University Press, 2000); Priscilla Hayner, *Unspeakable Truths* (New York: Routledge, 2001); Martha Minow, *Between Vengeance and Forgiveness: Facing History after Genocide and Mass Violence* (Boston: Beacon Press, 1998); Ruti G. Teitel, *Transitional Justice* (New York: Oxford University Press, 2001); Neil J. Kritz, ed., *Transitional Justice: How Emerging Democracies Reckon with Former Regimes* (Washington, D.C.: U.S. Institute of Peace Press, 1995); Robert I. Rotberg and Dennis Thompson, eds., *Truth v. Justice: The Morality of Truth Commissions* (Princeton, N.J.: Princeton University Press, 2000) [hereinafter *Truth v. Justice*].

22. Allison Marston Danner and Jenny Martinez, "Guilty Associations: Joint Criminal Enterprise, Command Responsibility, and the Development of International Criminal Law," *Vanderbilt Public Law Research Paper No. 04-09, Stanford Public Law Working Paper No. 87*, March 2004, available at http://papers.ssrn.com/sol3/papers.cfm?abstract_id=526202, last visited, October 7, 2004.

23. See generally *Truth v. Justice*.

24. See generally Minow, 9–24, 87–90; Hayner, 9–17.

25. Albie Sachs, "Honoring the Truth in Post-Apartheid South Africa," *North Carolina Journal of International Law and Commercial Regulation* 26 (2001): 799–810.

26. See Jorge Correa, "Dealing with Past Human Rights Violations: The Chilean

Case After Dictatorship," in *Transitional Justice: How Emerging Democracies Reckon with Former Regimes* 2, 478–94.

27. See Minow, 88, 122–32.

28. See Lawrence Douglas, *The Memory of Judgment: Making Law and History in the Trials of the Holocaust* (New Haven, Conn.: Yale University Press, 2001), 2–7.

29. See Lindsay Murdoch, "Belo Seeks War Crimes Justice for East Timor," *Sydney Morning Herald*, August 28, 2001.

30. Indeed, some victims challenged the Commission in court on these grounds. See *Azanian People's Organization (AZAPO) and others v. President of the Republic of South Africa and others* (CCt July 25, 1996), available at http://www.concourt.gov.za/files/azapo/azapo.pdf [hereinafter *AZAPO* case].

31. Richard Lloyd Parry, "Timorese Bishop Rejects Freedom Fighter's Call to Forgive the Guilty," *The Independent*, August 30, 2001 (noting that while Bishop Belo demanded international criminal trials, the former freedom fighter Xanana Gusmao was calling for amnesties and forgiveness).

32. See Minow, 122.

33. Danner and Martinez.

34. See Dumisa Ntsebeza, "The Uses of Truth Commissions: Lessons for the World," in *Truth v. Justice*, 164.

35. Hannah Arendt, *Eichmann in Jerusalem: A Report on the Banality of Evil* (New York: Viking Press, 1963), 233.

36. Douglas, 2; see also Judith Shklar, *Legalism: Law, Morals, and Political Trials* (Cambridge, Mass.: Harvard University Press, 1986).

37. Douglas, 2.

38. Ibid.

39. Ibid., 3.

40. Sean D. Murphy, "Progress and Jurisprudence of the International Criminal Tribunal for the Former Yugoslavia," *American Journal of International Law* 93 (1999): 95.

41. For discussions of how such transnational networks are formed and influence human rights policy, see, for example, Anne-Marie Slaughter, "A Global Community of Courts," *Harvard International Law Journal* 44 (2003): 191–219; Harold Hongju Koh, "A United States Human Rights Policy for the 21st Century," *Saint Louis University Law Journal* 46 (2002): 293–344; Margaret Keck and Kathryn Sikkink, *Activists Beyond Borders: Advocacy Networks in International Politics* (Ithaca, N.Y.: Cornell University Press, 1998); Annelise Riles, *The Network Inside Out* (Ann Arbor: University of Michigan Press, 2000); Jackie Smith et al., eds., *Transnational Social Movements and Global Politics: Solidarity Beyond the State* (Syracuse, N.Y.: Syracuse University Press, 1997).

42. But see Montgomery Belgion, *Victors' Justice* (Hinsdale, Ill.: Regnery, 1949), 42–131 (arguing that the alleged crimes were acts of war in which both sides were engaged and therefore did not warrant criminal punishment).

43. See ibid., 195; Ann Tusa and John Tusa, *The Nuremberg Trial* (London: Macmillan, 1983), 11–90.

44. See Charles E. Wyzanski, Jr., "Nuremberg—A Fair Trial? Dangerous Precedent," in *Whereas—A Judge's Premises: Essays in Judgment, Ethics, and the Law* (Boston: Little, Brown, 1965), 174–76 [hereinafter *Whereas—A Judge's Premises*].

45. Telford Taylor, *The Anatomy of the Nuremberg Trials: A Personal Memoir* (New York: Knopf, 1992), 28–33.

46. Robert Cover, "The Folktales of Justice: Tales of Jurisdiction," in *Narrative, Violence, and the Law: The Essays of Robert Cover*, ed. Martha Minow et al. (Ann Arbor: University of Michigan Press, 1995), 173, 196.

47. Charles Wyzanski, Jr., "Nuremberg in Retrospect," in *Whereas—A Judge's Premises*, 180, 189–90 (emphasis added).

48. Robert H. Jackson, *Report of Robert H. Jackson, United States Representative, to the International Conference on Military Trials* (Washington, D.C.: U.S. G.P.O., 1949), 437.

49. See Hansjörg Strohmeyer, "Making Multilateral Interventions Work: The U.N. and the Creation of Transitional Justice Systems in Kosovo and East Timor," *Fletcher Forum of World Affairs* 25 (2001): 107–24.

50. See ibid.; see also Wendy S. Betts, Scott N. Carlson, and Gregory Gisvold, "The Post-Conflict Transitional Administration of Kosovo and the Lessons-Learned in Efforts to Establish a Judiciary and the Rule of Law," *Michigan Journal of International Law* 22 (2001): 371–89.

51. For further discussion of the East Timor and Kosovo contexts and the use of hybrid courts there, see Laura A. Dickinson, "Transitional Justice in Afghanistan: The Promise of Mixed Tribunals," *Denver Journal of International Law and Policy* 31 (2002): 23–42 (describing the Kosovo and East Timor contexts).

52. See Paul Schiff Berman, "The Globalization of Jurisdiction," *University of Pennsylvania Law Review* 151 (2002): 527 (describing ways in which "the case against Pinochet appears to have stimulated a new round of human rights enforcement actions in South America").

53. See generally Minow; *Truth v. Justice*.

54. See Minow, 78.

55. See, e.g., ibid., 125–26.

56. See David Weissbrodt and Paul W. Fraser, "Book Review: Report of the Chilean National Commission on Truth and Reconciliation," in *Transitional Justice: How Emerging Democracies Reckon with Former Regimes*, vol. 2, at 470, 473 n 92 ("While

there was heated discussion about the historical interpretation of the Report [of the Chilean National Commission on Truth and Reconciliation], no one really disputed the facts"); Alex Borraine, "Truth and Reconciliation in South Africa," in *Truth v. Justice*, 141, 155 ("The TRC made it impossible, particularly for white South Africans, to continue to declare 'I did not know.'").

57. See, e.g., Shklar, 154.

58. *Ararat* (Miramax 2002).

59. Teitel, 13.

60. See Neil Kritz, "The Dilemmas of Transitional Justice," in *Transitional Justice: How Emerging Democracies Reckon with Former Regimes*, vol. 1, at xix, xix–xxx.

61. See *AZAPO* case; see also Terry Bell and Dumisa Buhle Ntsebeza, *Unfinished Business: South Africa, Apartheid & Truth* (Cape Town: Redworks, 2001).

62. See Hayner, 38.

63. Ibid.

64. Ibid.

65. See Rome Statute of the International Criminal Court, U.N. GAOR, 52d Sess., Annex II, at 4–5, U.N. Doc. A/CONF.183/9 (1998).

66. See Laura A. Dickinson, "Using Legal Process to Fight Terrorism: Detentions, Military Commissions, International Tribunals, and the Rule of Law," *Southern California Law Review* 75 (2002): 1454–55 (describing applicable treaties).

67. See UNTAET Regulation No. 2000/15 on the Establishment of Panels with Exclusive Jurisdiction for Serious Crimes, available at http://www.un.org/peace/etimor/untaetR/Reg0015.pdf.

68. See Statute of the Special Court for Sierra Leone, Appendix 2 Attachment, U.N. Doc. S/2002/246, at arts. 2–4.

69. See UNTAET Reg. No. 2000/11 on the Organization of Courts in East Timor, available at http://www.un.org/peace/etimor/untaetR/Reg11.pdf.

70. Albie Sachs, "South Africa's Truth and Reconciliation Commission," *Connecticut Law Review* 34 (2002): 1037–47.

71. See, e.g., Weissbrodt and Fraser, 461, 469.

72. Convention on the Prevention and Punishment of the Crime of Genocide, December 9, 1948, 78 U.N.T.S. 277.

73. Rome Statute of the International Criminal Court, U.N. GAOR, 52d Sess., Annex II, at 4, U.N. Doc. A/CONF.183/9 (1998), art. 7.

74. See Geneva Conventions on Protection of War Victims, August 12, 1949, 6 U.S.T. 3114, T.I.A.S. No. 3362.

75. See *AZAPO* case.

76. See "Editor's Introduction, Argentina," in *Transitional Justice: How Emerging Democracies Reckon with Former Regimes*, vol. 2, at 323–24; "Editor's Introduction,

Uruguay," in *Transitional Justice: How Emerging Democracies Reckon with Former Regimes*, vol. 2, at 383–84; "Editor's Introduction, Chile," in *Transitional Justice: How Emerging Democracies Reckon with Former Regimes*, vol. 2, at 453–54.

77. See Avril D. Haines, "Accountability in Sierra Leone: The Role of the Special Court," in *Accountabilities for Atrocities: National and International Responses*, 173.

78. See, e.g., Theodor Meron, "Classification of Armed Conflict in the Former Yugoslavia: Nicaragua's Fallout," *American Journal of International Law* 92 (1998): 236–42 (arguing that Balkans conflict was international in nature). Some have argued, however, that the conflict in the former Yugoslavia was not international in nature, leading to the exemption of some crimes committed from certain treaties arguably applying only to international conflicts. See ibid. (describing opposing views).

79. For example, the Security Council both condemned the invasion, UN Doc. S/Res/389 (1976), and called for Indonesian withdrawal from East Timor, urging all states to respect the territorial integrity of East Timor and the right of its people to self-determination, UN Doc. S/Res/384 (1975). The General Assembly also issued numerous resolutions criticizing the Indonesian annexation of the territory. See, e.g., GA Res 3485, UN Doc. A/Res/3485 (1975); GA Res 31/53, UN Doc. A/Res/31/53 (1976); GA Res 32/34, UN Doc. A/Res/32/34 (1977); GA Res 33/39, UN Doc. A/Res/33/39 (1978); GA Res 34/40, UN Doc. A/Res/34/40 (1979); GA Res 35/27, UN Doc. A/Res/36/50 (1981); GA Res 37/30, UN Doc. A/Res/37/20 (1982).

80. See, e.g., Thomas Buergenthal, "The United Nations Truth Commission for El Salvador," *Vanderbilt Journal of Transnational Law* 27 (1994): 502–3.

81. See Philip Shenon, "U.S. Releases Files on Abuses in Pinochet Era," *New York Times*, July 1, 1999, p. A12.

82. Philip Gourevitch, *We Wish to Inform You That Tomorrow We Will Be Killed with Our Families: Stories from Rwanda* (New York: Farrar, Straus, and Giroux, 1998).

83. See Laura A. Dickinson, "The Promise of Hybrid Courts," *American Journal of International Law* 97 (2003): 295–310.

84. See Seth Mydans, "U.N. and Cambodia Reach an Accord for Khmer Rouge Trial," *New York Times*, March 18, 2003, p. A5.

85. In April 2002 Bush appeared to reverse his pre-September 11 opposition to nation-building when he called for a new Marshall Plan to rebuild Afghanistan. See James Dao, "Bush Sets Role for U.S. in Afghan Rebuilding," *New York Times*, April 18, 2002, p. A1. In practical terms, however, it is far from clear that the administration is actively supporting robust nation-building. For example, the administration has not supported the expansion of the international security force in Afghanistan, currently only operating within Kabul, even though Afghan President Hamid Karzai and many humanitarian groups say such expansion is necessary for peace, security,

and reconstruction of the country. James Dao, "Lawmakers Urge Bush to Expand Afghan Force Beyond Kabul," *New York Times*, June 27, 2002, p. A11.

86. Dao, "Bush Sets Role for U.S. in Afghan Rebuilding."

87. Pierre-Richard Prosper, U.S. Ambassador-at-Large for War Crimes, "On Respect for the Rule of Law in Post-Taliban Afghanistan," *Connecticut Journal of International Law* 17 (2002): 433–36.

88. See Thomas J. Barfield, "On Local Justice and Culture in Post-Taliban Afghanistan," *Connecticut Journal of International Law* 17 (2002): 437–43.

89. See Laura A. Dickinson, "The Relationship Between Hybrid Courts and International Courts: The Case of Kosovo," *New England Law Review* 37 (2003): 1065–76 (discussing drawbacks of both purely domestic and purely international courts in Kosovo).

90. David Johnston and James Risen, "U.S. Seeks DNA of All Captives in Afghan War," *New York Times*, March 3, 2002, p. A1 (noting that 7,000–8,000 captured fighters are being held throughout Afghanistan).

91. Ibid.

92. William Spencer, "Establishing the Rule of Law in Post-Taliban Afghanistan," *Connecticut Journal of International Law* 17 (2002): 445–50.

93. Ibid.

94. Ibid.

95. Ibid.; see also U.S. Institute of Peace, "Rebuilding Afghanistan: A Framework for Restoring Security and the Rule of Law," January 15, 2002, available at http://www.usip.org/rol/afghan_mainreport.html.

96. See Betts et al.

97. R. Jeffrey Smith, "'Operational Relationship' with Al Qaeda Discounted," *Washington Post*, July 23, 2004, p. A1.

98. See John F. Burns and Dexter Filkins, "Iraqis Battle over Control of Panel to Try Hussein," *New York Times*, September 24, 2004, p. A1.

99. See Associated Press, "Critics Attack Secret Guantanamo Hearings."

100. See Brief for Respondents, *Rasul v. Bush*, 124 S. Ct. 2686 (1994).

101. *Rasul v. Bush*, 124 S. Ct. 2686 (1994).

102. See Neil A. Lewis, "Six Detainees Soon May Face Military Trials," *New York Times*, July 4, 2003, p. A1 (describing "unknown number of captives being held by the United States military at a group of undisclosed locations abroad").

103. See Lyle Denniston, "U.S. v. Detainees—'No Rights at All,'" *Scotusblog*, October 6, 2004, available at http://www.goldsteinhowe.com/blog/archive/2004_10_03_SCOTUSblog.cfm#109710137139109320, last visited October 7, 2004 (describing the government as arguing, in its most recent filings in the *Rasul* case on remand, "for a dismissal of all the detainees' challenges with no relief whatsoever").

104. Military Order of November 13, 2001—Regarding Detention, Treatment, and Trial of Certain Noncitizens in the War Against Terrorism, 66 Fed. Reg. 57, 833 (November 13, 2001). For further discussion of both the legality and the wisdom of the military commissions, see Dickinson, "Using Legal Process to Fight Terrorism," *supra* note 66.

105. See Neil A. Lewis, "Guantanamo Tribunal Process in Turmoil," *New York Times*, September 26, 2004, p. A29.

106. See Department of Defense, Military Commission Order No. 1, March 21, 2002, sec. 6.B(3).

107. See, e.g., Chris Hedges, "European Dragnet Captures New Clues to Bin Laden's Network," *New York Times*, October 12, 2001, p. B10. Indeed, "[s]ince Sept. 11, at least 23 foreign intelligence services—sometimes working with American intelligence, sometimes on their own—have disrupted terrorist cells and arrested hundreds of people around the world." James Risen and Tim Weiner, "Arrests Are Said to Have Disrupted Attacks," *New York Times*, October 21, 2001, p. B6; see also, e.g., John Tagliabue, "Italian Tapes Portray Young Arabs Operating on the Edges of Islamic Terror," *New York Times*, October 29, 2001, p. B4; John Tagliabue and Raymond Bonner, "German Data Led Us to Search For More Suicide Hijacker Teams," *New York Times*, September 29, 2001, p. A1; Warren Hoge, "Blair Says New Evidence Ties Bin Laden to Attacks," *New York Times*, November 15, 2001, p. B5. The CIA has even opened lines of communication with intelligence officials from several nations that Washington has in the past accused of providing state support for terrorism, including Syria, Libya, and Sudan. See James Risen and Tim Weiner, "C.I.A. Is Said to Have Sought Help From Syria," *New York Times*, October 30, 2001, p. B3; see also Douglas Frantz, "C.I.A. Leader asks Pakistan for Help in Bin Laden Hunt," *New York Times*, December 4, 2001, p. A1 (describing U.S. efforts to develop enhanced cooperation with Pakistani intelligence officials).

108. I use the appellations "Arab-Muslim world," and "Arab-Muslim governments" as shorthand for both the Arab countries of the Middle East and those countries with a predominantly Muslim population, such as Indonesia, Pakistan, and Malaysia. I certainly realize that because these countries are not monolithic, generalizations about them are inherently problematic. For the purposes of this essay, however, the term provides a convenient way to refer to a set of countries that, in U.S. foreign policy, is often distinguished from, for example, "Western Europe" (an equally problematic moniker).

109. Harold Hongju Koh, "The Case Against Military Commissions," *American Journal of International Law* 96 (2002): 343 n 41.

110. And of course the Arab-Muslim world does not have a monopoly on terrorism. Even some of the suspected perpetrators of the September 11 attacks, widely

believed to be members of the Al Qaeda terrorist network, are citizens of Western countries. For example, Zacarias Moussaoui is a citizen of France. Nor are all Al Qaeda members of Arab descent, as evidenced by the arrest of John Walker Lindh, a U.S. citizen apprehended while fighting for the Taliban and accused of belonging to Al Qaeda.

111.   See International Covenant on Civil and Political Rights, December 19, 1966, 999 U.N.T.S. 171, art. 2. One hundred and forty-eight countries have ratified the International Covenant on Civil and Political Rights, including Libya, Afghanistan, Syria, Kuwait, Iran, Iraq, and Egypt.

112.   Judge Amin El Mahdi of Egypt, for example, sits on the ICTY. United Nations, ICTY General Information, available at http://www.un.org/icty/glance/index. htm (last modified July 24, 2002).

113.   Convention for the Suppression of Unlawful Seizure of Aircraft, December 16, 1970, 22 U.S.T. 1641, 860 U.N.T.S. 105; Convention on Offences and Certain Other Acts Committed on Board Aircraft, September 14, 1963, 704 U.N.T.S. 219; Convention for the Suppression of Unlawful Acts Against the Safety of Civil Aviation, September 23, 1971, 24 U.S.T. 565, 974 U.N.T.S. 177; Convention for the Suppression of Terrorist Bombings, January 12, 1998, art. 2, S. Treaty Doc. No. 106-6, at 4, 37 I.L.M. 249, 253; Convention Against the Taking of Hostages, U.N. GAOR 6th Comm., 34th Sess., Supp. No. 39, at 2, U.N. Doc. A/C.6/34/L.23 (1979); Convention on the Prevention and Punishment of Crimes Against Internationally Protected Persons, December 14, 1973, art. 2, 28 U.S.T. 1975, 1978, 1035 U.S.T.S. 167, 169; Convention on the Physical Protection of Nuclear Material, March 3, 1980, art. 7, T.I.A.S. No. 11080, at 11; Convention for the Suppression of Unlawful Acts Against the Safety of Maritime Navigation, March 10, 1988, art. 3, S. Treaty Doc. No. 101-1, at 2–3, 27 I.L.M. 668, 674–75; Convention on the Marking of Plastic Explosives for the Purpose of Detection, March 1, 1991, arts. 2–4, S. Treaty Doc. No. 103-8, at 3–4, 30 I.L.M. 726, 727–28.

114.   See Arnold N. Pronto, "Comment," *American Society of International Law Insights* (September 2001), available at http://www.asil.org/insights/insigh77.htm.

115.   Sohail Hashmi, "Terrorism and Jihad" (November 9, 2001): 7, available at http://www.mountholyokeclubofnewyork.com/TerrorismandJihad.PDF; see also Sohail Hashmi, "The Terrorists' Zealotry Is Political Not Religious," *Washington Post*, September 30, 2001, p. B1.

116.   Hashmi, "Terrorism and Jihad," 6 (quoting Qur'an 2:190).

117.   Ibid.

118.   Ibid., 8. Hashmi notes that the first caliph, Abu Bakur, is recorded as advising:

Do not act treacherously; do not act disloyally; do not act neglectfully. Do not mutilate; do not kill little children or old men, or women; do not cut off the heads of the palmtrees or burn them; do not cut down the fruit trees; do not slaughter a sheep or a cow or a camel, except for food. You will pass by people who devote their lives in cloisters; leave them and their devotions alone. You will come upon people who bring you platters in which are various sorts of food; if you eat any of it, mention the name of God over it.

119. Ibid., 9.

120. Ibid.

121. Alan Cooperman, "Scholars Plan to Show How Attacks Violated Islamic Law; Muslim Jurists Sought to Draw Up an 'Indictment,'" *Washington Post*, January 20, 2002, p. A15.

122. See R. John Pritchard, "The International Military Tribunal for the Far East and Its Contemporary Resonances," *Military Law Review* 149 (1995): 27.

123. See ibid., 31.

124. See Charter of the International Military Tribunal for the Far East, January 19, 1946, art. 2, T.I.A.S. No. 1589, 4 Bevans 20.

125. Pritchard, 27 and n 3.

126. See, e.g., M. Cherif Bassiouni, "Nuremberg: Forty Years After," *American Society of International Law Proceedings* 80 (1986): 64.

Legalism and Its Discontents:
The Case of Reparations for Black Americans

JOHN TORPEY

On Tuesday, March 26, 2002, a young black lawyer named Deadria Farmer-Paellmann filed suit in U.S. District Court for the Eastern District of New York against FleetBoston Financial Corporation, Aetna Insurance, and a railroad company named CSX Corporation, their respective predecessors, and up to 1,000 "Corporate [John] Does" that, like the named companies, may have profited from American slavery. The suit sought damages and compensation for thirty-five million descendants of African slaves, although the plaintiffs asserted that any award would go not to individuals but toward a fund to improve health, education, and housing opportunities for blacks generally. According to Roger Wareham, one of several lawyers who prepared the legal action, "This is not about individuals receiving checks in their mailbox."[1] The suit—actually one of three suits seeking redress for slavery-related wrongs that were filed that day—reflected the recent upsurge of efforts to pursue "reparations" for blacks in the United States.

The announcement of the suits, which received considerable media attention, might have been expected to generate jubilation among those who have been promoting the idea of reparations as a means of rectifying the economic inequalities and social stigmatization endured by blacks in the United States. Yet the reaction to the suit by the best-known reparations activists was muted at best. Instead, those activists responded with notably faint praise. They seem to have regarded the Farmer-Paellmann suit as out of step with their larger political strategy for enhancing the living conditions of black Americans by means of reparations claims-making. Beyond demands for mere economic compensation, that strategy includes naming the U.S. government as a defendant in reparations lawsuits in order to highlight the fact that reparations are a matter not just of money, but of a national political responsibility to repair the broader damage caused by three centuries of slavery and segregation as well.

Notwithstanding their divergent aims, Farmer-Paellmann's suit and others filed by reparations activists elsewhere reflect a remarkable efflorescence in the use of law to address past injustices perpetrated by states, churches, and private firms. The transformation of political conflict into legal disputation—an old story in American life, observed already by Tocqueville 175 years ago[2]—is consistent with a larger human interest in the pacification of social relations, and this may be a successful way of achieving certain political ends during an age of retrenchment concerning racial equality and social justice more generally. This way of approaching political problems has been particularly facilitated in the United States by the 1966 codification of the modern class-action suit—a mechanism that was originally intended to help amalgamate small consumer claims, but that in the meantime has come to be used for vastly different purposes with much higher stakes.[3] Lawyers, always prominent in American public life, have played a crucial role in defining the terms on which political conflict is fought as the notion of reparations has grown more widespread. The litigiousness often regarded as a peculiarity of American society has increasingly gone global as a result. In view of the fact that much of the legal maneuvering with regard to past injustices that occurred elsewhere now takes place in courtrooms in the United States, one senses that Locke had it backward: it was not so much "in the beginning" that all the world was America, but rather "in the end."[4]

Yet there is a price to pay for doing politics through legal means. This mode of carrying on political disputes privileges lawyers over citizens and courtrooms over more widely accessible sites of debate and deliberation. The juridical pursuit of political aims is also vulnerable to being hijacked by people pursuing their own private agendas rather than the common good, especially when those political aims concern primarily economic matters. This kind of manipulation has had deleterious consequences for the wider political goals sought by those using the courts as a vehicle for broader purposes. Finally, it is not clear that legal casuistry is well suited for bringing about substantive social change; for such change to occur, legal maneuvering may provide some help, but popular mobilization is an essential element as well.

In the remainder of this essay, I explore the widespread turn toward the pursuit of political aims via legal means in the case of reparations for black Americans, as well as some of the pitfalls to which such a strategy is prone. I first discuss the political background to the resurgence of reparations politics among blacks. I then move on to an examination of the contemporary case being made for reparations for black Americans. I seek to show that although legal strategies may be valuable in advancing the agenda of racial equality in an age of relative stagnation in race matters, the pursuit of "reparations" for blacks also faces some very substantial obstacles. Legal stratagems may help promote an environment in which pressure to pass reparations legislation becomes powerful, but this outcome seems unlikely in the absence of a political movement exerting pressure outside the courtroom.

The Struggle for Reparations for Black Americans

Slavery, rather than territorial conquest, has generally been regarded as the most fundamental abrogation of the deep rhetorical commitment to freedom in U.S. history. Along with simple demographic facts that leave Indians a marginal population in most parts of the country, the problems of African Americans have therefore received more attention in American public life than those of indigenes, who have been the major focus of reparations politics in other settler (post)colonial contexts (especially in Canada and Australia). Few would argue that the "civil rights revolution" changed nothing for blacks, but many wonder how substantial the gains have actually been, particularly in view of large and persistent disparities between blacks and other groups in rates of incarceration, poverty, unemployment, mortality, and the like. The social and economic progress of blacks in the United States continues to be the subject of anguished if inconclusive debate.[5] The economic stagnation of parts of the black population, despite the achievement of legal equality in the 1960s and the emergence of a substantial black middle class, has perhaps inevitably prompted a resurgence of arguments asserting the existence of hereditary differences between races and claims that blacks are lazy or otherwise disinclined to work as hard as others.[6]

In the meantime, affirmative action, which many would regard as the appropriate approach to dealing with inequalities rooted in past injustices affecting blacks in the United States, fell from political favor and was forced to confront a serious challenge in the U.S. Supreme Court. This outcome came about in part because affirmative action, originally aimed at blacks, came to be extended to the waves of new nonwhite immigrants entering the country after the reforms of the mid-1960s, but more generally because it has come to be viewed by the majority as a violation of the American commitment to individual opportunity as opposed to policies benefiting groups.[7] One major consequence of the challenge to affirmative action was a renewed call among many, especially in the black intelligentsia, for "reparations" to blacks to make amends for the inequalities said by proponents to have been caused by slavery and segregation. In his discussion of the case for reparations for African Americans, for example, Robert Westley straightforwardly enunciated the relationship between the flagging popular support for affirmative action and the demand for reparations. Writing before the legal challenge was aired in the Supreme Court in 2003, Westley insisted, "Affirmative action for Black Americans as a form of remediation for perpetuation of past injustice is almost dead," and it is thus necessary to "revitalize the discussion of reparations."[8]

While this motivation for rejuvenating the discussion of reparations may be more prominent in the thinking of activists, one imagines that there may also be a more complex set of circumstances leading to this upsurge in reparations talk. Partially, of course, the movement was rekindled by the success of the Japanese American struggle for redress, which represents a frequent point of reference for black reparations activists. Yet there may be a more subtle cause for the burgeoning of concern with reparations. As a result of changes in immigration policies since the mid-1960s, the "face" of the United States has changed dramatically. Asians have arrived in substantial numbers, while the largest cohorts of new immigrants come from the United States's own backyard, Latin America. These demographic changes, along with a broader global embrace of "multiculturalism," have begun to subtly revise the traditional American perception of racial differences. Whereas "the American dilemma" at mid-century exclusively concerned the relationship between whites and blacks, the latter now jostle with waves of nonwhite immigrants who were not previously so significant a part of the population mix. With the postwar delegitimization of legally sanctioned racial discrimination of any kind, those groups have also been seen as deserving of greater respect and recognition. Against the background of multiculturalist agnosticism regarding the divergent historical trajectories of ethnoracial groups in the United States, the campaign for reparations might be said to symbolize the reassertion of the distinctiveness of the black experience vis-à-vis that of other nonwhites. However discriminated against or marginalized socially, no other nonwhite group could claim to have been systematically uprooted from their homelands and enslaved in North America. The black experience was unique in this regard, and the reasons for demanding reparations were as well.

Westley's remark also reminds us that the current round of reparations claims-making, which found expression in the Farmer-Paellmann suit, is hardly the first. Others have pursued reparations for blacks in the past, though with relatively little success. Indeed, the notion of some sort of compensation for the wrongs and the exploitation involved in American plantation slavery goes back at least to the Civil War era.[9] In early 1865, General William Sherman announced a plan to make available for settlement by freed blacks the Sea Islands and a portion of the lowlands south of Charleston, South Carolina. According to "Special Field Order No. 15," each family was to receive forty acres of land, and Sherman subsequently authorized the army to loan them mules. The promise of the two jointly gave rise to the notion of "forty acres and a mule." By June 1865, some 40,000 blacks had come to occupy 400,000 acres, and the Freedmen's Bureau planned to extend this pattern to a total of 850,000 acres of the land under its control. After taking office, however, President Andrew Johnson rescinded the Bureau's plan, forgiving Confederate owners and restoring to them their land. As a result, the freedpeople of the plantations were left with few resources and a deep sense of betrayal as they embarked upon the road to freedom.[10]

The bitter disappointment arising from the federal government's retreat from efforts to redistribute land to blacks after the war has given the phrase "forty acres and a mule" great resonance among subsequent campaigners for reparations. The symbolism for blacks of the number forty has thus come to parallel the way in which the number 442—deriving from the number of the heroic, much-decorated regiment of Japanese American soldiers during World War II—came to play an important symbolic role in the pursuit of redress for persons of Japanese descent interned in the United States during that war.[11] Just as H.R. 442, the bill mandating redress for interned Japanese Americans, was named after the 442d Regiment, Congressman John Conyers's H.R. 40—calling for a study commission to examine the question of reparations for African Americans—is drawn from the abortive possibility of distributing lands to freedpeople after the Civil War.

With the demise of Reconstruction after 1877 and the gradual imposition of segregationist legislation culminating in *Plessy v. Ferguson*'s ruling (1892) that "separate but equal" facilities were constitutional, blacks were compelled simply to fight for their basic civil rights and against the extralegal violence of such organizations as the Ku Klux Klan. The idea of reparations thus largely fell into abeyance until the upsurge of pressure for racial equality during the civil rights movement beginning in the 1950s. The Civil Rights Act of 1964 and the Voting Rights Act of 1965 constituted the movement's signal legislative victories, endowing blacks with the legal rights that had been nominally accorded to them in the post–Civil War amendments (the Thirteenth, Fourteenth, and Fifteenth), but that were rarely enforced after Reconstruction came to a close. But these legislative changes, significant though they were, hardly brought an end to police brutality, rat-infested ghettos, and sharp economic inequalities between whites and blacks. Meanwhile, the interracial movement that had spearheaded the campaign for those laws and for a larger "beloved community" subsided in the aftermath of its significant legislative victories.

Soon, along with other mobilized racial minorities, some black radicals in the United States began to see themselves as an "internal colony," a population exploited for its cheap labor—or simply left to make its own way—and kept under control not so much by laws as by untrammeled police violence.[12] Subsequent to Stokely Carmichael's 1966 declaration of "Black Power," the civil rights movement was gradually supplanted by the activities of the groups that would pursue the "identity politics" of the coming period, for which the black movement was a model. Those groups that could make a plausible case for a trajectory similar to the black experience would usher in a "minority rights revolution."[13]

In this context, the idea of reparations for slavery and legal segregation experienced a brief resurgence in the 1960s and early 1970s. At the time, the

notion may not have seemed so wild-eyed as it is sometimes thought to be, since no less a figure than President Lyndon Johnson had announced in 1965: "You do not take a person who, for years, has been hobbled by chains and liberate him, bring him up to the starting line of a race and then say, 'You are free to compete with all the others,' and still justly believe that you have been completely fair. . . . It is not enough just to open the gates of opportunity. All our citizens must have the ability to walk through those gates."[14] Johnson was effectively endorsing a notion of "affirmative action" of the sort that had been adumbrated in the civil rights legislation of the mid-1960s.

Yet there were many who felt that these notions did not go far enough, and that more concrete changes had to take place before blacks would be able to compete in the race of American life. "Queen Mother" Audley Moore, a one-time Garveyite and former communist, is often said to have been the first, or at least the first well-known person in the postwar period to raise the demand for reparations. The idea was soon incorporated into the political agendas of black radical groups, especially the Black Panthers, although the term was frequently interpreted to mean restitution or redistribution of land.[15]

The main episode that returned the idea of "reparations" to public awareness involved the so-called Black Manifesto of radical activist James Forman. The Manifesto was originally adopted by the National Black Economic Development Conference, which met in Detroit in late April 1969. According to Forman's own account, he worked out the text of the document with a number of activists from the Detroit-based League of Revolutionary Black Workers and proclaimed it to the conference with their support. The Manifesto demanded "five hundred million dollars in reparations from the racist white 'Christian' churches and the Jewish synagogues" in compensation "for the centuries of exploitation and oppression which they had inflicted on black people around the world." In the minds of its drafters, the Manifesto was not merely a claim for monetary compensation, but "a call for revolutionary action . . . that spoke of the human misery of black people under capitalism and imperialism, and pointed the way to ending those conditions." The promulgation of the Manifesto at the Detroit conference at first attracted little attention other than that of FBI Director J. Edgar Hoover and Attorney General John Mitchell. It received more notice, however, when

Forman delivered it—unscheduled and uninvited—to a dumbstruck congregation at the famously liberal Riverside Church in New York on Sunday, May 4, 1969. The Black Manifesto articulated a number of demands for economic improvements for blacks of the kind that would appear in subsequent efforts to obtain reparations, such as banks, universities, and job training programs designed to benefit blacks.[16]

The minister whose Riverside Church service had been interrupted, Ernest Campbell, eventually responded favorably to the basic outlook of the Manifesto, as did the Episcopal Church hierarchy. An article by Charles Willie, a black sociologist then at Syracuse University, wondered in print whether the document was "prophetic or preposterous," but was fundamentally sympathetic to the aims—if not the addressee—of the Manifesto. In a critique that would arise again later in the context of the recent lawsuits for reparations for slavery against private companies, Willie argued that the Manifesto's focus on the church was misguided because compensation from religious institutions cannot "absolve the government of what is government's responsibility."[17]

Yet the wider response to the Manifesto was unsympathetic, at best. Despite the fact that Forman had developed the Manifesto in collaboration with activists in the League of Black Revolutionary Workers, not all of that organization's members endorsed the cause. According to Michael Dawson, both rank-and-file adherents and leaders of the League saw the programs envisaged in the Manifesto as "a diversion from what should be the main thrust" of the group's efforts.[18] The mainstream National Association for the Advancement of Colored People (NAACP) also rejected the demands laid out in the Manifesto. In the pages of the *New York Times*, NAACP leader Roy Wilkins urged churchmen to "shun reparations as [a] delusion."[19]

Eventually, even those who had initially supported the aims outlined in the document backtracked as well. Worse still, monies paid by some churches to the Interreligious Foundation for Community Organizations, to which James Forman had urged payments to be made on behalf of the Black Economic Development Conference, were diverted, Forman wrote, "in very opportunistic ways. . . . This betrayal by greedy black churchmen was a serious disappointment."[20] The tensions between more radical and nationalist forces, on the one hand, and the black churches, on the other, would echo

down through subsequent black politics.[21] Ultimately, Forman's chronicle of the experience reads as a cautionary tale that anticipated the squabbles generated by reparations payments to the survivors of Nazi-era wrongs.[22]

Nonetheless, the notion of reparations had once again come to be associated with the injustices experienced by blacks in the United States. Within a couple of years after Forman's promulgation of the Black Manifesto, Boris Bittker, the Sterling professor of law at Yale, published his analysis in *The Case for Black Reparations*.[23] Arguing that blacks had suffered disproportionately among American racial and minority groups, Bittker suggested a number of ways to calculate the amount of compensation owed them. Irrespective of the method of calculation, however, the sums involved were very large indeed because the purpose was not merely to acknowledge and apologize for past wrongs but to redistribute wealth with the goal of enhancing black economic equality. Yet perhaps even more important than Bittker's suggestions about how to assess the amount due was his argument concerning the way in which the compensation should be paid. Bittker asserted that individual payouts would lead to fruitless expenditures on consumption, whereas what was needed was long-term investment. He therefore argued that payments should be made to blacks collectively in the interest of long-term institution-building.[24]

The book was soon reviewed by Derrick Bell, a civil rights activist and professor of law at Harvard whose visibility grew dramatically in the early 1990s when he tangled very publicly with that august institution over its failure to hire women of color on the Law School faculty.[25] Bell has long been an analyst of the "elusive quest for racial justice" who has despaired of "the permanence of racism" in the United States.[26] Given his demonstrated commitment to racial equality, Bell might have been expected to be enthusiastic about Bittker's proposals for a reparations scheme to enhance the conditions of American blacks.

Yet his review, entitled "Dissection of a Dream," concluded that the many constitutional and legal obstacles to such an undertaking were insurmountable. "Racial reparations," he wrote, "are more a vision than a legal possibility." In the end, according to Bell, the achievement of the aims set forth in Bittker's book depended not on legal disputation but on political developments. "Even if Professor Bittker had devised a fool-proof legal theory for black reparations litigation, few judges or legislators would be moved in the absence of some dramatic event, major crisis, or tragic circumstance that conveyed the necessity or at least the clear advantages of adopting a reparations scheme. . . . Legal analysis cannot give life to a process that must evolve from the perceptions of those responsible for the perpetuation of racism in this country."[27] Bell's emphasis on politics over legal disputation in the pursuit of reparations has considerable plausibility. Despite Bell's critique, however, Bittker's book remains influential among some of those who support the idea of reparations, though they tend to see its analysis as having been superseded by subsequent developments.[28]

Indeed, the response to Bittker's book at the time was "mild"[29] in part, no doubt, because the militancy of blacks and other minorities began to flag by the early 1970s. At that point, the idea of reparations for blacks largely went underground again until the late 1980s, in the immediate aftermath of the Civil Liberties Act of 1988 that recompensed Japanese Americans interned during the Second World War to the tune of $20,000 each. Soon thereafter, Detroit Congressman John Conyers resurrected the idea of reparations for blacks by proposing legislation to institute a commission to study whether blacks still suffer from slavery and segregation and, if so, to explore possible remedies. Under the symbolically laden rubric H.R. 40, Conyers introduced the bill into Congress in an environment that was flush with the reparations victory of a group that had been wronged, to be sure, but in a manner and to a degree that hardly seemed comparable to what black Americans had endured during their long sojourn in America. It is worth noting here that it was also in 1988 that John L. Lewis, the civil rights veteran and congressman from Georgia, submitted a bill for the creation of a National Museum of African-American History and Culture on the Mall in Washington, D.C., that has since come to fruition.[30]

In contrast to the success of Japanese American redress, however, Conyers's bill never got out of committee. Presumably the members of Congress realized that the mere installation of a commission of inquiry was likely to generate substantial pressures for some sort of reparations. Once the Commission on Wartime Relocation and Internment of Civilians (CWRIC) was in place to examine the factors that led to the Japanese American internments, the political momentum built steadily until Ronald Reagan was

forced to endorse the notion of redress. It took approximately eight years from the invocation of a congressional commission of inquiry to the signing of compensatory legislation.[31] At the same time, the members of Congress may simply be acting in accordance with the views of their constituents; a 1997 poll found that while two-thirds of blacks supported the idea of both an apology and compensation for slavery, two-thirds of white respondents resisted even an apology, and fully 88 percent opposed the notion of paying reparations.[32] In any event, the result is that Conyers's legislative proposal gets nowhere. Still, the issue of reparations for blacks has received greater public attention ever since Conyers put the issue back on the agenda,[33] and Conyers himself has said that he believes that reparations has now "entered the mainstream."[34] It is to these more recent developments that we now turn.

Reparations for Blacks in the United States: The Latest Chapter

Those backing the campaign for reparations for blacks in the United States have recently insisted more and more loudly that—after payments to Holocaust survivors, to persons of Japanese descent incarcerated as enemy aliens in North America during World War II, and to a variety of Indian groups—"it's our turn."[35] In 1994, during the early stages of the most recent wave of reparations claims-making, one observer correctly suggested that his readers "soon will be hearing that word [reparations] with greater frequency."[36] In the meantime, a number of city councils have adopted resolutions supporting the idea, and the City of Los Angeles has adopted an ordinance requiring every company doing business with the city to report whether it ever profited from slavery.[37] But whether the "campaign" for reparations ever becomes a successful "movement" probably depends on whether its backers succeed in creating a substantial popular base capable of pressuring lawmakers about the issue, just as Derrick Bell argued in the early 1970s.

While reparations talk spread during the second half of the 1990s, attention to the issue surged with the appearance, in 2000, of Randall Robinson's highly publicized book *The Debt: What America Owes to Blacks*.[38] Coincident with its publication, Robinson convened a meeting of a number of leading black politicians, intellectuals, and activists in the Washington, D.C., offices of the TransAfrica Forum, the organization he founded to lobby the federal government on American foreign policy with respect to Africa and the African diaspora (especially in the Caribbean).[39] The subject of the meeting, at which Congressman John Conyers was a keynote speaker, was to discuss "The Case for Black Reparations." Although no mention was made of the earlier Black Manifesto during the discussions, the portion of the TransAfrica Forum website chronicling the meeting includes a link to a text called "The Reparations Manifesto"; the heading of that document reads, "Restatement of the Black Manifesto."[40] Presumably some connection is being drawn to James Forman's demands of the late 1960s, but no mention is made in TransAfrica Forum's "Reparations Manifesto" of the culpability or responsibility of the churches. Instead, the document focuses on the liabilities of the U.S. government.

The issue of reparations for blacks soon became so prominent that it found its way into mainstream media and prime time television. Along with the attention and activism generated by Robinson's book among those supportive of the reparations idea, however, others who were less sympathetic were paying attention as well. On May 30, 2000, the conservative publicist David Horowitz wrote an attack on the idea of reparations in the online magazine *Salon*. The piece was headlined "The Latest Civil Rights Disaster," with the subtitle, "Ten reasons why reparations for slavery are a bad idea for black people—and racist too."[41] The article, which appeared in an outlet not widely consulted by nonintellectuals, generated little discernible echo.

But Horowitz, savvy as he is about a wedge issue, was not finished with the matter. In early 2001, he attempted to place ads under the "Ten Reasons" heading in the campus newspapers of a number of leading colleges and universities across the United States. Most of the newspapers declined to run the ad. Those that did saw copies spirited away from distribution boxes or had their editorial offices besieged by protesters—perhaps most notably at Berkeley, the proverbial birthplace of the Free Speech Movement. The student newspaper at Brown University published the ad, generating a fiasco. The furor provoked by the ad campaign stimulated a front-page article in the *New York Times* noting that "overlooked in much of the uproar over the [Brown University] newspaper's publication of the advertisement is the deeper national debate on reparations over slavery, which could have found fertile ground for discussion on this campus."[42]

Much ink was subsequently spilled on the controversy that Horowitz provoked, with published responses from even so distinguished a commentator as John Hope Franklin, chairman of Bill Clinton's "Dialogue on Race," who dismissed Horowitz's ad as a "diatribe."[43] Horowitz subsequently made considerable hay out of the matter, including a debating tour of college campuses with a representative of the National Coalition of Blacks for Reparations in America (N'COBRA), the major group working (in relative obscurity) on the reparations issue before Randall Robinson put it (back) on the map.[44] Horowitz also used the affair for his own fundraising purposes. He vigorously denounced the "hucksters" in the "racial shakedown racket" who were behind the "reparations scam," but he was apparently not averse to exploiting the issue for his own purposes.[45] A year or so after the controversy stirred up by Horowitz and his antagonists, the once-venerable organ of liberal opinion *The New Republic* also ran a lengthy, scathing attack on the idea of reparations—thinly disguised as a review of Randall Robinson's book *The Debt*—by Berkeley linguistics professor John McWhorter, a rising star on the right for his relatively conservative views on racial issues.[46] By this time, the matter of reparations had risen to become something of a *cause célèbre* in progressive circles, and a *bête noire* in conservative ones.

Despite being primarily a domestic U.S. issue, the debates about reparations that took place prior to the World Conference Against Racism (WCAR) in Durban, South Africa, in late summer 2001 put the matter on the worldwide political agenda. During the run-up to Durban, the prominent nongovernmental organization Human Rights Watch issued a document titled "An Approach to Reparations" that sought to bridge the gap between reparations for those who had themselves suffered wrongs and those who were seeking to rectify the long-term consequences of systems of domination and exploitation—that is, between "commemorative" and "antisystemic" reparations.[47]

In one of the most thoughtful and innovative interventions in the reparations discussion to date, Human Rights Watch proposed the creation of what would be "effectively truth commissions" to investigate "specific multiracial countries such as the United States, Brazil, and South Africa" that have been the foci of reparations debates because of their legacies of slavery and racial domination, as well as other bodies of inquiry "for specific countries that would examine the degree to which the slave trade and colonialism, as opposed to the subsequent practices of the post-independence government, have contributed to the destitution of the country's population."[48] Yet Human Rights Watch's nuanced approach to reparations, which sought to overcome the distinction between reparations for those who had directly suffered harms and those who suffer today from the *consequences* of earlier wrongs, especially the neediest among them, was soon lost in the flood. With the deterioration of discussion at Durban into shouting matches that included anti-Semitic remarks, the attacks of September 11, 2001, and the civil liberties and human rights challenges that soon followed, Human Rights Watch abandoned its plans to pursue the reparations inquiries that it had outlined. The Durban conference did issue a declaration that slavery was a crime against humanity, however, providing further fodder for reparations activists.

In the atmosphere created by *The Debt*, David Horowitz, and Durban, public opposition to the idea of reparations by a black person had come to appear something of a betrayal of other blacks. Yet Jack E. White, who had been present at the TransAfrica Forum gathering in early 2000, wrote in his column in *Time* that "the fight for slave reparations is a morally just but totally hopeless cause."[49] A columnist for *Time* might be written off by supporters of reparations as too mainstream, but the same cannot be said of the only other prominent contemporary left-wing black critic of the idea of whom I am aware, the New School University political scientist Adolph Reed. Reed's progressive credentials are difficult to impugn; he has for some years written the "Class Notes" column for *The Progressive* magazine. Yet Reed pulled no punches in his published discussion of the reparations cause, dismissing the pursuit of reparations as a "political dead end."[50] On the assumption that it was "so obviously a nonstarter in American politics," Reed sought in his commentary on the subject to make sense of why the idea of reparations had gathered such momentum in a political climate in which the fortunes even of affirmative action had declined substantially.

Reed argued that the idea of reparations had three relevant dimensions: material, symbolic, and psychological. He agreed that the economic wrongs inflicted on the American black population by slavery and legal segregation manifestly deserved to be remedied. He also understood the symbolic dimension of reparations, the yearning for public acknowledgment of the injustices of the past. But this, he asserted, "does not require the rhetoric of reparations," and it fit what he called "the Clintonoid tenor of sappy public apologies and maudlin psychobabble about collective pain and healing." But Reed was most critical of reparations activists' arguments with regard to the third, psychological dimension. In particular, he rejected their assumption that it is important "to restore or correct racial consciousness that the legacy of slavery is supposed to have distorted or destroyed." This notion he refers to as the "damage thesis,"[51] which maintains that blacks have been psychologically disturbed by their experiences of oppression. This approach to understanding the plight of blacks, he argues, "ensconces a particular guiding role for upper class blacks" who think they have escaped the psychological damage they diagnose among others.

Like many other critics, Reed finds insuperable the complications involved in reparations compensation—who would be the recipients? If payments were made to a corporate entity, how would that entity be held accountable? Reed subsequently extended this critique by arguing that it's one thing to compensate people who have directly suffered physical harms, and another to pay reparations to their descendants. Reed made the point in connection with a much-noted exhibition on the appalling history of lynching in the United States: "If there's a case to be made for reparations, based on existing precedents, it seems like this would be it. There are victims with names and culprits with names, and there's a specifiable harm."[52] In effect, Reed was distinguishing between "victims" and "the dispossessed"—which corresponds from the opposite perspective with a distinction between "perpetrators" on the one hand and "beneficiaries" on the other—in a manner that has been used by others to distinguish among different kinds of reparations claims, and to argue that reparations are only likely to be paid in the case of the former.[53] The compensation paid to the victims of the Rosewood massacre of 1923 and that recommended for those terrorized in the race riots in Tulsa, Oklahoma, in 1921 fit this pattern well; rather than being compensation for the generalized wrongs done to blacks historically under slavery and Jim Crow, these cases involved reparations for harms done to specific individuals and their families.[54] Yet even the lawsuit seeking to realize the recommendation for reparations to the surviving victims of the Tulsa race riot has so far been unsuccessful, on statute of limitations grounds.[55]

Ultimately, however, Reed's objections to the idea of reparations were political: "What strikes me as most incomprehensible about the reparations movement is its complete disregard for the simplest, most mundanely pragmatic question about any political mobilization: How can we imagine building a political force that would enable us to prevail on this issue?" Moreover, at a time when "common circumstances of economic and social insecurity have strengthened the potential for building broad solidarity across race, gender, and other identities," he argued, the "demand for racially defined reparations . . . cuts precisely against building such solidarity." In short, Reed opposed the idea of reparations as politically divisive—not with respect to some airy, nonexistent American "community," but rather with regard to those elements of American society who are worst off because of their shared class position and who might be mobilized to seek political and social change on that basis.

Reed's has remained a lonely voice on the left. Yet the difficulties of squaring the pursuit of reparations for black Americans with traditional left-wing politics become apparent in an article by Ben Dalby in the *International Socialist Review* addressing the problem of "Slavery and the Question of Reparations." Dalby shares Reed's view of Randall Robinson as "elite-oriented," but reserves his main criticisms for the latter's tendency to view the fundamental social divide that reparations is to ameliorate as *racial* rather than economic. Dalby argues that racism has always been used by "the ruling class" as a way of dividing workers along racial lines, to their disadvantage and to the benefit of that ruling class. Hence analyses that stress the advantages to all whites that have accrued from slavery and racism miss the mark: "The legacy of slavery and institutionalized racism has meant lower unionization rates, and lower wages for Black *and* white workers. . . . The potential combination of the struggle against racism with class consciousness was a constant danger." The correct answer to the reparations demand, therefore, is to "make the rich capitalists who benefited from slavery pay." Yet the ruling class shrinks from countenancing this demand, in this account, because its implications are too profound: "This is more than just resistance to paying out large sums of money. . . . [If blacks receive reparations, w]ho will we have to pay next, the Bushes and Rockefellers of this country might ask? American Indians demanding land and the billions stolen from them? The entire working class who have been systematically robbed for profit?"[56] The problem with this analysis is that it transforms "the working class" into a quasi-racial entity that persists relatively unchanged across generations. Nonetheless, the argument points toward a transformation of the idea of reparations from a race-based to a class-based demand. While perhaps having better prospects politically, one wonders whether the term "reparations" is useful in achieving what would amount simply to a policy of wealth redistribution, whether intended to fix *past* injustices or current and future ones. The *International Socialist Review*'s attention to the reparations demand nonetheless suggested the extent to which the idea of reparations had taken hold in left-wing circles, but the magazine's treatment also made clear that this was an awkward demand from the point of view of traditional left-wing, class-based universalism.

Adolph Reed's sharp critique of the campaign for reparations for blacks raised the unavoidable question of the political mobilization behind, and hence the practical feasibility of, reparations for blacks. There have in recent years been two main groups active in the reparations cause. First is the high-profile Reparations Coordinating Committee (RCC), which was initially co-chaired by Harvard Law School professor Charles Ogletree and by Randall Robinson. The RCC was first formed in 2000. The other group pushing the reparations idea—N'COBRA, the acronym of the aforementioned National Coalition of Blacks for Reparations in America—is less well known, though it has been in existence since 1987. The differences between the two groups are striking. The RCC includes some of the most visible and successful black intellectuals and professionals in the United States today. The involvement in the issue of such persons appears to reflect a disillusionment about the prospects for racial equality that is fuelled by their own evident success in American life; though this is by no means to impugn the integrity of their commitment to the issue, that commitment has something of the quality of a "survivor's guilt."[57] By contrast, those associated with N'COBRA are substantially less well-known, and have stronger links to traditions of black nationalism in the United States. The two seem a somewhat unlikely match.

Neither the RCC nor N'COBRA issued a ringing endorsement of the March 2002 suit filed by Deadria Farmer-Paellmann, which seems from their perspective to have been something of a maverick enterprise. Indeed, in an apparent effort to regain the upper hand for their own approach to reparations claims-making, the RCC's Ogletree observed disapprovingly on the op-ed page of the *New York Times* later the same month that the suit "is limited to FleetBoston, Aetna, CSX, and other to-be-named companies." In contrast, "the broader reparations movement seeks to explore the historical role that other private institutions and government played during slavery and the era of legal racial discrimination that followed. The goal of these historical investigations is to bring American society to a new reckoning with how our past affects the current conditions of African-Americans and to make America a better place by helping the truly disadvantaged."[58] In other words, the Farmer-Paellmann suit was confined to seeking mere monetary compensation, rather than aiming to stimulate a public debate about slavery, segregation, and their consequences, as the Reparations Coordinating Committee envisioned.

For its part, about three weeks after the filing of Farmer-Paellmann's lawsuit, the N'COBRA National Board issued a "Membership Advisory" indicating that while it "applauded" Farmer-Paellmann's efforts, it had declined her invitation to act as co-lead counsel because it was not informed of the pending lawsuit until twelve days before it was filed and the board did "not want to participate in a litigation strategy that has been developed and implemented . . . without the input of its legal team." More particularly, "it appears that the strategy developed may include not filing actions against the United States government," in contrast to N'COBRA's stress on "the central role that the government played in the enslavement of Africans and [that it] continues to play in maintaining the vestiges of slavery."[59] In short, the two principal organizations spearheading the recent drive for reparations for black Americans were inclined to keep their distance from the Farmer-Paellmann lawsuit, mainly because it was limited to suing private enterprises rather than the federal government. Their criticisms of Farmer-Paellmann for targeting only private companies paralleled Charles Willie's earlier critique of the Black Manifesto for directing its attack at the churches rather than what he regarded as the proper addressee, namely the government.

In addition to their stated objections, the reluctance of the RCC and of N'COBRA to go along with Farmer-Paellmann's suit may also have stemmed from the involvement of controversial reparations attorney Edward Fagan. The newly prominent lawyer earned considerable notoriety as counsel in some of the legal actions that brought in more than a billion dollars in reparations for Holocaust survivors in the late 1990s. Fagan's controversial involvement in the Holocaust-related actions garnered him a scathing front-page feature in the *New York Times* examining his often-questionable tactics and practices.[60] Yet Fagan was only getting started when he helped compel the Swiss to pay victims of the Holocaust for their suffering. Having moved on to help put together the Farmer-Paellmann suit in late March 2002, he was also the lead lawyer in a $50 billion class action suit against Citigroup, UBS, and Credit Suisse filed two months later on behalf of victims of South African apartheid. From the point of view of reparations activists, his participation in the Farmer-Paellmann suit was likely to complicate the perception of reparations as a political rather than a merely legal issue.

In all events, Fagan beat N'COBRA and the RCC off the mark, and thus preempted—at least to some degree—whatever strategy they may have had in mind. The fundamental problem here may not have been so much Fagan's possible huckstering as the difficulty of pursuing a legally oriented strategy for obtaining reparations in the absence of a broader grassroots movement supporting that demand. Until this time, the RCC and N'COBRA appear to have had at least formally an arms-length relationship, although Adjoa Aiyetoro, N'COBRA's chief legal consultant, was present as a participant at the TransAfrica Forum meeting on reparations in January 2000 and she and Charles Ogletree have long known one another personally.[61] Soon after the Farmer-Paellmann lawsuit was launched, however, N'COBRA and the Reparations Coordinating Committee issued a joint statement agreeing to work together more closely. The statement bespeaks the RCC's recognition that it is an undertaking of the contemporary equivalent of Dubois's "talented tenth" and an attempt to overcome the relative isolation of that group from the remainder of the black population. The planned cooperation between the two groups, according to the statement issued by N'COBRA, "links the RCC with the constituency of African Descendants that are both [N'COBRA's] clients and the beneficiaries of our work. . . . The breadth of the N'COBRA network assures the important linkage of the RCC to the broad-based grassroots movement for reparations."[62] The two groups apparently came to believe that they had to work together more closely if they wished to achieve their common goals.

Despite the rapprochement between the two organizations and the statement's invocation of a "broad-based grassroots movement," however, the evidence for the existence of such a movement has been weak. For example, March 21, 2002, was declared Reparations Awareness Day in the city of New York, but even a sympathetic observer from *The Village Voice* reported that an event in Brooklyn celebrating the occasion produced only a scene of "Ivy Leaguers and comfortable activists talking to each other" that was "replayed at reparations forums around the city."[63] Similarly, a Citywide Millions for Reparations Mobilization Rally scheduled to take place at the Harriet Tubman School in Harlem in May 2002 produced little discernible echo.[64] The Harlem event was intended to drum up support for the Millions for Reparations National Rally scheduled for Saturday, August 17, 2002, in Washington, D.C. Turnout for the rally was relatively meager—perhaps a few thousand—although RCC co-chair Charles Ogletree agreed with the *New York Times* account that it was a very "energetic" group.[65]

Oddly, the Millions for Reparations Rally was not organized by either the RCC or N'COBRA, but by a number of black nationalist groups including the National Black United Front, the New Black Panther Party,[66] and the United Negro Improvement Association, the group originally founded by the early twentieth-century Caribbean-born "back-to-Africa" leader Marcus Garvey. In addition to calling attention to the demand for reparations, the August rally was also supposed to honor Garvey on the 115th anniversary of his birth.[67] The Garveyite and Afrocentric infrastructure underlying the march bears witness to political scientist Michael Dawson's recent finding that, as a result of the relative weakness of other currents in contemporary black politics, "black nationalism is enjoying more grassroots success than it has had in three-quarters of a century"—that is, since Garvey was at the height of his influence.[68]

Yet Dawson's claim that "the language of reparations" is part of the "common understanding" of black politics is doubtful—or at least it doesn't tell us much about blacks' degree of commitment to seeing reparations achieved.[69] Examining the extent of support for reparations among black youth, one analyst argued that the urban black youth of the "hip-hop generation" are almost entirely unaware of the reparations lawsuits and their aims. A figure familiar to hip-hoppers, the impresario and founder of Def Jam records, Russell Simmons, pledged to promote knowledge of the reparations cause among his customers and to support research and action on the matter. Simmons also bankrolled the Hip Hop Summit Action Network, whose president, former NAACP president Benjamin (Chavis) Muhammed, had committed himself to getting out the reparations message to blacks. In a bid to take the campaign to the streets, Simmons developed plans for a publicity campaign based on the theme of "Forty Acres and a Bentley"—because, he said, the luxury car "has become the highest American aspiration for this generation, unfortunately." Whatever its appeal to the hip-hop generation, this choice of theme may not be well calculated to inspire enthusiasm about the idea of reparations among the nonblack segments of the population, who are likely to be crucial in determining the eventual political outcome of the quest for reparations. The bottom line, according to *The Village Voice* writer, is that if the reparations movement is going to get anywhere, "the lawyers and academics will have to roll up their sleeves, kick off their expensive shoes, and get their feet dirty walking the streets, looking for a way to bridge the divide" between "the old civil rights guard" and the "reigning hip-hop generation."[70]

If history is any guide, in order for the campaign to have any prospect of becoming a mass movement, reparations activists will need to gain the support of mainstream civil rights organizations and the black churches. Yet an examination of the website of the NAACP found no discussion of the issue, much less any stated position on the matter.[71] Notably, however, the NAACP website posts the results of several polls concerning the reparations issue. A poll created July 23, 2001, asks, "Will reparations help America address a long delayed moral obligation?" Thirty-four percent of the respondents said that it would, while 56 percent said that it would not. Another poll created in March 2002 indicates that 71 percent of the respondents oppose a governmental inquiry into possible reparations for slavery. Finally, in a poll created in early April 2004, soon after a judge dismissed a number of lawsuits against businesses that had allegedly profited from slavery, the NAACP asked whether respondents "agree or disagree with lawsuits for reparations against companies that insured slave ships." Fewer than one-third agreed, while 61.5 percent disagreed with such actions. It is unclear how the parameters of these polls were drawn, but the respondents were presumably NAACP members; in all events, the NAACP would appear at least to want these negative findings to be known to anyone viewing its website.[72] Given the apparent dearth of grassroots mobilization behind the reparations idea, perhaps the most striking feature of the campaign so far has been the relative absence from its ranks of the black churches. The pulpits have historically been the most reliable channel between elite black opinion and mass grassroots activism. One may reasonably regard with skepticism the hope that leaders of the hip-hop movement will substitute for the churches and play a substantial role in generating support for reparations, especially if Bentleys are the stated aspiration.[73]

Presumably the figures promoting the campaign for reparations envision the legal route as a catalyst that will generate enthusiasm for the reparations idea among both blacks themselves and the public at large. In order to assess this strategy, one should bear in mind that the civil rights movement did not emerge full-blown with sit-ins, boycotts, and marches on Washington; it took time for the movement to gather steam. It began in the unpromising, famously (though misleadingly) conformist 1950s, but ultimately led to a "second Reconstruction."[74] One of the sparks that eventually lit the fuse in the dark days of the 1950s was the decision in *Brown v. Board of Education*, which declared an end to the era of legalized segregation. In most accounts of the rise of the civil rights movement, the *Brown* decision is identified as a watershed episode. Gerald Rosenberg has disputed the widespread assumption that *Brown* was a key moment heralding the possibility of wider changes, however, arguing that political developments outside the courtroom were more decisive in actually achieving equal rights. Yet he relies on a positivistic methodology that assumes that one must find copious references to *Brown* in, say, the speeches of Martin Luther King, Jr., in order to demonstrate its significance for the civil rights movement. In fact, *Brown* had an immediate and welcome impact on many of those involved in the struggle for civil rights, and they saw the ruling as a beacon of wider changes.[75] Rosenberg is correct, however, to insist that court rulings in themselves do little to change matters "on the ground"; that requires political mobilization and enforcement of the law.[76]

One of the more striking conclusions of Michael Dawson's study *Black Visions* concerns the extent to which black political discussion and debate take place in terms that lead it to be extensively overlooked by the mainstream media. An important result is that political analysts tend to underestimate the significance of nationalist perspectives among blacks. Dawson shows that nationalism has been resurgent in recent years largely because of the widespread disillusionment—among even the country's most successful blacks—regarding the prospects for progress toward racial equality in the United States. The idea of reparations for blacks has bubbled along in the black nationalist underground for some years and has surfaced with some force since the late 1990s both because of the larger context of successful reparations claims by other groups and because of the high profile of some of the campaign's leading advocates.[77] Despite attracting the rhetorical support of many blacks, it has continued to be largely a marginal preoccupation of a relatively small though often highly visible group, and there is no sign that the wider society has grown appreciably more sympathetic to the idea of reparations for blacks in the United States since the latest round of reparations activism began.

Conclusion

Against this background, what is achieved by pursuing the seemingly unlikely goal of gaining reparations for the injustices suffered by blacks in American history, real though they have been? Employing the legalistic language of "reparations" may offer some advantages, but it entails substantial disadvantages as well. Supporters of reparations for blacks often point to the precedent set by the reparations paid to Jews for their Holocaust-related suffering, as well as to persons of Japanese descent for their unjust internment during World War II. These cases do, indeed, raise questions about why blacks might not similarly demand compensation for the wrongs to which they have been subjected and for their uncompensated contributions to the wealth of the contemporary United States. Yet there is something to the argument that payments to Holocaust survivors and interned Japanese

Americans are a different matter than compensation to those who are ("merely") the descendants of slaves, rather than themselves the victims of atrocities. It is for this reason that the lawsuits in the Tulsa Race Riot case seemed more promising than a more general attempt to rectify inequalities of wealth through the mechanism of reparations. As we have already noted, however, the lawsuit seeking reparations in that case was dismissed on statute of limitations grounds.[78] If the campaign for reparations for blacks is to be successful, in all events, the focus has to be shifted from *perpetrators* to *beneficiaries*, and this presents very difficult obstacles that arise from the fact that the people for whom the campaign is being undertaken—the most disadvantaged blacks in American society—are not necessarily the victims of actionable legal offenses, as were Japanese Americans.

To the extent that Americans have come to associate the term "reparations" with monetary payments to individuals, such a goal would seem likely to be a nonstarter politically, as a number of commentators on this issue—black and white—have suggested. Although many reparations activists actually seek such measures as college scholarship funds, small business loans, and educational programs designed to call greater attention to the history of racial oppression in America, for the uninitiated the use of the term "reparations" tends to conjure up images of monetary payouts that would have to be rather large to make any significant impact on individual blacks. In addition, the idea of individual payments raises eyebrows among those potentially responsible for the resulting tax burden. Some of the estimates of what would be owed for back wages, lost opportunities, and the like are, not surprisingly, astronomical sums.[79] The prospect of individual payments to black Americans, in the manner of the funds recently developed by the German government to compensate those exploited as slave labor under the Nazis, therefore seems dim.

Such individual payments are probably not, in fact, the objective of most supporters of "reparations" for black Americans. In response to some of these objections, Charles Ogletree has recently argued that "the billions, or perhaps trillions, of dollars that come from a successful reparations lawsuit not be distributed in the form of a check to every African-American," but that "all of the money be placed in a trust fund, administered perhaps through the churches or other reputable organizations in the community, and made available to the 'bottom stuck,' those African-American families that have not been able to realize the American Dream fully. . . . It is a paternalistic approach, of course, but one that is entirely necessary to overcoming the problems we face."[80] Yet if this is the objective, use of the term "reparations" in connection with the pursuit of these policy objectives may well be counter-productive, suggesting as it does the notion of individual payments. For this is simply a policy of redistribution of wealth to the black poor, which in any case is not an objective with strong prospects in contemporary American politics. The notion that the funds should be distributed by "reputable organizations in the community" is sure to provoke controversy, as Ogletree is well aware. More significantly, the notion that the money will become available through a single successful reparations lawsuit seems far-fetched. This is especially true in view of the fact that the Tulsa reparations suit—on which Ogletree stakes so much importance and which he claimed "avoids the modern critique of reparations lawsuits" (namely, that they must involve living victims)—has been dismissed since he wrote his memoir.[81]

> In the end, the use of legal stratagems such as lawsuits for reparations to achieve the goals of racial equality in the United States must be understood above all in tactical terms. Does the pursuit of reparations contribute to a better understanding of the ways in which slavery and segregation have created a society that frequently mistreats and denigrates blacks and denies them their full share in American life? Does it contribute to a more complete recognition of the role of blacks in creating the prosperity enjoyed by Americans? Does it contribute to improving the lives and opportunities of the most disadvantaged black Americans?

The legal path is appealing because the political context is so frustrating. "Court is the one place we can achieve what we can't achieve in the popular vote," Ogletree has said.[82] Yet this approach leaves the movement open to interlopers less interested in their political aims, and for whom the courtroom is the only venue in which they seek victory. Likewise, the pursuit of money—as opposed to the civil rights movement's search for equal legal treatment—raises hackles because it appears to invoke a notion of economic equality to which the United States has never had any commitment, constitutional or otherwise. Even if the issue were not so difficult, the march through the courts appears likely to be a long one; commenting on the prospects of success of reparations legal actions, NAACP Legal Defense Fund litigator Ted Shaw has said that these efforts are taking place "in a context in which the Supreme Court is as conservative as any we have seen in our lifetime," and "they will be hostile to anything we could bring."[83]

The juridification of politics is not necessarily auspicious when the goal is broad economic redistribution and the legal and political climates are so unpromising. Political scientist and longtime analyst of American racial politics Jennifer Hochschild put the matter succinctly when she argued that "using the court system to debate a deeply political and moral issue distorts the case for reparations by framing it in 'legalese'. . . . There are . . . deep costs to demanding monetary recompense for what was national policy for over three centuries—especially if there is no real chance of seeing the cash."[84]

The campaign for reparations for blacks has shown few signs of growing into a movement because there seems little prospect that the U.S. government is going to dispense largesse to a group defined by its race. In order to mount a serious challenge to the disparities of wealth and power that are widening in the contemporary period, it will be necessary to build an interracial movement to challenge contemporary inequalities that appeals to broad segments of the population.[85]

Notably, this was precisely the approach adopted by those supporting the University of Michigan in its efforts to defend the use of affirmative action in its admissions policies. Faced with a major court challenge, supporters of the policy rallied their forces, including representatives of corporate business, the military, academia, Jewish groups once opposed to "quotas," and others. These authorities warned that, without a diverse student body and, subsequently, a diverse corps of well-educated persons, the United States would eventually suffer damage to its legitimacy and well-being. Their arguments emphasized efficiency and effectiveness, the possibilities and promise of the future rather than the wrongs of the past.[86] In considerable measure, this view appears to have been crucial in gaining the (limited) support of the Court's swing vote in the Michigan law school case, that of Justice Sandra Day O'Connor. The result was that affirmative action seems to have been preserved, in a somewhat opaque form, for a generation.[87]

In the end, although racial inequality in the United States cannot be understood without some reference to the historical legacy of slavery, solutions will have to be couched in forward-looking terms that a politician can articulate, not in legal terms that stress the past violations of slavery and Jim Crow. These arguments must be able to address satisfactorily the gains—in many respects remarkable—that blacks have made in the last four decades. The project for a Museum of African-American History and Culture on the mall in Washington also seems a promising means of recognizing the role of blacks in American life and the almost biblical nature of their sojourn in the United States. At the same time, of course, it will do little to transform the conditions of the poorest blacks. The museum will address the cultural aspects of the historic wrongs that have been done to blacks, but not the economic wrongs. Ameliorating the latter will require a broader-based political movement devoted to greater economic equality for all Americans. Legal approaches alone are not enough.

Notes

I am grateful to the Social Science and Humanities Research Council of Canada for the funding that made this project possible.

1. No author, "Suits Ask Slavery Reparations," *Chicago Tribune*, March 27, 2002, sec. 1, p. 9; the suit itself can be found online at: http://news.findlaw.com/ legal-news/lit/slavery/. For further developments in the case, see Lori Rotenberk, "A Stern Judge Presides as Reparations Fight Begins," *Boston Sunday Globe*, August 24, 2003, p. A17.

2. See his oft-quoted observation, "There is almost no political question in the United States that is not resolved sooner or later into a judicial question." Alexis de Tocqueville, *Democracy in America*, trans. Harvey Mansfield and Delba Winthrop (Chicago: University of Chicago Press, 2000), 257.

3. Linda Greenhouse, "Judges Back Rule Changes for Handling Class Actions," *New York Times* national edition, September 25, 2002, p. A16.

4. John Locke, *Two Treatises of Government*, ed. Peter Laslett (New York: Mentor, 1965), Treatise II, §49.

5. For a spectrum of views concerning the progress of the black population in the United States—or the lack thereof—since the civil rights movement, see Orlando Patterson, *The Ordeal of Integration: Progress and Resentment in America's "Racial" Crisis* (New York: Basic Civitas, 1997), which sees the glass as half-full; William Julius Wilson, *The Bridge over the Racial Divide: Rising Inequality and Coalition Politics* (Berkeley: University of California Press, 1999), which sees the glass as half-empty but

open to improvement through a multiracial coalition politics that deemphasizes race in favor of a stress on class; and, at the most pessimistic, Michael Dawson, *Black Visions: The Roots of Contemporary African-American Political Ideologies* (Chicago: University of Chicago Press, 2002), which sees the glass as half-empty and with few prospects of improvement in sight.

6. Richard J. Herrnstein and Charles Murray, *The Bell Curve: Intelligence and Class Structure in American Life* (New York: Simon & Schuster, 1996). For a refutation of the biological arguments, see Joseph L. Graves, Jr., *The Emperor's New Clothes: Biological Theories of Race at the Millennium* (New Brunswick, NJ: Rutgers University Press, 2001).

7. See Hugh Davis Graham, *Collision Course: The Strange Convergence of Affirmative Action and Immigration Policy in America* (New York: Oxford University Press, 2002); and Wilson, *Bridge over the Racial Divide*. Also noteworthy are Robert Blauner's reflections on affirmative action in *Still the Big News: Racial Oppression in America* (Philadelphia: Temple University Press, 2001), 191–92.

8. Robert Westley, "Many Billions Gone: Is It Time to Reconsider the Case for Black Reparations?" *Boston College Law Review* 40, no. 1 (December 1998): 429, 432.

9. For a detailed discussion of these claims up until World War I, see John David Smith, "Historicizing the Slave Reparations Debate," paper presented at the conference "Historical Justice in International Perspective: How Societies are Trying to Right the Wrongs of the Past," German Historical Institute, Washington, D.C., March 2003. Smith is working on a book-length history of the idea of reparations among blacks in the United States.

10. Eric Foner, *A Short History of Reconstruction* (New York: Harper & Row, 1990), 32, 71–72. For a discussion of the failures of the Freedmen's Bureau, see W. E. B. Dubois, *The Souls of Black Folk* (New York: Dover, 1994 [1903]), Chapter 2, "Of the Dawn of Freedom," and, on the consequences of its failures, Jacqueline Jones, *The Dispossessed: America's Underclasses from the Civil War to the Present* (New York: Basic Books, 1992). John David Smith argues that the land was "probably" leased to the freedmen, but that the Order was misconstrued by blacks as "conveying outright titles to the property." See "Historicizing the Slave Reparations Debate," 7.

11. On the significance of the 442d Regiment in the Japanese American redress movement, see Mitchell Maki et al., *Achieving the Impossible Dream: How Japanese Americans Obtained Redress* (Urbana: University of Illinois Press, 1999), 153.

12. See the analysis in Robert Blauner's path-breaking *Racial Oppression in America* (New York: Prentice-Hall, 1972), insightfully revised and updated in Blauner, *Still the Big News*.

13. See John David Skrentny, *The Minority Rights Revolution* (Cambridge, MA: Harvard University Press, 2002), and Graham, *Collision Course*.

14. Quoted in Harvard Sitkoff, *The Struggle for Black Equality, 1954–1980* (New York: Hill and Wang, 1981), 228.

15. See Robin D. G. Kelley, *Freedom Dreams: The Black Radical Imagination* (Boston: Beacon Press, 2002), 118–20; Charles Ogletree, "Reparations, A Fundamental Issue of Social Justice," *The Black Collegian Online*, undated, http://www.black-collegian.com/news/special-reports/resparations2002-1st.shtml; and Arthur Serota, *Ending Apartheid in America: The Need for a Black Political Party and Reparations Now!* (Evanston, IL: Troubadour Press, 1996), Acknowledgments.

16. James Forman, *The Making of Black Revolutionaries* (Seattle: University of Washington Press, 1997 [1972]), 545, 547; for the Manifesto itself, see Arnold Schuchter, *Reparations: The Black Manifesto and Its Challenge to White America* (Philadelphia: Lippincott, 1970); see also Rhonda Magee, "The Master's Tools, From the Bottom Up: Responses to African-American Reparations Theory in Mainstream and Outsider Remedies Discourse," *Virginia Law Review* 79, no. 4 (1993): 882–84; and Dawson, *Black Visions*, 119.

17. Charles Willie, "The Black Manifesto: Prophetic or Preposterous?" *The Episcopalian*, September 1969, quoted in Schuchter, *Reparations*, 11.

18. Dawson, *Black Visions*, 206.

19. Maki et al., *Achieving the Impossible Dream*, 71, 252 n 35. It may be worth noting that the idea of reparations goes without mention in the recent book by Roger Wilkins, Roy Wilkins's prominent nephew, *Jefferson's Pillow: The Founding Fathers and the Dilemma of Black Patriotism* (Boston: Beacon Press, 2001).

20. See Forman, *The Making of Black Revolutionaries*, 549.

21. See Michael Dawson's discussion of the tensions between black nationalists and the churches in *Black Visions*, 107–8.

22. Alan Feuer, "Bitter Reparations Fight Reignited over Settlement," *New York Times* national edition, November 21, 2000, p. A22; Joseph B. Treaster, "2 Holocaust Survivors to Sue Group Set Up to Collect Insurance," *New York Times* national edition, September 25, 2003, p. A16; William Glaberson, "Judge Rebuffs U.S. Holocaust Survivors on Distribution of a Fund," *New York Times* national edition, November 22, 2003, p. A14.

23. Boris Bittker, *The Case for Black Reparations* (New York: Random House, 1973). Around the same time, R. S. Browne also published "The Economic Case for Reparations to Black America," *American Economic Review* 62, nos. 1/2 (1972): 39–46.

24. A brief discussion of Bittker's book and some contemporary updating of his proposals can be found in Darrell L. Pugh, "Collective Rehabilitation," in Roy Brooks, ed., *When Sorry Isn't Enough*, 372–73.

25. The story is recounted in Derrick A. Bell, *Confronting Authority: Reflections of an Ardent Protester* (Boston: Beacon Press, 1994).

26. See Derrick A. Bell, *And We Are Not Saved: The Elusive Quest for Racial Justice* (New York: Basic Books, 1987) and *Faces at the Bottom of the Well: The Permanence of Racism* (New York: Basic Books, 1992).

27. Derrick A. Bell, Jr., "Dissection of a Dream," *Harvard Civil Rights-Civil Liberties Law Review* 9, no. 1 (1974): 165. In recent years, Bell has apparently been converted to the idea of reparations; see the relevant discussion in his *Silent Covenants: Brown v. Board of Education and the Unfulfilled Hopes for Racial Reform* (New York: Oxford University Press, 2004), 73–76.

28. Roy Brooks has sought to update Bittker's analysis of the constitutional obstacles confronting reparations claims in Boris I. Bittker and Roy L. Brooks, "The Constitutionality of Black Reparations," in Roy Brooks, ed., *When Sorry Isn't Enough*, 374–38.

29. Magee, "The Master's Tools, From the Bottom Up," 903.

30. See Lynette Clemetson, "Long Quest, Unlikely Allies: Black Museum Nears Reality," *New York Times* national edition, June 29, 2003, pp. A1, A24; and Lynette Clemetson, "Bush Authorizes Black History Museum," *New York Times* national edition, December 17, 2003, p. A32.

31. This interpretation is advanced by Dennis C. Sweet III, an attorney in Jackson, Mississippi, who won a major settlement in the "fen-phen" diet drug case, in "Forum: Making the Case for Racial Reparations," *Harper's* (November 2000): 51. On the other hand, John Tateishi, a redress activist and now president of the Japanese American Citizens League, insisted in an interview with the author (San Francisco, March 3, 2003) that the achievement of redress legislation was anything but a foregone conclusion.

32. See Joe R. Feagin and Eileen O'Brien, "The Growing Movement for Reparations," in Roy Brooks, ed., *When Sorry Isn't Enough*, 343.

33. The *Philadelphia Inquirer* ran two full-page editorials endorsing the idea of a study commission on May 20 and 21, 2001, generating hundreds of letters from readers.

34. Interview with Congressman Conyers, Washington, D.C., March 27, 2003.

35. Conrad W. Worrill, "Millions for Reparations Rally: It's Our Turn," *The Black World Today*, April 1, 2002, available online at: http://www.encobra.com/Reparations%20Articles/millions_for_reparations_rally.htm.

36. Salim Muwakkil, "Time to Redress Slavery's Damage," *Chicago Sun-Times*, February 27, 1994, p. 45.

37. "The Business of Slavery and Penitence," *New York Times* national edition, May 25, 2003, "Week in Review," p. 4.

38. Randall Robinson, *The Debt: What America Owes to Blacks* (New York: Dutton, 2000).

39. The meeting took place on January 11, 2000; see http://www.transafricaforum.org/reports/roundtable011100_reparations.shtml#overview; a transcript is available at: http://www.transafricaforum.org/reports/roundtable011100_transcript.shtml.

40. See http://www.transafricaforum.org/reports/roundtable011100_manifesto.shtml.

41. See http://dir.salon.com/news/col/horo/2000/05/30/reparations/index.html.

42. See Diana Jean Schemo, "An Ad Provokes Campus Protests and Pushes Limits of Expression," *New York Times* national edition, March 21, 2001, pp. A1, A17; see also "Rhode Island: Debate Canceled," *New York Times* national edition, April 4, 2001, p. A15.

43. For an overview of the controversy, see http://www.murchisoncenter.org/reparations/resources.htm.

44. A videotape of Horowitz's debate with the N'COBRA representative Dorothy Lewis on April 4, 2001, at MIT is available from C-SPAN under the title, "Black Reparations Debate." See Horowitz's follow-up piece in Salon.com, "My 15 Minutes," at http://dir.salon.com/news/col/horo/2001/04/02/reparations/index.html.

45. See the website of Horowitz's publication "Frontpage Magazine.Com": http://www.frontpagemag.com/content/read.asp?ID=1 (accessed August 8, 2002).

46. John McWhorter, "Against Reparations," *The New Republic* (July 23, 2001): 32–38.

47. On this distinction, see my article "'Making Whole What Has Been Smashed': Reflections on Reparations," *Journal of Modern History* 73, no. 2 (June 2001): 333–58.

48. The document, dated July 19, 2001, can be found at: http://www.hrw.org/campaigns/race/reparations.htm#N_1_.

49. Jack E. White, "Don't Waste Your Breath," *Time* (April 2, 2001): 27.

50. See Adolph L. Reed, Jr., "Class Notes: The Case Against Reparations," *The Progressive* (December 2000), available at: http://www.progressive.org/reed1200.htm.

51. Here Reed refers to the study by Daryl Michael Scott, *Contempt and Pity: Social Policy and the Image of the Damaged Black Psyche, 1880–1996* (Chapel Hill: University of North Carolina Press, 1997).

52. Quoted in Postel, "The Awful Truth," *Chronicle of Higher Education*, July 12, 2002, p. A14; also available at http://chronicle.com/free/v48/i44/44a01401.htm.

53. See Mahmood Mamdani, "Degrees of Reconciliation and Forms of Justice: Making Sense of the African Experience," paper presented at the conference "Justice or Reconciliation?" at the Center for International Studies, University of Chicago, April 25–26, 1997, p. 6; quoted in Priscilla Hayner, *Unspeakable Truths: Confronting State Terror and Atrocities* (New York: Routledge, 2000), 164; and Mahmood Mam-

dani, "A Diminished Truth," in *After the TRC: Reflections on Truth and Reconciliation in South Africa*, ed. Wilmot James and Linda van de Vijver (Athens, OH: Ohio University Press, 2001 [2000]), 59. The distinction between "commemorative" and "anti-systemic" reparations that I made in "'Making Whole What Has Been Smashed': Reflections on Reparations" is analogous.

54. See Kenneth B. Nunn, "Rosewood," in Roy Brooks, ed., *When Sorry Isn't Enough*, 435–37; and Ross E. Milloy, "Panel Calls for Reparations in Tulsa Race Riot," *New York Times* national edition, March 1, 2001, p. A12. The final report of the Oklahoma Commission to Study the Tulsa Race Riot of 1921 can be found at: http://www.ok-history.mus.ok.us/trrc/freport.htm; see also Alfred L. Brophy, *Reconstructing the Dreamland: The Tulsa Race Riot of 1921* (New York: Oxford University Press, 2002); and James S. Hirsch, *Riot and Remembrance: The Tulsa Race War and Its Legacy* (Boston and New York: Houghton Mifflin, 2002).

55. See Lyle Denniston, "Judge Dismisses Riots Reparations Suit," Boston.com, March 23, 2004, available at: http://www.boston.com/news/nation/articles/2004/03/23/judge_dismisses_riots_reparations_suit?mode=PF.

56. Ben Dalby, "Slavery and the Question of Reparations," *International Socialist Review*, no. 26 (November–December 2002): 74–80.

57. See the evident frustration in Charles Ogletree, Jr., *All Deliberate Speed: Reflections on the First Half Century of* Brown v. Board of Education (New York: Norton, 2004); see also the discussion in Kathleen M. Sullivan, "What Happened to 'Brown'?" *New York Review of Books* 51, no. 14 (September 23, 2004).

58. Charles J. Ogletree, Jr., "Litigating the Legacy of Slavery," *New York Times* national edition, March 31, 2002, p. 9.

59. The statement can be found online at: http://www.ag-east.org/West/N'COBRA1.htm; accessed July 2, 2003.

60. Barry Meier, "Lawyer in Holocaust Case Faces Litany of Complaints," *New York Times* national edition, September 8, 2000, pp. A1, A21.

61. Interview with Charles Ogletree, Oak Bluffs, Massachusetts, August 21, 2002.

62. Dated on April 16, 2002, the document is available online at: http://www.encobra.com/Reparations%20Articles/relationship_between_rcc_and_n.htm, in the author's possession.

63. Adamma Ince, "No Masses, No Movement: Black Boomers Shout Reparations in the Court—But Go Silent in the 'Hood," *The Village Voice* May 22–28, 2002; available online at: http://www.villagevoice.com/issues/0221/ince.php.

64. See the announcement online at: http://www.thedrammehinstitute.org/.

65. Interview with Charles Ogletree, Oak Bluffs, Massachusetts, August 21, 2002; see also "Slavery Reparations Advocates Voice Demands in Washington," *New York Times* national edition, August 18, 2002, p. 23.

66. For an unflattering portrayal of the New Black Panther Party and its conflicts with the original group bearing that name, see Dean E. Murphy, "Black Panthers, Gone Gray, Fight Rival Group," *New York Times* national edition, October 8, 2002, pp. A1, A21.

67. See the announcements of these various organizations, available online at: http://www.nbufront.org/html/BushTelegraph/ReparationsMarch.html   (NBUF); http://afrikan.i-dentity.com/afrikan.net/html/article.php?sid=375 (NBPP); and http://www.ag-east.org/west/mfm-dc.htm (UNIA-ACL).

68. Dawson, *Black Visions*, 308. On Garvey and Garveyism, see Judith Stein, *Marcus Garvey: Race and Class in Modern Society* (Baton Rouge: Louisiana State University Press, 1986).

69. Dawson, *Black Visions*, 60.

70. See Ince, "No Masses, No Movement." The scene in the movie *Barbershop*in which reparations is discussed suggests that the idea is familiar, but generates little enthusiasm.

71. According to Feagin and O'Brien, however, the NAACP has come out in support of the idea: see "The Growing Movement for Reparations," 343. At an NAACP-sponsored event in which I participated in Oak Bluffs, Massachusetts, on August 26, 2002, however, NAACP Legal Defense Fund lawyer Ted Shaw stated that the organization had not endorsed the quest for reparations.

72. See http://www.naacp.org/polls/results.php (accessed July 20, 2004).

73. On this point, see Felicia R. Lee, "Hip-Hop Is Enlisted in Social Causes," *New York Times* national edition, June 22, 2002, pp. A13, A15.

74. On the deceptiveness of the apparent somnolescence of the 1950s, see Todd Gitlin, *The Sixties: Years of Hope, Days of Rage* (New York: Bantam, 1987), Chapter 1, "Cornucopia and its Discontents."

75. See, for example, William H. Chafe, *Civilities and Civil Rights: Greensboro, North Carolina and the Black Struggle for Freedom* (New York: Oxford University Press, 1980), 13, 42–44; and Harvard Sitkoff, *The Struggle for Black Equality, 1954–1980* (New York: Hill & Wang, 1981), passim.

76. On these points, see Gerald N. Rosenberg, *The Hollow Hope: Can Courts Bring About Social Change?* (Chicago: University of Chicago Press, 1991), Part I.

77. The latter interpretation was suggested by Charles Ogletree in my interview with him on August 21, 2002.

78. Charles Ogletree, one of the lead lawyers in the case, stated that the judgment would be appealed, and that "this has always been viewed as a marathon, not a sprint. There is a lot of fight left in our clients." Lyle Denniston, "Judge Dismisses Riots Reparations Suit," Boston.com, March 23, 2004.

79. See Dalton Conley, "Calculating Slavery Reparations: Numbers, Theory, and

Implications," in *Politics and the Past: On Repairing Historical Injustices*, ed. John Torpey (Lanham, MD: Rowman & Littlefield, 2003), 117–25.

80. Charles J. Ogletree, Jr., *All Deliberate Speed*, 292–93; see also Ogletree, "The Case for Reparations," *USA Weekend*, August 18, 2002, available at: http://www.usaweekend.com/02_issues/020818/020818reparations.html.

81. Ogletree, *All Deliberate Speed*, 290.

82. Chris Burrell, "Forum Explores Issue of Reparations," *(Martha's) Vineyard Gazette*, September 4, 2002.

83. Comments at the Oak Bluffs NAACP event on reparations, August 26, 2002.

84. Jennifer Hochschild, "The Price of Reparations," *Contexts* 1, no. 4 (Fall/Winter 2002): 4.

85. An example of the kind of argument I am making is William Julius Wilson, *The Bridge over the Racial Divide: Rising Inequality and Coalition Politics* (Berkeley: University of California Press, 1999). See also the report of the American Political Science Association's Task Force on Inequality and American Democracy, "American Democracy in an Age of Inequality," released June 2004, available at: http://www.apsanet.org/Inequality/taskforcereport.pdf.

86. See Diana Jean Schemo, "U. of Michigan Draws a New Type of Recruit," *New York Times* national edition, February 21, 2003, p. A18; and Diana Jean Schemo, "Doctors, Soldiers, and Others Weigh in on Campus Diversity," *New York Times* national edition, February 23, 2003, "Week in Review," p. 7.

87. See Nicholas Lemann, "A Decision that Universities Can Relate to," *New York Times* national edition, Week in Review, June 29, 2003, p. 14.

The Dilemma of Legality and the Moral Limits of Law

DAVID DYZENHAUS

Surely, the truly liberal answer to any sinister use of the slogan "law is law" or of the distinction between law and morals is, "Very well, but that does not conclude the question. Law is not morality; do not let it supplant morality."

—H. L. A. Hart[1]

To me there is nothing shocking in saying that a dictatorship which clothes itself with a tinsel of legal form can so far depart from the morality of order, from the inner morality of law itself, that it ceases to be a legal system. When a system calling itself law is predicated upon a general disregard by judges of the terms of the laws they purport to enforce, when this system habitually cures its legal irregularities, even the grossest, by retroactive statutes, when it only has to resort to forays of terror in the streets, which no one dares challenge, in order to escape even those scant restraints imposed by the pretence of legality—when all these things have become true of a dictatorship, it is not hard for me, at least, to deny it the name of law.

—Lon L. Fuller[2]

Introduction

In 1958 the *Harvard Law Review* published a debate between H. L. A. Hart and Lon L. Fuller that set the course for much of legal philosophy to this day. While Hart's positivist heirs have turned his version of legal positivism into an esoteric doctrine, deliberately detached from relevance to practice, Hart's 1958 essay was infused with practical relevance.[3] Almost forgotten by his heirs is that Hart engaged directly with a range of issues which today are grouped under the rubric of transitional justice—how a country seeking to escape from an unjust past should use law in the attempt both to come to terms with the past and to promote a better future. As we will see, Hart's argument bears directly on how best to understand the kinds of dilemmas that judges, lawyers, and those subject to the law face when the law is, or has been, used as an instrument of injustice. It bears both on the situation of citizens, judges, and lawyers in an unjust state and on the situation of those same actors confronted by the problem of how best to manage a transition from such a state to a just one. It also bears directly on important issues in more or less just states, where questions about the legal effect of the injustices of the past are hardly absent.

Hart claimed that we will do best if we understand the dilemmas individuals face in such situations in the terms suggested by the positivist Separation Thesis, the claim that there is no necessary connection between law and morality. However, I will argue that Fuller was right that the Separation Thesis brings mystery rather than light to these dilemmas, as it requires that we distort the predicaments which individuals face by seeing them in terms of a clean clash between the morality of conscience, on the one hand, and the law, on the other. As Fuller suggests, the dilemmas are more complex, better captured in the idea that they are dilemmas of legality, in which there is morality on both sides of the dilemma. Moreover, once we see this, we also see that the mystery infects more than Hart's suggestions about how to deal with the past; it extends into his treatment of the present and thus into that part of his argument that still frames debate today. I will argue that the reasons for this conclusion tell in favor of Fuller's antipositivist theory of law and what they tell is that law itself sets moral limits to what can be done in its name.

In the next section, I will set out in some detail that part of the debate between Hart and Fuller that pertains to the topic of transitional justice. As we will see, they focused on how to evaluate the work of Gustav Radbruch, a German legal philosopher who, in the light of his experience of the Nazi period, made some striking claims about the topic of unjust laws. Then, in the next section I will show that the case which Hart thought supported his positivist position and undermined Radbruch's in fact shows that Hart's position sheds darkness rather than light on the problem of how best to face up to unjust laws. However, I do not conclude that we should therefore opt for Radbruch. Rather, I argue that Radbruch's position should be rejected and Lon Fuller's preferred.

Hart and Fuller on Gustav Radbruch

In 1958, Hart defended the Separation Thesis in a three-part argument. In the first, he confronted the legal realists' claim that the Separation Thesis is undermined by the fact that judges must rely on their own values or moral convictions when they interpret particular laws. Against this claim, Hart argued that one should see both that values need not be moral and that, more importantly, in the cases on which the realists focused—cases in which there is disagreement about the law—there was likely no answer determined by law. Rather, the intrusion of value into law came about precisely because the law did not supply an answer so that the judge was left with no other resource to decide the issues than his own values. In the second part, Hart responded to the claim that the positivist slogan "law is law" encouraged lawyers to be complicit in, rather than resistant to, the moral iniquity of particular laws. In the last part, he answered a claim not about the connection between particular laws and morality, but between legal order as a whole and morality, namely, that legal order has to instantiate particular moral values.

The second and third parts of this argument have more or less vanished from view. The second has only recently received any serious attention in the English-speaking world.[4] The third was for a time the subject of a lively debate, since Fuller, while he contested all of Hart's claims, placed the burden of his response on the third. And in his later work *The Morality of Law*, Fuller sought to elaborate a position that there are principles of legal order that together make up an "internal morality of law."[5] However, Fuller's elaboration is widely considered to have failed. Hart and Joseph Raz are thought to have successfully demonstrated that Fuller's principles of legal order are best understood as principles which make law an effective instrument of power, and power can, of course, be exercised for evil as well as good purposes.[6] Moreover, Ronald Dworkin, who had previously joined wholeheartedly in the positivist critique of Fuller's position on the internal morality of law,[7] then eclipsed Fuller, becoming the leading critic of legal positivism. And Dworkin focused almost exclusively on Hart's argument about adjudication and value.

As I have suggested, a detailed analysis of Hart's argument and his vocabulary in the second part exposes tensions not only there but throughout his positivist position. Hence, I will seek to vindicate not only Fuller's critique of Hart's solutions to the dilemmas of legality, but also Fuller's insight that Hart's problems in this regard infect the whole of his position.

It is in this second part that Hart sets out the "truly liberal answer" in the epigraph to this essay as part of his counter to Gustav Radbruch's famous claim that legal positivism contributed to the failure of lawyers in prewar Germany to respond adequately to the Nazis' abuse of the legal order. Radbruch made this claim in short articles in 1945 and 1946.[8] Like his colleague at Heidelberg University, Karl Jaspers, who was engaged in writing a monograph on the moral responsibility of all Christian Germans for Nazi crimes,[9] Radbruch hoped to contribute to the moral reconstruction of Germany through encouraging critical reflection on the period between the world wars. Both were deeply humane men who had spent most of the period of Nazi domination in "internal exile" after the Nazis dismissed them from their chairs. Both thought it would be a mistake to see the crimes of the Nazis as totally discontinuous with the German past or to think that those responsible for the crimes were the few directly involved in murder, thus leaving the morality of the majority of ordinary Germans unbesmirched. At least part of the explanation for what happened, and so of guarding against any repetition, they argued, had to lie in the German institutions and traditions that predated the Nazi advent to power.

Hart's response to Radbruch is harsh. He accuses Radbruch of "extraordinary naivety" for holding the view that "insensitiveness to the demands of morality and subservience to state power in a people like the Germans should have arisen from the belief that law might be law though it failed to conform with the minimum requirements of morality." Hart does recognize that the positivist slogan "law is law" might have had a different history in Germany, acquiring a "sinister characteristic" in contrast to its English history, where it "went along with the most enlightened liberal attitudes." But even if that were the case, Hart asserts, "latent" in Radbruch's "whole presentation of the issues to which the existence of morally iniquitous laws can give rise" was "something more disturbing than naivety." For Radbruch had only "half digested the spiritual message of liberalism which he is seeking to convey to the legal profession." Everything Radbruch says, according to Hart, depends on an "enormous overvaluation of the bare fact that a rule may be said to be a valid rule of law, as if this, once declared, was conclusive of the final question: 'Ought this rule of law to be obeyed?'"[10] Instead, one should adopt the truly liberal answer and not let the fact that X is the law determine the issue whether X should be obeyed. And, we should note, Hart suggested later, in *The Concept of Law*, that one could not take seriously the claim that an antipositivist concept of law "is likely to lead to a stiffening of resistance to evil."[11]

Hart was well aware that the harshness of his judgments could only be accentuated by the fact that, as he described it, Radbruch and others, "like Ulysses or Dante," testified from the experience of a descent into hell, from which they brought a "message for human beings." He was also very aware that Radbruch's criticism of positivism involved an exercise of self-criticism, for Radbruch, on his own account, had before the Nazi advent to power put forward a basically positivist view of law.[12] However, it was precisely the power of the experience from which Radbruch spoke that bothered Hart, because that made Radbruch's appeal "less an intellectual argument" than a "passionate appeal." So Hart describes Radbruch's turn against positivism in religious terms—a "conversion" and a "recantation."[13]

For Hart, the only way to avoid talking "stark nonsense"[14] is to adopt the view of his positivist predecessors, Jeremy Bentham and John Austin, and see that the question of the validity of particular laws does not depend on their moral content. Rather, if "laws reached a certain degree of iniquity then there [is] . . . a plain moral obligation to resist them and to withhold obedience." Here he quotes with approval Austin's example of the man who is convicted of a crime punishable by death when the act he did was in fact trivial or even beneficial. The man objects to the sentence that it is "contrary to the law of God," but the "inconclusiveness" of his reasoning, Austin says, is demonstrated by the "court of justice" by "hanging [him] up, in pursuance of the law of which [he had] impugned the validity."[15]

Hart based his argument against Radbruch on the use of Radbruch's ideas by German courts after the war, on the way in which they relied on what is known in Germany as the "Radbruch formula." In Hart's summary, Radbruch asserted that enactments lack the force of law when they contravene fundamental principles of morality and thus "should not be taken into account in working out the legal position of any given individual in particular circumstances."[16] In order to illustrate the confusions Hart thought inherent in the formula, he relied on the decision of a German court in 1949 in a case where a woman was prosecuted for the offense of illegally depriving her husband of his liberty—a crime punishable under the German Code of 1871, which had remained in force.[17] In 1944, she had denounced her husband to the authorities for insulting remarks he had made about Hitler while on leave from the army. She wanted to get rid of him because she was having an affair. Under Nazi statutes, it was "apparently," Hart says, illegal to make such remarks though the wife was under no legal duty to report him. The husband was found guilty and sentenced to death, though it seems that he was not executed but sent to the front.

The wife's defense was that she had acted in accordance with the law—the statutes—and so had not committed any crime. But the court of appeal, despite the fact that the husband had been "sentenced by a court for having violated a statute," found her guilty of the offense of deprivation of liberty, because—quoting from the judgment—the statutes were "contrary to the sound conscience and sense of justice of all decent human beings."[18] Hart reports that the reasoning was followed in many cases, and these were "hailed as a triumph of the doctrines of natural law and as signaling the overthrow of legal positivism." But, he retorts, "the unqualified satisfaction with this result seems to me to be hysteria."[19]

Hart's point is that even if one applauds the objective of punishing the woman for "an outrageously immoral act," one should see that to achieve this a "statute established since 1934" had to be declared "not to have the force of law," and he thinks that the "wisdom of this course must be doubted." There were two other choices—leaving her unpunished or the "introduction of a frankly retrospective law . . . with a full consciousness of what was sacrificed in securing her punishment in this way." He then comments:

> Odious as retrospective criminal legislation and punishment may be, to have pursued it openly in this case would at least have had the merits of candour. It would have made plain that in punishing the woman a choice had to be made between two evils, that of leaving her unpunished and that of sacrificing a very precious principle of morality endorsed by most legal systems. Surely if we have learned anything from the history of morals it is that the thing to do with a moral quandary is not to hide it. . . . [T]here is an insincerity in any formulation of our

problem which allows us to describe the treatment of the dilemma as if it were the disposition of the ordinary case.[20]

Hart emphasizes that it is not a mere matter of form whether one leaves it to the court to invalidate the statute in the way it did, that is, by pretending that it was merely interpreting the law with no sacrifice of principle, or one requires that a statute be invalidated by a retrospective statute. For if we follow Radbruch's and the court's course and assert that "certain rules cannot be law because of their moral iniquity," we "confuse one of the most powerful, because it is the simplest, forms of moral criticism." So we should "speak plainly" and say that "laws may be laws but too evil to be obeyed."[21]

In 1958, Fuller responded to Hart by pointing out that the reliance by the wife on the Nazi statutes for the legality of what she did is rather more complicated than Hart allows. First, one of the statutes was aimed at wartime offenses committed in public, that is, at soldiers who incited others to disobedience. If one adopts the reasoning of the Nazi court which found that this offense could include within its scope remarks made to a civilian in private,[22] one is allowing the "interpretive principles applied by the courts of Hitler's government" to determine the legal issue.[23] The second statute was, Fuller comments, a "legislative monstrosity," "overlarded and undermined . . . by uncontrolled administrative discretion." It made it an offense punishable by imprisonment to make public utterances which insulted the "leading personalities of the nation," declared "public" "private" utterances which a person "realized or should have realized . . . would reach the public," and gave discretion over prosecution as well as definition of "leading personalities" to the minister of justice.[24] So Fuller asks whether it can be "argued seriously that it would have been more beseeming to the judicial process" if the postwar courts had studied Nazi interpretive principles and then "solemnly" applied them to ascertain the meaning of the statute? And he also asks whether, on the other hand, the courts would "really have been showing respect for Nazi law if they had construed the Nazi statutes by their own quite different, standards of interpretation?"[25]

Now it might seem that these points tend in the direction of support for the postwar court's decision. However, Fuller points out that he, like Hart, would prefer the solution of a retroactive statute and that Radbruch himself shared this preference. Moreover, Radbruch was well aware that his formula occasioned a moral dilemma and expressed concern about the dangers for the rule of law in refusing the quality of law to duly enacted statutes. The issue is, then, not whether there is a dilemma, but how to state it.[26]

Fuller clearly thinks that Hart's statement of the dilemma should be rejected because its solution—say that the law is too evil to be obeyed—is wrong-headed, at least if it is offered to judges. When a court "refuses to apply something it admits to be law," "moral confusion reaches its height." As Fuller, of course, recognized, Hart did not mean this solution to be deployed by a court but by a legislature. However, Hart does not, Fuller says, take into account the situation of "drastic emergency" in which the courts and Radbruch were living. If "legal institutions were to be rehabilitated in Germany it would not do to allow the people to begin taking the law into their own hands, as might have occurred while the courts were waiting for a statute."[27] Germany had "to restore both respect for law and respect for justice," and the attempt to "restore both at once" necessarily created "painful antimonies."[28]

"No pat formula," Fuller says, can resolve this problem. But legal positivism's response to the problem has no contact with its reality—it presents "opposing demands that simply shout their contradictions across a vacuum."[29] Indeed, Fuller claims that Hart's statement of the dilemma makes "no sense" for, once unpacked, it seems to amount to the following:

> On the one hand, we have an amoral datum called law, which has the peculiar quality of creating a moral duty to obey it. On the other hand, we have a moral duty to do what we think is right and decent. When we are confronted by a statute we believe to be thoroughly evil, we have to choose between those two duties.[30]

I believe that Fuller had the better of this exchange, and the rest of this essay will elaborate the argument for that belief. But before embarking on that task, it is important to have in mind that Fuller not only expressed doubts about the court's decision, but also about Radbruch's position. I will not be taking up Fuller's suggestion that a close look at German legal history would show that positivistic ideas had played a large role in getting German lawyers to accept that what is law is what is decreed from above, and that that attitude helped to make it possible for Hitler to come to power through the "exploitation of legal forms."[31] Nor will I take up his claim that German legal positivism was indifferent to the moral ends of law, that is, German lawyers did not suppose that their role required them to concern themselves with the moral purposes of statutes.[32] My focus is rather on Fuller's thought that German lawyers were also indifferent to what he called at the time the "inner morality of law"—later the "internal morality."[33] That is, German lawyers were indifferent to the conformity of law to fundamental principles of legal order.

In Fuller's view, attention to the internal morality would have helped German lawyers before the war maintain their fidelity to the ideal of law. After the war, German judges could have dealt better with cases like that of the informer wife had they focused on the deterioration of legality that he outlined in the second epigraph to this essay.

However, it is not the historical or sociological basis for this thought that concerns me, so much as Fuller's suggestion that the indifference to internal morality is part of Radbruch's new position after the war. For Radbruch's resort to notions of "higher law"—a morality that transcends positive law but which functions as a test for the validity of law—may itself, Fuller says, be "a belated fruit of German legal positivism." Someone with a positivist mindset might feel that the only way to "escape one law is to set another off against it, and this perforce must be a 'higher law.'"[34]

Fuller thus seems to be claiming that, despite Hart's vehement critique of Radbruch, there is a deep similarity between their positions. Indeed, his thought might have been that the vehemence was produced by the similarity. Both Hart and Radbruch resort to the idea of higher law in order to deal with the problems created by past legal injustice. For them the higher law is a law which has the power or force to invalidate another law. Thus they both in fact prefer the legal solution to come in the form of a frankly retroactive statute. The only difference is that Radbruch is prepared to allow judges to do what the legislature has not done or will not do, which means that he finds himself compelled to present what they are doing as legal. Thus he argues that extreme injustice is a kind of higher law, since it also can invalidate a law.

Recall that Fuller also preferred the retroactive statute. But he was anxious to state that his reason for this preference was not the positivist one that the statute would be "the most nearly lawful way of making unlawful what was once law." Rather, the statute would symbolize a "sharp break with the past," enabling the judiciary to "return more rapidly to a condition in which the demands of legal morality could be given proper respect."[35] In order to appreciate Fuller's point, one has to have a better grip on his claim that Radbruch's and Hart's positions are virtual mirror images and here a defense of Radbruch by Robert Alexy, Germany's leading philosopher of law, provides the starting place.

As we will see, Alexy suggests that Fuller's internal morality of law sets limits to the tolerable injustice of the positive law, but has to be complemented by the Radbruch formula that extreme injustice is no law. The complement is necessary for those situations of extreme injustice where the law that creates the injustice offends neither technical criteria of validity nor the internal morality of law. However, as I will show, Alexy concedes too much to Hart, thus bringing, inevitably in my view, Radbruch's position into line with Hart's. The closer we get to the situations with which the Radbruch formula or Hart's legal positivism are supposed to deal, the more Fuller's internal morality looks like the better bet. Indeed, as I will argue in the subsequent section, reliance on the Radbruch formula can actually undermine an attempt to deal with the past by legal means. And so I will conclude that the Radbruch formula should be rejected.

Positivism's Mysteries

Alexy has recently defended Radbruch's formula through an analysis of judgments by German courts after the war that dealt with the validity of Nazi statutes and of judgments after reunification which dealt with the lawfulness of prosecutions of border guards from the former German Democratic Republic (GDR) who had shot and killed East German citizens as they tried to escape to the West.[36] I cannot do justice to Alexy's complex argument here as I want to focus mainly on his claim that Fuller's internal morality of law can "complement but not replace Radbruch's formula"[37] that extreme injustice is no law, or, as Radbruch stated it:

> The conflict between justice and legal certainty should be resolved in that the positive law, established by enactment and by power, has primacy even when its content is unjust and improper. It is only when the contradiction between posi-

tive law and justice reaches an intolerable level that the law is supposed to give way as a "false law" [*unrichtiges Recht*] to justice. It is impossible to draw a sharper line between the cases of legalised injustice and laws which remain valid despite their false content. But another boundary can be drawn with the utmost precision. Where justice is not even aimed at, where equality—the core of justice—is deliberately disavowed in the enactment of a positive law, then the law is not simply "false law," it has no claim at all to legal status.[38]

As Hart was well aware,[39] part of the difficulty of the formula is that *Recht* means "right" as well as "law," and so there is an obvious tension in the phrase "*unrichtiges Recht*" in contrast to "unjust law," where there might appear to be no tension at all. "*Unrichtiges Recht*," that is, seems tantamount to the contradictory "unjust justice," whereas "unjust law," and especially "unjust law where we mean by law the enactments of those with power," seems perfectly coherent.

Alexy's main argument in support of Radbruch is that law, whether in the sense of particular positive laws or legal orders as a whole, necessarily makes a claim to "correctness,"[40] though we should keep in mind that the word he uses is not "*Geltung*" or "technical validity" but "*Richtigkeit*," which deliberately maintains the (ambiguous) characteristics of *Recht*.[41] According to Alexy, the claim to correctness includes Fuller's "internal morality of law," that is, generality, publicity, nonretroactivity, clarity or intelligibility, noncontradiction, possibility of compliance, constancy through time, and congruence between declared rule and official action.[42] But correctness goes further, maintains Alexy, since it includes what Fuller calls the "external morality" of law or substantive justice. And it has to go further because of the problem posed by extremely unjust laws that comply wholly or almost wholly with Fuller's principles.[43] If judges understand law's claim to correctness—its claim to include both the procedural internal morality of law and substantive justice—antipositivism will, contrary to Hart, stiffen resistance to evil. The issue, Alexy says, is not best captured by the situation of the individual judge facing an unjust law where it makes little substantive difference "whether he relies on Hart and refuses to apply an extremely unjust law on *moral* grounds or, with Radbruch, does the same by calling on *legal* grounds."[44] In both cases, the judge's decision will be influenced by factors other than the concept of law, namely, his calculation of personal costs.

However, things look different when one focuses not on the individual judge but on legal practice. If there is a consensus in legal practice that the legal character of law depends on the fulfillment of minimal requirements of justice, then there is "the capacity to provide resistance to the acts of an unjust state by dint of arguments which are juridical as well as moral."[45] Nevertheless, a "successful unjust regime" can use various tactics to override quickly such judicial resistance, so that resistance is effective only, and perhaps only for a time, against a "weaker unjust regime."[46]

Alexy also contends that the harm to the value of legal certainty is minimal since great harm comes about only through those antipositivist positions that propose a complete coincidence of law and morality. Radbruch's postwar position, in contrast, merely requires a slight modification of his prewar position in which legal certainty has an "unconditional precedence" over the other two values of law he identified—justice and purposiveness. According to the formula, only in cases of extreme injustice is the hierarchy—certainty, then justice, then purposiveness—adjusted so that justice trumps certainty. And then the adjustment is required, as otherwise the precedence of certainty over justice "could not be reconciled with the claim to correctness, which includes justice as well as legal certainty."[47]

Now the cases on which Alexy focuses in order to sustain his claim about the substantive justice requirement are those of German Jews who had been deemed by Nazi law to have lost their nationality on leaving Germany. After the war, questions arose about their rights to property because if the nationality law were valid they had lost these rights. Since there was no retroactive statute, nor would one be passed, everything depended on whether the courts could invalidate the nationality law. As Alexy puts it, the "decision for or against legal positivism . . . can have immense practical significance for the victim of a tyrannical regime."[48] And because he regards a law which strips people of their nationality in this way as an obvious example of extreme injustice, he approves the German courts' use of the Radbruch formula to vindicate these victims' rights.

In contrast, he rejects the reasoning of a German court which after reunification found that border guards of the German Democratic Republic (GDR) had acted unlawfully in shooting and killing people who attempted to escape to the West, and thus found them guilty of manslaughter, even though the guards had complied with the provisions of the Republic's Border

Law.[49] One reason for rejection is that it is not self-evident that the shootings were an extreme injustice, and the idea that the injustice must be extreme is supposed to be what keeps courts off the slippery slope of imposing contestable moral evalautions.[50] But much more important for Alexy is that the court in question interpreted the Border Law not in the light of the interpretive principles in use in the GDR, but in the light shed by the principles of the rule of law of reunified Germany. It followed that the guards could be said neither to have complied with a fundamental legal principle of proportionality, nor with the requirement that they regard life as the "most prized legal value." Alexy says of this judgment that, by interpreting the "former law of the German Democratic Republic in the light shed in the present by principles of the rule of law is [to pursue] . . . a covert kind of retroactivity which is worse than an open one."[51]

However, as Julian Rivers has pointed out, courts that pursued the line of argument Alexy condemns did try to put that argument on a basis which had a legal toehold in the GDR.[52] In particular, they appealed to the fact that the GDR had committed itself to upholding human rights by binding itself to the International Covenant on Civil and Political Rights which contains "pertinent rights to life and free movement."[53] Rivers portrays the latter appeal in Dworkinian terms as an interpretive turn, a move to a mode of constructive interpretation where the Border Law was not interpreted in accordance with what the GDR government wanted it to mean, as demonstrated by its implementation. Rather, it was interpreted in accordance with that government's commitments to human rights, as proclaimed to the international community. Hence, there are two inconsistent methods of dealing with the injustice of the Border Law. There is the method which declares the law invalid because unjust and the method which presupposes the law's validity but interprets it so as to find its implementation illegal.[54]

As we have seen, and as Rivers recognizes, the interpretive turn had been clearly foreseen by Fuller, though not by Hart.[55] Moreover, shortly after the 1958 debate between Hart and Fuller, H. O. Pappe pointed out that the case on which they focused has been misreported. In fact, the court and other courts which dealt with either the same or similar issues explicitly *rejected* a "higher law" argument, preferring to focus on interpretation of the law. They concentrated on matters such as the absence of a duty to inform and the pri-

vacy in which the remarks had been made in order to sustain the conclusion
that there had been an illegal deprivation of liberty in terms of the 1871 law.[56]
In addition, one court took into account the reliance of the informer on the
severity of punishment and a lack of due process in the military tribunals
which decided such cases. Pappe's elaboration of this "insight" of the court is
instructive:

> There was, despite the warped judgment of wide circles during the Nazi period, a
> lively awareness in the population that administrative and legal authority could
> be abused for the purpose of intimidation and suppression of opposition views.
> Sentences, which served the purpose of political terror rather than the realisation
> of the law, had actually led to a heightened popular sense of right and wrong
> rather than stifling it. This assumption was accepted by the Supreme Court as a
> matter of common knowledge; it had also been found to be correct by the jury. A
> mistaken belief in the legality of the court-martial procedure would be a defence
> only for a person who could not be expected to share the insights of ordinary
> members of the public. However, the facts of the case, as found by the jury, indi-
> cated that the accused, far from acting to reveal the crime, just wished to make
> use of the best means to get rid of her husband so that she could continue her
> adulterous way of life.[57]

Now Hart added a footnote to the reprinted version of "Positivism and the
Separation of Law and Morals" in which he summarized the respects in
which, on Pappe's account, he had the facts of the case wrong. He said that
Pappe's "careful analysis should be studied." But he did not seem to think it
had implications for his own account of the dilemma of legality; for he said
that the case as he had understood it could be treated as a "hypothetical
one."[58] In responding in this way, Hart failed to address Pappe's argument,
particularly the ways in which Pappe followed Fuller. For Pappe wanted to
draw a link between the "arbitrary interpretation" of the military tribunal
and what he termed the "objective deterioration of judicial independence
and of devotion to legal, in contrast to political, considerations."[59] In this regard, he drew attention to the little noticed fact that in 1958, Hart connected
his response to Radbruch to his response earlier in the same article to the legal realists.

   Recall that Hart rejected the legal realists' claim that from the fact that
when judges interpreted particular laws they had to rely on their own moral
convictions, one could demonstrate a connection between law and morality,

thus impugning the Separation Thesis. Hart's argument is in two steps. First, he argues that reliance on values is not equivalent to reliance on morality and second, that in the cases on which the realists focused—cases in which what the law required is in contest—there was likely no answer determined by law. In other words, at most—step one—the realists had shown a necessary connection between law and value, not law and morality. But in fact—step two—they had failed to show even this, since in the cases where judges had to rely on value, the reason for such reliance was precisely that the law could not be said to supply a determinate answer. The judge is in the penumbra of personal choice or discretion, rather than in the core of legal certainty.

The informer wife is the example that Hart relies on for the first step. That under the Nazi regime men were sentenced to death for criticism of the regime shows, he says, that the "choice of sentence might be guided exclusively by consideration of what was needed to maintain the state's tyranny effectively." A "decision on these grounds would be intelligent and purposive, and from one point of view the decision would be as it ought to be." But that "ought" is of course immoral; and thus we know that it cannot sustain a claim that the distinction is false between "law as it is and law as *morally* it ought to be."[60]

Pappe comments that to regard such intimidation "in the interests of the ruling party as the declared purpose of the German criminal law . . . is . . . an arbitrary assumption." Not only was the 1871 law in existence, but so was the large part of pre-Nazi law. Moreover, the judges were supposed to be independent and they had to choose "between applying the criminal law as established by statute, interpretation and precedent, and, on the other hand, obeying the shifting and often contradictory administrative directives of the government of the day." Finally, it has to be taken into account that a dictatorial government can of course make laws to achieve its ends, but cannot change the body of preexisting law wholesale. What it really desires is the ability to be able to decide arbitrarily. But it is unlikely to reveal its character by enacting a statute declaring that courts should follow government orders regarding the "definition and punishment of crime," since such a statute would "obviously not be law, even in Hart's sense." It is thus unsurprising, Pappe concludes, that the postwar courts should "have concentrated on questions of judicial interpretation and procedure rather than on that of the validity of statutory law."[61]

Once elaborated, Pappe's insight is even more powerful.[62] In using the two-step argument, Hart exposes a deep tension in his own position. On the basis of the second step, one should not make any concession that there was an "ought" for the judge to follow. The whole point of the second—and more important—step is to tell us that the judge is in the penumbra and so not under a legal duty to come to a particular decision. The ought is therefore one only from the perspective of a judge who says to himself, "I have a vast discretion in regard to how to decide and I must exercise it as I think the Party would want me to."

Now this judge clearly thinks that in some sense he ought to exercise his discretion in this way. But even to get to the stage of thinking that he has discretion in Hart's sense, he has to suppose that he is more or less free of a duty to use his independent judgment purely on the basis of the legal materials that would incline him to find that the remarks were not public, and so on. Moreover, if he has that freedom, then nothing he does has any relevance to the distinction between law as it is and law as it morally ought to be, since what he does is not determined by law. On closer examination, then, it seems that Fuller was right that Hart's distinction between law as it is and law as it ought to be is far from providing either the clarity or candor he claimed for it, whether one looks to the situation of the postwar German judge or that of the German judges during the Nazi era. I will now explain why the solution of the advocate of candor and of the clarity-serving aspects of a positivistic concept of law turns out to shed more mystery than light.

Hart's problems arise from the fact that he introduces the distinction between law as it is and law as it ought to be not in the context of judicial interpretation of the law, but in the context of an individual citizen confronting a morally bad law where the badness is apparent. The citizen's distinction, as we might think of it, is supposed to assist the citizen by telling him that there is a clean clash between conscience and the law. But in both of the judicial situations—the judge looking back on a bad past and the judge who confronts a bad present—in issue is what the law is. So it is not so evident that the citizen's distinction could be helpful to a judge.[63]

It is not even evident how the citizen's distinction could be helpful to a citizen during the Nazi era confronting the two laws on which the military tribunals relied in order to find guilt and sentence people accused of making disrespectful remarks. In order to provide the clean clash between legal and moral obligation which Hart envisages, the citizen would have to predict the tribunal's interpretation of those laws and rely on that prediction. It does seem that the wife did so rely, otherwise there was no point to the exercise of turning her husband in. But even if she could be confident in her prediction because the dominant practice of interpretation during the Nazi era was to interpret the law so as to keep the population in line, she was relying—according to Hart's distinction between core and penumbra—on an interpretive practice of use only in the penumbra and hence not on the law properly so called—the law in the core of certainty.

Indeed, since the wife had no duty to turn her husband in, she was at the point in time that she turned him in offending against the 1871 law which made it an offense illegally to deprive someone of his liberty. That is, prior to the moment when judgment was given, there was no law in existence that could remove the quality of illegality from her act. Hart's assumption that what she did was protected by the law would then seem to be based on the claim that it was the court's judgment that made legal an initially illegal act. But if that is right, then Hart's solution is stuck with the exact sin of judicial retroactivity of which he wanted to convict Radbruch. Not only is the husband convicted of a crime that was not a crime at the time he made the remarks, but the wife's wrongdoing under the 1871 law—the illegal deprivation of liberty—is retroactively made legal.[64]

There is another possibility. Hart might say that, like it or not, the court's decision was in the core, not the penumbra, just because an ordinary individual could confidently predict the court's interpretation of the law on the basis of a dominant judicial practice of using a particular criterion which does in many cases lead to a determinate answer. Put differently, because as a matter of fact—through that practice—that criterion has become part of the legal order's criteria for determining the law, and because the criterion does pick out one answer, the answer is fully—in the positivist sense—determined by the law.

There is much in Hart's later work, particularly in his account of the rule of recognition in *The Concept of Law*, that would support this different way of describing the situation.[65] And once the situation is so described, we have the almost clean clash between law and moral obligation after which Hart hankered. There is still the complication that the woman had no duty to turn him in, but she can at least rely on the claim that she violated no law.

But we get the clean clash at a high price. We have to give up on the idea that there was an alternative conception of law which led to a different conclusion. This is the solution given by a brave judge who says, "My duty is to the law, not to the Nazi Party, and the law, understood in terms of interpretive principles that underpin vast areas of the law which survives from the era before the Nazis, requires me to find the defendant not guilty."

Moreover, we pay that price even if we adopt the more complex description that the wife was relying not on the law, but on a prediction that the judges would exercise their discretion in a particular way. For on that description, neither of the two possible conclusions is privileged by the law so that, from the perspective of the core, each was equally valid. Since there was then no legal duty on the judge, he had to override at most his moral scruples—not his sense of legal duty—to get to the conclusion the wife wanted.

My point here is not, of course, that legal scruples are morally more weighty than moral scruples. It is that on the alternative picture of law, moral and legal duty overlap, since the judge's duty is conceived as an obligation of fidelity to something like Fuller's internal morality of law. The idea of a discretionary or penumbral decision is unhelpful to this judge, because his conclusion that the husband is not guilty is, in his view, fully determined by law.

Once we see that, we should also be able to see how confusing Hart's solution becomes on closer inspection. Imagine that the brave judge and a judge who accepted Hart's view, but was cravenly going to exercise the discretion he thought he had so as to maximize terror, retire to their chambers after hearing legal argument.[66] The two judges will not even be able to engage properly with each other, since the brave judge will argue in terms of the requirements of law, while the craven judge will make political arguments about the need to maximize terror, backed perhaps by his fears if he does not toe the party line. They will, as Fuller puts it, be shouting at each other across a vacuum.

Indeed, from the point of view of proper engagement, the brave judge has an easier time with a different judge—the judge who thinks that his legal

duty is to interpret the law in accordance with facts about the dominant interpretive practice of his time, which in turn leads him to facts, as he understands them, about the intentions of the regime as expressed in the two Nazi
statutes. This other judge, whom we can call the "plain fact" judge, has a
view of fidelity to law as positive law, which leads him to views about how
best to interpret the law so as to recover facts about legislative intention.

My claim is not that these two judges will refrain from shouting at each
other. Indeed, the shouting might be even more intense. But that would be
because they have something to disagree about. On the one hand, the plain
fact judge will argue that Nazi statutes are best interpreted in isolation from
pre-Nazi law and pre-Nazi interpretive practices, and in accordance with
what the judges both know to be facts about the intentions of those who enacted the statutes. The brave judge will argue that the statutes have to be
"read down" so as to avoid illegally depriving the husband of his liberty, so as
to preserve the distinction between public and private as much as possible,
and so as to avoid introducing a penalty from a statute designed to prevent
undermining of military morale into a situation where a soldier was speaking
in private to a civilian. He might also point out that the general situation of
legality was deteriorating in Germany and that judges should do as much as
possible, because it is their duty as judges to uphold the rule of law, to avoid
expanding more than was absolutely necessary the powers the administration
had under statute. His stand is that the judges' obligation of fidelity to law
requires them to be even more alert than in normal times to the need to give
expression in their judgments to the principles of the rule of law.

My imaginary example is, I'm sure, wholly imaginary. I doubt whether
there were in Germany in 1944 lawyers to put the argument that would sustain the brave judge's conclusion to the court, or judges on the court who
would entertain such an argument. I'm sure, that is, that the trial was very
much a summary one, dominated by 'tis/'tisn't arguments about what the
husband had said.

However, the example is not fanciful in—to use Alexy's term—"weaker
unjust regimes." In apartheid South Africa, for instance, legal challenges to
the executive had precisely the character of the argument that would sustain
the brave judge's conclusion.[67] Of course, in order for such arguments to be
made and on occasion accepted, there had to be a minority of lawyers who

were prepared to make them and a minority of judges disposed to accept such arguments. Moreover, when judges felt compelled to articulate the deepest reasons for their different interpretive approaches, these surfaced along the lines of the disagreement between the brave and the plain fact judge; no judge seemed to think the issue was how to exercise a penumbral discretion.[68]

I believe that this less extreme situation, the situation of the weaker unjust regime, is the better test for Hart's claims about the clarity and candor delivered by legal positivism. In this situation, the issue clearly is how judges should best understand the obligation of fidelity to law—to the rule of law. Those understandings form the starting point for the judges as they begin to make sense of the legal materials relevant to the particular case and thus they incline the judges toward their final conclusions about what the law requires. Hart's distinction, taken from the situation of a citizen confronting a law with a determinate and immoral content, is useless to such a judge, since the issue for the judge is what the content of the law is.

Hart sees this point to some extent, because he seems to want to tell the judges that they have misunderstood their own predicament. The issue, according to Hart, is not what the law is, as the judge is in the penumbra where no answer exists by definition. But to tell either the brave judge or the plain fact judge that he has misunderstood his predicament is entirely unhelpful. Hart seems to ask the brave judge to drop precisely what he needs to hold on to, if he is to reach the conclusion most consistent with the principles he understands to be intrinsic to the rule of law. In order to reach that conclusion, the brave judge has to hold on to an antipositivist conception of law—his sense that his obligation of fidelity to law requires him to understand law as necessarily aspiring to such principles. So to tell him that he should drop his antipositivism is, as he understands it, to tell him that he should give up on being a judge since he can no longer serve the law.

Things are even worse when Hart gives his advice to the plain fact judge. When that judge is told that he should conceive his predicament in positivist terms, his retort is that he already does so. He conceives of law as positive law with a determinate content which it his duty as a judge to ascertain. Where he differs from Hart is that his positivism is political in nature and gives rise to interpretive tests that seek to avoid judicial engagement in what he regards as politically illicit activity—letting his own moral convictions interfere in the determination of the content of the law. He never then gets to the point of finding that he has discretion in the sense that he is in a penumbra where law supplies no answer.

If there is any predicament for the positivist or plain fact judge, it is something like the predicament of Hart's citizen confronting the bad law, but it differs in one important respect. Once the plain fact judge has found out the content of the law, he might also find that that content is, by his own moral lights, offensive. So at the moment he applies the law he experiences, as Robert Cover described it, dissonance. He is, that is, in Cover's "moral-formal" dilemma, since his formal or positivistic tests that determine what law is come out with an answer that clashes with his conscience.[69] However, even that clash cannot be simply described. As Fuller pointed out, there is morality on both sides of such a dilemma.[70] The judge's conclusion is reached because of his sense of the morality of the role of office, so that he finds himself morally compelled as judge to decide against his conscience as citizen. Moreover, although I will have to come back to this point a little later to defend it properly, we have in place now the possibility that even the citizen's predicament is not as clearly described by legal positivism as Hart claimed; perhaps even there we will find that the only way to make sense of the dilemma as a genuine one is to see that there is morality on both sides.

Hart might answer that these points pertain only to the first part of his 1958 argument—the claim that judicial interpretation of the law happens for the most part in the penumbra. If, as he suggested in his brief response to Pappe, the laws under which the husband was convicted clearly required that conviction, then the Nazi era judges, as well as the postwar judges, were faced with the citizen's dilemma, what to do in the face of clearly unjust laws. Further, Radbruch and Alexy seem to agree with Hart on at least this issue. And we have seen Alexy make the additional claim that there is no difference from the perspective of the rule of law between the retroactivity involved when the legislature declares that a past law is invalid because it was unjust and when judges use their present interpretive practice to find that that law did not mean what the judges in the prior era thought it to mean.[71] Indeed, it is because Alexy, following Radbruch, accepts Hart's description of this situation that he then argues that Fuller's internal morality of law needs to be complemented by the Radbruchian claim that extreme injustice is no law.

My view is that Fuller's position on the internal morality of law does not require any complement by the Radbruch formula and that Fuller was right that Radbruch's reaction to the horrors of Nazi Germany was determined, against his intentions, by his positivistic assumptions. Indeed, there is almost a total affinity between Hart's and Radbruch's positions. Radbruch's postwar legal theory is positivism with a minus sign—laws are valid laws on the positivist understanding of legality except when they are extremely unjust.[72] My argument for this view starts with an analysis of a case recently decided in Canada by one of Canada's most respected courts, the Ontario Court of Appeal, a case in which for the first time, as far as I'm aware, Radbruch's formula has been relied on in an argument to a common law court.

The Head Tax Case[73]

In 1885 Canada enacted the Chinese Immigration Act,[74] which required immigrants of Chinese origin to pay a tax which was equivalent to two years' wages for a Chinese Canadian worker at the time. There was no equivalent statute aimed at other groups, and the motives in enacting it were explicitly racist. Because Chinese immigrants continued to arrive, in 1923 a new Chinese Immigration Act was passed which excluded Chinese immigration with narrow exceptions, thus preventing some of the immigrants from bringing their families to Canada.[.] This act was repealed in 1947.[76] The Canadian government has refused to extend any redress to the Chinese Canadian community, and so individuals within that community attempted to get redress through the courts—for both repayment of the tax and an apology.

The main argument made by the lawyers for the Chinese Canadians who sought redress—either individuals who actually paid the tax or their spouses or descendants—was that the government was under a legal obligation to disgorge the taxes collected because it had been unjustly enriched by the tax. That there was enrichment was clear but in *Mack v Attorney General of Canada*,[77] first the Superior Court of Justice and then the Ontario Court of Appeal found against the Chinese Canadians on the basis the claim of unjust enrichment could not succeed because the statute was a "valid juristic reason" for the enrichment.

Both courts recognized that the head tax was substantively unjust. Indeed, the Court of Appeal said at the beginning of its judgment that the head tax was one of the "more notable stains" on Canada's "minority rights tapestry"[78] and it rather curiously quoted this evaluation at the end.[79] But the courts decided the case by acceding to the attorney general of Canada's drastic motion to have the claim struck because it disclosed "no reasonable cause of action." The Supreme Court of Canada has indicated its agreement with this stance by rejecting an application for leave to appeal against this decision.

The lawyers did not argue that the Chinese Immigration Act was unconstitutional during the time of its operation. They were fully aware that the doctrine of parliamentary supremacy at the time the act was in force likely precluded any challenge to the validity of the statute on the grounds of its substantive injustice. Nevertheless, they argued that the injustice of the statute was recognized by Canadian courts at the time, by international legal norms, and by Canadian governments which signed onto various international conventions which prohibited racial discrimination. In addition, they argued that in the absence of redress by the government, the discriminatory status inflicted by the head tax is perpetuated, and that such discrimination violates the equality protection in section 15 of the Charter of Rights and Freedoms, the Canadian bill of rights that came into force in 1982. Their position was that the head tax's consequences reached into the present by perpetuating a discriminatory status on Chinese people.[80]

Justice Moldaver, who wrote the judgment for the three-judge bench of the Ontario Court of Appeal, did not dispute these claims, but found that they did not add up to a conclusion that racial discrimination was during the relevant period prohibited by customary international law. He relied on the claim of a scholar of international law that only in 1945 with the birth of the United Nations did individual rights break through from a "fragmentary perspective to a global aim."[81] Until then, the norms existed only as "pockets of enlightenment." But even if the lawyers had established that customary international law did contain a norm prohibiting discrimination, the judges said that they would have halted the action "because of the well-established principle that customary international law may be ousted for domestic purposes by contrary domestic legislation."[82]

The Court of Appeal did not hold that the existence of a statute would always provide a sufficient juristic reason to rebut a claim of unjust enrichment. But it held that, because the lawyers' arguments that the statute did not constitute such a reason were about international law and the Charter, and because these arguments failed in their own terms, they could not succeed in sustaining the claim about unjust enrichment. Here the Court of Appeal adopted the reasoning of Justice Cumming in the court below that before the courts could find that a statute did not constitute a juristic reason, it had to be shown that the statute was either "unconstitutional or ultra vires." But the Charter could not be relied on retrospectively to invalidate a statute, and a domestic statute ousts customary law for domestic purposes.[83]

This judgment, like the judgment in the court below, recharacterizes the lawyers' argument in order to suggest that it can be answered definitively, so definitively that it could be said to disclose no reasonable cause of action. However, the recharacterization is not total. For, as I will now show, to the extent that the lawyers relied on the Radbruch formula, they laid themselves open to this recharacterization.

For the most part, the lawyers did not argue that the fact that the statute was unjust and discriminatory meant that it was invalid. Rather, they argued that it could not be relied on as a legal reason by the government to retain the taxes. Here they could deploy extensive common law authority, including Canadian authority, that the test for unjust enrichment is not a mechanical or formal one, determined by categories where past courts have found for a claimant, but one of "good conscience." The court has an equitable discretion to adapt the common law so as to live up to the animating principle that no man should be allowed "unjustly to appropriate to himself the value earned by the labour of another."[84]

Their argument relied in part on English authority. In 1976 the House of Lords had to consider whether the Nazi citizenship law was a valid basis for imposing a tax on an individual. Lord Cross stated that a "law of this sort constitutes so grave an infringement of human rights that the courts of this country ought to refuse to recognise it as a law at all."[85] In addition, the Ontario Court of Appeal had previously found that a racist trust, established in 1923, could not be perpetuated because it had to "give way to current principles of public policy."[86] This decision, in the lawyers' view, is authority for the proposition that when "positive law enshrines extreme injustice courts acting in furtherance of their judicial duties must refuse to give legal effect to that injustice." By analogy, they argued that

> [r]etention of the funds paid pursuant to the Act is only possible if courts rely on a juristic reason profoundly at odds with the basic principles of the legal order. Holding that the *Chinese Immigration Act* constitutes a juristic reason for the continued enrichment of the defendant would not only amount to a contemporary validation of this racist legislation but would implicate the court—the ultimate custodian of rights—in its perpetuation. A judge determining whether the enrichment in this case is unjust is acting today, and must act in accord with the principles of the legal order as we understand them now. Therefore, it is submitted, a contemporary court must apply principles of racial equality in order to prevent validation and perpetuation of the racism embodied in the *Chinese Immigration Act.*[87]

The lawyers were fully aware that this was only an analogy and so they sought to weaken the juristic force of the statute by pointing out that the legislature which enacted it was highly unrepresentative, since until 1948 provinces were given the authority by a federal statute to exclude people from the franchise on the basis of race and some used it. The point of principle here is that "respect for democracy underlies deference to legislative choices" and so "courts ought to be wary about categorically granting such deference to legislatures that are profoundly undemocratic, particularly when the legislative choices place burdens on the very groups excluded from the democratic process."[88]

They also argued that they were not asking the courts to make a retroactive decision but to deal with a present harm, one which was clearly illegal by the standards of the present. The head tax's consequences reached into the present by perpetuating a discriminatory status on Chinese people. Indeed, the point of the tax was not to collect money, but to signal that Chinese people are of lesser status and so the retention by the government of those taxes amounts to a perpetuation of that status. Hence, there is a violation of the equality guarantee in section 15 of the Charter. Moreover, the lawyers protested that any decision to deal with the matter on a summary basis, that is, without going to a trial, would prevent the courts from addressing the full evidentiary record of discrimination. In particular, the courts would be unable to assess properly the fact that another group which had been discriminated against—Japanese Canadians—had been given redress, which might signal that the discrimination against Chinese Canadians is "somehow of less significance."[89]

However, the lawyers also invoked reliance on the Radbruch formula by German courts to invalidate statutes because of their injustice. But it is significant that when they put the Radbruch formula in their own words, it does not come out quite as invalidation; rather, it comes out as grounds for not deferring:

> The values of certainty or democracy that ordinarily require that the courts simply defer to the existence of legislation must at a certain point give way, in the very name of law itself, to the most basic of legal values which courts are dedicated to upholding. Otherwise, contemporary Canadian courts will perpetuate injustice instead of law and ... law itself will stand defenseless against the most iniquitous uses of its form.[90]

One might argue that there is little difference between declaring a statute to be invalid because it is extremely unjust and refusing to allow it to have legal effect because it is extremely unjust. But this distinction is one firmly embedded in the common law.[91] It has to be acknowledged that in the case of the Chinese Immigration Act, the refusal by a court to defer to it seems more drastic. Since the Act no longer exists, the only effect it could have in the future is to constitute a valid juristic reason for refusing to disgorge enrichment, so the refusal to defer to it also eradicates it from the legal landscape. But this fact suggests not that there is something wrong with the court's declaration, but that there is, and always was, something legally wrong with the statute. That is, the statute was legally flawed even at the time it was in force.

The flaw here is that the statute was akin to a bill of attainder, for it offended the rule of law requirement that all laws be general in nature, particularly when the law is punitive. A law which seeks to punish a particular individual or class of individuals is considered suspect from the point of view of the rule of law, because it violates one of the principles which we saw

Fuller identify as a principle of the internal morality of law. And, as T. R. S. Allan has recently argued, the principle of generality is one of the most important principles of the rule of law because it serves the value of equality before the law.[92]

That a court at that time might have rejected this argument should be irrelevant to a court dealing with the same issue today. In addition, the court dealing with the issue today is not confronted by the problem of whether it would reject this argument if it were the sole argument that confronted it in a challenge to a statute that is still on the books. Nor is the court dealing with the issue about whether it is unfair to impose on the past its contemporary interpretive practice. The only issue for the court is whether a statute that has been taken off the books constitutes a valid juristic reason. It suffices in this regard to show that the juristic force of the statute is severely undermined by the fact that the statute was akin to an act of attainder.

The statute's formal flaw from the point of view of the rule of law is a flaw because it is very closely connected with substantive injustice, but the violation is of a value that is legal as well as moral—a value that is part of law's own morality. The term bill of attainder seeks to pick out, without naming the particular act of injustice, what goes wrong when the law is used as an instrument by government to punish an individual or group of individuals. Hence, determining whether a statute is a bill or act of attainder is depends not as much on whether the statute names an individual or group of individuals; rather, it depends on whether it names them for the purpose of punishing them, where punishment means an affront to the value of equality. Such bills are presumptively tainted, whatever the particular injustice each wreaks; and so the onus will be on those who would maintain their validity to show that they are not bills of attainder.

That onus could not have been discharged by the various Canadian governments who participated in enacting and maintaining versions of the Chinese Immigration Act. The lawyers effectively showed that these governments frankly recognized that their motives were entirely racist; indeed, these governments paraded their racism as they felt entirely justified in their bid to get rid of the "scourge" of the "wily oriental."[93] But, as the lawyers also showed, the government's sense of justification had to be maintained against a backdrop of moral values that condemned what they did. Other Canadians condemned the act.[94] And in cases in nineteenth-century British Columbia, courts had held that municipal bylaws and provincial statutes that imposed special taxes on Chinese immigrants were either void or unconstitutional.[95] Further, at the same time that these governments were complicit in maintaining a racist statutory regime, they signed the various treaties or conventions that the Court of Appeal held constituted the "pockets" from which international customary norms prohibiting racial discrimination grew.[96]

The Court of Appeal did not address the lawyers' argument as I have described it, though my way of putting it, with the exception of the point about bills of attainder, is closer generally to the lawyers' own. In particular, the court did not address at all the nineteenth-century cases cited by the lawyers. The court did have an answer to those cases, that the provincial legislation offended the Canadian division of powers between the federal and the provincial legislatures and that the bylaws were enacted under delegated authority which cannot, on ordinary common law principles, be exercised in a discriminatory fashion unless the discrimination is explicitly authorized. However, the Ontario Court of Appeal might say the federal parliament was acting within its jurisdiction and has unlimited authority to override the common law. But that answer, it is crucial to see, depends on the very same suspect recharacterization process.

The court's recharacterization of the lawyers' argument and the fact that it ignored significant portions of it stem from a positivistic mindset, which adopts a binary vision of the legal world marked by the validity/invalidity distinction. For that mindset, unless there is a constitutional bill of rights in play, statutes are either valid or invalid, which means that they have either all their force or none. Such a mindset is not receptive to an argument that the authority of law is constituted by principles of an internal morality of law, since its vision of law is a top down one, as Fuller once put it, a "one-way projection of authority" from ruler to ruled.[97] The authority of law is constituted not by principles, but by the will of the sovereign, a will which is limited by only the explicit legal constraints on that authority; for example, the statutory provisions of the Confederation that set out the legal terms of Canadian federalism.

This positivist mindset can work in two ways. First, it can exclude judicial reliance on principles when it comes to interpreting a statute, as it inclines judges to use tests that seek to determine plain facts about legislative intention—what the sovereign in fact intended to communicate. Second, once a statute's content has been determined, by whatever tests, the mindset excludes judges from deciding what force should be given to that content by reference to the same principles. The head tax case is an example of the second kind of situation, but it is important to see that these two situations are not in substance different.

In the first, judges are determining from the perspective of the present what the content of the statute is in order to decide what the law is that they are to apply. In the second, they are determining the legal effects of a statute which had been applied in the past but which is no longer on the books. Now the second situation can, as we have seen, be complicated by questions about what the content of the statute was. So in the informer cases, and in the border guard cases, the courts could say that the statute had the content which those who claimed they were acting according to law ascribed to it, that is, the content which a typical judge of the time would have ascribed to it.[98]

As I have suggested, following Pappe and Fuller, this claim is itself the product of a positivist mindset, because it excludes the thought that a statute should always be understood in terms of the principles constitutive of the authority of law, even if the majority of judges at the time rejected those principles. So in this class of cases the interpretive issue is not contentious because of time, but because of a theoretical controversy about the authority of law. And here it should be noted that Canadian courts have not only explicitly adopted the antipositivist view that the authority of law is constituted by such principles, but have contended that these principles and more have always been part of the Canadian legal tradition. Thus, as the lawyers pointed out in argument, the Supreme Court of Canada said in its decision on the legality of Quebec secession not only that the rule of law and constitutionalism are and have always been organizing principles of the Canadian Constitution, but so also is respect for minority rights.[99] Further, it was at this point in their argument that the lawyers adduced the record of British Columbia courts which had struck down provincial legislation and municipal bylaws that imposed equivalents of the head tax. So if the issue were one about how to interpret a present law or a past law, it seems that Canadian courts should adopt the antipositivist method of interpretation.

However, as in the case of the Germans who had been stripped of their property by the Nationality Law and the Chinese immigrants who had to pay the head tax, the issue of how to interpret the law might not seem to arise as a theoretical issue about the authority of law because *whatever* test one uses to interpret the statute comes out with the same answer—it is an answer in what Hart calls the core. But, as I will now argue, the issue about the authority of law is just as controversial here as it is when one might say that the law's content has to be settled by interpretation.

Here Ronald Dworkin's distinction between the gravitational force of a law and its specific authority is useful. If a judge finds that the best interpretation of a law is one that shows the law to be a mistake from the point of view of the rule of law, but not sufficiently mistaken to be invalid, it will be the duty of the judge to try to confine the force of that law to the greatest extent possible, in order to prevent the mistake from spreading.[100] Judges, Dworkin asserts, owe only a "qualified deference to the acts of the legislature" even in a legal order where the legislature is supreme. Thus, when statutes contain mistakes, judges should limit their deference to the absolute minimum.[101]

On the basis of this distinction, I have argued in an analysis of cases dealing with the discriminatory laws of apartheid South Africa that it was the duty of judges who had no constitutional authority to invalidate such laws to try to confine them to the narrowest possible reading when it came to deciding what the scope was of the authority officials had to implement the laws. And this duty came about precisely because of the gravitational force of the legal principles of their common law tradition, in particular, the principle of equality before the law which requires that legislation be implemented fairly and reasonably unless the statute explicitly excludes such values.[102]

Suppose for example that Canadian judges had in the 1930s to decide between two interpretations of an ambiguous provision in a general immigration statute, one which permitted officials to exclude Jewish immigrants on the grounds of their race and one which did not. Suppose also that the racist interpretation was to some extent better supported by the text of the general immigration statute and that if judges took notice of clearer exclusions, for example, in the Chinese Immigration Act, the racist interpretation would look like the right one. My claim is that the judges would be failing in their duty as judges if they accorded the Chinese Immigration Act gravitational force in their interpretation of the general immigration statute. Rather, they should give the more benign interpretation of the general immigration statute, resting it on common law authority such as the nineteenth-century cases from British Columbia.

But if that claim is right, it follows that when a judge now asks about the legal force of the Chinese Immigration Act, he or she is under the very same duty to confine its force to what it most specifically enacted and thus not to give it any gravitational force at all. The reasons for taking this stance are overwhelming. Not only was the statute during the time it was in force inconsistent with Canadian commitments to equality, as evidenced in ratification of international instruments, the common law, and the record of parliamentary debates, but to let that force reach into present is in flagrant violation of the explicit values of the Canadian political and legal order. Moreover, as we have seen the lawyers argued, deference to the legislature that enacted the statute has to be even more qualified than would be the case if the legislature had merely made a mistake; deference has to be qualified because the very people who were targeted by the statute were subject to disenfranchisement.

It turns out, on this argument, that the very fact of the clarity of the Chinese Immigration Act, the fact that its meaning was so evident, makes the case of how to deal with it from the present perspective far easier than the issues raised by the border guard trials or the trials of the informers. Further, the head tax case did not involve the problem of imposing criminal liability for an act that was arguably legal at the time it was committed. So the question then becomes pressing of why the judges of the Ontario Court of Appeal, a court not known for its positivism, should have approached the matter from such a sternly positivist mindset?

A useful contrast here is the House of Lords decision on which the lawyers relied, where the judges had to consider whether the Nazi citizenship law was a valid basis for imposing a tax on an individual. We have encountered already Lord Cross's famous and rather Radbruchian dictum: a "law of this sort constitutes so grave an infringement of human rights that the courts of this country ought to refuse to recognise it as a law at all."[103] But there is another equally famous, or perhaps infamous, dictum from the case. Lord

Pearson disagreed with Lord Cross, saying:

> When a government, however wicked, has been holding and exercising full and exclusive sovereign power in a foreign country for a number of years, and has been recognised throughout by our government as the government of that country, and some legislative or executive act of that government, however unjust and discriminatory and unfair, has changed the status of an individual by depriving him of his nationality of that country, he does in my opinion effectively cease to be a national of that country and becomes a stateless person unless and until he has acquired some other nationality. ... Suppose then that the wicked government is overthrown. I do not think it would be right for the courts of this country on their own initiative to disregard that person's change of status which in fact had occurred and deem that it had never occurred.[104]

Lord Pearson's stance is not only positivistic, but it is exactly the stance of the judges of the Ontario Court of Appeal. The only difference between the cases is that in the Head Tax case, the court is not dealing with the statute of a foreign country, whose generally wicked government has been overthrown, but with a wicked law of a succession of Canadian governments, where the succession happened through peaceful democratic means and where there has been no dramatic break with the past.

But while the judges of the Ontario Court of Appeal were anxious to stress at the beginning and end of their judgment their view that their country's treatment of the people of Chinese origin represents "one of the more notable stains on our minority rights tapestry,"[105] they also seemed anxious to resist the analogy the lawyers sought to draw between the laws of Nazi Germany and of apartheid South Africa, on the one hand, and the Chinese Immigration Act on the other. Indeed, they reduced the lawyers' arguments on this score to an ignominious footnote to their last substantive paragraph: "We are not here concerned with facially valid laws enacted by a totalitarian or other despotic regime." The paragraph reads: "The doctrine of unjust enrichment is an equitable doctrine. However, even the broad purview of equity does not provide courts with the jurisdiction to use current Canadian constitutional law and international law to reach back almost a century and remedy the consequences of laws enacted by a democratic government that were valid at the time."[106] The combination here of point and footnote is a classic example of what Cover described as the judicial techniques used in

order to reduce the cognitive dissonance that ensues when judges find themselves confronted by the prospect of enforcing a law that is wicked by their
own moral lights.[107] Such judges elevate the "formal stakes" and ascribe "responsibility elsewhere" in order to distance themselves from responsibility
for complicity in perpetuating wickedness. They emphasize the impersonal
nature of the law's authority in order to claim that it is not the judges who
determine the law. Rather, the law speaks through them; they are merely the
mouths that pronounce its predetermined content.[108]

   What can explain the retreat of Canadian judges from a generally antipositivist stance, especially when it is a retreat by judges of perhaps the
most antipositivist court in the land? In my view, there are only two reasons
that can explain this fact. The first is the understandable reluctance of the
judges to recognize that in important respects their democratic country had
something significant in common with the racist totalitarian regimes of the
twentieth century. Indeed, this reluctance might well be manifested in the
fact that both courts agreed to adopt the drastic legal measure of finding that
the lawyers' arguments disclosed no reasonable cause of action. As the lawyers tried to argue, this measure meant that they were prevented from presenting the full moral record of the implementation of the statute to the
court. In particular, the courts then avoided being confronted properly by
the kind of stain that the head tax was and the tension inherent in their claim
that the stain was on a "minority rights tapestry." For if there were such a
tapestry, then their position that human rights sprang into being after the
Second World War like mushrooms is wrong—the tapestry was woven, as
the Supreme Court claimed in the *Secession Reference*, from the time of
Confederation in Canada, and the head tax was suspect from the point of
view of the rule of law, as evidenced in part by the British Columbia cases. In
Fuller's terms, the head tax was suspect both from the point of view of the
principles of the rule of law—the internal morality of law—and from what
Fuller thought of as the external morality of law, the moral values of the
time.

   The second reason is, I think, the general reluctance of courts to put
judges on the slippery slope where they would constantly be confronted by
arguments that they should be in the business of remedying the substantive
injustices of the past. But there is a slippery slope only if the issue is ap-

proached from the perspective of the Radbruch formula that extreme injustice is no law. If that is the issue, then judges are forced to be first and foremost moral philosophers, which, whatever their talents in this regard, is not their mandate.

If, however, the issue is the Fullerian one of justice in the "administration of the law,"[109] then the determination of what constitutes legal injustice, injustice from the perspective of the rule of law, is properly within their mandate. While they will still have to make a judgment that there is substantive injustice, they will not be called upon, at least initially, to distinguish between degrees of substantive injustice. As my analogy to bills of attainder shows, the presence of the legal injustice in the law is triggered by a substantive injustice that also is an affront to the morality of law. So what matters to the judges initially is not so much the enormity of the substantive injustice, but the fact that the form of law has been abused in order to wreak such an injustice.

In other words, and contrary to Alexy, Radbruchian arguments about substantive injustice should not, from the perspective of judges, play the role of being a sufficient reason to invalidate a statute. They are invoked not as a test for the validity of law, but because, from the perspective of the judges, it is the apparent legal injustice which first triggers the inquiry into substantive injustice. There is no slippery slope, then, as judgment about substantive injustice is limited by the requirement that there be an initial legal injustice that frames the subsequent substantive judgment. And I would venture, to the extent that postwar German courts relied on the Radbruch formula to deal with the present effects of the Nazi citizenship law, their reliance shows that Fuller was right that the resort to a higher law argument is the product of a positivist mindset. The resort is produced by a compulsion to understand the legal word in terms set by the valid/invalid distinction, rather than as a world that aspires to realize the principles of the rule of law.

This goes to show that the claim to correctness which Alexy rightly suggests is necessarily part and parcel of the constitution of legal order also requires that justice has at least equal standing with certainty in the hierarchy of legal values. Indeed, it shows that there is no hierarchy. All three of the values which Radbruch identified—justice, certainty, and purposiveness—have equal standing. But justice here is not substantive justice in the Radbruchian sense of an external standard of morality against which the positive law can be measured. Rather, it is justice in the administration of the law, or Fuller's internal morality of law.

Conclusion

Fuller was right, in my view, that the Radbruch formula is best understood as the reaction of a positivist to the problems which might result from a positivist theory of law. The very idea of a formula is one that fits a positivist mindset, one that searches for bright line tests for validity. As Fuller said, "[n]o pat formula" can deal with the complexities of the kinds of problems we have encountered in this essay. But to the extent that legal theory can offer anything useful, Fuller was also right that the idea of an internal morality of law, of the principles of the rule of law, is best suited to explain both what goes wrong, legally speaking, in wicked regimes, and how best to address, legally speaking, the wickedness of the past.

Recall that while Fuller saw much better than Hart the complexity of the question whether the informer's action had a legal warrant for her action, he expressed his own preference for a retroactive statute, although he said, this was for a different reason from Hart's and Radbruch's (positivistically inclined) preference for using a statute that it would be "the most nearly lawful way of making unlawful what was once law." In Fuller's view, the statute would symbolize a "sharp break with the past," enabling the judiciary to "return more rapidly to a condition in which the demands of legal morality could be given proper respect."[110] While Fuller, quite characteristically, did little to elaborate this point, its elaboration has the potential to unravel the links between justice in the administration of the law and substantive justice, between the internal and the external moralities of law.[111]

I cannot attempt this task here, but will only sketch its first step by adverting to what the editors of an excellent collection of essays on transitional justice call the "paradox of the probable and the unnecessary": "The impact of truth and justice policies on a new democracy depends on starting conditions or the initial balance of power; in other words, the more likely the implementation of such policies is because of a favourable balance of forces, the less necessary they are to ensure a process of democratisation."[112] But, as the editors also say, whatever the effect of such policies on democratization, they are "crucially important moral and political demands which are, even if imperceptibly, part of a changing climate that places respect for human rights at the forefront within and between national communities."[113]

In other words, we can place societies seeking to uncover from an unjust past on a continuum, ranging from those which—to recall Alexy's terminology—are "weaker unjust" regimes to regimes which were very strong unjust regimes. If we assume that the pitch of injustice varies with the strength of the regime, then the weaker unjust regimes are likely to have less to recover from than the stronger ones. Correspondingly, the weaker regimes are likely to have in place better resources for dealing with past injustice, most notably for our purposes, a judiciary and a legal profession which are not completely tarnished by the past and so are able to participate in rebuilding the institutions necessary for a successful transition.[114] The weaker regimes will, that is, have committed substantive injustices but not to the extent that they have also completely compromised the rule of law. They will thus not need to mark as sharp a break with the past, both its substantive and its institutional injustices, as their equivalents which are recovering from a strong and very unjust regime.

The conclusion to which this argument drives is then that there is, as Fuller suggests in the second epigraph to this essay, a limit to which legal institutions can be used as the instrument of substantive injustice without a very severe strain on their claim to be legal. Three further conclusions fall out of this one.

The first tells against the Radbruch formula, since it is the case that the challenge to positivism's Separation Thesis—the thesis that there is no necessary connection between law and morality—rests not on the claim that extreme injustice is no law, but on the claim that certain kinds of extreme injustice put a severe strain on legality.

The second tells against Hart, since it indicates that Hart's positivist solution—disobey the law if it is in severe conflict with your conscience—is not only far from helpful when it comes to judicial dilemmas in the face of injustice, but of little help where it seems most at home—the case of a citizen or legal subject facing an unjust law. For the subject, there will usually be morality on both sides of the dilemma as long as there is law involved, because in order for law to be involved there will be some compliance with the internal morality of law.[115] To the extent that the claim that law is involved becomes less sustainable, the individual might be faced with all sorts of dilemmas, but they will not be dilemmas of legality. It is hardly surprising, then, that when a morally obnoxious law is enacted in a properly functioning democracy, the dilemma of legality becomes most acute. In such a democracy the law side of the dilemma is heavily freighted with morality. But that also suggests that there is some connection between the internal morality of law and democracy, at least in that democracy might be seen as the institutional fulfillment of the aspirations of the rule of law.

The third conclusion pertains to the burgeoning academic field of inquiry known as transitional justice. I have argued elsewhere that the thought that there is such a field depends on various distinctions, of which two are relevant here.[116] There is a distinction between transitional and stable societies and a distinction between just and unjust societies. Transitional justice is then the study of societies in the process of transition from a relatively stable but unjust regime to a stable and just regime. But as we can see from the head tax case, there is no sharp distinction between societies either in terms of stability and instability or in terms of justice and injustice. Rather, there is a continuum, so that no society should ever be complacent about either its stability or its justice. Indeed, in a country like Canada, whose inhabitants are generally considered to have an enviable quality of life, one might perhaps have to be especially vigilant. For in such a country the injustices of the past might more imperceptibly shape the lives of groups who are supposed to enjoy the same equality before the law of all within its borders.

Notes

I thank Robert Alexy, Evan Fox-Decent, Arthur Glass, Dimitrios Kyritsis, Thomas Mertens, Mayo Moran, Julian Rivers, Mike Taggart, and Lars Vinx for their comments on drafts of this essay. An earlier version was presented to a seminar at Amherst College and I thank all who participated in the discussion for their suggestions and comments.

1. H. L. A. Hart, "Positivism and the Separation of Law and Morals," reproduced in Hart, *Essays in Jurisprudence and Philosophy* (Oxford: Clarendon Press, 1983), 49, 75.

2. Lon L. Fuller, "Positivism and Fidelity to Law—A Reply to Professor Hart," *Harvard Law Review* 71 (1958): 630.

3. I will address in this essay neither the current debate within legal positivism between "exclusive" and "inclusive" legal positivists nor a recent neo-Benthamite revival in legal positivism. For discussion of the first two, see "Positivism's Stagnant Research Programme," *Oxford Journal of Legal Studies* 4 (2000): 703 and for discussion of all three, see my "The Genealogy of Legal Positivism," *Oxford Journal of Legal Studies* 1 (2004): 39.

4. Here Stanley Paulson provided the impetus in two seminal articles— "Radbruch on Unjust Laws: Competing Earlier and Later Views?," *Oxford Journal of Legal Studies* 15 (1995): 489, and "Lon L. Fuller, Gustav Radbruch, and the 'Positivist' Theses," *Law and Philosophy* 13 (1994): 313.

5. Lon L. Fuller, *The Morality of Law* (New Haven: Yale University Press, 1969, revised edition).

6. H. L. A. Hart, "Lon L. Fuller, 'The Morality of Law,'" in Hart, *Essays in Jurisprudence and Philosophy*, 343. Joseph Raz, "The Rule of Law and Its Virtue," in Raz, *The Authority of Law: Essays on Law and Morality* (Oxford: Clarendon Press, 1983), 210.

7. Ronald Dworkin, "Philosophy, Morality, and Law: Observations Prompted by Professor Fuller's Novel Claim," *University of Pennsylvania Law Review* 113 (1965): 672.

8. Gustav Radbruch, "Fünf Minuten Rechtsphilosophie" and "Gesetzliches Recht und übergeseztliches Recht," reproduced in Erik Wolf and Hans-Peter Schneider, eds., *Radbruch, Rechtsphilosophie* (Stuttgart: KF Koehler, 1973, 8th ed.).

9. See Karl Jaspers, *The Question of German Guilt* (New York: Fordham University Press, 2000; translated by E. B. Ashton, first published in Germany in 1947).

10. Hart, "Positivism and the Separation of Law and Morals," 74–75.

11. H. L. A. Hart, *The Concept of Law* (Oxford: Clarendon Press, 1961), 210.

12. Hart, "Positivism and the Separation of Law and Morals," 72–73.

13. Ibid., 72–74.

14. Ibid., 73. The phrase is John Austin's, quoted from Austin, *The Province of Jurisprudence Determined* (Library of Ideas ed., 1954) 185, but Hart clearly adopts it as his own.

15. Hart, "Positivism and the Separation of Law and Morals," again quoting from Austin.

16. Ibid., 74.

17. Here I follow Hart's account, ibid., 75–77, pretty well verbatim, though without quotation marks except when I want to emphasize Hart's choice of language.

18. Ibid., 76.

19. Ibid.

20. Ibid., 76–77.

21. Ibid., 77.

22. For an intriguing exploration of the public/private divide in this context, see Vandana Joshi, "The 'Private' Became 'Public': Wives as Denouncers in the Third Reich," *Journal of Contemporary History 37* (2002): 419.

23. Fuller, "Positivism and Fidelity to Law—A Reply to Professor Hart," 653–54.

24. Ibid., 654.

25. Ibid., 655.

26. Ibid., 655–56.

27. Ibid., 655.

28. Ibid., 657.

29. Ibid.

30. Ibid., 656.

31. Ibid., 659. In "Lon L. Fuller, Gustav Radbruch, and the 'Positivist' Theses," Paulson argues against this causal thesis. In *Legality and Legitimacy: Carl Schmitt, Hans Kelsen and Hermann Heller in Weimar* (Oxford: Clarendon Press, 1997), I argue not that legal positivism prepared the way for Nazism, but rather that it was incapable of providing lawyers with a resource to resist it. This argument builds on Fuller through the work of Hermann Heller, since the central claim is that legal positivism empties the principle of legality of content, thus permitting law to be used as mere instrument of power.

32. Fuller, "Positivism and Fidelity to Law——A Reply to Professor Hart," 659.

33. Ibid., 659.

34. Ibid., 660.

35. Ibid., 661.

36. Robert Alexy, "A Defence of Radbruch's Formula" (translated by David Dyzenhaus), in Dyzenhaus, ed., *Recrafting the Rule of Law: The Limits of Legal Order* (Oxford: Hart Publishing, 1999), 15.

37. Ibid., 35.

38. G. Radbruch, "Gesetzliches Unrecht und übergesetzliches Recht," quoted in Alexy, "A Defence of Radbruch's Formula," 15–16, Radbruch's famous essay was first published in 1946 in the first volume of the *Süddeutschen Juristen-Zeitung*, 105–8.

39. Hart, "Positivism and the Separation of Law and Morals," 74.

40. Alexy, "A Defence of Radbruch's Formula," 26–27.

41. Ibid., 27–28. Alexy offers the following powerful example in support of the necessity of the claim to correctness. A minority of the people in a country suppresses the majority but are honest about the injustice of their rule. So they decide to enact a constitution which has as its first provision: "X is a sovereign, federal and

unjust Republic." As he points out, the oddness of this provision goes beyond its immorality; it seems somehow "crazy." And that craziness stems from a contradiction—"a claim to correctness is necessarily bound up with the act of giving a constitution, and in such cases it is above all a claim to justice." Once we see this, we can no longer understand law as the "commands of the powerful."

42. Fuller, *The Morality of Law*, especially the section replying to critics at 187–253.

43. Alexy, "A Defence of Radbruch's Formula," 34–35.

44. Ibid., "A Defence of Radbruch's Formula," 30, his emphasis.

45. Ibid., 30–31.

46. Ibid., 31. Alexy mentions one further way in which an anti-positivist concept of law might stiffen resistance. In an unjust state an official has to consider the risk that in the future an antipositivistic concept of law will prevail and so that his judgment in the unjust state will be found invalid because the law on which it is based is later deemed unjust. Ibid., 31–32.

47. Ibid., 32–33.

48. Ibid., 19.

49. Ibid., 19–21.

50. Ibid., 22, 34.

51. Ibid., 21. For a different view, see A. James McAdams, *Judging the Past in Unified Germany* (Cambridge: Cambridge University Press, 2001), Chap. 6.

52. Julian Rivers, "The Interpretation and Invalidity of Unjust Laws," in Dyzenhaus, *Recrafting the Rule of Law*, 40.

53. Ibid., 50–51, at 51.

54. Ibid., 52–53. Rivers points out that the issue was then moved up a level, as both methods were challenged before the Constitutional Court because they violate the Basic Law's prohibition against retroactivity of criminal offences. The Court deemed both methods to be retrospective in the prohibited sense, but then ruled that reliance on the law of the land for one's claim that what one did was legal is predicated on the "normal case of an act committed in the Federal Republic of Germany under conditions of democracy, the separation of powers and the protection of human rights," 55. Rivers mentions that Alexy, in a comment on this case, has suggested that the Radbruch formula should provide an implicit limiting clause to the principle of nonretroactivity, 56

55. Indeed, Rivers argues that there is a basis for understanding Radbruch as engaged in the interpretive turn; ibid., 59–60.

56. H. O. Pappe, "On the Validity of Judicial Decisions in the Nazi Era," *Modern Law Review* 23 (1960): 260.

57. Ibid., 268–69.

58. Hart, "Positivism and the Separation of Law and Morals," note 43 at 75.

59. Pappe, "On the Validity of Judicial Decisions in the Nazi Era," 271.

60. Hart, "Positivism and the Separation of Law and Morals," 69–70, at 70.

61. Pappe, "On the Validity of Judicial Decisions in the Nazi Era," 271–72.

62. He confined himself to a short comment on this issue; ibid., note 34 at 271. But this note, combined with the discussion at 272 of what Pappe calls an "unqualifiedly sociological theory of law," provides a rich basis for my discussion.

63. For a powerful argument which reaches the same conclusion, see Thomas Mertens, "Radbruch and Hart on the Grudge Informer: A Reconsideration," *Ratio Juris* 15 (2002): 186, 200–204. See also Kenneth I Winston, "Introduction," in Winston, ed., *The Principles of Legal Order: Selected Essays of Lon L. Fuller* (Durham, NC: Duke University Press, 1981), 16–23. As Winston perspicuously argues, Hart's legal theory addresses only one mark of legal authority—the final determination of the content of the law. Hart thus misses the other mark of authority, its congruence with legal principles. Attention to this other mark—ordinarily, the province of the judge—brings one almost inevitably into an internal perspective on law which is out of kilter with positivist claims about discretion and the Separation Thesis. On these last points, see Frederick Schauer, "Fuller's Internal Point of View," *Law and Philosophy* 13 (1994): 285, for an apparent concession that there is this second mark and that attention to it has these effects, all the time arguing that it is still important to maintain a positivistic, external point of view.

64. I realize that there is something odd about this claim, since strictly speaking Hart would say there was no law on this matter, just a penumbral issue waiting for judicial resolution, a resolution which from the perspective of law could legitimately go either way. Since it was neither true nor false that what the husband did was a crime, one couldn't know whether the wife was doing something illegal until the court gave its decision. But the oddness, in my view, lies in the convoluted descriptions which his position requires and not in my attribution of problems to the position. Mertens, "Radbruch and Hart on the Grudge Informer: A Reconsideration," 201–2, points out that Radbruch and the court wished to avoid finding the Nazi law invalid because that would lead to the consequence that the judges should be prosecuted. So they focused on the issue of the wife's guilt in turning her husband in under a valid law.

65. Hart, *The Concept of Law*, Chap. 6.

66. In a well-known essay, Fuller dealt with similar issues; see "The Problem of the Grudge Informer," Appendix to Fuller, *The Morality of Law*, 245. The minister of justice seeks advice from several deputies about how to deal retrospectively with grudge informers from an era very much like the Nazi one. The first deputy takes the position that nothing can be done. There was a valid law and a uniform practice of

adjudication. The second argues that nothing should be done because the past era was one of chaos to which juristic terms have no application. The third rejects either/or solutions. He points out that there was not complete chaos; rather there were large pockets of legal order. He argues that one can discriminate between lawful acts and abuses of the law, such as the act of the grudge informer. The fourth says that such picking and choosing amounts to the kind of arbitrariness experienced in the past. Thus he advocates a carefully thought out and drafted, duly enacted, retroactive law. The last argues that no law can deal with the complexity of the cases. He expresses satisfaction with the fact that the grudge informers are being dealt with by street justice.

67. And in the case in which social democrats challenged the federal take over of the Prussian government in 1932, a take over which set the stage for Hitler's abuse of legality, the lawyers for the social democrats adopted just this structure of argument to the court; but their argument fell on deaf ears; see my "Legal Theory in the Collapse of Weimar: Contemporary Lessons?," *American Political Science Review 91* (1997): 121.

68. See both my *Hard Cases in Wicked Legal Systems: South African Law in the Perspective of Legal Philosophy* (Oxford: Clarendon Press, 1991) and *Judging the Judges, Judging Ourselves: Truth, Reconciliation and the Apartheid Legal Order* (Oxford: Hart Publishing, 1997).

69. Robert Cover, *Justice Accused: Antislavery and the Judicial Process* (New Haven, CT: Yale University Press, 1975), Chap. 13. Of course, the brave judge will also find that his interpretations of the law do not always, or even often in an unjust regime, coincide with the dictates of his conscience.

70. See further Mertens, "Radbruch and Hart on the Grudge Informer: A Reconsideration," 203.

71. See also Rivers, "The Interpretation and Invalidity of Unjust Laws."

72. Stanley Paulson argues that Radbruch is not best understood as having disavowed his prewar positivistic legal theory; see "Radbruch on Unjust Laws: Competing Earlier and Later Views?" and "Lon L Fuller, Gustav Radbruch, and the 'Positivist' Theses."

73. For materials relating to this case, see http://www.law.utoronto.ca/visitors_content.asp?itemPath=5/7/3/0/0&contentId=658. This is the website established for a conference on the head tax case, held at the Faculty of Law, University of Toronto in April 2003. The proceeds from this conference will be published as David Dyzenhaus and Mayo Moran, eds., *Calling Power to Account* (Toronto: University of Toronto Press).

74. The Chinese Immigration Act 1885, SC 1885.

75. The Chinese Immigration Act 1923, SC 1923.

76. The Immigration Act, SC 1947.

77. Mack v. Attorney General of Canada (2001), 55 O.R. (3d) 113 (SCJ), upheld (2002) 60 O.R. (3d) 737 (CA).

78. Ibid., Paragraph 1.

79. Ibid., Paragraph 52.

80. They did argue, rather more tentatively, that section 15 also gives rise to a right of redress.

81. Francesco Capatorti, "Human Rights, the Hard Road Toward Universality," in *The Structure and Process of International Law: Essays in Legal Philosophy Doctrine and Theory*, R. St. J. MacDonald and Douglas M. Johnston, eds. (The Hague: Martinus Nijhoff Publishers, 1983) 977, at 983.

82. Mack, Paragraph 32.

83. Ibid., Paragraphs 48–50.

84. Dickson CJ, in Petkus v. Becker (1980) 2 SCR 834, at 844.

85. Oppenheimer v. Cattermole [1976] AC 249, at 278.

86. Canada Trust Co. v. Ontario Human Rights Commission (1990), 74 OR (2d) 481 at p. 496 (CA).

87. Factum, Paragraph 106.

88. Ibid., Paragraph 107.

89. Ibid., Paragraph 134. The lawyers argued that section 15 of the Charter arguably gives rise to an independent right of redress, one that is in accord with a developing human rights norm. This amounts to an obligation on the state to promote the achievement of equality for those who have been disadvantaged by the injustices of the past. Again, the summary nature of the proceedings did not permit this novel claim to be argued properly.

90. Ibid., Paragraph 103.

91. For example, Canada's Supreme Court has held that administrative tribunals may rely on the Charter to decide whether a provision in the tribunal's constitutive statute offends constitutionally protected values. The oddness of a body using its authority to pronounce on the validity of the source of its authority—the statute—is mitigated by the fact that, as the Court reasons, the force of the tribunal's decision pertains only to the case before the tribunal. Since the offending provision is declared of no force and effect for the parties alone, the statute, including the offending provision, remains valid.

92. T. R. S. Allan, *Constitutional Justice: A Liberal Theory of the Rule of Law* (Oxford: Oxford University Press, 1999). Fuller himself does not have a principle of equality as one of his principles of the internal morality of law, but, as Allan successfully argues, the package of principles, as well as the claim that together they make up a morality, require the principle of equality if Fuller is not to be turned into

a proponent of a rather formal, positivistic understanding of the rule of law. (For exactly this transformation, see Joseph Raz, "The Rule of Law and Its Virtue"). See further my discussion in the Conclusion.

93. Factum, Paragraphs 5 and 8, quoting from House of Commons Debates.

94. Ibid., Paragraph 42.

95. Regina v. Corporation of Victoria (1888) 1 B.C.R. Pt. II 331 at 333 (S.C.); Regina v. Mee Wah (1886) 3B.C.R. 403; Tai Sing v. Maguire (1978) 1 B.C.R. Pt. I 101 at 106 (S.C.); R v. Gold Commissioner of Victoria District (1886), 1 B.C.R. Pt. II 260 at 262 (Div. Ct.). Indeed, the rule of law argument about bills of attainder merely raises to a higher level the administrative law argument that delegated authority has to respect the principle of equality.

96. A court may not respond here that immigration is a privilege and so the rule of law arguments in the text do not apply. See also Singh v. Canada (Minister of Employment and Immigration) [1985] 1 SCR 177. Indeed, until the point that Canada decided to put a stop almost altogether to Chinese immigration, it tried to have its cake and eat it too in a particularly cynical way. That is, it sought to benefit from importing people branded as low status and so made vulnerable from the outset to economic exploitation. Canada thus introduced into its domestic law a contradiction. In some respects, Chinese immigrants were regarded as equal. In others, they were regarded as inferior, for example, by federally sanctioned provincial disenfranchisement and by the attempts by provincial governments and by municipalities to emulate the brand of the head tax. But because they were regarded as equal unless the law explicitly undermined their equality, a court should be estopped from saying that since they chose to come to Canada despite the head tax, they were not subject to punishment in the sense relevant for designating a statute a bill of attainder.

97. Fuller, The Morality of Law, 207.

98. See Carl Schmitt, Gesetz und Urteil: Eine Untersuchung zum Problem der Rechtspraxis (Munich: C. H. Beck, 1969), 52.

99. Reference re: Secession of Quebec, [1998] 2 SCR 217, at paragraphs 32 and 81, cited at paragraphs 39 and 40 of the factum. At paragraph 40 of their factum, the lawyers quoted these lines from paragraph 81 of the judgment in Mack: "It should not be forgotten that the protection of minority rights had a long history before the enactment of the Charter. Indeed, the protection of minority rights was clearly a consideration in the design of our constitutional structure even in the time of confederation. Although Canada's record of upholding the rights of minorities is not a spotless one, that goal is one towards which Canadians have been striving since Confederation, and the process has not been without success. The principle of protecting minority rights continues to exercise influence in the operation and inter-

pretation of our Constitution." The remaining two organizing principles are federalism and democracy.

100. Ronald Dworkin, *Taking Rights Seriously* (London: Duckworth, 1977), 121–23. I am putting a rather Fullerian spin on Dworkin's distinction here.

101. Ibid., 37.

102. Dyzenhaus, *Hard Cases in Wicked Legal Systems*, Chap. 3.

103. Oppenheimer v. Cattermole, at 278.

104. Ibid., 265. As it happens, this disagreement made no difference to the result. Despite the fact that the majority of the House of Lords agreed that they should not recognize the Nazi citizenship law, the appellant had not taken the steps required by postwar German law to regain his citizenship.

105. Mack, Paragraphs 1 and 52.

106. Ibid., Paragraph 53.

107. Cover, *Justice Accused*, 229–38.

108. Hence the judges failed to live up to their own description of the task they faced when evaluating a claim about unjust enrichment. In Paragraph 51 of Mack, they agreed with the lawyers that they had to take into account values such as "moral balancing," "good conscience," and "injustice." The factors, they said, are "part of the foundation of the equitable doctrine of unjust enrichment." Here they relied on Supreme Court authority to the effect that fairness or justice alone is not sufficient to sustain a claim of unjust enrichment. The courts have to strike a balance between "predictability" and "certainty," on the one hand, and justice and equity, on the other. And in order to do that, the law "defines what is so unjust as to require disgorgement in terms of benefit, corresponding detriment and absence of juristic reason for retention."

109. To use a phrase of Hart's against him—see Hart, "Positivism and the Separation of Law and Morals," 8. Note that the Fullerian equivalent of Alexy's constitutional provision, note 41 above, that announces its injustice is a statute that declares that an official's act is valid even when it is unreasonable, unfair, beyond his authority, or treats those subject to his decision unequally. Any of these statements would, I think, amount to a more particular way of the legislature announcing what no legislature has ever announced—that its laws are intended to be unjust. See my "The Justice of the Common Law: Judges, Democracy and the Limits of the Rule of Law," in Cheryl Saunders and Katherine Le Roy, eds., *The Rule of Law* (Sydney: Federation Press, 2003), 21.

110. Fuller, "Positivism and Fidelity to Law—A Reply to Professor Hart," 661.

111. Though see Chap. 4 of Fuller, *The Morality of Law*, "The Substantive Aims of Law," explored in my "Aspiring to the Rule of Law," in T Campbell, J. Goldsworthy,

and A. Stone, eds., *Protecting Human Rights: Instruments and Institutions* (Oxford: Oxford University Press, 2003), 195. As Fuller's position is made more substantive, and if Radbruch's position on extreme injustice is attached more to specifically legal injustices, the two might seem much closer than I depict them in the text. Both Robert Alexy and Julian Rivers have suggested to me that Radbruch's formula is much more in tune with a Fullerian understanding of the rule of law than I recognize. For my attempt to deal with this point, see my "The Juristic Force of Injustice" in *Calling Power to Account* and for vigorous counter argument, Julian Rivers, "Gross Statutory Injustice and the Canadian Head Tax Case" in the same volume.

112. Alexandra Barahona De Brito, Carmen Gonzalez-Enriquez, and Paloma Aguilar, *The Politics of Memory: Transitional Justice in Democratizing Societies* (Oxford: Oxford University Press, 2001), 314.

113. Ibid.

114. See my *Judging the Judges, Judging Ourselves.*

115. See Dworkin in his response to critics in Marshall Cohen, ed., *Ronald Dworkin and Contemporary Jurisprudence* (London: Duckworth, 1984), 258–59, as discussed in *Hard Cases in Wicked Legal Systems*, Chap. 10, especially 250–57.

116. Here I rely on two essays: my review article "Transitional Justice," *International Journal of Constitutional Law 1* (2003): 163; and "Judicial Independence, Transitional Justice and the Rule of Law," *Otago Law Review 10* (2003): 345.

The Conditions of Surrender:
Reconstituting the Limits at Conflict's End

ROBIN WAGNER-PACIFICI

A legal world is built only to the extent that there are commitments
that place bodies on the line.

—Robert Cover[1]

Prologue

Surrenders of the political and military sort are quintessentially *situations
at the limit*. They involve giving up in order to end ongoing conflicts when
one party reaches the limit of its endurance.[2] The undoing of sovereign
power in surrender and its accrual to the victor occur as the actual violence
of the conflict is both invoked and stanched. Endings of conflicts are difficult, and endings that designate victor and vanquished and that accomplish
the undoings of power are particularly difficult and dangerous. Where do the
fixed rules, the recognized bodies, and institutions of law enter the acts of
surrender? Where and how do the might and violence of war pass the baton
to the conventions of law? Is law imposed during surrenders or is it conjured
out of the exchanges and transactions of force and power?

Law does not get the parties to the scene of surrender; calculations about
waning force or political support or provisions do that. The moment of law's
entrance here is always extra-legitimate. The arbitrariness of a superior might
in battle that appeals to a certain authority only becomes legitimate after it
finds its shape in the process of codification. Law is present in its conven-
ing—the parties to a surrender must invoke or must generate rules of conduct that are authorized by law (either codified or customary). If the parties
share a common worldview, they can more easily depend on traditional notions of authority and rule-bound process. But in any event, the previous
enmity means that any mutually accepted law must be, to a significant extent, emergent. On the other hand, the radical suspendings and undoings of

surrender are the work of a sovereign power that operates (through its forceful dominance) outside the sphere of law while deposing a sovereign power that surrenders. So perhaps the zone of surrender is best described as one in which overt, illegitimate violence hands off to the realm of covert and/or legitimate violence that is, precisely, law.[3] The terms of surrender and the reconfigured power relations that are engendered are best understood as temporary suspensions of bellicose violence.

How are these temporary suspensions soldered and sustained? In this essay, I will detail the recomposing and reconstituting work of material and symbolic transactions (exchanges of gestures, documents, signatures, soldiers, swords, pens, hostages, and oaths) that occur at the convergent site of surrender. These actions have the force of law while keeping the law of force in a state of suspended animation.

Surrender's Law

This essay begins with three propositions that connect the study of surrender to the study of law's limits. The first proposition is that it is analytically critical to elaborate the on-the-ground constitution of the law in socially and politically liminal moments and spaces. This proposition is analogous to the charge launched by scholars such as Chandra Mukerji to study the material culture of political regimes in order to track the peregrinations of power. In the case of her own work, this involves analyzing the gardens of Versailles under the reign of Louis XIV. Relevantly, she articulates the "*naturalization* of lawfulness and power, which was explicitly cultivated in the gardens of Versailles."[4] In the case of the work at hand, I wish to study the "material culture" of surrender. This approach to law purposefully moves both forward and backward in its analysis. It incorporates documents, discourses, and actions that announce themselves as embodiments of law. But it also incorporates documents, discourses, cultural objects, and actions that are not such obvious embodiments.[5]

The second proposition of this essay is that these transactions and exchange of objects occurring in moments such as those of military surrender come to have the *force of law* as they reconstitute relationships. Here the emphasis is on the way in which force and law are inextricably yoked together even as situations of ongoing violence are halted. For example, law can forcefully end the reign of force; law can justify and legitimate force; force can announce itself as the exception that operates beyond law (the "sovereign exception"), or force can back up (enforce) law.

The final proposition is a methodological one borrowed from Foucault. In this essay, and the larger study of surrender out of which it comes, surrender is viewed as a gap—in power relations, in history, in temporal and spatial fields. It must thus be studied as a gap, the representation of which flows through varied media. These mediations respond to the tension between the programs of the antagonists, to the complex and contradictory mandates of self-undoing in surrender, and to the above-mentioned liminal nature of the material brought in to span the gap. Thus, as W. J. T. Mitchell wrote about Foucault's essay on the Velazquez painting, *Las Meninas*, I too will attempt to develop a strategy of "holding open the gap between language and image [that] allows the representation to be seen as a dialectical field of forces, rather than a determinate 'message' or referential sign."[6]

The Problem of Surrender

What does it mean to be a subject who says, "I surrender," or to be a recipient of the statement, "I surrender," or to be a witness of an interchange of surrender? What happens to the subjecthood of the surrendering self, the surrendering army, and the surrendering sovereign as they surrender their selves to others? And what, analytically, does it take to grasp these social entities performing and interacting in such a moment of extremis? Surrenders are never quite what they seem—they may be part relinquishment of power and identity, part exchanges (handing over), part termination of conflict or resistance, and part salvaging operations. For all the variations on modalities of surrender (more or less emphatic asymmetry between the victor and the vanquished; more or less severe consequences incumbent upon the act), surrenders entail performances of the self in a moment of existential extremis. Hinge mechanisms of the flows of power, they illuminate the adjudication of victory and defeat in social life.

I would argue that surrenders, their signings and exchanges, their ceremonies, and their symbolic representations, are acts that mark and redraw the conceptual edges of social, political, and juridical time, space, and identity. They emerge out of the disordered spatiality and temporality of the battlegrounds and besieged cities of violent conflict, and assert a reordering. In this edge-work, they are akin to other transactional encounters that demand a convergence and a divergence at a designated boundary: foundings, resignations, secessions, inaugurations, and marriages. All of these are boundary events that reconfigure the world as they enact a transformation. They constitute both ends and beginnings and map the material landscapes of political, territorial jurisdiction, and the symbolic landscapes of solidarity and power. The assumed clarity of the structural intervention of surrender seems intuitively to contrast with the ambiguous leveling of such things as "peace accords." Yet withal, surrenders are themselves complicated ways of ending conflicts, with many contingent variations on their enactments, and with their own ambivalences and ambiguities.

The methodological approach of this study is to follow the semiotic phases of surrender—the *performative* phase (in which the act of surrender is accomplished with speech acts—"I surrender," "I promise to lay down my arms"—signatures on documents, and strategic exchanges of weapons and troops); the *demonstrative* phase (in which speeches, gestures, ceremonies, postures, positions, and so forth do the work of pointing out the transformations that are about to be, are being, or have been performed); and the *representative* phase (in which the accomplished surrender is "copied" and its meaning is historically sedimented). These phases have a complicated and variable chronology and it must be clear that understanding surrender requires suspending a strict linear accounting of their progress. While any event of social, political, or legal transformation can be interpreted via an application of this rubric, the specificity of surrender as an event that is an undoing as much as it is a doing, pushes this analytic scheme to its epistemological limits. The surrender then becomes an ontological telling of the halting of violence and resistance, of an undoing, or of the loss of an ongoing situation.[7]

The pauses of surrenders, unlike those of suspension of arms or truces, appear to gather themselves together or concentrate about the point of exchange and transaction at their centers. Arms must be laid down, promises to withhold from future fighting must be made and witnessed. The vanquished must accept the reality of loss. These actions, of both a performative and a demonstrative nature, take place *within* the pause and allow the parties to traverse it. Unlike other types of termination, surrenders as pauses seem to involve more than the usual suspense about surprise resumption of fighting, about sneak attacks, and so forth. Because the nature of surrender entails the radical submission/abnegation of oneself to another (the collective self and the individual self both relevant here and often synecdochically linked), the pause of surrender brings with it the earlier noted transformation of social and political identities and existential orientations. Thus the pause of surrender constitutes a truly liminal space and time during which the new order can only emerge once the old order goes through a kind of historical vanishing point.

The Etymology of Surrender

The English language is full of terms of authoritative transaction that derive their authority from language itself: juris-*diction*; sub-*scribe*; re-*sign*. Sur-*render* is one of these terms, and we turn to linguistic roots in order to begin to render the meaning of surrender. The *Oxford English Dictionary*, in its entry for "surrender"[8] as a noun, lists "sure render" and "surrendre" as other renderings of the word. The first meaning listed is that which pertains to law: "The giving up of an estate to the person who has it in reversion or remainder, so as to merge it in the larger estate . . . specifically the yielding up of a tenancy in a copyhold estate to the lord of the manor for a specified purpose." Thus, surrender is immediately linked to *space*, by way of its territorial referent, to *time* in its signifying of re-version or re-mainder, and to the accumulations of *power* ("so as to merge it in the larger estate"). These spatial, temporal, and political reconfigurations move through the designating institutions of the law, however they are initially impelled. The second, more general, meaning is given as: "The giving up of something (or of oneself) into the possession or power of another who has or is held to have a claim to it; especially (Military, etc.) of combatants, a town, territory, etc. to an enemy or a superior. In wider sense: Giving up, resignation, abandonment."

Three things are striking about these definitions. First, the persistent suggestion of a *prior* claim in the essential meaning of surrender—there are always those who are held to have a claim to the self or thing surrendered. Second, one is always surrendering something to someone else—whether that be the lord of the manor, the sovereign,[9] the court, another claimant, or the enemy or assailant.[10] And finally, the concept "enemy" is linked, and yet also distinguished from "superior."[11] These issues demonstrate the relational nature of surrender—there is always a recipient of the surrendering act, which recipient must be recognized as some kind of sovereign authority.[12] As well, they suggest ambivalence about the nature of that relationship between victor and vanquished, an ambivalence that is contingently resolved through the literal and figurative conditions of each surrender.

A clue to the first issue (that of the prior claim) can be found in the etymology of the root word "render" in surrender. The *OED* defines "render" as a verb with the Old French root of rendre, the popular Latin root of rendere (an alteration of prendere) and of classical Latin as reddere, the meaning of which is "to give back." In fact the very first of some seventeen meanings for render that are provided in the *OED* is: "To repeat (something learned); to say over, recite." Repetition is then at the very linguistic heart of surrender. But not just rote repetition, for the second, though noted as now somewhat rare, definition of render is "To give in return, to make return of." Here repetition is return, as one renders thanks for some prior gift. And thus notions of recompense and proportionality are brought to bear as render gets drawn into the modality of the gift and gift giving.

What is clear even from these dictionary definitions is that the oscillation between meanings that point to a transcendent truth, buttressing the social acts of rendering and surrendering (the mythological notion of return) and meanings that are derived from and enacted by consensually validated performances (performatives subscribed to by witnesses and/or revivifying legal claims), reveals a fundamental tension. One needs especially to come to terms then with the essential mythos of return in the linguistic and symbolic roots of such situations of social exchange as surrender. With all the assumed glory of the victor in surrender, it is puzzling that the very terms of the scene themselves (sure render, surrender, sur rendre) do not allow the victor the claim of first movers.

Similarly, there is also no last mover or final surrender—even as each new victor hopes to have put the matter to rest. By their very cyclical natures, surrenders cannot be definitive.[13] They must be repaid. While surrenders may, in their extremism, seem to be the very essence of conclusiveness and finality, they are revealed to harbor an idea of provisionality. Today I surrender to you—tomorrow you will surrender to me. As the wheel of historical fortune turns, the idea of re-taking is too much at the heart of the surrender, and the vanquished must of necessity be drawn back into the cycle.

The Transactions and Exchanges of Surrender

Surrenders demand convergence as the warring sovereigns (or their military proxies) meet to communicate and perform the giving up and giving over. The exchanges of surrender perform, demonstrate, and represent the realignments of power, hierarchy, and control when one party surrenders to another. They establish a meta-threshold: of time, of space, of violence, and of sovereign power. Convergence without transaction and exchange simply recapitulates a siege—some gesture must bridge the gap. Similarly, separate transactions without convergence cannot cauterize a conflict. One of Robert E. Lee's generals, E. P. Alexander, recalled Lee considering ordering his troops to disperse rather than to formally surrender, and his rejection of that option. According to Alexander, Lee stated:

> If I should order this army to disperse, the men with their arms, but without organization or control, and without provisions or money, would soon be wandering through every State in the confederacy, some seeking to get to their homes and some with no homes to go to. Many would be compelled to rob and plunder as they went to save themselves from starvation, and the enemy's cavalry would pursue in small detachments.[14]

Analysis of the exchanges that both constitute and cross the limit of the conflict must identify their *interactional* aspects, their *material* aspects, and their *symbolic* aspects. Turning over the key to a city, for example, may be viewed as a social interaction between the giver and the receiver, as a material exchange of a concrete object (heavy or light, functional or not, old or newly minted) at a particular time and place, and as a symbolic gesture denoting accessibility, power, and control. In all of these incarnations, the exchanges involved in the termination of conflict create what Lewis Coser, following Georg Simmel, claimed to be, "a social process dependent upon, but not directly deducible from its pursuits."[15] In other words, also following Simmel, the actions of termination of a conflict are distinct from both the actions and goals of the conflict itself or those of the periods of peace that abut the conflict on either end.

In taking its own shape (or shapes) this key moment of transition retains a significant element of ambiguity. Even where the victor and the vanquished are clearly identified, there are important variations in the manner in which this identification is marked and its consequences made apparent. If the surrendering exchanges are viewed as a type of compositional system with vectors of exchange, some kind of balance between what art historian Rudolf Arnheim calls the centric and the eccentric tendencies must be achieved. Short of total annihilation, no vanquished party can render up absolutely everything to the victor. As Arnheim writes: "Neither total self-centeredness nor total surrender to outer powers can make for an acceptable image of human motivation."[16]

Something essential about the key element of ambiguity in surrender exchanges in bound up in this variable balancing. There is the palpable sense of both functional and semiotic danger in the actions associated with surrender in war. Having reached the point where a desire to surrender on the part of the projected defeated party meets a willingness to grant and/or accept surrender terms on the part of the imminent victor, the parties must still bring the fighting to a halt and cross the threshold to peace. Analysts of war note the particular dangers of such transactions and their on-the-ground contingencies and interpretations. Randy Collins notes that: "Surrendering in the midst of combat conditions can be a physically very dangerous act, since it requires communicating to enemy soldiers, who are still expected to be menaced and getting the signal accepted. Given the victory frenzy that frequently occurs among the conquering side, many troops are killed in the action of surrender, or even shortly thereafter."[17]

This most dangerous moment of a conflict is far from straightforward. For combatants to go from a condition of attack (or readiness to attack) to a condition of retreat or cease-fire involves physical and existential circuit switching of the most extreme nature. Armies that have maintained discipline in the ranks during the fighting may indeed experience the kind of release that Collins identifies. This release may actually derail the anticipated conclusion of the fighting itself, instigating renewed hostilities.

The perils associated with moments of surrender highlight the work of the attendant promises, oaths, demonstrations, gestures, and representations. These actions attempt to fix the event, align its meaning for all participants, and assure its trajectory. But dis-alignments and uncertainty are always present: hybrid genres of action may signal differently and set off diverse interpretations; strategic actors may see arrangements as either temporary or permanent, as it suits them; surprise attacks when the enemy's guard is down may give a lie to promises to desist. And the perils are not only physical. There are also existential perils to be navigated, and they are most obvious in the more *ceremonial* moments of surrender. Political scientist Marc Ross claims that all surrender ceremonies contain a combination of elements of both recognition and degradation[18] (with attendant ambiguities about the consequences). Thus the sequence of exchanges will tend to be highly structured and reflexive as they seek to fend off or cultivate ambiguity.

The Conditions of the Surrender Delivery

The exchanges of surrender are indeed subject to existential and semiotic ambiguity. One way to deal with such ambiguities is to establish rules to conventionalize the transactions. In early modern Europe, the "consciously cultivated and painstakingly perfected art of war"[19] involved the development of conventions of warfare generally and the conventions of surrenders specifically. Siege warfare became the norm as important towns and forts, defended by increasingly sophisticated guns and cannons, reworked the moral and strategic landscape of emergent absolutism.[20] Surrenders after a siege were among the most highly conventionalized transactions ending a war. For example, a large breach in the wall of a town or fortress signified that defeat was imminent and the defending commander was both forced and allowed to surrender at that point (with dire consequences for refusal): "It was a law of war that if a place refused to surrender when a practicable breach had been made in the body of the works, when there remained no hope of succor, and the attack was compelled to have recourse to the assault, the garrison was granted no quarter, the place was open to sack and the commander hanged."[21] Other norms concerned the manner in which the defeated troops might exit, the positions in which they might carry their weapons and flags, and the fates of deserters. Several of these conventions will be discussed below. Here, it is important to note that even within these rules there were contradictions. One rule called for a garrison to surrender when it had still at least two days' supplies of rations and ammunition. Another rule called for the fortress to hold out until all stores had been exhausted. Actions that might be interpreted as heroism could alternatively be interpreted as foolhardiness. Thus, even within this highly conventionalized context, the meaning and consequences of surrendering exchanges were highly contingent upon interpretation.

The Conditions of the Unconditional

Unconditional surrender seems to push surrender to its conceptual limits. Such surrenders self-consciously announce their breaks with all customary or codified law, requiring at least the residual condition of an agentic interlocutor with whom the victor might "compose the peace." Unconditional surrender appears not to be able to sustain the "I" of the one surrendering (one who indeed is surrendering his very self), that sustaining being a condition of social transactions.

Of course, this is only the most extreme interpretation of unconditional surrender. Attempts to pin down the meaning of this term, both its official and its unofficial connotations, have been unsuccessful. In February 1945, a Gallop Poll in the United States asked a series of questions about public attitudes toward the policy. Tellingly, the poll began the series of questions with: "Will you tell me what the term 'unconditional surrender' means to you?" Here the possibilities were numerous and highly detailed. They ranged from (1) "Complete surrender—surrender without any provisions; surrender with no advance peace terms; acceptance of the dictated peace terms of the Allies; no compromise; no clauses," to (2) "Surrender—end of fighting; whole place gives up," to (5)"Change form of government, get rid of Nazis," to (7) "Take everything away from them, give up everything, no longer exists as a nation," to (8) "No future wars, permanent peace," to (10) "Fight until the last man; kill them all," with other meanings in-between. Results of the poll showed that 52 percent of those responding understood unconditional surrender to mean that the United States would dictate the surrender with no advance peace terms, no compromises, no clauses. Eleven percent understood it to mean stripping the enemy of all power, all arms. Another 9 percent believed it meant taking everything from the Germans to the point of destroying the enemy as a nation. Finally, 4 percent thought it meant that the United States would take possession of everything and would govern Germany.[22]

The line between unconditional surrender and total destruction or annihilation is revealed to be a confusing one in these possible responses. Redundancies ("whole place gives up," "take everything away") may reflect the psychological and political nervousness of a war-weary public. The slight, but crucial, variations of both tone and signification engage discourses of revenge, hegemonic control, or targeted destruction.

The most explicit and ultimately successful formulation of the "unconditional surrender" demand in modern warfare was that developed during the Second World War by Franklin Roosevelt at the January 24, 1943, press conference at Casablanca. Certain "unconditional surrender" precedents did exist in the history of warfare, however, most often in regard to the surrender of a specific fort or garrison. Such a formulation meant that "the military personnel of the captured fort [would] be taken prisoner and confined under the rules of war until the end of hostilities."[23] Application of these terms to larger social and political entities, such as cities or states, was more problematic.

Looking for meaning in historical precedents would not have been entirely fruitful. One example, the unmet demand for the unconditional surrender of Carthage by Rome in the Third Punic War, entailing the surrender of territory, cities, and populace, did lead to the eventual sacking and destruction of all of Carthage in 146 B.C., although such may *not* have occurred had Carthage actually surrendered unconditionally. Generally, outright refusal of surrender by the incipiently vanquished, whether of the negotiated or unconditional kind, could indeed lead to sacking and destruction.[24]

In the modern epoch, in accord with evolving international law, wars often ended with negotiations and a peace treaty between the belligerents.

Thus Roosevelt's demand for "unconditional surrender" had no successful modern precedent. American general John J. Pershing did make the argument for demanding unconditional surrender from the Germans at the end of World War I, but was not successful in getting other generals, specifically the British, to agree. As Wolfgang Schivelbusch writes:

> A further quarter of a century and the Second World War were required for the idea of unconditional surrender to be fully accepted. The significance of this change is signaled by the adoption of the American "surrender" instead of the British "capitulation." ... An army that capitulates in the traditional sense lays down its arms but retains its status as a legal entity. An army that surrenders is subjugated in toto to the authority of the victor.[25]

Years later, Roosevelt himself claimed to come up with the term while thinking about Ulysses S. Grant's nickname:

> We had so much trouble getting those two French generals [De Gaulle and Giraud] together that I thought to myself that this was as difficult as arranging the meeting of Grant and Lee—and then suddenly the press conference was on and Winston and I had had no time to prepare for it, and the thought popped into my mind that they had called Grant "Old Unconditional Surrender" and the next thing I knew I had said it.[26]

It is important to highlight the convention-breaking nature of Roosevelt's declaration. For one thing, the eventually codified policy's combining of political and military surrender was historically remarkable.[27] Justification by the Allies for the "unconditional surrender" involved indexing the enemies as similarly unprecedented in nature. Thus the Allies termed the Axis powers "not normal belligerents," and the war that they had initiated "aggressive."[28]

And then there was the fact that the very war trajectory by which Germany might be brought to the state of an unconditional surrender would probably entail the collapse of any authority capable of actually performing the surrender (performatives of such nature requiring the authority to be, precisely, authorized, viz. felicitous, in carrying out the surrender). Thus:

> [T]owards the end of March 1945, the British government became convinced that once Germany had been completely overpowered, there would in all probability no longer be any military or civil authority capable of signing such an instrument of surrender. As a consequence, the victors would have to resort to a different procedure and unilaterally proclaim total German defeat and their assumption of

supreme authority in Germany. Accordingly, the surrender document was re-drafted by the European Advisory Commission into the form of a declaration.[29]

Ultimately, the members of the German High Command did sign the military surrender instrument at General Dwight D. Eisenhower's headquarters in Reims. But it is analytically interesting that in the case of Germany, the *unconditional* nature of the demand coincided with the *absence* of any sovereign authority with which it would be possible to negotiate.

Such problems of authority and symmetry find partial solutions in the decoupling of military and political authority. If the victor pronounces no recognizable political authority with which to negotiate the surrender, it might accept a military authority as a kind of signing proxy. Such was also the case in the U.S. Civil War, as generals Ulysses Grant and Robert E. Lee signed a surrender instrument in their capacities as military officials, and as generals William Sherman and Joseph Johnston attempted to sign a surrender instrument in similar capacities. Just after the signing of Grant and Lee's surrender instrument at Appomattox, President Abraham Lincoln made a speech in which he clarified the nature of these negotiations: "Unlike the case of a war between independent nations, there is no authorized organ for us to treat with. . . . We simply must begin with, and mould from, disorganized and discordant elements."[30]

The delicate navigation of the boundary between military and political authority was evident in certain mis-steps and reconfigurations. For example, during the Sherman/Johnston meeting, a Confederate cabinet member, Secretary of War John Breckinridge was initially rejected as a participant by Sherman, who would not recognize or negotiate with a Confederate politician. Sherman changed his mind when "Johnston explained that Breckinridge was also a major general."[31] Ultimately, Sherman himself, a military man, would be accused by (post-Lincoln assassination) newly inaugurated President Andrew Johnson and his cabinet of overstepping his boundaries in his attempt to forge a much more political manifesto out of his negotiations with Johnston. General Grant was sent by the president to meet with Sherman to terminate and make null Sherman's surrender "Memorandum."

The final conceptual conundrum presented by the "unconditional surrender" formula is bound up with the semiotic phases of surrender. In order for transformations and exchanges like surrenders to be successful, specified actions and renderings must be generated, witnessed, and accepted. The very blankness of the "unconditional" formulation seems self-annihilating. The practical and the phenomenological coincide here. As historian Raymond O'Connor writes about the application of the doctrine to the surrender of Italy during World War II: "The presence of numerous 'conditions' in both the long and short-term documents . . . revealed a disposition toward flexibility in interpreting and applying the doctrine." Lest one think this only the case with belligerents who were soon to be transmuted into allies, O'Connor goes on to write: "What the formula could not eliminate was the necessity for specific terms in any armistice or surrender document. Essential items . . . the disarmament and disposition of troops, the release of prisoners, the administration of internal affairs."[32]

The sheer fact of the existence of specified agents, times, and places for the performance of the speech acts associated with surrendering made the unconditionality of the surrender only reachable asymptotically. Beyond that, a more generalized "sense" of the surrender might stand in for specified conditions when complicated messages were entailed. A director of the Overseas Branch of the Office of War Information during World War II quoted an anonymous source who stated, precisely, the sense that Roosevelt wanted to convey to the citizens in the Axis coalition at war's end:

> [Roosevelt] wanted to rule out any pledge or offer like the Fourteen Points and still convey to the enemy peoples the idea that they would be treated generously by the Allies. He thought that the story of Grant and Lee at Appomattox would convey this idea . . . what he especially wanted to bring out was Grant's gesture in letting the confederates keep their horses. The President felt that this incident from American history would help the enemy peoples to realize that they were facing chivalrous foes who did not desire to impoverish them or humiliate then but who would treat them with magnanimity.[33]

Here, the allegorical power of the Grant/Lee reference was meant to reassure the *peoples* of the Axis countries while the "unconditional surrender" demands were directed toward the soon-to-be former authorities. Such historical analogies and policy genealogies relied upon what I am terming the network of cross-witnessing. The nature of this network is to be constantly augmented and revised. In this case, the conditions and exchanges of World

War II were brought into alignment with those of Appomattox as chains of actors and their interpreting witnesses pointed contemporary audiences in the right direction, toward the right interpretation.

The ultimatum demanding Japan's "unconditional surrender" issued at the conclusion of the meeting in Potsdam in July 1945, the "Potsdam Declaration," took a different form than that issued to Germany. One significant difference hinged around the recognition of the continuation of the Imperial dynasty under Emperor Hirohito. Such a recognition was complicated—how could surrender be unconditional when the vanquished could successfully demand, as did the Japanese, a condition that went to the heart of its own *endogenous* authority? The mechanism by which such a nuanced navigation of the questions of conditionality and authority proceeded was one comprised of nearly coterminous "lumpings and splittings."[34] Thus, the concept of unconditional surrender was alternatively targeted at the military forces, at the Japanese government, at the Emperor, and at the whole entity named "Japan." These associations came in and out of focus in the various documents generated over the course of the waning days of the war. For example, Point Thirteen of the Potsdam Declaration said: "We call upon the Government of Japan to proclaim now the unconditional surrender of all Japanese armed forces. . . . The alternative for Japan is prompt and utter destruction."[35]

However, the Japanese acceptance of this Declaration seemed to insert its own condition: "The Japanese Government is ready to accept the terms enumerated on July 26, 1945 . . . with the understanding that the said declaration does not comprise any demand which prejudices the prerogatives of His Majesty as Sovereign Ruler."[36] And the complications of balancing what I would term the "compositional system" of surrender become most clear in the American response to this qualified acceptance:

> [F]rom the moment of surrender the authority of the Emperor and the Japanese Government to rule the state shall be subject to the Supreme Commander of the Allied Powers who will take such steps as he [General Douglas MacArthur] deems proper to effectuate the surrender terms. The Emperor will be required to authorize and ensure the signature by the Government of Japan and the Japanese Imperial General Headquarters of the surrender terms necessary to carry out the provisions of the Potsdam Declaration.[37]

This exchange of messages culminates in an American response that is constructed of several nested actions. On the one hand, it functions as a performative speech-act, *ordering* the emperor and the Japanese government to subject themselves to the supreme commander of the Allied Powers. At the same time, it *demonstrates* or indexes a series of embedded authority structures that must authorize each other in order for the surrender to proceed. The emperor is positioned as the authorizing institution that must guarantee the signature of the government of Japan and the Japanese Imperial General Headquarters. That signature, in turn, will perform the surrender. In Austin's terms, the chain of constative and performative speech acts is deployed in overt fashion, with a kind of fabulous simultaneous constitution/recognition of subsidiary authority structures. The emperor's role retains its singularity in some important authorizing sense. And yet he must submit himself in turn to the supreme commander of the Allied Powers: "The Emperor will be *required* to authorize and ensure the signature." This hierarchical and nested construction allowed, precisely, for the insertion of a condition into the unconditional, that being the retention of the Imperial sovereign in Japan.[38]

Ultimately, "unconditional surrender" operates as a kind of theoretical ground zero of surrenders generally, a conceptual vanishing point that keeps disappearing (is it all territory, is it all sovereign authority, is it all armaments, is it the entire nation and its people) as the transactions of surrender work themselves out.

The Structure of the Surrendering Exchange: Gift, Contract, Demonstration

At the conclusion of the peace, people, objects, and speech acts are exchanged across (former) enemy lines. It is also true, meaningfully, that people, objects, and speech acts can be explicitly withheld or retained at such moments. But these *nonexchanges* also participate in and constitute a kind of compositional field of exchange. If a defeated soldier is allowed to retain his sword, for example, such permission references both an object and a medium of exchange. The victor gives a kind of "gift" to the vanquished. In a paradoxical way, he gives him "back" his own sword.

Giving back, the idea of a return, recalls the etymological origins of "surrender," in which that which is rendered to the victor is thusly designated as lawfully "always having been" the victor's. And when the category of victor extends to include the victims of the vanquished, as it did after World War II, the giving of reparations is explicitly restorative: "Wiedergutmachung was Germany's term for the reparations, literally meaning 'to make good again,' that is to return to former conditions."[39] Following the unconditional surrender of Germany, these reparations signify that the former conditions were the proper conditions. Unconditional surrender and reparations combine to heighten the normative inflection of the embedded idea of "return" in surrender.

Such exchanges reveal how extraordinarily complex the temporal looping involved in surrender accords and exchanges can be. Postwar reparations of the sort that Germany was compelled to pay after World War I and II have, according to legal scholar Ruti Teitel, precisely a hybrid temporal extension. They assist in the suturing work of the transactions in the present, they restore and thus revive the past, and they point toward a new equilibrium in the future.[40]

But equilibrium is not always the goal or the outcome of surrender exchanges. There can, and often is, stability without equilibrium. Hannah Arendt links the desire for stability in politics to the faculty of making promises and to the laws of contract: "We may trace it back to the Roman legal system, the inviolability of agreements and treaties (pacta sunt servanda)."[41] Agreements may bring stability after a period of enmity and war, but agreements of the surrendering sort rarely bring equilibrium. A survey of surrenders reveals a high degree of contingency in these transactions. What gets exchanged? Who gets to keep what? Who must give what to whom? These contingent arrangements deliver a tone and a sense to individual surrenders that then take shape as essentially in the business of, alternatively, humiliation or re-equilibrium, or magnanimity.[42]

But even within the highly contingent situation of specific wars and their endings, there are formal models, ideal types, of exchange relationships that each case may, more or less, resemble and embody. These models include the gift, the contract, and the debt, among others, and it is possible to analyze the exchanges of surrender as variously approximating these forms. Each of these models assumes and relies upon an extant *system* of exchange for their functioning. And thus, the question of the first mover (or first transfer) is raised once again. Simmel's attempt to theorize the physiognomy of exchange, in his essay titled, precisely, "Exchange," circles in on his own sense of a first mover. Simmel writes: "I hold it to be completely possible that the forerunner of socially fixed exchange was not individual exchange, but a form of transfer of possessions that was not exchange at all—[rather] something like robbery. Interindividual exchange would then have been nothing other than a peace treaty."[43]

Thus Simmel ties the origins of a system of exchange to an originary act of property alienation and to conflict-ending peace treaties. Given this, it is not surprising that exchange transactions are so central to surrender.

But what of the various codified systems of exchange that surrender transactions may mirror? We begin with the gift, one among several media by which social relations are organized and reorganized.[44] Many of the objects exchanged during surrender ceremonies can be understood as types of gifts—keys, swords, supplies, freedom from captivity, and so forth as will be described below. As a fundamental social form of exchange, social theorists from Marcel Mauss, Pierre Bourdieu, Jacques Derrida, Maurice Godelier, to Viviana Zelizer have analyzed the gift. These theorists all agree on one thing: gifts are paradoxical objects of exchange. Of the many paradoxes of the gift, a key one is that which relates to its ontological claim—the gift claims to be, as Pierre Bourdieu put it, "an inaugural act of generosity."[45] Yet there are certain clear systemic expectations for gift-giving and repaying. Gifts need to be appropriate to the situation, they need to be proportional to expectations that involve, among other things, restitution, and they imply time limits or terms: "The difference between the gift and every other operation of pure and simple exchange is that the gift gives time . . . but this gift of time is also a demand of time. The thing must not be restituted immediately and right away . . . there must be waiting—without forgetting."[46] And it is precisely this delay between occasions of gift giving and counter gift giving that allows each gift to appear "inaugural."

The significance of this "inaugural" appearance lies in the gift's self-representation as un-coerced, voluntary, or unmotivated. A *free* giving over has nothing to do with force or violence. Yet exchanges in surrender are not thereby inappropriately interpreted within the paradigm of the gift, as one might assume given surrenders' forced nature and violent backdrop. For gifts are, according to their many analysts, never inaugural, never unmotivated, never without a history, and never completely uncoerced, regardless of their idealization. Here is the link between gifts and violence. We might recall Simmel's speculative understanding of the evolutionary origins of codified exchange—from robbery to peace treaty to exchange. The exchange may be said to domesticate the violence that, under another name, set off the series of transfers in the first place. But domestication may also be a form of mis-recognition. And the confusion about the nature of gifts given in ceremonies of surrender has precisely to do with what Bourdieu terms such "symbolic violence": "the gentle, invisible form of violence which is never recognized as such, and is not so much undergone as chosen, the violence of credit, confidence . . . gifts, gratitude . . . all the virtues honored by the code of honor—cannot fail to be seen as the most economical mode of domination."[47] Surrenders are principally about the cauterization of violence and the re-imposition of lawful relations. But, if the exchanges that are the medium of surrenders' transpiring (here read through the gift paradigm) are really violence under a different, symbolic rubric, violence persists through the acts of surrender itself.

What kind of gifts are these? What is the directionality of the transactions? In other words, who is giving what to whom? Are there simultaneous, or co-inciding, gifts and repayment of gifts? Are there different orders of gifts (e.g., symbolic objects and freedom)? Finally, is there a kind of poison infused in the gifts that the vanquished give to the victor, the expectation of return in the future metamorphosing into the dream of revenge? These questions reveal how complicated and point-of-view dependent is the analysis of the mechanisms of exchange in surrender.

Taking one example, one might view the victor's giving the vanquished permission to surrender as a kind of gift. It may be a gift of life (as opposed to annihilation) or of partial autonomy or of freedom from slavery. Alternatively, looked at from the agentic vantage point of the vanquished, the act of surrender itself may be viewed as a gift to the victor: "Victory . . . involves yielding of the vanquished. By the very act of declaring himself beaten, he achieves a last assertion of his power. With this act, as Georg Simmel has said, 'he actually makes a gift to the victor.' The capacity of making gifts is a measure of autonomy."[48]

Regardless of the point of view, the exchange of gifts of a variety of types and orders during ceremonies of surrender works to bind the giver and the receiver in the temporally extensive way that Teitel articulates in her analysis of the meaning of reparations. This binding is, and must be to varying degrees, always tainted and dangerous. The scene out of which it emerges is one of violence, enmity, and destruction. And the undeniable (however temporary) asymmetry of the victor and the vanquished foreground the symbolic violence of gifts given in surrender.

The joining, or shaking, of hands may more readily suggest a contractual exchange than that of a gift. In fact, I have yet to encounter a representation of surrender that features an actual handshake at the key moment of exchange between victor and vanquished. Near-handshakes, demurred handshakes, or handshakes in the prelude to the surrender are more the norm and suggest, as the following section on objects and gestures of exchange will demonstrate, that the surrender handshake can only be approached asymptotically. Most typically, figures of the vanquished kneel or bow or stand at attention as they face the victor and their fates. Nevertheless, certain aspects of surrender exchanges may evoke the legal paradigm of contract (contract defined by the *OED*. "In a legal sense: An agreement enforceable by law. a. An accepted promise to do or forbear; b. An agreement which effects a transfer of property; a conveyance").

The fact that the surrender terms must, to varying degrees, be a function of collaboration of both parties to conflict helps make surrenders contract-like.[49] This is so even if the only acts of collaboration are the signing of the signature by the vanquished and the desisting of fighting. Inevitably copies of the surrender instrument and terms are distributed to both sides, such copies acting as a kind of written "contract" and record of what transpired at the surrender ceremony. Yet contractual compatibility and coordination of the actions and exchanges at the point of surrender do not imply symmetry or mutual satisfaction. Attempts may be made by the defeated party to translate surrender agreements into more symmetrical programs and pledges than they actually prescribe. Linguistic translations provide a flexible medium for such attempts, as the bilingual Christian-Islamic thirteenth-century surrender pact between al-Azraq and King James of Aragon reveals. Alternating lines of Arabic and Castilian texts demonstrate variant interpretations: "[T]he Christian text makes al-Azraq a vassal and partner, while the Arabic text merely agrees to a three-year truce . . . and implied no real subordination to the infidel."[50]

Other attempts fail even in the effort to be translated (literally and metaphorically) and make it into the historical record. At the end of World War II, the German general Alfred Jodl made an apparently impromptu hortatory speech immediately after signing the surrender documents in May of 1945 in Eisenhower's Reims headquarters. In this speech he attempted to reequilibrate the outcome of the surrender, through making maximalist claims about Germany's war experiences. Speaking in German, Jodl declaimed: "With this signature the German people and the German armed forces are, for better or worse, delivered into the victor's hands. In this war, which has lasted more than five years, both have achieved and suffered more than perhaps any other people in the world. In this hour I can only express the hope that the victor will treat them with generosity." As Douglas Botting recounts: "Complete silence greeted this plea from Jodl. No written translation was made of it."[51] The very absence of any translation of this unprogrammed intervention reveals the importance of the scribe's role in codifying the meaning of such transactions. The clear decision not to *officially witness* this speech meant that it would have virtually no temporal or, most importantly, archival extension and consequence.

Another example in which the mutually binding qualities of "normal" contracts were expressly rejected as the governing paradigm for surrender comes from the U.S. Civil War. Section 4 of the 14th Amendment to the U.S. Constitution codifies the decision of the victorious Union not to assume the debts incurred by the Confederacy during the war. The relevant part of the section reads: "But neither the United States nor any State shall assume or pay any debt or obligation incurred in aid of insurrection or rebellion against the United States, or any claim for the loss or emancipation of any slaves; but all such debts, obligations, and claims shall be held illegal and void."[52]

Finally, the vectors of the exchanges of surrender may be understood as demonstrations of agency and responsibility. The compositional system that emerges from the transfers highlights the ultimate ground of legitimacy. First movers and final arbiters are located via actions that are both practically effective and symbolically exemplary. In one of the letters that Grant sent to Lee in the complicated epistolary prelude to the surrender of the Lee's Army of Northern Virginia, he wrote:

> The results of the last week must convince you of the hopelessness of further resistance on the part of the Army of Northern Virginia in this struggle. I feel that it is so, and regard it as my duty to shift from myself the responsibility of any further effusion of blood, by asking of you the surrender of that portion of the Confederate States army blood, known as the Army of Northern Virginia.[53]

In the matter of ultimate responsibility, then, Grant implies that inasmuch as both parties had engaged in armed conflict, both generals had some responsibility for the "effusion of blood." But inasmuch as the outcome of further fighting was, after great Confederate losses, destined to favor the Union, Grant was taking it upon himself to "shift from myself the responsibility" in exchange for the Confederate's surrender. Responsibility is effectively transferred, in this communication, though not, interestingly, authority. Grant designates himself the arbiter of the course of the war and gives himself the autonomy to either maintain responsibility for its ongoingness or to divest himself of it. But the transaction must take the form of an exchange—responsibility is transferred to Lee, who must, in turn divest himself of it by the only option available to him, surrender.

The Objects of Exchange

What kinds of things are exchanged in surrender transactions, as victor and vanquished reconstitute their worlds? The actions and objects of surrender exchanges can be divided into four categories: (1) originary objects of contention in the conflict; (2) secondary objects of contention that emerge during the conflict or opportunistically present themselves at the point of surrender; (3) objects and actions that comprise the mechanics of surrender exchanges; (4) symbolic objects of authority and solidarity.

Originary and Secondary Objects of Contention

> Not the act of tracing boundaries, but their cancellation or negation is the
> constituting act of the city.
>
> —Giorgio Agamben[54]

Simultaneous and conflicting claims of ownership, jurisdiction, control, or authority over people, territory, resources, sacred objects, or worldviews form the background of many wars. The relevant objects of contention may indeed contingently ignite a conflict and they may remain in the sights of the antagonists over the course of the conflict to become the focus of its termination. As Lewis Coser writes, "The more restricted the object of contention and the more visible for both parties the clues to victory, the higher the chances that the conflict be limited in time and extension."[55]

These originary objects of contention may be said to have the imprint of the "inalienable" about them. They are the focal points of conflict precisely because they are experienced as essential to the identity of the regime or the collective entity claiming possession of them. In this regard, it is useful to think about the distinction made by Marcel Mauss between alienable things that are part of the ongoing systems of exchange across social groups and those that are kept out of exchange. Commenting on Mauss's distinction, Maurice Godelier notes that it is precisely this inalienable core that allows the system of exchange to be set into motion.[56]

These objects may have variable physical and symbolic physiognomies. They may be crucial towns or forts or other military units, they may be borders themselves or national capitals.[57] They may also be sacred relics or objects of traditional authority, the alienation of which is tantamount to a loss of essence.[58] Thus it is not surprising that many of these original objects of threatened or forced alienation appear as central figures in the ceremonies and transactions of surrender. Nor is it surprising that similar objects emerge over the course of a conflict as focal points for exchange at the conclusion of the peace, taking on something of the essential or of an identity-articulating or reinforcing quality. They include territory, legal rights and responsibilities, warriors and populations, and flags, gems, medals, and emblems.

One method by which historians have come to identify war "in a legal sense" is the degree to which conflicts "led to important legal results, such as creation of a state, territorial transfers, or changes of government."[59] Such obvious reconstitutions of territory and social organization can be most actively worked out during surrender negotiations. Once again, the apparent subordination of the vanquished and the superiority of the victor provide only the first approximation for predicting what the reconfigured landscape (both literal and figurative) will look like after the transactions. New, expanded borders can represent a real challenge to the victors, who must now police them: "On the one hand, terms of settlement that include giving up territory will increase the relative strength of the winner in the current war. On the other hand, by withdrawal the loser may gain more defensible borders."[60]

Jurisdiction over territory must be further parsed into several types of control: military, political, economic, legal, religious. These different kinds of rights do not necessarily all align, as cities or castles or garrisons move back and forth across the antagonists' divide. Defeated residents or citizens, variably configured, might be left with economic autonomy but religious restrictions; traditional authority but political and military strictures; territorial autonomy but political dependency, and so forth. Further complicating these variable formulations is the possibility of alternative interpretations of the "same" surrender treaty, as has already been demonstrated. Language is key here as is the relative weight given to different channels of performative action. What, for example, becomes more meaningful and binding, speech or writing? Discussing the case of the 1840 Treaty of Waitangi in New Zealand, when forty-six Maori chiefs gave the queen of England sovereignty over their territories, Roger Chartier notes:

> For the English, the Maori chieftain's signing of the text ceding "to Her Majesty the Queen of England, absolutely and without reservation, all the rights and powers of sovereignty" was an unambiguous recognition of the colonizers' political domination. This was not the case with the Maori. First the term translating "sovereignty" in the vernacular version of the treaty (kawnatanga) meant only acceptance of British administration, not the abandonment of power over the land; second, the fact of signing the treaty had no particular value for the Maori, since what they considered essential were spoken words and promises made orally.[61]

Surrender treaties may also engage a dual-action mechanism whereby territory is theoretically alienated from the vanquished upon defeat and surrender, and then immediately given "back" in a gesture of magnanimity. Thus,

in the thirteenth-century Christian/Muslim surrender agreement signed by
Prince Alfonso and King James of Aragon and by al-Azraq, "The prince *con-fers* the two main castles on the Muslim's family "to give, sell, pledge" or use
entirely according to al-Azraq's wishes."[62] These gestures are as practical as
they are symbolic, with calculations about the feasibility of territorial alienation in the long run. In like manner, Louis XIV returned Franche-Comté to
the Spanish in 1668, after dismantling its fortress, stating that: "Franche-
Comté, *which I handed back,* could be reduced to such a state that I could be
its master at any time, and my new conquests, firmly established, would
open a more certain entry into the rest of the Low Countries."[63]

The Case of Civil Wars

In the case of civil wars, territory becomes particularly charged as secession presents unique challenges. As an object of exchange during surrender
procedures, the territory that seceded and must now be reabsorbed (in the
case of victory of the original sovereign entity) is a conceptual conundrum.
How ought this territory, which was always still considered present during
the civil war by the victor, to be now re-presented by the rendering foe? Civil
war thus takes to an expressive extreme the etymological deep structure of
the notion of return in surrender—to render back that which was always,
really, rightfully possessed by the victor. In the case of the American Civil
War, these complex conceptualizations and administrations were given further resonance by the historically extant tension between regionalism and
federalism in that country. On the occasion of his Farewell Address, President George Washington himself felt compelled to weigh in on this tension:
"The name of American, which belongs to you in your national capacity,
must always exalt the just pride of patriotism more than any appellation derived from local discriminations."[64] Almost seventy years later, Confederate
General Robert E. Lee makes the following intervention during the Appomattox surrender meeting with General Grant: "There is one thing I would
like to mention," Lee replied, "The cavalrymen and artillerists own their own
horses in our army. Its organization in this respect differs from that of the
United States." A participant of this meeting, Lieutenant Colonel Horace
Porter of the Union delegation noted that: "This expression attracted the

notice of our officers present as showing how firmly the conviction was ground in his mind that we were two distinct countries."[65]

The legal entity of the Confederacy, never recognized as such by the Union in any case, was nevertheless destroyed by the surrenders of the Southern generals. Beyond raising the simple paradox of how one undoes that which was never recognized by one's conquerors to exist, questions were raised as to how to re-invoke recognition of the Southern states the status of which, as states, re-emerged at the end of the war. Lincoln's approach was pretty straightforward and had everything to do with the varieties and predictability of, precisely, exchange relationships with these states. Objects and agents would go from the north, and especially from Washington, to the south, and objects and agents (representatives, population, taxes, commercial products, mail) would come from the south to the north: "Once the war is over, Lincoln wants to establish normal commercial relations with the former Confederate states as soon as possible. The cabinet agrees. The executive agencies should resume their traditional functions in the South: the Treasury Department would proceed to collect revenues; the Interior Department would set its surveyors and land and pension agents to work; the Postmaster General would reestablish mail routes."[66] The very objects of contention acted to reconstitute the country through being reinserted in a system of *ongoing* normalized exchange.

The Fates of Warriors and Civilians

Along with territory and rights of residents or citizens, the actual status of entire populations and military forces is bound up in the contentious competition of wars.

The fates of soldiers are often decisively decided during negotiations of surrender. Will they be captured, arrested, and tried for various crimes, including (in cases of civil wars) treason or the more historically recent "crimes against humanity"? Will they be allowed to return to their homes and take up civilian life? Will they be conscripted or enslaved by the victorious forces?

Even with the codification of conventions of war in the seventeenth and eighteenth centuries, there were variations on a theme of soldier exchange. Of the early modern Spanish soldier, historian Lorraine White notes that:

[U]nlike men in England's armies who swore to do "loyall true and fythefull srvice' " to Queen Elizabeth I, there is no evidence that common soldiers who enlisted in Spain's royal armies actually swore an oath. Given the multinational, not to mention multi-confessional composition of many of Spain's armies, along with the presence of mercenaries, perhaps this is not surprising . . . transfers of allegiance were frequent after major defeat, though this was perhaps truer of foreign soldiers in Spain's peninsular armies in the 17th c.[67]

Thus was allegiance to one or another monarchy and army a highly contingent thing and thus were armies and monarchs or governments not entirely in control of their military forces. Another key thing about such allegiance shifting is that it demonstrates the willingness of antagonists to absorb rather than prosecute former enemy soldiers. As well, victorious forces might allow deserters or traitorous soldiers who had gone over to the enemy lines to escape unharmed when exiting the defeated forces stronghold.[68]

Retreating and surrendering soldiers were of course always in a certain amount of danger. Even when it appeared that provisions had been made to protect the defeated forces, as they were exchanged, they might instead be attacked. In the surrender of the parliamentary foot at Lostwithiel in 1644 England, "The parliamentary army was to have a convoy of a hundred royalist horse, which in turn was to be safely convoyed back to the king." Instead, the Cornish people attacked the parliamentarians on their way.[69] Often it has mattered to whom soldiers, and civilians, would be permitted to surrender. In World War II, German general Karl Dönitz kept up the fighting in the east even as it was clear that the Allies were definitively victorious in order to allow German soldiers and civilians to escape to the west in order to surrender to the British and the Americans rather than to the more volatile and punitive Soviet troops.

Civilian populations have experienced varied fates upon surrender agreements, from enslavement to exile to freedom. In the *Obsidio Bredana*, written in the mid-seventeenth century by the Jesuit Confessor of Spanish general Ambrogio Spinola, during and after Spinola's successful siege and conquest of the town of Breda, there is a map etched by the artist Theodore Galle that reveals thousands of refugees fleeing, on foot and in carriages, through the breach in the walls: "Etiquette required that the defeated should leave through a breach in the city wall."[70] Buttressing this pictorial image is Hermannus Hugo's transcribing of the "Articles of Surrender" at Breda that included Number 3: "Freedom of movement and belongings to citizens and inhabitants," and Number 5: "It shall be granted to the [Protestant] preachers of the word to depart freely with their wives, children, family goods and movables, without all offence or damage."[71] In all cases, the movement of populations within and across reconstituted borders is an essential part of the remaking of the world.

Finally, beyond the territory, population, and military forces that ignite or emerge over the course of conflicts, there are objects of great symbolic value to the contending parties that are exchanged at the conclusion of the peace. These include flags, medals, emblems, and gems. The focalized attention given to such objects serves several purposes. Within the press and chaos of battle itself, they can serve the function of drawing psychic attention of the warriors and mitigating the natural fear.

These symbolic tokens often take the form of flags, the flying of which tracks and maps the territorial shifts at stake in the conflict. During the surrender ceremony on board the USS *Missouri* in Tokyo Bay on September 2, 1945, a historic flag would announce victory and possession. The American flag, originally flown by Matthew Perry when he entered Tokyo Bay ninety-two years earlier, was recalled to Japan especially for this ceremony and mounted on a bulkhead of the USS *Missouri*. In these cases of symbolic objects focused upon as proof of ownership and authority, the metonymic power of them is put in high relief. These are flags that have literally lived through and survived encounters and battles. The traces of their histories remain on them as they are caught up in the transactional systems of surrender.

As in the case of flags, other objects present a complex essence—part object of contention, part symbol of reconstituting relations, part booty. Such objects as precious gems get caught up in the ceremonies and performances of ownership, power, identity, and fealty that flow through surrendering exchanges. The fascinating case of the famous jewel, the Koh-I-noor, handed over to Queen Victoria's representative Governor General Lord Dalhousie, during the surrender of the Maharajah of Lahor in 1849, demonstrates this complex of transactional meanings. Years after the gem was taken from the Maharajah, Queen Victoria herself met the Maharajah, brought him to live temporarily in one of her own residences, and commissioned a portrait to be painted of him. As recounted in anthropologist Brian Axel's study of the Sikh diaspora, a strange and powerful scene occurs during one of the sittings for the portrait. A lady of the court is instructed by Queen Victoria to ask if the Maharajah would like to see, once again after so many years, the Koh-I-or. His reply reveals much about the power and symbolism of the objects in surrendering exchange:

> Yes indeed I would! I would give a good deal to hold it again in my hand! Why? Because I was but a child, an infant, when forced to surrender it by treaty; but now I am a man, I should like to have it in my power to place it myself in her [Queen Victoria's] hand. ... After a quarter of an hour examining the gem, Duleep moved deliberately to where her Majesty was standing, and, with a deferential reverence, placed in her hand the famous diamond, with the words: "It is to me, Ma'am, the greatest pleasure thus to have the opportunity as a loyal subject, of myself tendering to my Sovereign the Koh-I-noor!" Whereupon he quietly resumed his place on the dais, and the artist continued his work.[72]

The Koh-I-noor is thus worked and re-worked in a performed cycle of possession, dispossession, repossession and "voluntary" alienation. The coercive nature of gifts, their sublimated violence, and the many-layered system of relations they constitute and reflect are all exposed in the Maharajah's rendering up, for the second time, the famous jewel.

Transactional Objects of the Process of Surrender

Surrenders need to be managed as a series of decisions and actions must occur at certain times and places. At the most basic, existential, level, food and provisions must begin to flow across the enemy divide. The halting of the fighting and the restructuring of relationships between human agents and between collective entities and authority structures must all be accomplished via contingent negotiations. Terms are proffered, debated, rejected, or accepted. Credentials authorizing representation of collectivities and sovereignties are presented. Letters go back and forth across antagonist lines. Oaths are then taken, promises and pledges are made, orders are given—a whole series of performative speech acts constitute the very stuff of the surrender.

Most surrenders are preceded by a chain of letters and documents that flow back and forth across the conflict's divides. In the three main case studies of my larger investigation of surrender, that at Breda in 1625, at Appomattox in 1865, and in Tokyo Bay in 1945, these missives hammered out the terms of the surrender instruments and authorized the eventual signers of these terms. Before the performative act of signing could occur, the authority and legitimacy of the signer needed to be assured. As always, the legal and political force of such transactions relies upon the tricky dialectic between the performative and the constative. This dialectic is often exposed for its logical and practical complexity when there is disalignment or potential disalignment. Two cases of such awkward fitting are especially clear here (and they will be described below)—the case of General Sherman's thwarted surrender Memorandum with the Southern general Johnston, and the case, already introduced, of the authorization by the Japanese emperor of the signers of the World War II Instrument of the Surrender of Japan.

When the course of the conflict begins to become clear, the imminent victor will usually proffer terms to the soon-to-be defeated. Toward the end of the siege at Breda, initial terms were indeed offered by Spanish general Spinola to Justin of Nassau, the Dutch general defending the town. As recorded by Hermannus Hugo, Spinola's Jesuit chaplain and memoirist:

> Spinola confirmed once again by these letters [that were intercepted from the Dutch] of the penury of their provision, and advertised of the slow coming of their help . . . thought good to try Justin's mind, by demanding of him to render it up. For this purpose he sends the Trumpeter of Count Salazarius with his letters privily . . . that he would make him offer of reasonable conditions, if he would treat with him of a composition.[73]

Ultimately, the Dutch would come to accept to "treat with him of a composition" and terms of the surrender agreement were copied and sent back and forth for the signatures of both generals.

In the case of Appomattox a series of letters between Grant and Lee circled in on the surrender of Lee's Army of Northern Virginia and the provisional terms of the surrender. The terms derived from President Lincoln's magnanimous stance, codified as the River Queen Doctrine, toward a South he greatly desired to be reconciled with:

> to get the deluded men of the rebel armies disarmed and back to their homes . . . let them once surrender and reach their homes, [and] they won't take up arms again. . . . Let them all go, officers and all, I want submission and no more

bloodshed. . . . I want no one punished; treat them liberally all around. We want those people to return to their allegiance to the Union and submit to the laws.[74]

But it was left to the two generals to maneuver their way to a time and a place of meeting and exchanging documents and signing onto the agreed upon terms. Grant writes about this correspondence at some length in his *Memoirs*, reproducing the letters and recalling the terrible headache that he suffered during the several days leading up to final acceptance. Lee's final letter read: "I received your note of this morning on the picketline whither I had come to meet you and ascertain definitely what terms were embraced in your proposal of yesterday with reference to the surrender of this army. I now request an interview in accordance with the offer contained in your letter of yesterday for that purpose." Upon receipt of this letter, Grant writes in his memoirs: "When the officer reached me I was still suffering with the sick headache; but the instant I saw the contents of the note I was cured."[75]

Approximately a week after the signing of the surrender instrument at Appomattox by Grant and Lee, General Sherman was to meet with General Johnston to perform a similar operation for all remaining active troops. Over the course of some ten days, these two men hammered out a Memorandum, or Basis of Agreement, that was broad and sweeping in its reach. It called for Confederate armies to be: "disbanded and conducted to their . . . state capitols, there to deposit their arms and public property in the state arsenals"; for federal courts to be reestablished throughout the land; for the U.S. president to recognize existing state governments as soon as their officials took loyalty oaths to the Union; and for all citizens to be guaranteed "their political rights and franchises . . . as defined by their constitution."[76] In spite, or perhaps because, of its grandeur and sweep, this Memorandum was as noted above, rejected by President Johnson. The lack of civil, political authority on Sherman's part made his autonomous decision to go beyond the terms laid out at Appomattox illegitimate. He was, in brief, not authorized to sign the document he forged (note the double entendre embedded in that word).

Finally, in the case of the surrender of the Japanese to the Allies at the end of World War II, much of the work of the letters that prepared the way for the surrender focused on the status of the emperor and the Imperial monarchy in Japan. As discussed above, the "Unconditional Surrender" of Japan made obviously problematic the maintenance of the Imperial dynasty as authoritative. The conditional recognition of the emperor's authority was nested in the more overarching authority of the supreme commander for the Allied Powers. Yet in a fantastical kind of performative looping mechanism, only the emperor could authorize the Japanese foreign minister to sign the Instrument of Surrender.

> By the Grace of Heaven, Emperor of Japan, seated on the Throne occupied by the same Dynasty changeless through ages eternal, To all to whom these Presents shall come, Greeting!
>
> We do hereby authorise Mamoru Shigemitsu, Zyosanmi, First Class of the Imperial Order of the Rising Sun to attach his signature by command and in behalf of Ourselves and Our Government unto the Instrument of Surrender which is required by the Supreme Commander for the Allied Powers to be signed.[77]

It was powerfully clear that Douglas MacArthur was indeed the supreme authority and that the emperor could not act autonomously to make policy or direct the fate of Japan. Nevertheless, it is interesting to analyze the beginnings of the eight paragraphs of the Instrument of Surrender (in the English version) for what they reveal about this complex and internally cross-referencing system of authorization. The first paragraph begins: "We, acting by command of and in behalf of the Emperor of Japan, the Japanese Government and the Japanese Imperial General Headquarters, hereby accept the provisions." The second paragraph starts with: "We hereby proclaim the unconditional surrender to the Allied Powers." The next three paragraphs "hereby command" Japanese forces to cease hostilities and surrender. But then, there is the strangely worded sixth paragraph that begins: "We hereby *undertake for* the Emperor, the Japanese Government and their successors to carry out the provisions of the Potsdam Declaration." These words, "undertake for," are confusing in their forcefulness and the directionality of their agency. Finally, the last paragraph reasserts MacArthur's command status: "The authority of the Emperor and the Japanese Government to rule the state shall be subject to the Supreme Commander for the Allied Powers." Thus the Instrument begins with the "command of" the emperor of Japan and ends with the subjection of this same commanding authority. This document and the debates about the agents responsible for it, on both sides of the completed war, demonstrate just how complicated the credentializing process can be—those credentials that authorize, those that undo authority, and those that authorize a redoing or shifting of authority.

Surrenders call forth the world-changing *final* commands and orders that definitively end a conflict. These are orders that stand literally on the brink of their own mortality. This aspect may be what gives them a kind of poetic, elegiac quality. They have the *authority* to undo but the *pathos* of self-immolation. The speeches in which the defeated commanders give these last orders contain a mixture of reflection, description, hortatory words, admonitions, and performative speech acts. They thus constitute intricately hybrid documents. All of these things are obvious in Robert E. Lee's "General Orders Number 9":

> After four years of arduous service, marked by unsurpassed courage and fortitude, the Army of Northern Virginia has been compelled to yield to overwhelming numbers and resources. I need not tell the brave survivors of so many hard fought battles, who have remained steadfast to the last, that I have consented to the result from no distrust of them. But feeling that valor and devotion could accomplish nothing that would compensate for the loss that must have attended the continuance of the contest, I determined to avoid the useless sacrifice of those whose past services have endeared them to their countrymen. By the terms of the agreement officers and men can return to their homes and remain until exchanged. You will take with you the satisfaction that proceeds from the consciousness of duty faithfully performed, and I earnestly pray that a Merciful God will extend to you His blessing and protection. With an increasing admiration of your constancy and devotion to your country, and a grateful remembrance of your kind and generous considerations for myself, I bid you all an affectionate farewell.[78]

Lee has crafted his "order" from the verbs "compelled," "consented," "determined," and "prayed." His order emerges out of the sentiments of affection and his description of brave service rendered by his troops. Such a document raises important questions about how one recognizes an order, a command. A speech act full of indexical expressions locating the war and the soldiers in time and in place (including the words with the still unresolved territorial and legal referent "countrymen" and "your country") functions, in fact, as an order. The terms of the surrender agreement are embedded, almost hidden, in the middle of the text, not quite an afterthought but not the main message. Lee's own authority to order the soldiers to surrender appears to need no external legitimization—he does not refer to the government of the Confederacy and his reference to God is only aimed at auguring God's protection of the soldiers.

Pledges, Oaths, Promises, and Pardons

Along with the presentation of credentials and letters of agreement and instruments of surrender, there are other processual objects and speech acts that make surrenders actually happen. These include pledges, oaths, promises, and pardons. They are often embedded in the formal documents and speeches that constitute and carry forward the surrenders. Sometimes they appear in the preludes, sometimes in the aftermath, doing the work of preparation or solidification.

This class of speech acts can refer either to the past or can point to the future. They are in the business of normalizing postconflict relations and reorganizing ties of fealty. Together they form a class of guarantees—guarantees that the fighting will actually stop, that those who surrender will not be arrested or enslaved or killed, that those who surrender will not reactivate their animosity and violence after being exchanged, that those who are victorious will accept the redefinition of political selves of the vanquished, and so forth. We, in the United States, have had our own recent experience of a political surrender replete with promises and oaths. Presidential candidate Al Gore, grudgingly acknowledging his defeat more than a month after the election was held in 2000, gave a nationally broadcast speech in which he referred to an exchange he had just had with his opponent George W. Bush: "Just moments ago I spoke with George W. Bush and congratulated him on becoming the 43rd president of the United States. And I promised him that I wouldn't call him back this time."[79] The promise not to call back after acknowledgment of defeat is a powerful and necessary mechanism of this transactional apparatus.

Pledges or promises occur on both sides of the victory divide and can invoke future behavior and relations to deal with past offenses. They participate in the attempt to suture the world torn by war and bind parties together in recognizable, predictable ways. They also reveal the nuances of the power dynamics in the conditions of the exchanges. In these acts, the victor may be obliged to promise the vanquished certain conditions in exchange for their surrender. Hermannus Hugo transcribed the Instruments of Surrender at Breda in his *Obsido Bredana* (it is interesting to note that there were actually two such instruments drawn up, one for the governor and garrison, one for the magistrates and burgers). Exhausted by the long and arduous siege, with Spain's military resources already stretched thin, Ambrogio Spinola had been anxious to extract a surrender agreement from the Dutch. He was thus willing to accede to many of the demands of the Dutch, including the demand: "That *pardon* and *forgetfulness* be both *promised* and *performed*, of all those things which were committed by the citizens and inhabitants of Breda . . . whether committed before, or after the recovery of the city in the year 1590."[80]

This first of fifteen Articles of Surrender insists explicitly on its pledge to pardon "all things" done by all people in Breda during the period from 1590–1625 (the most recent period of Dutch control). It is sweeping in its concrete (unconditional) referent and in its temporal demarcation. Not enough that the pardon will be promised and *performed* (a proto-Austinian parsing of the performative) but the crucial element of *forgetfulness* powerfully responds to the inherent cyclical element of surrender. Forgetfulness invokes a break from the past, a linear orientation to time, an escape from the deep structure of such exchange systems as the gift.

The exact nature of such speech acts as pledges is, as befits the liminality of the situation of surrenders, contingent and shifting. When embedded in an Instrument of Surrender or a newly revised constitution, they take on a clearly legal imprint. When inserted into the text accompanying a magazine's lithograph, as was the case after the surrender at Appomattox in the U.S. Civil War, the pledge may act more as a religious or moral assurance. On Palm Sunday, 1865, *Harper's Weekly* published a two-page print by Thomas Nast. In the print, two scenes are displayed side by side. On the left is a drawing of "The Savior's Entry into Jerusalem" and on the right is a rendering of "The Surrender of General Lee and his Army to Lieutenant General Grant." The analogy-making work of this print is stunning in its explicit yoking together of salvation, religious revelation, and the surrender of the Confederacy to the Union. Here, I want to focus on the caption under "The Savior's Entry into Jerusalem." In this caption, Nast assumes the reconciling voice of the North: "We hold out the olive branch to our erring and mis-guided brethren of the Southern states and *pledge* to all of them who are loyal a hearty welcome to all the benefits of our free Republic."[81] The Confederate soldiers are thus described as erring and misguided, not criminal or traitor-ous, but the pledge is quite specifically directed to only those who are (now) loyal.

In some cases, the victors may refuse to make the legally binding type of pledges to the vanquished, preferring to have the freedom to deal with the defeated in an unfettered manner. It was with the precedent of Wilson's World War I Fourteen Point Pledge in mind that the Western Allies in World War II and Roosevelt in particular explicitly ruled out such pledges.[82] However, as we have seen, it was through the deployment of the Appomattox example that Roosevelt wanted to make the indirect, *moral* pledge to the people of Germany, that the Allies would treat them fairly.

The foundational logic of symmetrical actions often requires oaths and pledges on the part of the vanquished to match the pledges of the victors. But what if the vanquished refuse to swear oaths of loyalty to the victor? This dilemma was confronted toward the end of the Civil War when very few of the many thousands of captured Confederate soldiers would swear an oath of allegiance to the Union.[83] Brigadier General Joshua Lawrence Chamberlain, the Union officer designated to organize the ceremony of the surrender of the Confederate troops, recalled a Rebel officer who articulated this resis-tance: "Chamberlain recalled telling a Rebel officer that the good will that soldiers from both armies exhibited at Appomattox augured well for the fu-ture. 'You're mistaken sire,' the Confederate replied with undisguised bitter-ness. 'You may forgive us but we won't be forgiven. There is rancor in our hearts . . . , which you little dream of. We hate you sir.'"[84]

An oath of loyalty may indeed incorporate an acceptance of the pardon tendered by the victor. In that sense, it refers not just to a past that is cauter-ized through the swearing of the oath, but to the future as an assurance of future conduct. Legal scholar Ruti Teitel usefully differentiates between Abraham Lincoln's proposal of eliciting loyalty oaths from former support-ers of the Confederacy, which were largely prospective and solidarity-making in their orientation, and what were termed the "iron clad oaths"; "whereby deponents would attest to past allegiance to the Union as a condition for future public service. Anyone who had broken his oath to support the Constitution would be disqualified from public service."[85] The latter oath announced a consistency of identity and fealty across time and was therefore nonfoundational (perhaps almost antifoundational) in its impact and motivation.

Instruments and Weapons of War

As a practical matter, the weapons and instruments of war must be relinquished by the vanquished (or destroyed by them in advance of the moment of surrender)[86] and turned over to the control of the victors. This action ensures the inoperability of these weapons in any potential reinvigorated violent conflict between the antagonists. Of course the manner by which the armaments of war are exchanged bespeaks the symbolic potency attached to machines of destruction and their handling. The symbolic variations on a theme of laying down of arms will be discussed in the next section. Here it is important to note how very critical the exchange of weapons is for the actual halting of violence.

The actual fact of disarming an eventually defeated foe was very much in the mind of Roosevelt, early on in the progress of World War II. In a speech delivered in October 1942, he contemplated the war's end and declared: "It is clear to us that if Germany and Italy and Japan—or any of them—remain armed at the end of this war, or are permitted to rearm, they will again, and inevitably, embark upon an ambitious career of world conquest. They must be disarmed and kept disarmed."[87] In fact, as the formula for unconditional surrender came to be codified and communicated to the Axis forces, it was decided, in mid-1944, to use the precise term "bedingungslose Waffenniederlegung" (laying down of weapons) in American propaganda broadcast to the enemy (an answer, then, on the part of the State Department, to the Gallop Poll's question about the meaning of unconditional surrender). As Michael Balfour wrote about this decision: "Once a government's armed forces have laid down their weapons, the government becomes powerless to resist—except passively—any orders which the conqueror may choose to give, while the 'conditions' presented to it or to its armed forces are better described as 'requirements,' since little or no argument is possible about them."[88]

Symbolic Objects of Authority and Solidarity

The same weapons and instruments of war that are laid down for the purpose of cauterizing the violence are also laid down (or not) for symbolic purposes. The line between the practical and the symbolic in these exchanges is a permeable one. This is clear in the famous case of Grant's decision to allow the Confederate officers to keep their swords and to allow the officers and troops to keep their horses and their baggage. In this decision, the identity of these items was conceptually and legally altered. They were, after the surrender agreement was signed and ratified, no longer instruments of war. They were instantly domesticated by Grant:

> I take it that most of the men in the ranks are small farmers, and as the country has been so raided by the two armies, it is doubtful whether they will be able to put in a crop to carry themselves and their families through the next winter without the aid of the horses they are now riding, and I will instruct the officers I shall appoint to receive the paroles to let all the men who claim to own a horse or mule to take the animals home with them to work their little farms.[89]

As long as the farmers are "small" and as long as the farms are "little," the fairytale metamorphosis of the identity of the horses could proceed.

On the other hand, Grant's own magnanimity was apparently prompted by a bit of humiliation on his own part. General Lee had come to the meeting at Appomattox dressed in a new uniform and wearing a beautiful sword. Grant writes in his Memoirs that "In my rough traveling suit, the uniform of a private with the straps of a lieutenant-general, I must have contrasted very strangely with [Lee]."[90] As well, Grant's aide, Horace Porter wrote that it was the very sight of this sword hanging at Lee's side that inspired Grant to reject the "unnecessary humiliation" of requiring the officers of the Confederacy to surrender their swords. A strange and not entirely predictable exchange network of honor and humiliation thus emerged. Lee bedecked in a most honorable military attire and Grant in his scruffy, literally degrading private's uniform. Lee claiming, as he did, that he wore this uniform because he thought he would be taken prisoner by Grant and wanted to do so honorably. Grant used the occasion of his own humiliation to avert the humiliation of the vanquished.

Beyond the practical and the sociologically symbolic nature of the exchanges or giving-back of such weapons as swords in the modern era, there is the powerful psychoanalytic potency of these exchanges. Much of Porter's recollections about the Lee sword and much of Grant's own *Memoirs* concern the focus of the two protagonists of surrender on this sword during the Appomattox discussions. A shining, hanging, synecdoche, the sword caught everyone's attention and called forth a series of myths about its fate and personified participation in the event. According to Porter, Grant's attention is drawn to the handsome sword and he subsequently concocts his remanding plan for the Confederate officers. But then, unable to let go of the topic, Grant apparently was compelled to explain to Lee the absence of his own sword: "I started out from my camp several days ago without my sword. . . . I have generally worn a sword, however as little as possible, only during the actual operations of a campaign." Lee responds: "I am in the habit of wearing mine most of the time. I wear it invariably when I am among my troops, moving about through the army."[91] A story developed and spread throughout the country that Lee actually surrendered his sword to Grant and that Grant then handed it back. Grant's refutation of this story in his *Memoirs* is itself noteworthy, but the protest goes beyond clarification. "The much talked of surrendering of Lee's sword and my handing it back, this and much more that has been said about it is the purest romance. The word sword or side arms was not mentioned by either of us until I wrote it in the terms."[92] Romance indeed: a mythical exchange of masculinity, of potency, of the unacknowledgable (it "was not mentioned by either of us") aspect of war, and of surrender of man to man.

Tributes, Demonstrations, and Gestures

Weapons importantly figure in the ceremonies, tributes, and demonstrations of surrender. The conventions of war-craft determined specific positions of honor or dishonor upon exiting a garrison or town in a posture of surrender. Swords worn at the side were honorable, under the arms and pointing to the rear were dishonorable. Sabers drawn and resting on the shoulder pointing upward and muskets pointing upward were honorable. Sabers in their scabbards were dishonorable.[93]

But there were several other channels and media of communication and identity reconstituting involved in these ceremonies: "To march with drums beating, trumpets sounding, and colors flying was a distinction; flags furled and the drums and trumpets silent was humiliating."[94] General Grant assigned the task of planning a formal day of surrender for the Army of Virginia, April 12, 1865, to Joshua Chamberlain. Chamberlain arranged for the Union soldiers to "carry arms" and raise their muskets in a salute to the surrendering foe. Grant himself admonished the troops not to engage in "demonstrations [cheers] in the field."[95]

Art historians Brown and Elliot maintain that the conventional manner of depicting surrender is as a "pageant of triumph and humiliation," in which the victor is either positioned above the vanquished or sitting while the vanquished kneels in abjection. In the three principal cases of this study, the surrender of Breda, Appomattox, and Japan, such traditional demonstrations of the asymmetry of power at conflict's end is either specifically rejected or much muted. And it is in precisely the bodily gestures of orientation and extension at the center of the compositional field of exchange that these variations are expressed.

Anthropologist William Hanks writes that: "In many . . . cases of demonstrative reference, a crucial role is also played by the execution of bodily gestures simultaneous with the utterance, such as pointing, directed gaze, handing the object over, cocking the head, or pursing the lips."[96] The lion's share of gestural deixis is formulated and expressed by the central protagonists at the signing of the surrender agreements and the surrounding ceremonies. Liminal moments such as these are all about directionality, literal physical directionality as de facto territorial realignments are made law, historical directionality as the past is both negated and recovered and the future prescribed, and social and political directionality as relations of power and solidarity are rerouted. A certain predictable quotient of ambivalence and contradiction is necessarily present.

This ambivalence and contradiction are evident in, precisely, posture, orientation, and gesture. It is as if the entire conflict and its trajectory were condensed in the central site and acts of exchange. Art historian Rudolf Arnheim discerns such a central condensation in works of art, and he terms it the "microtheme": "The microtheme presents at some prominent center of the work, usually in the middle, a small, concentrated version of the subject that is played out in the composition as a whole. . . . Such microthemes can be discerned remarkably often, especially in the action of hands, whose expressive behavior finds its place quite frequently in the middle of a work."[97] The relevant composition here is the structured series of actions that draw antagonists together to "compose" a surrender. The theme may be the expression of hierarchy, or of magnanimity, or of loyalty, or of humiliation. Or, more complexly, it may be a combination of these things as victor and vanquished must both work in tandem and must demonstrate clear distinctions. The actual signers of the agreements, the bearers and deliverers of the keys, the swords, the weapons, the flags, and so forth, present the concentrated microtheme at the center of this world.

Certainly, the actions of hands and other parts of the body caught up into the gestural program (as A. J. Greimas terms it) are key and necessarily draw the attention of the cross-witnessing network. Handshakes, both those that are offered and performed, and those that are anticipated but refused, figure prominently in this program. Both historically and semiotically the handshake enjoys a close proximity to violence (deferred or anticipated). Handshakes operate as proxies for violent interaction. For example, what is really interesting about the interpretation of the handshake as a demonstration that ones hands are, precisely, empty of weapons, is that it acknowledges the latent social expectation of violent encounters, particularly true following a war. We encounter actual handshakes and deflected or deferred handshakes in many of our surrender "compositions."

In the case of Appomattox, Grant and Lee do shake hands in the preliminary moments of the surrender talks, but this gesture gets confused and fragmented in the many prints and reproductions made after the fact. Most often the hands of the two generals are portrayed signing a document or, in the case of Lee, holding on to his sword. But in a *Harper's Weekly* Nast print of the imagined scene, Grant is drawn tentatively extending his hand to Lee, while Lee stands staunchly self-contained, left hand on his sword, right hand not shown but most likely on his hip. Another example comes from the period of preparing and transporting the Japanese surrender delegation at the end of World War II when American Colonel Craig Mashbir was confronted with the head of the Japanese surrender delegation, General Masakazu Kawabe en route to the Philippines. William Craig writes about the encounter:

"Looking casual in suntans and no tie, Mashbir said in fluent Japanese, 'I have come to meet you.' Kawabe saluted and Mashbir returned it. Then the Japanese put out his hand to Mashbir, who instinctively brought his own forward. At the last second, he realized that such a greeting was inappropriate, and jerked his hand back as though it were burned."[98]

Swords, muskets, horses, soldiers, letters, Memoranda, handshakes, keys, pens, turbans,[99] and so forth transmute into a whole series of transitional objects that constitute the flow of exchange across the borders of surrender. They are absolutely crucial and the various manners in which they are directed and received give particular shape and meaning to the event. Together, they participate in giving the act of surrender the force of law.

Sites of Exchange

In order for all of these exchanges and demonstrations to occur, the principals to concluding the peace must come together at a point of contact and convergence. They must focus on each other and on the artifacts of the surrender agreement. They need, in other words, a site of surrender. This space, however it is selected, is itself transformed by dint of its designation as the surrender site. As it is readied for the surrender, it must empty itself out of a fixed identity and nature. I would argue that this space must become liminal, even empty (sometimes literally so as, for example, souvenir hunters ransacked poor Mr. Wilmer McLean's home after the Appomattox agreement was signed there), a context for metaphysical transformations. War is to be displaced by peace, instruments of death are to be transmuted into instruments of domesticity (swords into ploughshares). In this, it shares something with the emptiness of "spaces" of founding. Working through the writings of Hannah Arendt and Jacques Derrida on the acts of founding a republic, Bonnie Honig refers to each theorist's articulation of this necessary, although problematic, blank space. With Arendt she writes, "Political action has no anchor . . . it 'has as it were nothing to hold on to; it is as though it came out of nowhere in either time or space.'" From Derrida, she takes the idea that "God is the name Derrida gives to whatever is used to hold the place of the last instance, the place that is the inevitable aporia of founding."[100] In a manner both analogous and obverse, I am making such a claim for the emptiness of the "space" of surrender. But as foundings emerge *out* of their originary aporia, or break, from that which is known or that which is past, surrenders may be understood to disappear *into* an aporia, or vanishing point, of dissolution, undoing.[101] After which, the world is made anew.

The (former) schoolhouse (scene of the surrender of the German military to Eisenhower in May 1945), the (former) siege perimeter (site of the surrender of Justin of Nassau to Ambrogio Spinola in June 1625), the (former) farmhouse (the site of the surrender of Lee to Grant in April 1865), the (former) battlefield (the site of the surrender of Cornwallis's proxy to American General Benjamin Lincoln, Washington's proxy in October 1781), all transmute from sites experiencing the trauma of war into sites that, as Thomas Dumm claimed for the analogous contexts of letters of resignation, "contribute to bringing a traumatic experience to a conclusion . . . to contain it and to remove its effects."[102] They are to be the first of an outwardly expanding circle of "pacified social spaces," as Norbert Elias described the civilizing consequences of the emergence of a monopoly of force.[103] And they are positioned as a provisional, conceptual borderland between the past and the future, the former territorial alignments and the reconstituted ones.

The space of surrender must also be empty because of its function as a medium, a host for actions that are undertaken in extremis and under duress. Its image is as meaningful as its practical and strategic location. Similar to Roland Barthes idea of the "somehow empty image [of a city's center] needed for the organization of the rest of the city," the "emptiness" of the site of surrender is directly related to the reorganized world that it anchors.[104] This is not to say that some surrender sites are not tendentious. The main deck of the battleship USS *Missouri*, with its powerful guns much in evidence, appears to deviate from this rule. Nevertheless, such things as the sight of American soldiers and sailors casually draping themselves over these guns to get a better look at the proceedings and the actual construction off the main deck of an elaborate platform for newsreel cameramen and newspaper photographers, reveal a temporary domestication of the space of the battleship precisely in the service of establishing it as a site of surrender, momentarily emptying it of its violent essence.

As always, the choice of the site of surrender itself reflected the renegotiated power dynamics occurring at conflict's end. This includes power dynamics within one party's forces as well as between the opposed parties. For example, according to William Craig: "The choice of the Missouri as the surrender site had its origins in Washington and reflected the intense rivalry between Army and navy."[105] Thus from one point of view, the army wins as Supreme Allied Commander Douglas MacArthur conducts the ceremony, instead of Admiral Chester Nimitz (although Nimitz does sign), but the navy also wins with the location of the ceremony, the battleship *Missouri* anchored in Tokyo Bay.

In surrenders oriented toward magnanimity, toward the defeated foe, the process by which a setting for surrender is chosen is overtly one of negotiation and attempted symmetry. Thus does Ambrogio Spinola send a message to Justin of Nassau, via the offices of a mediator (Henry of Bergues, blood relative of house of Nassau and familiar with the language and customs the United Provinces): "wherefore that he should the next day come to meet them out of the city halfway and declare what conditions he required, to be put in writing and our guards standing near adjoining."[106] The prescription of meeting halfway reflects more than a predictable mandate for caution (no one ventures too far into the field) in an ongoing battle. It is clearly metaphorical in its meaning as well. By the same token, in two of the final surrender-prelude letters between generals Grant and Lee, Grant wrote, first, "I will meet you, or will designate officers to meet any officers you may name for the same purpose, at any point agreeable to you, for the purpose of arranging definitely the terms upon which the surrender of the Army of Northern Virginia will be received"; and then "I am at this writing about four miles West of Walker's Church and will push forward to the front for the purpose of meeting you. Notice sent to me on this road where you wish the interview to take place will meet me."[107] Generosity and magnanimity thus flow in a synchronic manner through the many media that converge to deliver the peace.

Convergence and Divergence

The drawing together at a physical point of exchange of the parties to surrender suggests a connection between physical space and mental space. In order for the antagonists to conceptualize and attend to the varied performative, demonstrative, and representational matter that must materialize

and flow in the event, continuity and convergence seem imperative. Perception requires this kind of point of focus.[108]

The burden on perception is even greater because of the complex existential tasks involved in surrendering. A nation, a political party, a juridical territory, a royal line—all or any of these may stand on the brink of disappearance in such occasions. The vanishing point of history cannot be entered easily. Thus the perception and structuring of the "spatial field" as anthropologist William Hanks terms it, is exceptionally marked. This is why gestures, such as handshakes or bows or salutes, or signatures come to matter so much. An analysis sensitive to the political semiotic of these interactions can illuminate how they gather to assume the force of law. This is a *social* world in the unmaking and the making. Hanks insists on this point: "[T]he spatial field of deictic reference is not simply egocentric but sociocentric, mediated by the socially defined physical configuration of the participants."[109]

It is through the aegis of the exchanges of surrender that the new social and political and legal relations are forged and codified. The vectors of these exchanges are inflected with the political attitudes and emotional stances of both the giver and the receiver in any particular case. They also, themselves, set off new chains of probable future relations. Sworn oaths can lead to solidarity, the giving over of a precious gem can foster a sense of indebtedness or resentment, the disarming of a nation can lead to an assumed obligation to take control of that nation's entire operation, the return of a horse and a sidearm can recapitulate and revive an idea of individual autonomy against that of collective enthusiasm.[110] As these items and gestures and identities disappear into the historical vanishing point of surrender, they must reappear under a different paradigm. In this way, the compositional apparatus of the actual ceremony of surrender can, perhaps, be best understood via the analysis of the vanishing points in Renaissance paintings. But such an analysis would be extended in its reach to incorporate not just the spectator, but the participants as well as they attempt to gain a perceptual purchase on the proceedings. Thus Louis Marin writes: "We may theoretically consider that in the vanishing point, in its hole, the things represented gradually disappear . . . or that from the viewpoint [of the spectator] they gradually appear to be distributed in the represented space."[111] The redistribution of things represented emerges out of the agreements, exchanges, and instruments of surrender and demonstrates a new world. The exchanges of surrender thus suture the chasm in the ruptured historical narrative while they also provide the perceptual and conceptual apparatus to stare into the breach.

Surrenders reveal limits, create limits, and cross limits. Normal, lawful relations, having been sundered by the conflicts and violence of the preceding belligerence, need to be reconstituted "on the ground." Transactional work at the limits is dense and busy, both practical and symbolic, as new identities and relationships are soldered. In is in this edge work that law finds itself renewed.

Notes

This essay takes up the issue of the exchanges of surrender, which issue forms the basis of Chapter 3 in my forthcoming book, *The Art of Surrender: Decomposing Sovereignty at Conflict's End* (forthcoming 2005, University of Chicago Press).

1. Robert Cover, *Narrative, Violence, and the Law: The Essays of Robert Cover*, ed. Michael Minow, Martha Minow, and Austin Sarat (Ann Arbor: University of Michigan Press, 1995), 208

2. Of course, the terms of surrender agreements, as will be shown, can vary widely, with more or less degrees of "undoing" of the vanquished.

3. The work of Max Weber, Robert Cover, Giorgio Agamben, Pierre Bourdieu, and Lewis Coser, among others, develops analyses of this complicated interdependency of violence, power, and law. All struggle to track the basic asymmetry of the force/law dialectic. This asymmetry is well captured in the following statement of the British foreign minister during the parliamentary debate over the impending war against Iraq in September 2002: "Law without force is no *law*; force without law is no *law*." But of course, force without law is still *force*.

4. Chandra Mukerji, "Unspoken Assumptions: Voice and Absolutism at the Court of Louis Xiv," *Journal of Historical Sociology* 11, no. 3 (1998): 301. Emphasis mine.

5. In this, the approach is similar to that described by Michael Biggs in his study of cartography, in which, absent conventionalized and legitimized maps of realms, jurisdiction is gauged through sedimented social relations: "The geographical extent of entities such as the county or kingdom was in turn defined by tradition and relationships. The oldest villagers were asked to whom they owed allegiance where they paid taxes and bought salt, and which courts judged local disputes. Actual relationships with royal authority thus determined the realm's spatial extent and not the re-

verse." Michael Biggs, "Putting the State on the Map: Cartography, Territory, and European State Formation," *Comparative Study of Society and History* 10 (1999): 386.

6. W. J. T. Mitchell, *Picture Theory* (Chicago: University of Chicago Press, 1994), 64.

7. In his book *Lee at Appomattox and Other Papers*, Charles Francis Adams recounts the following scene between General Robert E. Lee and Henry Wise, a former governor of Virginia. Wise, having grown impatient with General Lee's refusal to see that he was in an endgame with General Grant during the waning days of his campaign in the U.S. Civil War responds tellingly to a question posed by Lee: "Growing more serious, General Lee inquired what he thought of the situation. 'Situation?' said the bold old man. 'There is no situation! Nothing remains General Lee but to put your poor men on your poor mules and send them home in time for spring ploughing.'" Charles Francis Adams, *Lee at Appomattox and Other Papers* (New York: Houghton, Mifflin, and Co., 1902), 7.

8. *Oxford English Dictionary—Online Edition* (Oxford: Oxford University Press, 2001).

9. *Oxford English Dictionary* definition 1b states "To give up (letters patent, tithes) into the hands of the sovereign." *Online Edition*, 2nd ed. 1989.

10. Ibid. *Oxford English Dictionary* definition 2 states "To give up (something) out of one's own possession or power into that of another who has or asserts a claim to it . . . to give up the possession of (a fortress, town, territory) to an enemy or assailant."

11. The earliest examples provided for both of these meanings come from the fifteenth century.

12. The absence of such an authority at conflict's end militates against surrender as an option for termination. Referring to the imminent end of the European phase of World War II, Reiner Hansen writes that: "Towards the end of March 1945, the British government became convinced that once Germany had been completely overpowered, there would in all probability no longer be any military or civil authority capable of signing such an instrument of surrender. As a consequence, the victors would have to resort to a different procedure and unilaterally proclaim total German defeat and their assumption of supreme authority in Germany. Accordingly, the surrender document was redrafted by the European Advisory Commission into the form of a declaration." Reiner Hansen, "Germany's Unconditional Surrender," *History Today* 45, no. 5 (1995): 6.

13. It is interesting to note here that contemporary theorists and practitioners of "conflict resolution" never use the term surrender. According to political scientist, Marc Howard Ross, it is not in their vocabulary—partly for its imperialist loading

and partly because surrender is, despite its apparent clarity, understood not to ever really resolve things.

14. Adams, *Lee at Appomattox and Other Papers*, 25.

15. Lewis A. Coser, "The Termination of Conflict," *Journal of Conflict Resolution* 5, no. 4 (1961): 348.

16. Rudolf Arnheim, *The Power of the Center* (Berkeley: University of California Press, 1988), 2.

17. Randall Collins, "Violent Conflict and Social Organization: Some Theoretical Implications of the Sociology of War," *Amsterdams Sociologisch Tijdschrift* 16, no. 4 (1990): 72.

18. Marc Ross.

19. William McNeil, *The Pursuit of Power* (Chicago: University of Chicago Press, 1982).

20. Cf. Mukerji, "Unspoken Assumptions: Voice and Absolutism at the Court of Louis XIV," 286.

21. John Wright, "Sieges and Customs of War at the Opening of the Eighteenth Century," *American Historical Review* 39, no. 4 (1943): 631.

22. Thanks to Barry Schwartz for providing me with this polling instrument and its results. The poll goes on to ask subjects their opinion about requiring unconditional surrender of "our enemies," and about making public the fact that the United States was requiring unconditional surrender.

23. Anne Armstrong, *Unconditional Surrender* (New Brunswick: Rutgers University Press, 1961), 14. See also Quincy Wright, "How Hostilities Have Ended: Peace Treaties and Alternatives," *Annals of the American Academy, Political and Social Science* 392 (1970): 55.

24. Compare the case of the war between the Athenians and the Melians in 416 B.C., which followed the Melian refusal to surrender sovereignty, Heinz Waelchli and Dhavan Shah write that: "After a siege that lasted from the summer of 416 BC to that winter, the Melians surrendered to the Athenians, who killed all men of military age and sold the women and children for slaves. Subsequently, the Athenians sent out five hundred colonists and inhabited the island themselves." Heinz Waelchli and Dhavan Shah, "Crisis Negotiation between Unequals: Lessons from a Classic Dialogue," *Negotiation Journal* 10, no. 2 (1994): 138.

25. Wolfgang Schivelbusch, *The Culture of Defeat*, trans. Jefferson Chase (New York: Henry Holt and Co., 2003), 310.

26. Roosevelt quoted in John L. Chase, "Unconditional Surrender Reconsidered," *Political Science Quarterly* 70, no. 2 (1955): 260.

27. "Indeed the demand for political capitulation was unprecedented in international law. In contrast to armistice treaties, international law regarded, and con-

tinues to view, surrender as a purely military agreement concluded between the armed forces of the warring parties." Hansen, "Germany's Unconditional Surrender," p. 2 of downloaded article.

28. Wright, "How Hostilities Have Ended: Peace Treaties and Alternatives," 57.

29. Ibid., 3.

30. Quoted in Jay Winik, *April 1865: The Month That Saved America* (New York: HarperCollins, 2001), 215.

31. Edwin Cole Bears, "We Have to Save the People: Efforts to End the War after Lee's Surrender Collide Head-on with Politics—and the Murder of a Peacemaker," *Civil War Times*, May 2000: 41.

32. Raymond G. O'Conner, *Diplomacy for Victory: FDR and Unconditional Surrender* (New York: W. W. Norton and Co., 1971), 60.

33. John L. Chase, "Unconditional Surrender Reconsidered," 263.

34. Cf. Eviatar Zerubavel, "Lumping and Splitting Notes on Social Classification," *Sociological Forum* 11, no. 3 (1996) 421–33.

35. Quoted in William Craig, *The Fall of Japan* (New York: Dial Press, 1967), 66–67.

36. Ibid., 125.

37. Ibid., 145.

38. For the debate within the Truman administration about the consequences and advisability of retaining the emperor, see Kyoko Inoue, *MacArthur's Japanese Constitution: A Linguistic and Cultural Study of Its Making* (Chicago: University of Chicago Press, 1991), 6–7, 1; and Craig, *The Fall of Japan*, 59. Chapter 4 of my forthcoming *The Art of Surrender* addresses the question of sovereignty in surrenders most directly, and this decision is taken up again there.

39. Ruti Teitel, *Transitional Justice* (Oxford: Oxford University Press, 2000), 24.

40. It is not always clear who will be paying reparations to whom. As late as February 1865, President Abraham Lincoln had returned from an unsuccessful peace conference with representatives of the Confederacy off Hampton Roads and "suggested to his cabinet that the United States pay the insurgent Southern states $400 million as compensation for their lost slaves—if they surrendered by April 1. The Union cabinet was unanimous in its rejection." Winik, *April 1865: The Month That Saved America*, 34.

41. Hannah Arendt, *The Human Condition* (Chicago: University of Chicago Press, 1958).

42. Of course, the network of cross-witnesses has various degrees of freedom to confirm or negate the interpretation of these tendencies in their performative, demonstrative, and representational actions.

43. Georg Simmel, "Exchange," in *Georg Simmel: Individuality and Social Forms*, ed. Donald Levine (Chicago: University of Chicago Press, 1971), 67.

44. Perhaps implicitly suggesting a link between the arts of war and the giving of gifts, Chandra Mukerji writes about humanity's sustained engagement with armaments and their deployment: "These acts of material assault are just as much material means of organizing relations as gift-giving." Chandra Mukerji, "The Political Mobilization of Nature in 17th Century French Formal Gardens," *Theory and Society* 23 (1994): 655.

45. Pierre Bourdieu, "Structures, Habitus, Power: Basis for a Theory of Symbolic Power," in *Culture/Power/History: A Reader in Contemporary Social Theory*, ed. Geoff Eley Nicholas B. Dirks, and Sherry Ortner (Princeton: Princeton University Press, 1994), 166.

46. Jacques Derrida, *Given/Time I. Counterfeit Money*, trans. Peggy Kamuf (Chicago: University of Chicago Pres, 1992), 41.

47. Bourdieu, "Structures, Habitus, Power," 186.

48. Coser, "The Termination of Conflict," 348.

49. Writing about forced resignations, surrenders of a sort, Thomas Dumm describes a similar dynamic: "The receipt of the letter is crucial to the resignation because it is the moment of communication, the act of transmission of the sign of resignation . . . the letter of resignation becomes a collaborative act." Thomas Dumm, *A Politics of the Ordinary* (New York: New York University Press, 1999), 55.

50. Robert I. Burns and Paul E. Chevedden Burns, "A Unique Bilingual Surrender Treaty from Muslim-Crusader Spain," *Historian* 62, no. 3 (2000): 524–25.

51. Douglas Botting, *From the Ruins of the Reich: Germany 1945–1949* (New York: Meridian Books, 1985), 90.

52. U.S. Constitution, Amendment 14, Section 4.

53. Letter from U. S. Grant to R. E. Lee, April 7, 1865, reproduced in Ulysses Grant, *Personal Memoirs of U. S. Grant*, vol. II (New York: Charles Webster and Co., 1886), 478.

54. Giorgio Agamben, *Homo Sacer: Sovereign Power and Bare Life*, 85, trans. Daniel Heller-Roazen. (Stanford, CA: Stanford University Press, 1998).

55. Coser, "The Termination of Conflict," 349.

56. Maurice Godelier, *The Enigma of the Gift*, trans. Nora Scott (Chicago: University of Chicago Press, 1999), 19.

57. Coser notes that for some nations "the capitol symbolizes the very existence of the nation, then its fall will be perceived as defeat and will lead to the acceptance of the terms of the victor." This he claims was true for Paris in 1971 and 1940. "The Termination of Conflict," 350.

58. Kim Lane Scheppele writes abut the surrender of the Hungarian army at the end of World War II and the capture of the Holy Crown of St. Stephen. The crown guard "only agreed to turn the crown over to the Americans if they got not just a

property receipt, but also a statement saying that the crown had been given 'asylum' in America." "Counter Constitutions," unpublished manuscript (2002).

59. Wright, "How Hostilities Have Ended: Peace Treaties and Alternatives," 52.

60. H. E. Goemans, *War and Punishment: The Causes of War Termination and the First World War* (Princeton: Princeton University Press, 2000), 33.

61. Roger Chartier, *On the Edge of the Cliff: History, Language, and Practices*, trans. Lydia G. Cochrane (Baltimore: Johns Hopkins University Press, 1997), 87.

62. Burns and Chevedden, "A Unique Bilingual Surrender Treaty from Muslim-Crusader Spain," 523. Emphasis mine.

63. Quoted in Roger Chartier, *Forms and Meanings: Texts, Performances and Audiences from Codex to Computer* (Philadelphia: University of Pennsylvania Press, 1995), 44.

64. James D. Richardson, "President Washington's Farewell Address, September 17, 1796," in *A Compilation of the Messages and Papers of the Presidents 1789–1897* (Washington, DC: U.S. Congress, 1899).

65. Horace Porter, "The Surrender at Appomattox," *Civil War Times*, May 2000, p. 70.

66. Winik, *April 1865*, 217.

67. Lorraine White, "Spain's Early Modern Soldiers: Origins, Motivation and Loyalty," *War and Society* 19, no. 2 (2001): 43. These soldiers included Italian, English, German, and Burgundian troops along with Spanish and Flemish ones.

68. Wright, "Sieges and Customs of War at the Opening of the 18th Century," 642: "Covered wagons which would not be examined were to permit the garrison to bring with unseen deserters from the enemy. Were these deserters to march with the troops they would be instantly recognized and the victorious general would be under the necessity of having them shot or hanged which he wished to avoid."

69. Barbara Donagan, "Codes and Conduct in the English Civil War," *Past and Present* 118 (1988): 88.

70. Simone Zurawski, "Notes to New Sources for Jacques Callot's Map of the Siege of Breda," *Art Bulletin* 70, no. 4 (1988): 633.

71. Hermannus Hugo, *Siege of Breda: By the Armes of Phillip the Fourth*, trans. Cataine Barry (Ilkley: Scholar Press, 1975), 142.

72. Brian Axel, *The Nation's Tortured Body: Violence, Representation, and the Formation of the Sikh Diaspora* (Durham: Duke University Press, 2001), 51–52.

73. Hugo, *The Siege of Breda*, 129.

74. Winik, *April 1865*, 68.

75. Grant, *Personal Memoirs*, 485.

76. Winik, *April 1865*, 294.

77. National Archives of the United States, *The End of the War in the Pacific:*

Surrender Documents in Facsimile (Washington, DC: U.S. Government Printing Office, 1945).

78. Quoted in Winik, *April 1865*, 194.

79. Transcript of concession speech of Al Gore, *New York Times*, Dec. 14, 2000, p. A26.

80. Article 1, Surrender Agreement between Magistrates and Burgers of Breda and Ambrogio Spinola, transcribed in Hugo, *Siege of Breda*, 138.

81. Thomas Nast, *Harper's Weekly*, May 20, 1865, pp. 312–13.

82. Cf. Hansen, "Germany's Unconditional Surrender," 6.

83. Winik, *April 1865*, 131: "Of the several thousand Confederate soldiers taken prisoner by the Federals after th[e] battle of Five Forks on April 1 [about a week before Appomattox] not even a full 100 would swear the oath of allegiance to the Union."

84. Gary Gallagher, "'There Is Rancor in Our Hearts ... Which You Little Dream of': The Outward Civility of the Appomattox Surrender Hid a Terrible Secret: A Shared Animosity that Would Not Heal for Generations," *Civil War Times* May 2000: 54.

85. Teitel, *Transitional Justice*, 154.

86. General Jonathan Wainwright of the U.S. Army in the Philippines during World War II, wrote about his actions immediately after his decision to surrender to the Japanese: "Then I order the men of Corregidor and the other fortified islands in the bay to destroy all remaining weapons of greater than .45 caliber before noon, as well as all other military and naval stores, equipment and ships." *General Wainwright's Story: The Account of Four Years of Humiliating Defeat, Surrender and Captivity*, ed. Robert Considine (New York: Doubleday and Co., 1946), 120.

87. Armstrong, *Unconditional Surrender*, 18.

88. Michael Balfour, "The Origin of the Formula: 'Unconditional Surrender' in World War II," *Armed Forces and Society* 5, no. 2 (1979): 291.

89. Grant quoted in Porter, "The Surrender at Appomattox," 70.

90. Grant, *Personal Memoirs*, 490.

91. Porter, "The Surrender at Appomattox," 74.

92. Grant, *Personal Memoirs*, 494.

93. John Wright writes of a defeated garrison found guilty of sedition: "Then the infantry marched out without muskets, carrying only their swords; but these could not be worn by their side and were carried drawn and under their arms, pointing to the rear." Wright, "Sieges and Customs of War at the Opening of the Eighteenth Century," 639

94. Ibid., 641.

95. Henry Elson, The *Civil War through the Camera* (Springfield MA: Patriot, 1912), pt. 16.

96. William Hanks, "Metalanguage and Pragmatics of Deixis," in Hanks, *Intertexts: Writings on Language, Utterance and Context* (New York: Rowman & Littlefield, 2000), 69.

97. Arnheim, *The Power of the Center*, 76.

98. Craig, *The Fall of Japan*, 241.

99. Brian Axel reproduces a historian's account about the work with turbans: "In the eighteenth and nineteenth centuries, an Indian would place his turban at the feet of the conqueror as a sign of complete surrender. This was also used in a metaphoric sense to ask a great favor of someone, indicating a willingness to become their slave." Axel, *The Nation's Tortured Body*, 59.

100. Bonnie Honig, "Declarations of Independence: Arendt and Derrida on the Problem of Founding a Republic," in *Rhetorical Republic: Governing Representations in American Politics*, ed. Frederick M. Dolan and Thomas L. Dumm (Amherst: University of Massachusetts Press, 1993), 210–13.

101. A discussion of the complex nature of the "vanishing point" in pictorial representations of surrender is developed in chapter 2 of my forthcoming book.

102. Dumm, *A Politics of the Ordinary*, 54.

103. Norbert Elias, *The Civilizing Process: Power and Civility*, trans. Edmund Jephcott, vol. II (New York: Pantheon Books, 1982), 235. "When a monopoly of force is formed, pacified social spaces are created with are normally free from acts of violence."

104. Roland Barthes, quoted in Arnheim, *The Power of the Center*, 114.

105. Craig, *The Fall of Japan*, 300.

106. Hugo, *The Siege of Breda*, 129.

107. Grant, *Personal Memoirs*, Letter of April 8, 1865, p. 626, and Letter of April 9, 1865, p. 486.

108. Randall Collins makes a similar point about perception on the battlefield itself: "the individual overcomes fear by displacing his attention to symbolic tokens which structure the perceptual field among the chaos of the battlefield." Collins, "Violent Conflict and Social Organization," 69.

109. Hanks, "Metalanguage and Pragmatics of Deixis," 90.

110. For example, in the formulation of the Unconditional Surrender policy of World War II, "Secretary Hull objected to the policy [of Unconditional Surrender] not only on tactical grounds but also because he felt that it "logically required the victor nations to be ready to take over every phase of the national and local governments of the conquered countries, and to operate all governmental activities and

properties. We and our Allies were in no way prepared to undertake this vast obligation." Chase, "Unconditional Surrender Reconsidered," 278

111.   Louis Marin, "Toward a Theory of Reading in the Visual Arts: Poussin's
'The Arcadian Shepherds,'" in *The Art of History: A Critical Anthology*, ed. Donald
Prezoisi (Oxford: Oxford University Press, 1998), 268.

Bound by Law? Alien Rights, Administrative Discretion, and the Politics of Technicality: Lessons from Louis Post and the First Red Scare

BONNIE HONIG

This paper is dedicated to the memory of Michael Rogin

Nothing is more striking to the European traveler in the United States than the absence of what we term Government, or the Administration. Written laws exist in America and one sees that they are daily executed; but although everything is in motion, the hand which gives the impulse to the social machine can nowhere be discovered.

—Alexis de Tocqueville

[The new science of administration] is not of our making; it is a foreign science, speaking very little of the language of English or American principle. It employs only foreign tongues; it utters none but what are to our minds alien ideas. . . . If we would employ it, we must Americanize it . . . radically, in thought, principle, and aim as well. It must learn our constitutions by heart; must get the bureaucratic fever out of its veins; must inhale much free American air.

—Woodrow Wilson

Against the Exceptionalism of the State of Exception

Emergencies are one of the occasions on which governmental power and prerogative are expanded. Critics of such government expansion tend to appeal to courts to resist executive powers' new reachings. In the United States' near-emergency setting since September 11, 2001, many courts have blocked Justice Department efforts to put its claimed national security needs above individual rights to due process, some citing concerns about the indefiniteness of the War on Terror.[1] But historically in the United States, court interventions in times of more explicit emergency have had little impact on the expanded exercise of state power.[2] Often courts, certainly the Supreme Court, have explicitly deferred on such matters to executive branch claims of national security needs.[3] This deference is one of the reasons liberal and legal theorists tend to think of emergency politics as exceptional. The courts don't *normally* defer, so the solution to the problems that arise when they do defer (problems such as rights violations, undue administrative power) is to restore normal legal order either immediately or when the appropriate time comes (although emergency-occasioned changes often outlast the emergency that occasioned them).[4]

The tendency to treat emergency politics as exceptional or as sui generis is encouraged by Carl Schmitt's term for the phenomenon: the state of exception. This is a condition in which ordinary law is legally suspended and sovereign power operates unfettered, by way of decision. Schmitt's apparent defense, and even celebration, of decisionism combined with his own known Nazi party involvement, have led many to criticize him for promoting a dangerously immoral and warlike conception of politics.[5]

But to say that the state of exception is that in which decision takes over need not mean that all powers redound to a single unaccountable sovereign dictator, though that is the term Schmitt himself used, and that was his apparent meaning. Nor, contra Schmitt, need it necessarily mean that sovereignty is unified in and by way of the singular decision. In the context of American liberal democracy, decisionism has a place, but it is somewhat differently described: here, emergency politics occasion the creation of new administrative powers and the redistribution of existing powers of governance from proceduralized processes to discretionary decision, from the more proceduralized domains of courts to the more discretionary domains of administrative agency.[6]

Such agencies are decisionistic by design: highly discretionary, relatively unaccountable, for the most part ungoverned by the requirements of due process, and even possessed of law-making power of their own, they are referred to by their proponents (like the Progressives) as efficient, flexible agents of good political judgment and by their critics as dictatorial and unaccountable. Where proponents of administrative discretion see administrators as responsible agents entrusted to humanize and particularize the law that might otherwise be a blunt, harsh instrument, its critics see only the arbitrary, capricious rule of man taking the place of the rule of law. Simply put, then, in an American context, something like the decisionism that Schmitt approvingly identifies with a dictator goes by the name of discretion and is identified (approvingly or unapprovingly) with administrators and with administrative governance.

This way of thinking about decisionism takes emergency politics out of their exceptionalist context and sets them in the context of larger struggles over governance that have marked American liberal democracy for over a century.[7] On this account, emergency-occasioned "trade-offs" between, for example, security and rights, are not, *contra* Carl Schmitt and others, sui generis. Debates about them belong to larger debates about the risks and benefits to democracies, in emergency as well as nonemergency settings, of administrative versus judicial power, rule of man versus rule of law, efficiency versus fairness, speedy versus fully deliberative decision making, outcome versus process orientations, and secrecy versus transparency or publicity.[8] The focus on security versus rights, to which we are driven by the government's use of its powers to imprison, detain, deport, and de-naturalize in times of emergency, does not capture all the dimensions of emergency politics. The security versus rights perspective tends to deflect attention away from the more fundamental issue: the (re-)distribution of governing powers and the mechanisms by which they may or may not be held accountable. The liberty versus security debate is, from the perspective of administrative jurisdictional jockeying, a second or third order issue: important, to be sure, but it is the tail, not the dog.

The to and fro between administrative and judicial governance is most visible in exceptional settings that are least domesticated (emergency, national security, immigration politics, border policing, colonial governance).[9] But the to and fro is not itself exceptional. It is a quotidian jurisidictional jockeying among bureaucrats, administrative political appointees, judges, lawyers, civil libertarians, as well as citizens and activists from all across the political spectrum. It is part of a larger pattern of daily, ongoing vying for power.[10]

As part of that pattern, critics of administrative discretion and civil libertarians tend to respond to executive expansions of discretionary power not with counter-politics, per se, but with claims of rights. They try to rejudicialize the terrain in question in two ways: they turn to courts and contest the relocation of decision-making power from normal judicial settings to administrative sites,[11] and (or) they press for the expanded judicialization of nonjudicial sites by, for example, claiming that people have procedural rights of due process even in nonjudicial settings.[12] Such causes seem obviously worthy of support, but they offer no guarantees. For one thing, historically, even when courts have maintained jurisdiction, they have tended nonetheless to suspend their jurisdictional autonomy and to defer to executive branch claims in times of emergency, a tendency metaphorized for most Americans by the name Korematsu. And second, proceduralization itself cuts many ways: think of the recent call by Alan Dershowitz to proceduralize or judicialize torture. Dershowitz proposes that government interrogators who use torture be required to seek the issuance of a warrant by a magistrate "authorizing nonlethal torture." When we require government torturers to get judicial approval, we risk domesticating torture, Dershowitz concedes. But, he goes on to argue, since torture will go on anyway, we may as well bring it into law's fold and secure the protections and benefits of judicial procedure, both for ourselves as a society and for those being "interrogated."[13]

Thus, for those who want to put human rights and the dissenting politics they are meant to protect onto more certain ground, merely participating in the to and fro of judicialized processes versus administrative discretion will not be adequate. It may be necessary, but it will not be sufficient. The two poles operate in an oppositional yet partnered relation and the terrain they together stake out is too formal to really grapple with the political issues at stake. To illustrate this point and to seek a third option, let me turn now to the case of Louis F. Post, assistant secretary of Labor during the First Red Scare. Because he fought for procedural rights and due process during the arbitrary round-ups of the Palmer Raids, Post is often lauded as a principled proceduralist who anticipated later Court rulings on the rights of noncitizens. But Post was no mere proceduralist. He began his career in post–Civil War South Carolina, documenting the testimonies of Ku Klux Klan members detained under President Ulysses S. Grant's suspension of habeas corpus. About Grant's decision to suspend habeas corpus in order to break the Klan, Post never protested. For Post, a champion of proceduralism in 1919–

20, proceduralism was not a good in itself—it was simply one of law's many mechanisms, a mechanism whereby all sorts of political aims could be pursued.

Louis Freeland Post and the First Red Scare

On April 28, 1919, a homemade mail bomb arrived at the office of Ole Hanson, the Seattle mayor who had crushed a strike by shipyard workers just three months earlier. A day later, another bomb arrived at the home of former Senator Thomas Hardwick, exploding and maiming the unfortunate person who opened the package on Hardwick's behalf. Postal authorities located thirty-two other bomb packages before they were delivered. (Sixteen had been held back for insufficient postage, an oversight that also stalled some of the 2001 anthrax mailings). These had been sent in a likely bid for May Day delivery to, among others, John D. Rockefeller, Postmaster General Albert Burleson (who had used his powers to censor newspapers and other organs of opinion that were critical of the U.S. war involvement), Judge Kenesaw Mountain Landis, and other enemies of organized labor as well as immigration restrictionists. Some with more liberal leanings were also on the list of addressees: Senator Hardwick, Justice Oliver Wendell Holmes, Secretary of Labor William B. Wilson, and others.

The April bombings were followed by another round six weeks later, in June, when a new series of bombs exploded in eight different cities at the same hour. One of these—a suicide bomber, an Italian anarchist from Philadelphia—damaged Attorney-General A. Mitchell Palmer's house hurting no one but himself. Even with the technologies of communication and transportation of the early twenty-first century, it is a great feat of coordination to get a series of bombs to explode in eight different cities at the same time. How much more impressive is such a feat, and more terrorizing, in a time in which communications and transportation are primitive by comparison with ours? It seems hardly surprising, then, that a sense of vulnerability overtook the nation. As one historian put it, "Terrorism had come to America's own doorstep. . . . There had been terrorist attacks in the United States before, but nothing so coordinated and menacing. Most of the previous attacks were isolated bombings, conducted by self-proclaimed anarchists. This was different. During the latter half of 1919, the threat of terrorism sent Americans into a frenzy of fear."[14] We can understand this, perhaps, by analogy to our own current context. There had been previous terrorist acts on the United States as well—the attempted World Trade Center bombing in 1993 and the attack on the *USS Cole*. Both of these were troubling and yet neither really "prepared" people for what happened on 9/11.

The villains of the First Red Scare[15] are still relatively well known, but one of the period's heroes is all but forgotten. Louis Freeland Post, assistant secretary of Labor, defended the rights of the foreign born against those like Attorney General Palmer and J. Edgar Hoover (a mere twenty-four years old at the time and already head of Palmer's General Intelligence Division, also known as the antiradical division), who sought in wholesale deportations a solution to the anarchist threat and the problem of dissident action in the United States. Mindful of the recent Third International, the aim of Palmer and Hoover was "to destroy the Union of Russian Workers and the new Communist Party."[16] From late 1919 to early 1920, a series of raids known as the Palmer Raids swept up five to ten thousand (estimates differ) aliens and lined them up for deportation under the Sedition Act of 1918.[17] Outraged by the arbitrariness of the Justice Department's actions, Post took action when the opportunity arose.

Until 1920, John W. Abercrombie, solicitor general for the Department of Labor, worked in tandem with Commissioner of Immigration Anthony J. Caminetti, going so far as to issue five thousand blank deportation warrants for use by Palmer's agents. When in March, Abercrombie left the Labor Department to run for the Senate, Post took charge of deportation oversight and stopped the Labor Department's cooperation with Caminetti's Immigration Bureau and Palmer's Justice Department. Taking advantage of the language of the Sedition Act that created the Department of Labor, Post usurped, in accordance with the law, the de facto power of the commissioner of Immigration to decide the fates of detained aliens. Post "asserted the right to decide deportation cases without prior briefing [i.e., by Caminetti or his agents] and ordered that all records be sent to Washington for his personal review."[18] This move was continuous with earlier efforts made by Post, ever since he took his position as assistant secretary of Labor in 1913, to consolidate the power of the Labor Department over its bureaus.[19]

Having claimed jurisdiction and the power of decision, Post then began to whittle away at the category of deportability. First, he got Labor Secretary Wilson to rule that membership in the Communist Labor Party was not a deportable offense. A "student of radicalism," Post persuaded Wilson that the Communist Labor Party was more moderate than the Communist Party of America. Since only the latter did not disavow the use of violence, it could only be membership in the latter that was, strictly speaking, a deportable offence.[20] This directly contradicted the less-nuanced position of J. Edgar Hoover, who insisted that "both organizations have arbitrarily pledged themselves to overthrow the Government of the United States ... therefore ... the Communist Labor Party and persons who are members thereof fall within the provision of the Act of Congress approved Oct. 16, 1918."[21]

Second, Post decided, again contra Hoover, Palmer, and Caminetti, that what he coined "automatic membership" was not grounds for deportation. Automatic membership meant that a person was taken to be a member of the Communist Party if his or her name was found on their rolls. But the party padded its rolls, listing inactive or unpaid former members and borrowed names from lists of other related but nonidentical organizations. Post insisted that no one could be deported simply for having his or her name on a list. Some evidence had to be shown that the person in question consented explicitly to membership in the outlawed party.[22] This requirement substantially raised the evidentiary bar.

Third, and most radically, Post applied to administrative cases standards of evidence and due process that normally would have been thought at the time to obtain only in judicial settings, not administrative ones.[23] "Since deportation was not a criminal proceeding, and the prisoners were not citizens, Caminetti, Palmer, and Hoover claimed that the constitutional guarantees of right to counsel, to confront one's accuser, reasonable bail and habeas corpus were not applicable."[24] Post took the opposite view, repeating over and over that aliens facing deportation deserved constitutional protections of habeas corpus no less than citizens, and that protections traditionally thought of as attached to criminal investigations should apply also to administrative processes if not as a matter of law then simply as a matter of fairness. Fairness, after all, is what those protections were designed to capture or secure; or, in more purely procedural terms, those protections are proxies for an

otherwise elusive fairness. Deportation—even if it is an administrative matter—must be fairly administered, Post argued, and so it made sense to follow
those existing rules and procedures (the criminal law's due process, etc.)
that, in other venues, serve as proxies for fairness.[25]

In short, Post bound himself by law. Claiming he had no choice because
he was bound by rights that he himself attributed to those whom others
(including some of the courts) thought rightless, Post used his discretionary
power to limit his discretionary powers again and again. For example, he
ruled that aliens' self-incriminating statements could not be used against
them if those statements had been made without benefit of counsel.[26]

Finally, Post used all his powers of reasoning and all of the law's resources
to find in favor of aliens marked for deportation whenever possible. He employed the distinction between political and philosophical anarchism to the
benefit of those charged (only the former was actionable under the law). And
he second-guessed the self-incriminating statements of detainees. Here is his
account of his decision in the case of a self-professed anarchist, a well-known
activist from Mexico named Flores-Magon.

When asked about his political beliefs, Flores-Magon said he was a "communist anarchist." But Post did not take him at his word.

> I considered what his saying he was an anarchist meant. And if I had stopped
> there I should have been obligated to deport him. . . . I should have done as I did
> in the case of Emma Goldman, whose case stood wholly on that one word. She
> said she was an anarchist and I deported her and I should have done the same in
> his case. But I found on reading further [the record of Flores-Magon's interview]
> his meaning of the word did not tally with the definitions of anarchism as anyone
> who has investigated the subject knows; and because it did not tally, I came to the
> conclusion he was a man in favor of government and not opposed to government
> and that determined the case. . . . I decided to cancel [the warrant] because he
> was not an anarchist within the meaning of the law. (p. 230 HT).[27]

It will be apparent from this line of reasoning that almost anyone (with
the exception of the unfortunate Emma Goldman) could in such a way be
found not to be an anarchist, or at least not to be in violation of the law. Post
used the law and the rule of law's procedural requirements to create technicalities that would undo or counteract the Sedition Act's intended (at least
its deniably intended) and unintended effects.

In this way, in three months, Post and two assistants, working ten hour days and deciding as many as 100 cases per day, managed to free 2,000, 3,000, or perhaps even as many as 6,000 (estimates differ) detainees. One historian refers to Post's actions as an "insurrection against Palmer." Indeed it was, and Palmer knew it.[28] When, by the spring of 1920, Post had canceled the warrants of most of the detainees and released them, Palmer was livid: he charged Post with abusing his discretionary power and "demanded that Post be fired for his 'tender solicitude for social revolution.'"[29]

Post was not fired but he was called before the House Committee on Rules to answer Palmer's charges.[30] Was Post implementing the Sedition Act or was he using his discretionary power to undo it?[31] The public's impression and that of the members of the Committee was that when Post canceled a deportation warrant, he was in effect freeing an "alien after he was found guilty and ordered deported." (Indeed, one of his antagonists at the hearing of the House Committee on Rules snipped: "We have given you time to empty the jails as far as you could" [Mr. Johnson, Chair of the House Committee on Rules, p. 254, HT].) Post countered with the legally more precise claim that "Cancelling [*sic*] a deportation warrant is nothing more than finding a verdict for the defendant." That is, a warrant (which is all Palmer and Hoover could issue) was merely a charge, not a finding. It began a process of investigation, rather than marking the end of one. This clarification turned the tide of public opinion in Post's favor.[32] The Committee was not so quickly won over, though, and moved to take issue with Post's most radical invention: the rules under which Post decided the cases of the charged aliens.

A Democratic Administrative Power?

Post's discretionary decision to apply the more stringent criminal procedure rules to an administrative process was one of the core issues before the Committee on Rules. Post defended himself, deploying ideals of Americanism, constitutionalism, separation of powers, and limited government, appealing to an ideal of self-limiting administrative power that could otherwise be limitless in its reach, arbitrary in its application, despotic in its actions.

> My contention is that when the executive department of the Government is the absolute judge of whether a man shall remain in this country or not, and the

courts will not interfere, we should see to it that no injustice is done to the man.
. . . And that is the reason—not that I am applying absolutely criminal law to
administrative process, although I think the principles of criminal law, the protections of criminal law, ought to be accorded; yet I know that we cannot accord
them as criminal law. But I can take from the criminal law its humane, its just, its
American, its constitutional principles of protection to the liberty of the citizen
and apply it when I am acting for the executive department of the Government.
And I doubt if the Senate of the United States will condemn that attitude. . . . I
have drawn from the criminal law its principles which recognize the rights of the
individual and especially his right to a fair trial, to a fair decision as to whether he
is guilty or not, before he is penalized in any way. And to send a man who has
been here 10 or 15 or 20 years—to take him away from his family and send him
out of the country on an administrative warrant, a mere police warrant, until it
gets to the Secretary of Labor, is to penalize him and to penalize him in a very
drastic and very un-American way. (pp. 80–81, HT)[33]

Post emphasized the administrative character of the warrant to underline
the finality of the judgments involved: "we should be all the more careful in
judging these cases because he [the alien who has lived here ten or fifteen
years] has no redress in the courts when an administrative judgment is given.
And therefore I say that there are principles of the criminal law which ought to
be applied by the administrative department of the Government unless there
is the strongest reason, in each individual case, for not applying them."[34]

Post's appeal to an ideal of a self-limiting executive power did not move
the committee, at least not right away. One questioner, in particular, could
not fathom why an executive branch administrator possessed of broad discretionary power would bind himself by judicial rules and procedures which,
in the absence of such self-binding, would be inapplicable. "Mr. Garrett.
'Congress has passed this act; it has made it administrative; and it has put it
in the hands of executive officers to enforce. . . . I would say that it was a fair
presumption that Congress intended, in the passage of that act, irrespective
of the differences between the rights of aliens and the rights of citizens under
the Constitution of the United States, to eliminate the rules that would be
applicable in court." To this Post responded (in what must have been at least
partly mock horror): "In other words, the United States Government—
because this is the exact point—when a complaint is made against a man
under this law and the case comes before the Secretary of Labor, he must de-

port the man, whether the man is innocent or guilty? You did not mean that?" Garrett demurred, of course, but Post went on: "That is the issue, however. . . . The issue is: Not whether those who violate the law shall be deported, for we are deporting them . . . but whether those who have not violated the law shall be deported" (HT, pp. 80–81).[35] With criminal procedures acting as a proxy for fairness, and with a commitment in place to the imperfect proceduralism presupposed by the rules of criminal justice, there was no extra-procedural place from which to call "guilty" those who were not legally deportable according to the legal and procedural lines drawn and followed by Post.

And then there were the borderline cases. Throughout, Post admitted that although his own decisions were fully within the law, another might have decided the same cases another way, even using the same criteria (e.g., pp. 68, 230, 248, HT). Having usurped the power of decision, and having legally defined the boundary of decision as narrowly as possible and embraced the ensuing "constraints," Post took full responsibility for the decision that remained, even owning a certain inclination to favor people facing hardship. For example, in cases where the person in question was, say, the father of dependent children born in the United States, Post said that person should be given "the benefit of the doubt" (p. 78, HT): "I think that some humanity should come into the trial of these cases when there is some doubt as to guilt" (p. 79). This led to another typical exchange:

> The Chairman (interposing). "Yet if there had been enough men of that kind in the country to endanger the country, the fact that they had children born here that they would have to be separated from if they were deported, would not be any mitigation of the offense, would it?"
>
> Mr. Post. "Did you understand me to say anything to the contrary?"
>
> The Chairman. "No; and yet we should be keen to detect those who are keen to overthrow the Government of the United States."
>
> Mr. Post. "I said I was not keen to do it on flimsy evidence, and where there was any doubt. I never refrained from doing it in any case where the membership in the organization was clear, no matter what the hardship was. I could not sleep at night for thinking of some of the cases where the man had to be sent out. They were good, hard-working and useful men, who would have made good American citizens; but it was proved that they were members of this organization, even though they did not know what its purpose was; even though they thought they

were joining an organization of men from their own country; even though they thought that they were going to school. I have deported such men, because the evidence showed that it was clear that they belonged to the organization." (HT, pp. 78–79; emphasis added)[36]

With such oratory, delivered in a public venue and reported on daily in the nation's newspapers, Post sought to (re)humanize those whom Palmer and Hoover had successfully demonized. But Post knew that humanism, counter-Americanism, and oratory were not enough (neither to change the nation's path nor to save himself and the ideals—and calm—he represented). They were necessary but not sufficient to his cause. Their resources were not powerful enough to undo the effects of his opponents' demonological politics, at least not right away. Post was a lawyer, though he had practiced only briefly and thirty years before. He knew the law well and exploited its resources to the best of his abilities, which were considerable. Reviewing thousands of cases in a matter of weeks, he almost always found the detail, technicality, or doubt that might warrant a detainee's release.

Palmer and Hoover cast Post as an arbitrary, untrustworthy administrator whose aim was to undo the law. They claimed, by contrast, to be law's servants, operating in adherence to the requirements of the Sedition Act and the will of the legislators who passed it. Post responded by casting himself as law's strictest adherent and casting his opponents as arbitrarians and securitarians whose own decisionism was poorly cloaked by pseudo-legality. The success of his strategy depended largely upon whether Post's use of technicality would persuade or enrage the public and the members of the House Committee on Rules.

The Politics of Technicality—Or, Law Knows No Limits

Post's use of technicality to limit the range of the Sedition Act is reminiscent of the strategy whereby rabbinical interpreters in effect abolished the death penalty in Judaism. Working with biblical law, divinely authored, the rabbis could not simply change the law. They had to be more subtle and creative than that. So instead, they *legalized* the death penalty out of existence, creating such demanding procedural requirements that no one could be sentenced to death under the law. Here is a summary of their reasoning:

They required that the culprit be warned by two witnesses immediately before he committed the unlawful act carrying the death penalty (after all he may not know the act is illegal or punished so severely and how can you hold him liable for death for transgressing a law that he never knew?); that he respond, "Even so, I am going to do it" (because he may not have heard the warning), that he commit the act within three seconds of hearing the warning (for otherwise he might have forgotten the law he had just heard and therefore could not be held responsible); that the witnesses not be related to each other or to the culprit; and that there be at least one judge on the court who votes to acquit him (for otherwise the court might be prejudiced against him).[37]

These requirements are familiar to any student of the rule of law: publicity, intentionality, evidentiary requirements, impartiality, and so on.[38] But the rabbis extend them, comically, to the point of cartoonishness. Here interpretation, upon which the law depends for its animation, preservation, and application, is (also) used to undo the law.

Without interpretation, law, which is general and broad, can never be applied, implemented, or understood.[39] Without interpretation, law is insensitive to particularity and nuance. Such sensitivity, however, can lead to the creation of technicality, which is a product of working in law's nuances. And technicality seems to violate the basic premises of the rule of law: technicalities are rarely public because they are usually the products of arcane professional knowledge that makes sense only to lawyers and judges (or rabbis). Technicalities tend to be discovered or invented post hoc, they are not normally broadcast in advance as the rule of law requires.[40] Often they apply only to an individual case, and not to a general class of cases, and so they violate the rule of law's generality requirement. In short, technicality, a necessary presupposition of the rule of law (an outgrowth of interpretation and implementation), also threatens to corrupt or undo the rule of law.[41]

This doubleness of technicality is explored weekly (actually, now daily, no—hourly) on the television show, *Law and Order*, whose title suggestively both couples and severs the relation between its two terms—law and order. The "and" severs *and* couples. The title's doubleness is apt because the show's recurring theme is the district attorney's office's efforts to outwit defendants by creatively finding in law hitherto unsuspected traps, resources, and incentives—technicalities—by way of which order (but perhaps not law, at least not in the rule of law's usual sense of the term) can be maintained and the guilty punished. The ample literature on overcharging documents such practices in the real world.[42]

The ambiguous tactics of *Law and Order*'s infinitely creative and sometimes unprincipled (or overly principled) D.A. are presented as heroic, for the most part. In popular discourse, however, the term technicality still has a bad name. It is a term that brings to mind not a mechanism whereby order or justice might be secured but rather a mechanism whereby law's aims are subverted by sly criminals or their lawyers, as in: "he got off on a technicality." But note how this phrase, now a popular synecdoche for all the ways in which technicality—by implication, a cheap lawyerly trick—betrays the rule of law, actually turns on an assumption that Louis Post did not share and to which the rule of law does not commit us: it assumes or invites us to assume a coincidence between the rule of law's procedural ideals and its substantive rightness. The phrase's force relies on the assumption that the law's proceduralism is perfect, that the rule of law, if only unhampered by crooked devices such as technicality, will imprison only the guilty and free only the innocent. When we say "he got off on a technicality," we imply he is guilty but was not found to be so under law not because the law errs, but rather because the law erred in this instance only because it was exceptionally corrupted by a lawyerly device.

However, if we step out of the ideological prejudice (because that is what it is) that leads us to assume a match between procedural and substantive justice (that is, if we insist, with John Rawls, that all procedural fairness is at best imperfect or pure but never perfect),[43] then we should be able to see that technicality, no less than proceduralism itself, is a device available for capture by parties from all sides with a wide variety of agendas, a device whereby all sorts of ends, just or unjust, might be sought, as indeed they are on *Law and Order*. The instrument itself (technicality) does not prejudge nor predetermine the worth of the end in question. In Post's hands (and in those of the rabbis), technicality was used, in my view, to good ends. And administrative power (about which the rule of law's advocates are always wary and dubious) was made to serve laudable political goals. As it happens, those goals, in this instance, coincided with the larger goals of the rule of law: the protection of vulnerable individuals from arbitrary state power.

Moreover, as it happens, those larger goals could not in this instance have been secured by the rule of law per se. It needed to be supplemented (in the sense of undecidably both supported and corrupted) by the humor, cleverness, idealism, humanism, prerogative, and administrative decision that Post (no less than the rabbis who preceded him and to whose tradition he in some way surely belongs) brought to the rule of law and on behalf of which he pressed the rule of law into service. As aliens subject to administrative power, the detainees lacked the rights Post attributed to them. Post used his administrative powers to grant them rights they did not have juridically. He also advised them to invoke the writ of habeas corpus while in detention, even though he knew no court would likely side with them.[44] He understood the power and powerlessness of law. He knew that law cannot be pressed into new directions unless claims, even—or especially—illicit ones, are made in its name and using its terms. And then Post (before the Committee, in his practice at the Labor Department, in relation to the Justice Department) acted as if these rights, which had no juridical existence apart from his own contestable administrative rulings, bound him. All by itself, the rule of law did not secure nor mandate that outcome. And Post never implied that it did. He was inaugurating a new discourse, or reestablishing an old one, and he seems to have understood that the only way to succeed was by claiming to be bound by the very thing he was trying to bring into being. In so doing, he repeated the operation performed by the American founders when they declared independence in the name of *we, the people*, although that people, in advance of the new republic's constitution, did not yet exist.

Thus, when one of Post's more antagonistic questioners asked a question that might well have been posed in some form to the rabbinical reformers of Judaism's death penalty,[45] "You realized, of course, Mr. Secretary, that all of these rules that you had laid down—or the imposing of these deportation regulations—that every one of them operates to make it more difficult to deport the alien?," Post not only accepted the implied criticism, he embraced it: "Every rule in the interest of personal liberty makes it more difficult to take personal liberty away from a man who is entitled to his liberty" (p. 247–48, HT).[46] That entitlement, possessed even by the most vulnerable alien and secured in this instance by one man's discretionary administrative power and further legitimated by way of the device of technicality, was the check used by one executive agency to force itself as well as other loci of executive power to pause and be humbled.

Of course, the fact that the Justice Department had failed to "find more than four firearms and a few tons of propaganda pamphlets in the possession of the four thousand supposedly violent revolutionaries they arrested," only helped establish Post's case that aliens were people too and perhaps even good Americans (even if not citizens).[47] The bombings of 1919 had been real and devastating in their coordination; they had induced in most Americans a real and not unwarranted sense of vulnerability. But fears of cabals and networks of anarchists poised at the ready to attack the United States were waning in the face of little evidence to support them and in the face of doubts, prompted and fed by Post and his supporters, regarding the arbitrary administrative powers used by the Justice Department to fight those specters.

⌐

It is often said that the First Red Scare ended when the country chose hedonism over politics, shifting its focus from Italian anarchists to American flappers, from homemade bombs to homemade whiskey.[48] But couldn't we just as well say, shouldn't we just as well say, that the Red Scare ended when the country—and even a hostile Congressional Committee—chose democracy over despotism and fairness over arbitrariness in the exercise of governmental power? Because that is what happened (for one brief moment, anyway: Sacco and Vanzetti were yet to come).[49] The Committee on Rules found in Post's favor. Soon after, Palmer's political career was destroyed (he had been planning to run for the presidency) when he testified, much less effectively than Post, before the Committee regarding the Justice Department's handling of what Post came to call (and many others came to think of as) the "deportations delirium."[50] It was a huge victory for Post. But J. Edgar Hoover survived and went on to thrive.[51]

It is tempting to think the whole history of the American state's development into a national security state over the course of the twentieth century can be summed up by simply doing the math: Post was seventy-one years old at the time of these events; Hoover was twenty-four and lived for a half century after Post, perfecting and using the policing and surveillance techniques he first developed as head of Attorney General Palmer's antiradical division. Hoover was in this period already keeping files on various liberals, including Post, Louis Brandeis, and Felix Frankfurter, as well as black leaders like Marcus Garvey and labor leaders as well. It would be only four years until Hoover got the opportunity he needed to institutionalize his techniques and the demonological perspective that animated them. In 1924, Hoover was made head of the Federal Bureau of Investigation. Post died just five years later and his initiatives, by contrast, were never institutionalized. They passed out of the Department of Labor with him, months after the hearings, when the president he served left office. It is ironic that, of these two administrative exercisers of discretion, the man who stood up boldly for the rule of law never succeeded in institutionalizing his ideals so that they could survive, law-like, in his absence, while the man who stood for discretionary executive power eventually succeeded in creating an institution that would, even well after his own death and for a very long time to come, exercise power arbitrarily, in ways consonant with his own personal, often paranoid, vision.[52]

Until now, I have treated Hoover and Post as villain and hero, respectively. But my aim is not simply to write a history of great men. If Post and Hoover are of interest to us now, it is not only because the story of their engagement may inspire us to act well in challenging settings, but also because they name and order twin impulses in American political culture that may be in conflict, but nonetheless together drive our national responses to emergencies (real or imagined). American political culture has within it elements that are both demonological and inclusive, particularistic and universalistic, securitarian and willing to take risks, in favor of both discretionary and proceduralized power, and oriented toward both a centralized powerful administration and a fractured or divided and chastened sovereignty. The challenge for democratic activists is how to mobilize the energies of the latter in each of these pairings in order to offset and balance, not necessarily thwart, the former. The problem we face is that our contemporary political scene is dominated largely by impulses personified by Hoover and no longer also by those personified by Post. We are living in an era that is, as it were, *post*-Post because of the particular way the two impulses traced here played themselves out. The rights-centered future of American politics won out in the period after Post's victory, a period in which Post was blackballed from the public lecture circuit by supporters of Palmer and Hoover. It was not the chronological facts of the matter (Post's age; Hoover's youth) but rather the political battles that were won and lost after Wilson's departure from office that paved the way toward that future—our present. We are left with the civil libertarianism that animates the courageous rights-centered arguments of people like David Cole, but without the Progressivism and Henry Georgeism that breathed life into Post's. We are left, in short, with only the shadows of the rights for which Post fought. Some of those rights are now more firmly entrenched juridically than they were then, and this has led many to talk about how much "progress" the last century witnessed regarding rights. But these rights are not lodged in anything like what Post had—a visionary counter-politics that sought to stand up to executive power over-reachings in the settings of everyday as well as emergency politics. Denuded of such a context, contemporary liberal rights—fought for by lawyers, legal elites, and decided upon by courts—are important but inadequately able to generate the forms of collective action needed to counter the color-coded, securitarian, emergency politics of governance with which democratic citizens in the United States have been confronted since 9/11.

Conclusion: Law's Agency—Or, The Limits of Law

Louis Post is said by one historian to have "anticipated Supreme Court rulings of half a century later."[53] Noncitizens facing administrators (in nonemergency settings) do now have some of the procedural rights that Post discretionarily granted to Palmer's detainees in 1920. But the term "anticipation" operates in an end-of-history temporality that credits law with all the agency (phenomena—like rights—are not real until the law says they are), and leaves to people like Post only the perspicacity or good fortune to line up on the right side of the law before (or after) the law has spoken (or in anticipation of its one day doing so).[54] Moreover, that end-of-history temporality implies that law only steps forward, never back. Yet, at the moment, in the not-quite-emergency setting of the War on Terror, noncitizens and some citizens—enemy combatants and others—are denied many of the procedural rights granted their predecessors by Post. Finally, to identify Post's struggle as an *anticipation* of what came later is to misidentify the "rights" for which he struggled as the same things as the rights for which others struggle now.

But the rights that Post valued were embedded in a quasi-Progressive politics quite different from the liberal politics in the context of which contemporary rights advocates operate.

Post did not anticipate the law. He used all the law's resources and even invented some in order to render the Constitution more democratic, that is to say, to render it more responsive to the needs, rights, and views of the actually existing people over whom government power was brought to bear.[55] And, for better or worse, the law—through the agency of other interpreters, administrators, judges, and activists—eventually found its way to some of the democratic commitments and ideals that so moved Louis Post.

Post pursued many substantive Progressive goals while at Labor. Specifically, he sought to develop labor arbitration procedures so as to diminish strike violence and to improve the Labor Department's services to black labor. His innovations were short-lived. They were swept aside when he was pushed into the defense of proceduralism—as we all are—by the demands of emergency and demonological politics, which made survival rather than world-building a priority. (Or, better: in the context of demonological politics, proceduralization *is* world-building, albeit what is built is a barer world than we might otherwise seek.) In the realm of proceduralization, a dangerous realm in 1920, as now, Post took advantage of the ambiguity that left others in doubt as to whether it was he or the law that was the primary agent of his controversial administrative decisions. If some concluded that the "law made him do it," then so much the better for both him and the law.

But the question of whether Post made law or acted at law's behest can only take us so far. It is important also to pose the critical questions that lie beneath it: What is at stake in depicting Post as either bound by law or as law's author? In other words, for those who turn to it, what problem is law's agency supposed to solve?

Attributing agency to law is a move made by those anxious to hold fast the distinction between the rule of law and the rule of man. Faced with the undeniable impact of variable human agency on the rule of law's supposedly univocal, predictable governance, scholars of law and legal historians seek to excise or domesticate those elements of the rule of law that appear dangerously decisionistic (e.g., interpretation, implementation, technicality). One solution is institutional: authorized or sanctified in one way or another, or

legitimated by their norms or practices, institutions like the Rabbinical San-
hedrin or the U.S. Supreme Court interpret or make law through authorized
processes, forms, and norms that are said to transcend and bind the agency
of any mere human.[56]

The historian Lucy Salyer takes this institutional approach in her book,
Laws Harsh as Tigers, which seeks to explain why hostile, nativist lower court
judges decided cases in favor of Chinese petitioners seeking entry to the
United States at the turn of the last century. Salyer casts law as possessed of
an agency of its own—the judges were "captives of law," she says—but she
also locates that agency in particular institutions: the judges were con-
strained, by "the court's norms and traditions" and moved by their "institutional mission." She is undoubtedly correct. Institutions do set expectations,
generate grammars, and set out norms that are internalized by their members. But individuals then go on to act variously upon those norms and, in
their variety, they at some point "decide."[57]

Salyer's allusions to the courts' institutional mission occur within a larger
theoretical framework that works, perhaps unwittingly, to shore up and rele-
gitimate judicial power, insulate it from the charge of decisionism, and direct
that charge instead at administrative power. In this framework, in which Salyer as well as diverse proponents of the judicialization of procedure operate
(e.g., Martin Shapiro, Andrew Arato, Jurgen Habermas), *the rule of law*,
which is identified with law-disciplined judges, norm-bearing lawyers or legal
elites, and rights-bearing clients, is juxtaposed to *the rule of man*, which represents arbitrary power exercised over rightless persons by unaccountable
administrators with too much discretion and a focus on efficient outcomes,
not justice.[58] Yet the rule of law as a system of governance postulates both
judicial and administrative power.[59] And the binary distinction between rule
of law and rule of man is overdrawn and misleading.

To contest the binarism of the distinction between the rule of law and the
rule of man as it operates in contemporary scholarship is *not* to deny the important differences between administrative and judicial settings. People have
access to a wider array of procedural rights and protections when confronting state power in judicial arenas than when confronting state power in administrative arenas. Those procedural rights and protections may be nuga-
tory or they may be invaluable; it depends on the political and legal context

in which we try to claim or (re)take them.[60] Either way, however, the real differences between administrative and judicial settings do not underwrite the longer list of binaries that structures the arguments of those who champion the rule of law over its demonized, administrative other: efficiency versus justice, outcome versus process, decision or discretion versus norms, caprice versus regularity. These do not map neatly onto administrative versus judicial power. Some unholy mix of all these considerations informs administrators and justices alike in their exercises or easements of state power. Administrators can be nuanced, careful, and even self-limiting, while judges can be brutal, ambitious, and overreaching, as we well know. Proper judicial procedures don't always secure just outcomes. And courts are not the only public institutions guided by norms. Public administration (particularly as practiced by the Progressives) is no less structured by ideals, norms, and grammars than are courts. True, the ideals, norms, and grammars that motivate the two institutions may differ (hence the different rights and privileges possessed by their respective petitioners), but those differences exceed and confound the binary demands of the opposition—rule of law versus rule of man—in which the former is assumed to be superior to the latter.[61]

The logic of what Michael Rogin called demonological thinking is very much at work here.[62] Legal scholars and political theorists take something that is unsettlingly inside of the rule of law (variable, fallible interpretation, application, implementation, invention, technicality), cast it outside, and call it decisionism so that the rule of law is kept pure of its delegitimating taint. Decisionism is then identified with emergency politics, the state of exception, and its very foreign proponent, the legal theorist turned Nazi jurist, Carl Schmitt; or it is identified with the rule of law's other, administrative power, whose partnership role with more judicialized institutions in the United States is largely disavowed and whose position in relation to the rule of law is (re)cast as simply adversarial, rather than supportive or supplementary. Similarly, the so-called state of exception is disavowed, rendered exceptional, marked as a suspension of law rather than seen as part (even if an extreme part) of the daily rule-of-law-generated struggle between judicial and administrative power.

A politics of foreignness is also deeply at work here. A confident sense of the alienness of administrative power in relation not just to the rule of law but also to the United States is furthered by sentiments like those voiced by Alexis de Tocqueville and Woodrow Wilson in the quotations that opened this paper. Wilson (president at the time of the Palmer Raids and responsible for the appointment of Post and other Progressives to executive branch agency positions) suggests that administration is itself a foreign practice and therefore guided (if guided at all) by principles developed elsewhere and in need of Americanization.[63] Tocqueville's rumination suggests, also misleadingly, that although the United States has some administrative machinery, it is (perhaps by contrast with France) really a rule-of-law state, not (also) a bureaucratic one.[64] Or better, it suggests that one can have the rule of law without being implicated in mechanisms of governance: administration, implementation, and decision.[65]

Unfortunately, efforts to insulate law (and the United States) from the Others of decision and administration themselves contribute to the rule of law's undoing, for the rule of law is partly legitimated by its claim to be an instrument of self-rule, after all, and so it depends upon (or as Oakeshott would say, it postulates) the very human agency that many of the rule of law's proponents are committed to disabling or marginalizing for the sake of the equity, regularity, and predictability that the rule of law is also said to require and deliver.[66] With the disavowal of all that goes by the name decisionism, with the quest to bind ourselves everywhere by law, we disavow something else too: our human inaugural powers, which law *refuses but also offers* to its subjects: it refuses human agency when it aspires to regulate, command, and police us but it also, of course, remains dependent upon us, its subjects, to interpret and implement and even undo the law (perhaps even as its [co]authors). Lest this promisingly undecidable dimension of law be obscured, liberal democratic regimes need a third way, or perhaps a better way, of thinking about the two that we have. Perhaps somewhere between the rule of law and the rule of man, or on the terrain of their jurisdictional struggle, we might, together with Louis Post, find or enact the rule of men or people: plural and riven, plainspoken and arcanely technical, lawlike and lawless, all at the same time.

That is the terrain on which dissenting politics have, in the past, sometimes found fertile ground. And a good thing too; because a simply procedural, rights-centered politics (whether under the rubric of rule of law or that of rule of man) simply cannot stand up to America's politics of counter-subversion. Michael Rogin argued that one of the biggest consequences of the American government's historical countersubversive focus on security has been the atomization of political association.[67] This is something the current focus on individual rights inadvertently aids and abets. Rogin tracked the effects of three episodes of American countersubversion—the genocide of tribal Indians, the destruction of labor unions, and finally, under McCarthyism, the effort to make dangerous any sort of dissenting political affiliation. If Rogin was right, then there is nothing mysterious about the much-discussed decline of civic involvement in America. The only way to reverse it is to combine our worthwhile insistences on rights with a reclamation of the human inaugural political powers that motivated Post and on which dissenting and founding politics in this country have always depended.

Notes

I thank Austin Sarat for inviting me to write an essay for this volume and providing me with the occasion for further research on this topic. Sarat, Lawrence Douglas, and Martha Umphrey all provided valuable commentary on an early draft. Versions of this essay were presented at the University of Missouri at St. Louis, The Johns Hopkins University, Berkeley, UCLA, Amherst College, the 2003 American Political Science Association convention, the American Bar Foundation, and Princeton University. I thank all those in attendance as well as those who organized those fora and invited me to present my work. In particular, I am grateful to Lyman Sargent, Richard Flathman, Bill Connolly, Jane Bennett, Shannon Stimson, Wendy Brown, Hanna Pitkin, Marianne Constable, Ali Behdad, Kirstie McClure, Peter Myers, Stephen Macedo, and especially Juliet Williams. Bill Novak and Terry Halliday, my colleagues at the American Bar Foundation, took time to discuss new literatures with me, as did Jill Frank. John Comaroff, Iris Young, George Kateb, Marcie Frank, Larry Glickman, Linda Zerilli, and George Shulman were, as always, great interlocutors. For research assistance, I am indebted to Ella Myers, Lida Maxwell, and Laura Ephraim.

1. See especially *United States v. Zacarias Moussaoui*, Criminal No. 01-455-A (2001). Over the objection of federal prosecutors, Moussaoui continually pressed for and was granted the right to interview and cross-examine witnesses in Guantanamo Bay by Judge Leonie Brinkema. Also see *United States v. Satter*, 02 Cr. 395 (2002). Most recently, enemy combatant cases have been decided in favor of individual rights over government security claims. In *Falen Gherebi v. George Walker Bush, Donald Rumsfeld*, No. 03-55785 (2003), the 9th Circuit Court found that when detentions

are indefinite, detainee rights must prevail over security circumstances and challenges. In *Rasul v. Bush*, No. 03-334 (2004), the Supreme Court found that the United
States has sufficient dominion in Guantanamo to establish habeas corpus jurisdiction over detainees held there. And in *Hamdi v. Rumsfeld*, No. 03-6695 (2004), the
Supreme Court declared that citizen detainees cannot be held indefinitely without
due process rights to dispute the facts and legality of their detention. The Court's rationale? In a time of war such as this one the need to detain citizens indefinitely may
be allowed an executive *authorized by Congress, provided detainees are given an opportunity to present evidence* regarding facts of their enemy combatant status before a
neutral decision-maker.

2. In spite of my noting that the emergency was *more explicit*, less controversial,
in other past cases (e.g., *Korematsu, Milligan*) than in present ones (Guantanamo
Bay), I note that there may be some Whig history at work here. What looks uncon-
troversial to the backward-looking gaze may well have looked contestable and confusing in the present moment. This is an issue that has been explored at length by
Friedrich Nietzsche (*On the Genealogy of Morals*, trans. Walter Kaufmann [New
York: Vintage Books, 1989] and *Thus Spoke Zarathustra*, trans. Walter Kaufmann
[New York: Penguin Books, 1985]) and Hannah Arendt (*Between Past and Future*
[New York: Penguin, 1993]), as well as, most recently, by William Connolly (*Neuro-
politics* [Minneapolis: University of Minnesota Press, 2002]). I discuss the politics of
temporality at length in "The Time of Rights" (*The New Pluralism*, ed. David Camp-
bell and Morton Schoolman, forthcoming 2006).

3. The classic example is the majority decision in *Korematsu v. U.S.*, 323 U.S. 214
(1944), as well as the Jackson dissent in that case. The earlier decision in *Milligan*
(which found, contra Lincoln, that where civilian courts are open, military courts
cannot be used) was issued in 1866, after the war's end. The decision, *ex parte Merriam*, issued in Maryland court by Taney, was issued during wartime, 1861, and did
challenge Lincoln's suspension of habeas corpus, arguing that the possibility of suspension, listed in Article I, should be seen therefore as a congressional power, not an
executive one. Since *Merriam* was decided in 1861, during the Civil War, it is one of
several exceptions to my claim that courts *generally* defer to executive power in times
of emergency. But Taney's decision had no impact on Lincoln's conduct. See Clinton
Rossiter, *Constitutional Dictatorship: Crisis Government in the Modern Democracies*
(New Brunswick: Transaction Publishers, 1948, 2002), Part IV.

4. Perhaps mindful of the courts' probable deference, David Cole and Jack
Dempsey insist repeatedly (*Terrorism and the Constitution* [New York: New Press,
2002]) on the irregularity of the war on terrorism, on its likely infinitude, and its
unspecified character.

5. Typical and among the most unrelieved in his criticism is William Scheu-

erman, *Between the Norm and the Exception* (Cambridge: MIT Press, 1994), Chapter 1.

6. Analogously, and prior to this struggle between judicial and administrative power, courts themselves were disciplined into the predictable and proceduralized institutions demanded by the rule of law as we have now come to understand it. In the post-revolutionary United States, military courts were used to break the independence and unruliness of jural freedom, an institution that was once, in Akhil Amar's words, a fourth branch of government. See Shannon Stimson's wonderful and now timely *The American Revolution in the Law* (London: Macmillan, 1990) and Amar's *Bill of Rights* (New Haven: Yale University Press, 1998).

7. Scheuerman would agree with this point but he would, I think, very much resist its identification with Schmitt, whom Scheuerman sees as totally and unrelievedly decisionistic, by contrast with the history of American liberal democracy. In short, while Scheuerman would agree that the American state has generated many discretionary components of governance that are inadequately accountable to the people over whom they rule, he seems to think it risky indeed to use Schmitt in any way to highlight or identify such dimensions of America's larger politics, insofar as we risk, thereby, taking on board Schmitt's irredeemably fascist conception of law (on Scheuerman's account) and passing on the superior aspiration to weigh in (as Scheuerman does) on the rule of law side, by (for example) calling for the expansion of simple legal language and regularity (e.g., *Between the Norm and the Exception*, p. 212 passim).

As William Scheuerman notes in his book, and as William Novak first pointed out to me, the idea that there is a connection between emergency law and administrative law is a point made by Neumann in *Behemoth* (London: V. Gollancz Ltd., 1943). But Neumann's point is a bit different: Neumann criticizes and delegitimates administrative law by noting that its paradigmatic model is the emergency. I am interested in the converse, in thinking about emergency politics in the context of larger and more mundane struggles for state power between advocates of administrative discretion (not necessarily illegitimate, in my view) and proponents of judicial review.

8. Such "settings" include both emergency times and spaces because, *contra* Carl Schmitt and Clinton Rossiter, emergency powers are not just temporal; they may be spatial. Or, better, even when they are temporal, they are also always spatial. For example, in a time of national emergency, we are not all equally subject to emergency rule—some have the wealth or power or profile to opt out of many constraints and remain uncriminalized and even, in some cases, uncriminalizable by new security measures.

9. As Lucy Salyer notes: immigration politics and law are taken to be exceptional in American law, even in American administrative law—a "maverick" she says citing Peter Schuck, "anomalous," and even an "outlaw" body of law. As Schuck puts it,

"probably no other area of American law has been so radically insulated and divergent from those fundamental norms of constitutional right, administrative procedure, and judicial role that animate the rest of our legal system." Indeed, says Schuck, in immigration law "government authority is at its zenith and individual entitlement is at the nadir." Quoted in Salyer, *Laws Harsh as Tigers* (Chapel Hill: University of North California Press, 1995), xiv. See also David Cole, *Enemy Aliens* (New York: New Press, 2003, 30 passim) on the Ashcroft Justice Department's appropriation of immigration law as a tool in detaining people for investigation in the War on Terror.

But Salyer goes on to suggest that the area of immigration law is less an outlaw than Schuck and others assume. Chinese petitioners in the context of the Chinese Exclusion Act were savvy users of law and courts and were surprisingly successful in the federal courts, even when standing before nativist judges, because those judges were bound by institutionalized norms of the court and would not allow even their own nativism to stand in the way of judicial norms of due process. She argues, however, that immigration law, which is still largely administrative, should be further judicialized.

That is, Salyer's study of a time and a place in which the contest between rule of law and administrative governance is visible (or rather is rendered visible by her historical research) accepts and resecures the governing terms of current normative debates: the opposition between administrative law or rule of man and the rule of law, judicially enforced, the same opposition that governs Scheuerman's work. One merit of Louis Post's case, detailed below, is that it troubles that opposition and highlights the ways in which the rule of law's proceduralism is always dependent to some extent on *some*one's administrative or judicial decision. Mere proceduralism lacks direction, nuance, and meaning and offers no guarantees regarding the justice of its outcomes. With this point, we enter into large and ongoing debates in legal theory, which I refer to throughout and discuss briefly in the conclusion.

10. In recontextualizing emergency politics in an ongoing institutional setting, I position myself somewhere between Clinton Rossiter and Lucy Salyer: For Rossiter, "crisis government in this country has been a matter of personalities rather than of institutions" (*Constitutional Dictatorship*, 210). For Salyer, administrative discretion has played too large a part in the still exceptional arena of immigration politics (*Laws Harsh as Tigers*, see note 9 above), but that discretion has also been mediated in hitherto unappreciated ways by courts, and by law in its institutionalized settings. I am looking at emergency politics as a moment in that larger institutional struggle between judicial and administrative power (studied by Salyer in the mostly non-emergency area of immigration politics), while also emphasizing more approvingly than Salyer, I think, the extra-procedural and not always law-governed role played in

that struggle by the personalities (Rossiter) and decisions of judges, administrators, elites, legal clients, and all sorts of political actors.

11. See Andrew Arato, "The Bush Tribunals and the Specter of Dictatorship," *Constellations* 9, no. 4 (Winter 2002), and Cole, *Enemy Aliens*.

12. In *Laws Harsh as Tigers*, Lucy Salyer studies approvingly the process whereby Chinese would-be immigrants sought the expansion of judicial protections while dealing with highly discretionary and not very accountable administrators of the Chinese Exclusion Act. The literature on scholarly calls to proceduralize discretionary administrative agency is glossed in and exemplified by Martin Shapiro in *Who Guards the Guardians? Judicial Control of Administration* (Athens: University of Georgia Press, 1988).

13. Alan Dershowitz, *Why Terrorism Works* (New Haven, Conn.: Yale University Press, 2002), Chapters 4 and 5.

14. Bruce Watson, "Crackdown!" *Smithsonian* 32 (February 2002): 52.

15. Although at the time, of course, it was not so called (the Second Red Scare had not yet occurred). The events were referred to by Post as the "Red" Crusade. The above summary of events draws on William Leuchtenburg, *The Perils of Prosperity 1914–32* (Chicago: University of Chicago Press, 1958).

16. Charles Howard McCormick, "Louis Freeland Post," *American National Biography*, vol. 17, ed. John Garraty and Mark C. Carnes (New York: Oxford University Press, 1999), 731.

17. A vivid sense of the fears surrounding these raids is given by Clancy Sigal, a Hollywood screenwriter whose 2002 op-ed provides an excellent counter to Leuchtenburg, who downplays popular fears at the time. Says Sigal: "The anarchist threat was terrifying, just as the terrorist threat is now. Most Americans supported Attorney General Palmer's campaign against the 'Reds'—an ill-defined menace that went far beyond the small group of actual anarchists that was blamed for pretty much anything that smacked of social conflict—including at various times, the women's suffrage movement, a Chicago race riot, and a wave of paralyzing industrial strikes." Sigal's parents were at high risk in such a setting: "foreign-born, Jewish, radical labor organizers, who had actively participated in several turbulent strikes, [they also] had no fixed address and were living in sin. They were arrested, jailed and almost deported during the infamous Palmer Raids of 1920 and 21 [*sic*]." Later, Sigal learned from his mother that his father had been beaten by federal agents on his way to jail. Both were released later, she after a few days, he after a few weeks, and were not deported, though many of their friends were. "The raids," Sigal continues, "were a living presence at our house. At a later time, when J. Edgar Hoover's FBI came around to question me during the cold war, my mother politely met them at the door, invited them in for coffee and charmed them out of their intended purpose.

But she was pale and terrified when I got home. In an understandable slip of the tongue she said: 'The Palmers have been here. What have you done?'" Clancy Sigal, "John Ashcroft's Palmer Raids," *New York Times*, 13 March 2002, p. A25.

18. Dominic Candeloro, "Louis Post and the Red Scare of 1920," *Prologue: The Journal of the National Archive* 2, no. 1 (Spring 1979): 44. Caminetti resisted the takeover, of course, but Post replied that "power over deportation matters had never been given to the bureau [of immigration] and that Caminetti was merely an agent who had been assigned to brief cases for him." As Post later put it in his testimony before the Committee on Rules, "The Commissioner General of Immigration is not the dictator to the Secretary of Labor in warrant cases. It has been assumed by the committee that makes this complaint [the charges made by the Committee on Rules] that he is the dictator in effect, and that the Assistant Secretary [Post himself] was culpable for overruling him." But this assumption was wrong, Post insisted over many hours of testimony, in which he repeatedly characterized the immigration commissioner as a "sheriff" to the Department of Labor and as a mere advisor and, finally and most brutally, as possessed of "no more authority than the private secretary of a Secretary would have." U.S. House, Committee on Rules, *Investigation of Administration of Louis F. Post, Assistant Secretary of Labor, in the Matter of Deportation of Aliens*, 66th Cong., Apr. 27, 30 and May 7, 8, 1920: 227, hereafter cited as HT.

19. Dominic Candeloro, "Louis Freeland Post: Carpetbagger, Single-taxer, Progressive," Ph.D. diss., University of Illinois at Urbana-Champaigne, 1970, 155–65 inter alia.

20. "The mere innocent member who is guilty of nothing but joining an organization. . . . I don't think that any man with an *American mind* would wish to have that kind of man deported without showing some evidence that he was culpable." HT, 263.

21. Quoted in Candeloro, "Post: Carpetbagger," 45, citing Palmer's testimony before the House Committee on Rules. Secretary of Labor Wilson held open hearings on this matter and "stunned Hoover and the Justice Dept" when he ruled "that membership in the Communist Labor party was not a deportable offense because members were not required to know of or subscribe to the Party's goals or tactics as a condition of membership; he flatly rejected Hoover's brief and argument on the subject." Richard Gid Powers, *Secrecy and Power: The Life of J. Edgar Hoover* (New York: Free Press, 1987), 118.

22. "In other words, the principle 'Once a member, always a member,' is not true, in my judgment, in these cases, provided there is a withdrawal from membership in good faith." HT, 77.

23. Thirty years later, Hannah Arendt articulated one of the insights that motivated Post: that an innocent but stateless person subject to administrative state power could paradoxically improve her position by breaking the law and gaining

thereby the scrutiny but also the procedural protections to which those accused of criminal law violations are subject or have a claim. *Origins of Totalitarianism* (San Diego: Harcourt Brace, 1979), 286–87.

24. Candeloro, "Post: Carpetbagger," 46.

25. Post said he had Court decisions backing him in this view but none finessed the question (discussed below) of whether it was incumbent on an administrative procedure to hold itself to the more stringent requirements of criminal law. Thus, it is true, as Charles Howard McCormick says, that Post's legal position *anticipated* later court rulings. McCormick, *American National Biography* (cf. Candeloro, who says that "Post's dedication to upholding the procedural rights of the defendants anticipated Supreme Court rulings of half a century later" ["Post: Carpetbagger," 46]). I will quarrel with that term—"anticipation"—below. McCormick mentions specifically *Wong Yang Sun v. McGrath* 339 U.S. 33 [1950] and *United States v. Brignoni-Ponce* 422 U.S. 873 [1975]. Post himself invoked an 8th Circuit Court of Appeals case, *Whitfield v. Hanges* 222 F. 745 [1915], when he said in his testimony, "an alien, once lawfully admitted and resident in this country . . . has the same constitutional rights, except as to voting and purely citizenship rights . . . that the citizen has," and Post added, this "is good *American* doctrine." HT, 223, emphasis added.

26. Regarding his disregard for statements made by aliens without benefit of counsel, Post said to the House Committee: "If there is any objection to that stand that I took, the quarrel is with the United States district judge in the West and with the Supreme Court of the United States in its unanimous decision. I based that on the principle of the case of *Re Jackson*, in the U.S. District Court for Montana, in which the decision was by Judge Bourquin; and on the case of *Silverthorn v. The United States*, which was an appeal taken to the Supreme Court and decided January 28, 1920." HT, 78.

Post's ruling on this matter directly reversed an earlier change introduced by Hoover: In response to a pamphlet that advised aliens not to answer questions without benefit of counsel, Hoover amended immigration regulations "to delay the right to a lawyer until the case 'had proceeded sufficiently in the development of the facts to protect the Government's interests.' The amendment took effect on Dec. 31, 1919, one business day before the raids began." Cole, *Enemy Aliens*, 120 and passim.

27. Two other considerations entered into the case for Post, which he mentions at other times at the hearings: Magon had six American born children dependent upon him and, as a dissident, would very likely have been killed had he been returned to Mexico. Thus, Post said that even had he found Magon deportable, he would have imprisoned him in the United States until such time as he could be assured of the man's safety in Mexico.

28. Leuchtenburg, *Perils*, 79. Cf. McCormick, *American National Biography*.

29. Leuchtenburg, 80. Cf. Watson, "Crackdown!" Leuchtenburg says that thanks to Post, of the 5,000 arrest warrants sworn out in late 1919, "only a few more than 600 aliens were actually deported." Ibid., 81.

30. Salyer (*Laws Harsh*, 239), Cole (*Terrorism*, 123), and others suggest Post was impeached or "brought up on impeachment charges," referring to the hearings referred to here. In fact, he was not impeached. An impeachment resolution was introduced "unostentatiously," by Kansas congressman Homer Hoch. But the resolution "did not come formally before the House" and although it should then have gone to a preliminary inquiry by the Committee on the Judiciary, "the Speaker referred it to the Committee on Rules" (whose record is here referred to as House Testimony [HT]). In Post's view, the Speaker took a wise course: "[T]he Judiciary Committee is a judicial branch of the House. It could not gracefully dispose of such a resolution without reporting its judgment. But the Committee on Rules is a political branch which could, without any breach of judicial deportment, smother the whole proceeding if it discovered that the impetuous Mr. Hoch had gone off on a false scent. Like the nearsighted hunter of the familiar anecdote, the Speaker aimed to hit if the object were a deer, but to miss if it were a calf." Louis Post, *The Deportations Delirium* (Chicago: C. H. Kerr, 1923), 232–34. Thanks to Stephen Daniels for pressing me to clarify this point.

31. This, in a nutshell, is the recurring question in the literature regarding administrative power: Lucy Salyer parses it by way of a quotation from attorney Max Kohler, who criticized the Bureau of Immigration's exercises of administrative power under Ellis Island Immigration Commissioner William Williams (1911): "The discretion wielded by men like Williams to interpret law turned immigration officials from 'law-enforcers' into 'self-constituted law-maker[s].'" *Laws Harsh*, 154.

32. Even such "unfriendly" witnesses as the *Spokesman-Review* (a newspaper so characterized by Post) were entirely persuaded by this clarification. Post, *Delirium*.

33. Note how Post here meets Hoover on his own ground, vying with him for the right to be called the truest American and casting his opponents' violations of proceduralism as un-American. Post found support in this from the rhetoric of District Court Judge George W. Anderson, who reviewed Justice Department activities in hearing *Colyer v. Skeffington* 265 F. 17 (1920) and said: "Talk about Americanization! What we need is to Americanize people that are carrying out such proceedings as this. We shall forget everything we ever learned about American Constitutional liberty if we are to undertake to justify such a proceeding as this." Quoted in Salyer, *Laws Harsh*, 238.

Note too Post's key phrase above—"on an administrative process warrant, a mere police warrant until it gets to the Secretary of Labor." Post signals here his determination to divide the role of accuser from judge in deportation cases. He was very aware that a "police mentality" "develops in institutions such as the Immigration

Bureau, in which those who issue the warrants are the very same people as those who ultimately decide the cases" (HT, 229 and 239 ff.). Unsurprisingly, then, and largely for these structural reasons, the whole spirit of the Bureau, he said, "was the police office spirit of keeping the alien out or putting him out without much regard to facts" (HT, 229). "Most of the men in this service that I have come into contact with are perfectly honorable and honest men and intend to be good officials" (HT, 239). And later "I am not making any imputation against the man: it is human nature—he would naturally feel that it was up to him, if he has asked for a warrant, to see that that warrant was not asked for thoughtlessly, and so as a rule he would be very apt to find that the man whose arrest he had asked for had, upon examination, turned out to be what he had supposed he was in the beginning. Consequently, a police spirit develops naturally. . . . The effect of that is to turn that inspector into a police investigator" (HT, 246). In short, the problem was structural and so was the solution: separation of investigative and decision powers.

34. Post, *Delirium*, 254, emphasis added. Notably, with the phrase "strongest reason," Post leaves room for emergency/state of exception considerations.

35. That is not the *only* issue, however. Another is the separation of powers. Post's first response to Garrett's first iteration of the question cited above lights on this: "For myself, I do not see how Congress can compel the executive department of the Government to do anything other than execute the law that it passes" (HT, 81) (i.e., presumably, Congress cannot compel the executive to implement the law in any *particular* [as Oakeshott might say] *adverbial* fashion).

36. Here Post presents himself as bound by law, though in a different sense than I point to in this essay's last section. Here Post emphasizes his own feeling that he was forced by the law of the land and the responsibilities of his office to do things he thought wrong and unwarranted. By way of protest, Post referred repeatedly to the *usefulness* of the men he was forced to deport. The criterion of usefulness is fully at odds with the more deontic norm of individual liberty to which he also appeals, but it is unsurprising, as a political and historical matter, that Post would appeal to both. On the tension between them, see Linda Zerilli, chapter 3, *Feminism and the Abyss of Freedom* (University of Chicago Press, forthcoming).

37. Interestingly, Elliot Dorff and Arthur Rosett point out, this requirement of a divided bench "is the exact opposite of the requirement in American law for a unanimous jury." *A Living Tree: The Roots and Growth of Jewish Law* (Albany: State University of New York Press, 1988), 225. I am indebted to Bob Gibb of the University of Toronto for calling this text to my attention.

38. As Dorff and Rosett point out, some of these requirements (I would say all of them) are "extensions of principles that are reasonable in a different form" (ibid., 226). Even basic inference is precluded lest it corrupt the chain of direct sense data

evidence. The testimony of witnesses who saw a man with a knife enter a room and then saw him leaving minutes later with the same knife, bloody, in his hands, is insufficient for a capital conviction. Only the most empirically indubitable sense data are acceptable and the result, of course, is that nothing that meets these evidentiary and procedural standards will ever be found in the empirical world. The rabbis knowingly defend their amendments (not of the death penalty but of death penalty judgments and the procedures whereby they are reached) as a reasonable requirement given the severity of the punishment in question, but in so doing they call attention to the indefensibility of capital punishment itself, not to any real evidentiary or procedural rigor—("*Even so, I am going to do it*"?).

39. For a useful summary of the debates among Hart, Dworkin, and others on the need of law for interpretation, see Austin Sarat and Thomas Kearns, "A Journey Through Forgetting: Toward a Jurisprudence of Violence," in *The Fate of Law*, ed. A. Sarat and T. Kearns (Ann Arbor: University of Michigan Press, 1991), 236, 247, and passim. Note that since it is the generality and breadth of law that stage the scene for the problem/solution of interpretation and technicality, generality and breadth cannot per se, *contra* William Scheuerman, serve simply as the solutions to the problem of arbitrary administrative power. "Between Radicalism and Resignation: Democratic Theory in Habermas' *Between Facts and Norms*," in *Habermas: A Critical Companion*, ed. Peter Dews (Oxford: Blackwell, 1999). Also, Scheuerman, *Between the Norm and the Exception*.

40. This is contrary to the example of the rabbis, which is unusual in this regard: they did broadcast the technicalities in advance. That is because they did not do case law, per se, they debated matters of interpretation apart from particular cases, using hypotheticals, mostly unlikely and fanciful ones intended precisely to stretch the law and test its capaciousness. These contrived hypotheticals are the very sort that R. M. Hare charges utilitarianism's critics (such as Bernard Williams) with using deliberately and unfairly to discredit that moral and political theory. *Moral Thinking* (New York: Oxford University Press, 1981), 19.

41. On the various requirements of the rule of law, see Lon Fuller, *The Morality of Law* (New Haven, Conn.: Yale University Press, 1969) and William Scheuerman's discussion, by way of John Locke, in *Between the Norm and the Exception*. For a recent case of the political use of technicality, see "The Way We Live Now," *New York Times Magazine*, 28 September 2003, p. 19: "Librarians Unite: Three Technically Legal Signs for Your Library" [regarding the Patriot Act]:—We're sorry! Because of national security concerns, we are unable to tell you if your Internet-surfing habits, passwords, and e-mail are being monitored by federal agents; please act appropriately.—The F.B.I. has not been here. (Watch very closely for the removal of this sign).—Q. How can you tell when the F.B.I. has been in your library? A. You can't.

The Patriot Act makes it illegal for us to tell you if our computers are monitored; be aware!" (from www.librarian.net).

42. Thanks to Laura Beth Nielsen on this point.

43. See John Rawls, "Fair Equality of Opportunity and Pure Procedural Justice," in *A Theory of Justice* (Cambridge: Belknap Press of Harvard University Press, 1999), 83–90.

44. "The Supreme Court has held that Congress has turned this whole matter over to our administrative department of the Government; that the question of whether an alien shall be allowed to continue to reside in the United States is a question of sovereignty and belongs on the Executive side of the Government and not on the judicial side. Consequently the courts have refused, on writs of *habeas corpus*, to interfere with the decisions of the administrative side of the Government in these cases unless there is absolute lack of jurisdiction. Where there is no evidence at all to support the case for deportation, the courts will interfere on *habeas corpus*. But they will not review the merits of the case, because they say, it is a question of sovereignty turned over to the Executive department of the Government and they have no right to cross the line." Post, *Delirium*, 253.

45. Actually, the question *was* posed. Dorff and Rosett cite Makkot 1:10, in which the rabbis try to change the norms that surround death penalty judgments: "A court which has put a man to death once in a seven year period is called 'a hanging court.' Rabbi Elazar ben Azariah says, 'Even once in seventy years.' Rabbi Tarfon and Rabbi Akiva say, 'Were we members of the court, no person would ever be put to death.' [Playing Garret to Post's Akiva,] Rabban Simeon ben Gamliel retorted: 'If so, they would multiply the shedders of blood in Israel.'" Dorff and Rosett, *A Living Tree*, 225.

46. This response seems to have utterly turned North Carolina Congressman Edward Pou, who then suddenly expressed his admiration for Post—"I want to say, Mr. Secretary, that my feeling is that in what you have done, speaking for myself, I believe you have followed your sense of duty absolutely" (HT, 248)—and ceased his questioning which, until that point in the proceedings, had been vigorous and aggressive.

47. Candeloro, "Post: Carpetbagger," 50.

48. Leuchtenburg makes a move in this direction when he says "The election of Warren G. Harding, amiable but bumbling Republican presidential candidate in 1920, marked a desire for release from political turmoil and a chance to enjoy the pleasures of peace. . . . The 1920's, despite their chauvinism and conservatism, were hostile to the spirit of the Red Scare; the decade was one when interest in politics was at its lowest ebb in half a century, and Palmer was defeated less by liberal opponents than by the hedonism of the age." Leuchtenburg, *Perils*, 81.

49. Since the Sacco and Vanzetti case was just months away and their execution a full seven years later, this statement of mine risks appearing at best Panglossian. I

don't mean, however, to imply that with Post the forces of democratic good triumphed over evil, merely to say that a lot rides on how we render these moments in American history and to call attention to the anti-political scripts that govern our reception of these events now. Did Americans abandon Palmer because they preferred to party? Or because they were disgusted by his methods? Or both?

50. *The Deportations Delirium* is the title of the book Post wrote about his role in the events recounted here.

51. Though it was thought and actually hoped that Hoover, who replaced the corrupt Billy Burns, would, as one reporter put it, ""forget the teachings of Mr. Palmer under the more intelligent leadership of Mr. Stone [who had fought Palmer's crusade and was the new attorney general charged with cleaning up government after the Teapot Dome scandal]. It would be worth a great deal to the American people to be assured that the Department of Justice is what the name signifies and not the Department of Hysteria and Intolerance." Powers, *Secrecy and Power*, 146. In short, it was hoped, ironically, that Hoover would prove to be more Post than Palmer. This must have irked Hoover who lost every direct public battle he had with Post. One of Hoover's responses was to save a nine-stanza poem (excerpted below) about Post in a scrapbook along with a colored-in newspaper photo of Post. Says Powers, "Hoover may have been the artist, he may have been the poet." *Secrecy and Power*, 121–22.

The Bully Bolsheviki
Disrespectfully dedicated to "Comrade" Louie Post

In every city and town
To bring on Revolution
And the old USA to down

They'll soon be raising hell again
In every city and town
To bring on Revolution
And the old USA to down

. . .

And when he's lost his nice fat job
And is looking around for some work
They'll ask him to come to Russia
With the Bolsheviks he'll lurk

The poem instantiates the demonology Rogin studied. Here was Post, a Declaration of Independence radical, tarred as a Bolshevik for standing up for procedural fairness and depicted as Russian for his efforts to limit executive power in a divided government system that is supposed to be committed to such institutional (self-)

limitation. I guess Hoover saw the truth of what I am arguing here—that Post was no mere proceduralist, that he was using proceduralism and technicality as ways to pursue substantive political goals with which Hoover was very much in disagreement.

52. Salyer might see less irony here than I do. She admires Post and his actions, but of the Progressives in the 1900's, she notes.: "Even Progressives who were sympathetic to immigrants' concerns failed to endorse the proceduralist definition of the rule of law, advocating instead better personnel and more elaborate administrative review." *Laws Harsh*, xviii. In this as in most other things, Post defies our categories; he was a Progressive, but a qualified one—he championed proceduralism in a way most Progressives did not. On the other hand, Post's version of proceduralism was, as I remarked above, hardly absolute and it was administrative not judicial.

53. Candeloro, "Post: Carpetbagger," 46. Cf. 55: "Post's legal training and human sympathies allowed him to anticipate the judicial trend toward greater attention to the rights of the accused."

54. This picture of law as its own agent, with lawyers and other legal actors just along for its progressive ride, is well conveyed by the movie, *Civil Rights and Wrongs: The Fred Korematsu Story*.

55. Candeloro attributes Post's steadfast refusal to be swept up in the anti-Red hysteria to his "deep roots in the democratic radicalism of the Declaration of Independence and the Bill of Rights." "Post: Carpetbagger," 55.

56. Hence the arguments in legal and political theory about how judicial deliberation is more than mere preference-based voting. Similarly, deliberative democrats distinguish aggregative from deliberative democracy: in the former, raw preferences are added up, while in the latter, preferences are transformed and authorized to rule by a legitimating deliberative process. See Iris Young, *Inclusion and Democracy* (Oxford: Oxford University Press, 2000) on the distinction between aggregative and deliberative democracy, and arguments for the superiority of the latter.

57. Salyer, *Laws Harsh*, 57. See David Millon who concludes that all judicial interpretation, therefore, is always political. Review of *The American Revolution in the Law*, by Shannon Stimson, *Law and Social Inquiry* 18 (1993).

58. See Shapiro, *Who Guards the Guardians?*

59. Michael Oakeshott is one of the few theorists of the rule of law who owns the enforcement and policing traits of the rule of law, calling the former "postulates" of the latter in his essay, "The Rule of Law," *On History and Other Essays* (Totowa: Barnes and Noble, 1983) and in *On Human Conduct* (Oxford: Clarendon Press, 1975).

60. As I have argued elsewhere, such "taking" is a quintessential democratic practice. See Chapters 4 and 5 of *Democracy and the Foreigner* (Princeton: Princeton University Press, 2001).

61. On the differing and overlapping institutional norms of judges and adminis-

trators, see Donald Horowitz, *The Jurocracy: Government Lawyers, Agency Programs and Judicial Decisions* (Lexington: Lexington Books, 1977).

62. Michael Rogin, "American Political Demonology: A Retrospective" in *Ronald Reagan, the Movie* (Berkeley: University of California Press, 1987). My debt to Michael Rogin's work in this essay is large. Indeed, I hope this essay can function as a response to an obituary for Rogin written by Stephen Greenblatt shortly after 9/11. Greenblatt appreciates Rogin's substantial contributions to our thinking about the role of paranoia in American politics, but then adds: "I want, with an urgency I have never felt before, to phone Mike Rogin. I want to know what he makes of the massive intensification of the national security state. I want to know what happens to his concept of political demonology when there actually are deadly enemies, when they seem genuinely demonic, and when American boundaries have indeed been revealed to be permeable." Greenblatt, "In Memory of Michael Rogin," *London Review of Books* 3 January 2002. With this, Greenblatt undermines what I take to be Rogin's most important insight: demonology has little to do with the reality (or not) of one's enemies. Although the term *demonology* seems to suggest that one's enemies are the products of a popular or cultural imagination, the exteriorized reflections of some internal disorder, phantoms cast out and then disavowed, this need not be the case. One's enemies can be real and external and one can still demonize them, or not; one can make one's real enemy stand for a range of things that are opposed to one's idealized self-image, or not. Demonology has to do with how one experiences enmity, how one lives it, how one's politics are branded or warped by it. Demonology involves projecting all that we fear onto an other and representing ourselves as pure of any such demonic traits, even as we exhibit behavior startlingly like that of our foe (which we justify by saying we have to counter their subversion using their weapons or lose). In short, just because someone is really out to get you does not mean you are not paranoid; and just because our enemy is really real does not mean we have not also demonized our foe. Perhaps the best way to answer Greenblatt's question and to gain some perspective on our own particular challenges is to recall the lived reality of earlier enmities, which Rogin called demonological or counter-subversive not because they were false (they were not) but because of how they were lived. This is one of my aims in writing about Post here.

63. Woodrow Wilson, "The Study of Administration," *Political Science Quarterly* 56 (December 1941): 486. Recall that Judge George Anderson's inspiring indictment of the Justice Department also played the foreignness card in this way—see n. 33 above.

64. See Sheldon Wolin, *Politics and Vision* (Boston: Little Brown, 1960), for a democratic perspective on bureaucracy's ills and also for an exploration of a middle way between rule of law versus rule of man, by way of Calvin's ideal magistrate. On the latter point, on which I expand elsewhere, I am indebted to Eldon Eisenach.

65. The same demonological or purifying logic is discernable in Ronald Dworkin's work as well, in which certain "decisionistic" elements of judicial procedure are excised, undone, or tamed by way of an emphasis on the ineluctable workings of norms in the practice of legal interpretation and, in Dworkin's later work, on the importance of moral rules. (Oakeshott too, his account of law's postulates notwithstanding, gives a purified account of what the rule of law is [*On History and Other Essays*, op. cit.]. Others stress the effects of the norms of the legal profession, or bemoan their ineffectiveness, for the same reasons.) Austin Sarat and Thomas Kearns note this dimension of Dworkin's arguments, rightly capturing the domesticative effect of his interpretative norms. They counter by identifying the law in its entirety with the decisionism that Dworkin seeks to excise by way of interpretative norms. Then, since law is now all decision, they charge that law, as such, is violent. "Journey through Forgetting," 247 passim. But, oddly, insofar as the intent of Sarat and Kearns is to criticize the rule of law's ideological self-presentation, they repeat the terms of that self-presentation. They repeat the rule of law's prejudice, according to which decision, or the rule of man, is as such violent. They only contest the claim that goes with that, the claim that the rule of law, by contrast, is not.

66. Although of course, regularity and predictability are no less available for capture by diverse parties than is technicality. For example: John Ashcroft's defenders say that it is on behalf of regularity and predictability—uniformity—that he issued in September 2003 a directive limiting the use of plea bargains in federal prosecutions. The directive requires federal prosecutors to charge defendants with "the most serious, readily provable offense" in every case and, with some exceptions, not to engage in plea negotiations thereafter. Reactions to the new directive replay the binaries studied here: According to William W. Mercer, an attorney in Montana, fairness is precisely what the directive should achieve. "It's meant to minimize unwarranted sentencing disparities among similarly situated defendants." But one man's fairness is another's efficiency. For Alan Vinegrad, a former United States attorney in Brooklyn, the change represents a philosophical shift from "a focus on justice [to] more of a focus on efficiency." In the space between directive and implementation lies discretion: "if history is any guide," the *New York Times* reports, "local prosecutors will retain substantial flexibility but will exercise it quietly and early, before rather than after charges are filed." In other words, every directive, like every law, has its nuances and technicalities, available for exploitation by law's users. Adam Liptak and Eric Lichtblau, "New Plea Bargain Limits Could Swamp Courts, Experts Say," *New York Times*, 24 September 2003.

67. *Ronald Reagan, the Movie*, p. 73.

At the Mercy Of

ADAM SITZE

In *Homo Sacer I: Sovereign Power and Naked Life,* Giorgio Agamben takes up Carl Schmitt's argument that the conditions of possibility for juridical order can be understood by examining the sovereign power to declare a "state of exception."[1] In the exception, the same sovereign who has "the legal power to suspend the validity of the law, legally places himself outside the law."[2] Sovereign power, which is at once inside and outside of juridical order, thus marks a definitive limit of law.[3] If, as Hegel argues, "a thing is what it is, only in and by reason of its limit," and if, as Hegel goes on to suggest, the limit of a thing is also the hinge through which it both *is* and *is not,* then to think at the limit of law will necessarily require us to think through law as it manifests itself in the moment of its negation, which is to say, its preservation through cancellation.[4] It thus makes sense that Agamben would take as the point of departure for his writings on law the example of the sovereign exception Schmitt himself seems to emphasize most: the sovereign's legal suspension of law in the declaration of a state of emergency.[5] But while the relevance of this example can be amply supported by Schmitt's texts and their immediate political conditions, to understand Schmitt's theory of exception solely through the state of emergency is to risk obscuring a more counterintuitive example of the same. Consider that, in *Political Theology,* Schmitt mentions the power to grant pardons and amnesties as an instance of the "'omnipotence' of the modern lawgiver," and that, more recently, Jacques Derrida has argued that forgiveness operates precisely as a sovereign exception.[6] What understanding of law would we receive by thinking its limit through this set of examples, rather than through the example of the state of emergency? Would we be obliged to include the institutionalized iterations of forgiveness (grace, pardon, and amnesty) among the powers by which, as Agamben would put it, sovereign power can abandon naked life?[7] If so, how then would we make sense of what seems to be the relative occlusion or submersion of these iterations in Agamben's own thought? If the powers of pardon and amnesty can, on Schmitt's own terms, exemplify the sovereign exception, yet if Agamben's inquiry forecloses on this exemplarity by pre-supposing a near synonymy between state of exception and state of emergency, then won't Agamben in effect spare pardon and amnesty from his otherwise complete break with every form of unlimited, undivided sovereign power? If so, wouldn't Agamben's inquiry then exercise something like the same sovereign power it absolves from dissolution? But supposing this were the case, what would be the point of calling attention to the implication of Agamben's thought in the suspension of law it attempts to understand? Since, as Hannah Arendt writes, forgiveness is neither thought's condition nor its consequence,[8] it is all the more strange that Agamben would seem to grant the sovereign right of grace immunity from his struggle to release life from the sovereign ban. The possibility that Agamben's own inquiry gives it-self over to the very sovereign power from which it attempts to find a way out would then oblige us to take even more seriously Agamben's warning that the sovereign ban is not merely one among many new objects for the philosophy of law, but a potential that is constitutive of philosophy itself—one that, as Arendt might put it, we should at once acknowledge and escape, comprehend and resist.

Constituting Power

To enter into these questions, I turn to a reading of Søren Kierkegaard's 1849 *The Sickness Unto Death: A Christian Psychological Exposition for Up-building and Awakening*, a text written under the pseudonym "Anti-Climacus." I read this text not as a work of existentialism, but as one of the primary yet occluded points of reference in relation to which Schmitt formulated his theorems of juridical-political decisionism.[9] Approached from this angle, the central question posed by *The Sickness Unto Death* is not the aesthetic, psychological, or theological problem of the inward person whose persistence in silent concealment from the ethical is either demonic or di-

vine.[10] It is instead the specifically juridical-political problem Agamben
touches upon in the opening sections of *Homo Sacer I* under the heading of
"constituting power."

The concept of constituting power, introduced by Emmanuel-Joseph
Sieyès in 1789, refers, in a textbook sense, to power "situated outside the
State; it owes nothing to the State, it exists without it, it is the spring whose
current no use can ever exhaust."[11] In some instances, it can be "identified
with the constituting will of the people or nation."[12] True to its origins, constituting power thus belongs to a "democratico-revolutionary tradition"
which, Agamben notes, "wants to maintain constituting power in its sovereign transcendence to every constituted order."[13] In this, Agamben argues,
"constituting power" may be distinguished from "constituted power" in the
same way Walter Benjamin distinguishes "law-creating violence" from "law-
preserving violence."[14] Like the latter, constituted powers "exist only in the
State: inseparable from a pre-established constitutional order, they need the
State frame, whose reality they manifest."[15] One of the defining features of
contemporary politics, Agamben claims, is that constituting power is caught
in a bind.[16] Because there is no constituting power that does not implicitly or
explicitly aim at its completion in the law-preserving violence of a constituted power, and because constituted power internally excludes constituting
power within its framework in the form of an infinitely revisable constitution, it is difficult to find a solid theoretical basis for the distinction between
constituting and constituted power.[17] Antonio Negri argues that this theoretical difficulty is a patently political problem, since revolutionary transformation of an unjust social order will remain unthinkable without the
ability to think constituting power on its own terms, independently from the
state that implicitly or explicitly enframes it. But Agamben suggests that the
problem has a deeper root. The really difficult question is not whether some
ostensibly uncontaminated preexisting source of "good" constituting power
has been suppressed or polluted by the "bad" constituted power of the state.
Rather, Agamben argues, the problem is that constituting and constituted
power become indiscernible at the same limit that defines the relation between the inside and the outside of juridical order. The indistinct status of
this threshold opens up a space at once constitutive of law (because it calls
law into being) and exterior to it (because it is both prior to and other than

law).[18] Constituting power is able to pass seamlessly into unlimited, undivided sovereign power because its position at the constitutive limit of juridical-political order enables it both to join and to separate constituting and constituted power.[19] The pressing problem is not, then, that constituting power is suppressed by constituted power, but that sovereign power can administer the articulation of one to the other from a position that is simultaneously interior and exterior to both. Sovereign power here amounts to the negative in a Hegelian sense.

To begin thinking through a constituting power free not from constituted but from sovereign power, Agamben argues, is to cease thinking of constituting power as a merely political concept, and to think of it instead as a more primary problem of ontology, namely, as a problem of potentiality. Agamben understands "potentiality" not in the Hegelian sense (where everything potential, implicit, or *Ansich* develops naturally and by necessity into the actual, explicit, or *Fürsich*), but in a strict Aristotelian sense, where "potentiality," taken on its own terms, is always also a "potentiality to not (do or be)."[20] To "affirm the autonomous existence of potentiality" is to think through a "potentiality that can not pass over into actuality."[21] This approach illuminates the problem of constituting power, Agamben argues, because it shows how constituting power finds itself able to found a new political-legal order. Only by understanding potentiality as a potentiality to not-be can we understand how constituting power can constitute itself in a sovereign manner—"which is to say," Agamben adds, "without anything preceding or determining it (*superiorem non recognoscens*) other than its own ability not to be."[22] From this angle, it becomes clear that "an act is sovereign when it realizes itself by simply taking away its own potentiality not to be, letting itself be, giving itself to itself."[23] The "potentiality not to," Agamben argues, is thus "the ontological root of every political power."[24]

It is this root that I want to rethink by rereading *The Sickness Unto Death*. The resolutely past tense of the text's opening argument—that the self must be ground*ed* transparently in the power that establish*ed* it—positions it as a thesis concerned with the sovereign conversion of constituting into constituted power.[25] The fact that Anti-Climacus will arrive at this thesis by considering the ontological mode of a "potential not to be" only further situates the text within the unusual dialectic of potentiality and im-potentiality that, for

Agamben, defines constituting power itself. But the most basic reason that *The Sickness Unto Death* should be read alongside *Political Theology* and *Homo Sacer I* is that its distinction between forgiveness and amnesty grounds an opposition to the very idea of constituting power, and does so in the same passages where it argues *against* the undoing of the problem that Agamben, in *Homo Sacer I*, calls a "knot."[26] Anti-Climacus's attempt to administer the relation between constituting and constituted power hinges on an iteration of forgiveness as an irreducibly undemocratic power.

Climacus or Anti-Climacus?

The passages of *The Sickness Unto Death* where these arguments appear consist of a set of extremely sharp dialectical turns that each pivot on the concept of "relation." Kierkegaard's approach to the concept is derived from his opposition to the account of relation that dominated nineteenth-century Danish Hegelianism.[27] For Hegel, a self only grasps its being if it grasps itself as Spirit, where Spirit is understood as a self-alienating synthesis of antithetical terms.[28] In Hegel's dialectic, the self posits itself by negating or superseding the relation between terms such as the infinite and the finite, the temporal and the eternal, freedom and necessity, and actuality and possibility. Hegel conceives relation as mediation, and mediation as the movement of the negative; for Hegel, relations appear in order eventually to disappear.[29] Kierkegaard departs from this dialectic by arguing that the true being of the self exists not in a relation between two (where the self posits itself through the negation of relation as mediation), but in a movement of relation without negativity, which is to say, in the movement of a third that emerges and subsists in between the opposed terms of the Hegelian dialectic.[30] Self-reflection, in this view, is not *the negation* of relation, but *the positive movement* that takes place in the self-relation of relation itself. Only when a relation relates itself to itself positively *as* a relation, rather than as self-negating mediation, can a relation posit the self.[31]

With this intervention, Kierkegaard reveals a paradox that the Hegelian dialectic refuses to confront. If the self *itself* posits the relation that, relating itself to itself, *is* the self, that relation cannot truly count as a third, since it would merely be the act of the self *by itself*. But if that relation is posited *by another*, then the relation that is the self will not derive from the self. If the self *itself* posits the third, the third is not a third; but if the third is posited *by another*, the self is not itself.

For Kierkegaard, this paradox bears witness to the kind of relation that the self is. It attests not to the unity of self and other in the negative's alienation of the self from itself (as Hegel's phenomenology attempts to do), but to the unity of the self with the infinite or unlimited power that posited the self in the first place.[32] Since sin is not the kind of negativity the self can negate by itself, in and through its own essential negativity, the self's attempts to grasp sin through self-dirempting Spirit will remain an insufficient basis for self-knowledge. Only by giving in to one's establishment by infinite or unlimited power, and by finding oneself grounded transparently in this power, can one truly know thyself.

What Kierkegaard calls "despair" (a.k.a. the sickness unto death) is the refusal to find oneself grounded in this power.[33] For the Christian, who, unlike the pagan and the natural man, does not fear death but finds hope in death, despair is a fate worse than death.[34] Despair is the death in life that follows from a failure to grasp the life in death, where "life in death" consists of the unlimited and infinite possibilities that define the being of the Christian God. Because there is no way to grasp this life in death except by actually dying to the world, Kierkegaard defines despair in a strict sense as *the inability to die*.[35] Despair is the condition of living death that emerges when one wants to die to the world (and thereby gain eternal life) but cannot. It is the impotence [*afmægtig*] of the self to will itself to die to the world.

The cure for despair—which, in the simplest terms, is to die to the world—gains its potency only when the self can find itself grounded in the power that constituted it.[36] That power is the infinite and unlimited possibility of God. "The formula that describes the state of the self when despair is completely rooted out is this: in relating itself to itself and in willing to be itself, the self is grounded transparently [*grunder Selvet gjennemsigtigt*] in the power [*Magt*] that established [*satte*] it."[37] Despair thus poses an interesting ontological problem. Its potency does not follow the usual rule that governs relations between the modes of "actuality" and "possibility." In the Megarian account of entelechy, "actuality" is superior to "possibility"; no potentiality can exist that does not also lead to and exhaust itself in an act.[38] In the case of

despair, however, the actuality of despair is not at all superior to the possibility of despair. On the contrary, Kierkegaard argues, the highest ontological
category in the case of despair is "not to be in despair." What would it mean
"not to be in despair"? If it were even possible to achieve such a state, it
would mean negating, at every instant, the ever-present potential to be in despair. In the case of despair, then, the highest ontological category is not the
actualization of the potential to be in despair (to actually *be* in despair) but
the potential *not to be* in despair. The highest ontological category in the case
of despair is, in a word, im-potentiality.

But this poses a problem. How can the self achieve the impotentiality of
despair? If the self *itself* accomplishes this impotence, it will not have
achieved impotence, since it will have actually accomplished something,
even if what it has accomplished is its own impotence. The self cannot
therefore accomplish despair's impotence—it cannot not be in despair—by
itself. It is impotent to achieve its own impotence. Because, for Kierkegaard,
the self exists in a state of potentiality [κατὰ δύναμιν], the self's attempts to
draw on its own powers to achieve despair's impotence only reproduce its
own potentialities, and thus achieve the exact opposite of despair's impotence: despair's "potentiation" [*Potentsation*]. These "potentiations," Anti-
Climacus writes, are predicated on the error of grasping despair's movements
according to the "laws of motion."[39] Even if something like a "gravity of sins"
does exist, as Anselm suggests, such gravity will nevertheless remain unintelligible in terms of Newtonian physics.[40] But it is in exactly these terms that
the despairing self grasps its relation to itself when it conceives that relation
in Hegelian terms.[41] The self that attempts to derive itself from itself without
presupposition can only do so by attempting to negate sin—that is, by emptying sin of its *gravitas*, or, in Anti-Climacus's metaphor, by unloading the
ballast of sin from the balloon of the self. But sin is not the kind of negative
that can be sublated—raised to a higher level—through negation. The paradox of sin, according to Anti-Climacus, is that by emptying sin of its *gravitas*,
the self actually prevents its own ascent. The self's acts of impotence are, as
acts, by definition contradictory: its attempts to achieve impotentiality by
negating its own potentiality only intensify its despair and hasten its descent.

We can thus understand why Kierkegaard chose to publish *The Sickness
Unto Death* under the pseudonym "Anti-Climacus." Kierkegaard's pseudo-

nyms are not *noms de plume* but *personas* that name the mode of poetic production of the text to which they are attached.[42] *Climax* (or "ladder") refers to a rhetorical figure where mounting propositions form a series in which each rises above the preceding in force or effectiveness.[43] When he published his 1844 *Philosophical Fragments* under the pseudonym "Johannes Climacus" (a sixth-century monk who authored a text called *Ladder of Paradise*), Kierkegaard signed the text with the name of the rhetorical figure that governs its logic. Climacus's *Fragments* shows how the strongest postulate of Christian transcendence—the idea that God descended to earth in the form of a man, and guaranteed man's salvation through his own self-sacrifice—carries with it the potential to plot its own downfall. The concept of "incarnation" brings God and humanity into a proximity capable of abolishing their qualitative difference. The name Kierkegaard gives to Climacus's error is "monism" or "immanentism."[44] As developed by theologians like Anselm and philosophers like Descartes and Spinoza, this error amounts to the related postulates that God's nature is not distinct from the natural world; that God's omnipotence is immanent to the substance of the world itself; that God's omniscience is comprehensible through the laws of reason and as the reason of laws; that humanity is capable of its own absolution; and that, as a result, humanity is capable of being the source of its own sovereignty.

Anti-Climacus opposes Christianity's potential for immanentism not only by prioritizing descent over ascent, but also through a peculiar rhetorical device: the merciless categorization of despair into genres and species. This categorization is neither proto-psychological nor positivist. *Categoria* (or "accusation") has the rhetorical effect of "reproaching a person with his wickedness to his face."[45] The function of categorization in *The Sickness Unto Death* is precisely this: to force the reader to recognize him- or herself in one of the many categories of despair, up to and including the aspiration to absolve oneself of despair, such that the reader realizes that there is no escape from despair except to dwell transparently in the power that constituted the self. Thus, when a man takes offense at the idea that his sin can be forgiven, when he arrogates to himself the power to absolve or negate his own sins, Anti-Climacus will say that he finds himself in the genre of despair called "defiance." The specificity of this genre, Anti-Climacus continues, is that the defiant man's attempt to absolve himself does nothing more than actualize a potential posited by Christianity itself. He rages against the power to which he owes the realization of his own impotence.[46] Anti-Climacus's mercilessly deductive categories form neither a syllogism nor a taxonomy. They are an indictment and a trap. The dialectic they set into motion is designed to leave the reader no choice but to descend to what Kierkegaard calls the "absolute decision."[47]

Taken as a single dialectic, Kierkegaard's opposition of Anti-Climacus to Climacus carries implications that pass beyond the order of the theological. Ernst Kantorowicz has shown how the antithesis between grace and nature allowed medieval theorists of sovereignty to argue that a king could be both immortal and mortal, without his mortality yet reducing him to the same plane as his subjects or his immortality rendering him sacrilegiously equivalent to God. When God "leapt" into the king at his anointment and consecration, grace conferred upon him the divine *potestas* that, by nature, belongs to God alone.[48] Through the maxim *deus per naturam, deus per gratiam*, which, according to Kantorowicz, foreshadowed the mystic fiction of the King's Two Bodies, the king could thus resemble both God and man while also remaining above the latter and below the former.[49] In the process, the concept of grace—which could just as easily be interpreted, on the model of a kind of Eucharist, to confer upon every vessel of the Spirit the sovereign capacity to judge all while being judged by none—was instead reduced to a prerogative of exclusively royal and priestly institutions.[50] At stake in the dialectic of Climacus and Anti-Climacus is the scope and meaning of political theology itself.

What Is an *Auctor*?

The Kierkegaardian pseudonym, a cipher for the *poesis* of the text to which it is assigned, is also the trace of a text written at the limit of law. The pseudonym permits Kierkegaard to accept as an empty formality his legal culpability as an author, but only in order to then be able to more completely separate that culpability from the substance of what he takes to be his religious responsibility.[51] When Kierkegaard claims to "speak without authority," as he often does, he should then be understood to be refusing the modern concept of authorship in order to restore the danger of writing under the sign of the sacred and the profane.[52] Kierkegaard's pseudonyms draw on naming power in order to do away with names, especially that name which mediates life and writing through the institution of property-based authorship. The pseudonyms announce writing that abandons its relation to law in order to rest transparently in the power that constituted it.

In his 1933 text *Kierkegaard: Construction of the Aesthetic*, Theodor Adorno argues that the kernel of truth in Kierkegaard's pseudonyms can be discerned only by reading those pseudonyms both against the conceit of Kierkegaard's claim to poetry and against Kierkegaard's own unique style of exegesis. Adorno suggests that the mythical—untrue—content of Kierkegaard's texts can only be disclosed by treating his metaphors so literally that those metaphors gain autonomy from the texts they ostensibly only embroider.[53] Adorno's approach holds true for Kierkegaard's relation to Schmitt as well. If Schmitt could cite Kierkegaard's theological passion narratives in support of his theory of political sovereignty, it is not simply because of the way Schmitt torqued Kierkegaardian concepts (exception, concrete situation, occasion, decision, etc.).[54] It is also because an integral part of the intelligibility of Kierkegaard's own text already derives from its analogies to specifically juridical-political problems.[55] These analogies, which amount to a royalist attack on the possibility of establishing a democratic constitution, embed in Kierkegaard's text in advance the possibility of a reading like Schmitt's. By taking these analogies as the most literal expression of the pseudonym Anti-Climacus, we can see that, despite diverging from *The Sickness Unto Death* thematically, *Political Theology* nevertheless subscribes to the problematic it introduces. The question that the latter, like the former, poses for itself (or, rather, that is posed to each in and through its sociogenesis) is how to restore to the sovereign the constituting power usurped from it by the monist, immanentist multitude.[56] In response to this question, which was forced to the fore by the events of 1848, Schmitt comes up with much the same solution as Kierkegaard: decisionism *over and above* the multitude becomes necessary under political conditions that render judgment *within* the multitude impossible.

In Schmitt's work, this response emerges most clearly in the concluding pages of his 1919 text *Political Romanticism*. At the close of a study which opens by scorning the naïveté of anarchists and humanitarians who deny original sin and thereby secularize God into a "genial subject," Schmitt argues that the political romantic's unending stream of aesthetic value judg-

ments amount to an "inability to decide"—"a way out of the either-or"—
that, in the concrete, both implicitly calls for and explicitly correlates with
the most unromantic decisionism.[57] To read Schmitt on his own terms is to
recognize in this argument the genesis of his 1923 critique of parliamentary
democracy, where Schmitt argues that the paralysis caused by liberalism's
unending, open discussions prepares the way for dictatorial decisionism.[58]
But to read Schmitt alongside Kierkegaard is to find in this argument a repetition of the two modes of *either-or* set forth in the two volumes of Kierkegaard's 1843 *Either/Or*, the very form of which duplicates the relations of
mutual exclusivity revealed by its content. In volume I, Kierkegaard's pseu-
donymous "A" praises the pleasures offered by the disinterested *either-or* of
aesthetic judgment (where a certain formalism, indifferent to its object, lets
anything go: "either this one or that one will be good, so long as it is beautiful"), while in volume II, Judge Wilhelm clarifies the necessity of understanding the *either-or* of judgment in its decisive, ethical, mutually exclusive
sense (where its only interest is to deliver a verdict: *either* guilt *or* innocence).[59] In *Political Romanticism*, as in *Political Theology*, Schmitt develops
his jurisprudence by augmenting arguments already outlined by one or another of Kierkegaard's conceptual personas. *Political Romanticism* finds its
voice by resuming Judge Wilhelm's, while *Political Theology* takes up the
cause of Anti-Climacus. Schmitt's thesis that "all significant concepts of the
modern theory of the state are secularized theological concepts" thus hides
its intellectual debt in plain sight.[60] Far from springing fully formed from
Schmitt's forehead, it converts into political ontology Schmitt's confusion
over his own status as *auctor*. Schmitt's theory of the political, which reduces
the latter's very existence to a decision on the friend-enemy distinction, is
built from powers invented by Kierkegaard. Before it was possible for a sovereign decision to constitute the reality of the political, it was first necessary
to presuppose, in Adorno's words, "the prerogative of thought, as its own
law, to found reality."[61]

Democracy and the Unforgivable

We can trace Schmitt's artifice in more detail by returning to Kierkegaard's account of the impossibility of a democratic constitution, which

takes place in Section B(b) of Part Two of *The Sickness Unto Death*. Kierkegaard offers that opposition in the form of an extended analogy between theological and political powers. The objective of the analogy is to define "defiance." "Defiance," in Kierkegaard's categorization, is "not to will to be oneself."[62] Since the self is, for Kierkegaard, defined as a sinner, the "defiance" of not willing to be oneself consists in not willing to be a sinner. Defiance commences with the sinner's decision to absolve the self of sin oneself.[63] Yet because the self is in a state of sin, the self that absolves itself of sin by drawing on its own powers will merely intensify the very sin it seeks to absolve. The self that absolves itself thus saves itself from disgrace and disintegration only in the most paradoxical manner. It adds consistency to itself by sinning more consistently. It fabricates or forges the consistency of substance through the sheer strength [*Kraft*] of consciousness. In this attempt at absolute knowledge, the self decides that sin is an accidental, not necessary, part of itself: that, in short, the self can forgive itself. But by positing this possibility itself, the self appropriates for itself a power that, in the strict sense, can only be given by God. Instead of giving itself up directly before God as a sinner, which would involve surrendering itself to God's mercy or forgiveness, the defiant self decides to absolve itself even of the very idea of forgiveness. The "potentiation" of sin is "an effort to give stability and interest to sin as a power by deciding once and for all that one will refuse to hear anything about repentance and grace."[64] "Defiance" is being "in despair to will to be oneself—a sinner—in such a way that there is no forgiveness."[65]

The paradox of defiance, as we have seen, is that the sinner's attempt to defy God's power of forgiveness actually presupposes that same power. It is to illustrate this paradox that Kierkegaard turns to an analogy between defiance and the political. "Just as one becomes self-important in politics by belonging to the opposition and eventually comes to prefer to have an administration just to have something to oppose, so also there is eventually a reluctance to do away with God—just to become even more self-important by being the opposition."[66] Defiance is so attached to its own abstract capacity to oppose that its opposition not only presupposes but also begins to posit the position it opposes. Its utter rejection of Christianity reproduces a Christian substrate. This is why Kierkegaard classifies defiance as a specifically Christian sin.[67] Like all of the other modes of despair, its very possibility is predicated on Christ's claim to forgiveness: because defiance would not exist without that claim, defiance is impossible without Christ. Even the possibility of opposing forgiveness is thus opened up by Christianity itself, and is a possibility that falls under or belongs to the provenance of Christianity.

Anti-Climacus returns to this political analogy when he attacks the doctrine of immanentism and monism. The main thrust of his opposition derives from the argument that grace [*Naaden*] can only be a movement from God to man, not a movement from man to God. This essentially Pauline argument, which doubles as a prescription for the cure of the "potentiation" of despair, culminates in a paradox Sylviane Agacinski, in a formulation to which I will return, articulates nicely: "one can obtain grace only by not seeking to obtain it."[68] The only way for the concept of incarnation to be grasped, without also inciting the brazen defiance of a humanity that decides to absolve itself, is for the concept of the incarnation to be counterbalanced with the concept of atonement, which permits oneness with God only on condition that the sinner first ask forgiveness for his originary sin.

Anti-Climacus's turn to atonement to attack immanentism pivots on an argument about the concept of individual sin. Without the concept of individual sin, both judgment and forgiveness become impossible.[69] Yet without the concept of forgiveness, Christianity would dissolve into the immanentism incited by the doctrine of incarnation; it would in effect cease to exist. Anti-Climacus's attack on immanentism thus requires an argument against whatever forms of political community would dissolve the category of the individual, and with it the possibility for judgment, sin, and forgiveness. To name these communities, Anti-Climacus invokes the form of life Aristotle, in the *Politics*, calls *zoe*. "If men are first permitted to run together in what Aristotle calls the animal category [*Dyre-Bestemmelsen*]—the multitude [*Mængden*]—then this abstraction, instead of being less than nothing, even less than the most insignificant individual human being, comes to be regarded as something—then it does not take long before this abstraction becomes God."[70] In the passage of the *Politics* to which Anti-Climacus refers, Aristotle discusses the principle of democracy, namely, "the principle that the multitude ought to be supreme."[71] Anti-Climacus's conflation of the "animal category" with the concept of the "multitude" reminds us that Aristotle's discussion of the "political animal" draws upon two distinct terms for life. Though these terms are, as Agamben writes, "traceable to a common etymological root," they are also "semantically and morphologically distinct: *zoe*, which expressed the simple fact of living common to all living beings (animals, men, or gods), and *bios*, which indicated the form or way of living proper to an individual or a group."[72] Anti-Climacus's interest in the category of *zoe* is transparent: it helps him clarify the absurdity that follows logically from an immanentism like Spinoza's. If the essence of God is permitted to pass into existence without paradox or difficulty (as it does, Kierkegaard argues, in Spinoza's philosophy), one cannot deny that "a fly, when it is, has just as much being as the god."[73] The absurd conclusion of immanentism, in other words, is an inability to distinguish between limited animal life and divine power, knowledge, and being. Only by taking immanentism to this extreme does the absurdity of the thesis of the "God-man" become apparent.

> And then, *philosophice* [philosophically speaking], the doctrine of the God-man becomes correct. Then, just as we have learned that in governments the masses intimidate the king and the newspapers intimidate the cabinet ministers, so we have finally discovered that the *summa summarum* [sum total] of all men intimidates God. This is then called the doctrine of the God-man, or that God and man are *idem per idem* [the same].[74]

If the possibility of "offense" or defiance is posited by Christianity itself, Anti-Climacus suggests, it is because the doctrine of the incarnation obscures the inordinate concession by which God made himself man. Once one forgets this concession, all spheres of existence collapse into disorder. Democracy exemplifies this collapse. Anti-Climacus continues with his analogy by suggesting that

> [t]he doctrine of the God-man has made Christendom brazen. It almost seems as if God were too weak. It seems as if the same thing happened to him as happens to the good-natured person who makes too great concessions and then is repaid with ingratitude. It is God who devised the teaching about the God-man, and now Christendom has brazenly turned it around and foists kinship on God, so that the concession that God has made means practically what it means this days when a king grants a freer constitution [*friere forfating*]—and we certainly know what that means: "he was forced to do it."[75]

The "concession" Anti-Climacus mentions in this political analogy is perhaps less a reference to the famous revolutions of 1848 (which would only reach Denmark in March 1849, when Danish citizens successfully petitioned King Frederik VII for a democratic constitution) than an evocation of the papal amnesty that preceded the Italian revolution in particular (about which more in a moment). Yet however much the political analogies in *The Sickness Unto Death*, written in 1848, bear traces of that year's events, Anti-Climacus's attack on democratic rule cannot be limited to those events alone.[76] Anti-Climacus's political analogy is rather an opposition to the event of democracy itself. It implies the more general thesis that democratic constitutions are not won by a people through revolution (as the Greek *kratos* ["supremacy" or "victory"] would imply), but are merely given to a people when the royalty gives up its sovereignty. As such, Anti-Climacus's opposition extends just as much to the 1789 Declaration of the Rights of Man and Citizen—to the very emergence of the idea of human rights—as it does to the end of the epoch of royalism and the advent of the principle of democratic legitimacy. To recollect the origins of popular sovereignty in the king's gift and to put the multitude back in its place, Anti-Climacus will emphasize that a concept of individuality follows logically from the dogmatic teaching on sin.

> The teaching about the sin of the race has often been misused, because it has not been realized that sin, however common it is to all, does not gather men together in a common idea, into an association, into a partnership ("no more than the multitude of the dead out in the cemetery form some kind of society"); instead, it splits men up into single individuals and holds each individual fast as a sinner, a splitting up that in another sense is both harmonized with and teleologically oriented to the perfection of existence.[77]

But sin is only the necessary condition for the specifically Christian doctrine of atonement. The sufficient condition of that doctrine is the forgiveness of sins. The qualitative differences between man and God disregarded by immanentism can be reinstated only through an emphasis on the concept of forgiveness. The forgiveness of sins is the power the multitude can never appropriate as its own. It thus provides Anti-Climacus with the basis for a uniquely Christian opposition to the multitude's demand for a freer constitution.

> By means of the teaching about sin and particular sins, God and Christ, quite unlike any kings, have protected themselves once and for all against the nation, the people, the crowd, the public, etc. and also against every demand for a freer con-

stitution [*friere forfating*]. . . . The teaching about sin—that you and I are sinners—a teaching that unconditionally splits up "the crowd," confirms the qualitative difference between God and man more radically than ever before, for again only God can do this; sin is indeed: before God. In no way is a man so different than God as in this; that he, and this means every man, is a sinner, and is that "before God."[78]

When the multitude finds itself relating to sin directly before God, its potency dissolves; it is no longer able to "intimidate" and thereby to acquire its own constitution by force. The qualitative distinction between multitude and divine power is reinstated, the right to any purely human right eliminated. We are here squarely in the domain Ernst Bloch would call "relativized natural law," where a natural law exemplified by grace is given as a gift from above to sinners trapped in fallen nature below.[79] Forgiveness enables the suppression of popular democratic sovereignty by allowing for the division and individualization of the multitude's guilt. What remains most unthinkable and impossible for immanentism, and what is therefore the decisive principle of the qualitative difference between God and man, is the capacity to forgive sins.

> As sinner, man is separated from God by the most chasmic qualitative abyss. In turn, of course, God is separated from man by the same qualitative abyss when he forgives sins. If by some kind of reverse adjustment the divine could be shifted over to the human, there is one way in which man could never in all eternity come to be like God: in forgiving sins.[80]

With this, Anti-Climacus arrives at his strongest argument. To drive it home, he will add a last word on the analogy between theological and political power. To explain the difference between the omnipotence and omniscience required for divine forgiveness, on the one hand, and the limits of law, on the other, Anti-Climacus will consider the extreme juridical-political situation that demands the provision of amnesty.

> Of course, we men have learned, and experience teaches us, that when there is a mutiny on a ship or in an army there are so many who are guilty that the punishment cannot be applied, and when it is the public, the esteemed, cultured public, or a people, then there is not only no crime, then, according to the newspapers (upon which we can depend as upon the gospel and revelation), then it is God's will. How can this be? It follows from the fact that the concept "judgment"

corresponds to the single individual; judgment is not made *en masse*. People can be put to death *en masse*, can be sprayed *en masse*, can be flattered *en masse*—in short, in many ways they can be treated as cattle, but they cannot be judged as cattle, for cattle cannot come under judgment. No matter how many are judged, if judging is to have any earnestness and truth, then each individual is judged.[81]

Given Anti-Climacus's scorn for what he earlier called the brazenness and ingratitude of the multitude, we might trace the sociogenesis of his analogy to the unusually broad amnesty on political crimes in the Papal States granted by Pope Pius IX on July 16, 1846.[82] Far from quieting the *Risorgimento* into subdued thankfulness, Pius's amnesty only spurred it on, until, in 1848, Pius was forced to concede a constitution and, in 1849, a republic.[83] Anti-Climacus's oblique reference to what he could not but have understood as Pius's error also implies a canny knowledge of the way amnesty marks a constitutive limit to the democratic rule of law. The oath and covenant of 403 B.C., which together comprise what Nicole Loraux has called the "exemplary" amnesty, relied on a basic miscount to restore democracy to Athens in the wake of its *stasis*. Loraux shows how this restoration was predicated on prosecuting only the smallest possible number from among the oligarchic party: the amnesty released from punishment all but the thirty most guilty oligarchs.[84] Here, as in *The Sickness Unto Death*, amnesty indexes the limit to law that is the innumerable itself. The multitude, by virtue of its sheer quantity, can be neither guilty nor innocent. Its errancy, guilt, or sin—its *hamartia*—simply exceeds and exhausts law's capacity to substitute judgment for truth and justice.[85] Mass guilt neutralizes the possibility for measure that is judgment's indispensable condition.

> Now when so many are guilty, it is humanly impossible to do [*gjøre*] this, therefore one has to give up [*opgiver*] the whole thing. It is obvious that there can be no judgment: there are too many to be judged; it is impossible to get hold of them or manage to get hold of them as single individuals, and therefore judging has to be given up [*opgive*].[86]

But where judgment has to be given up, so too must forgiveness be abandoned. Law can neither prosecute nor forgive mass guilt. Anti-Climacus's point is clear: the sheer quantities involved in mass guilt expose the qualitative limit distinguishing law from divine truth and justice. Where law is incapable of measuring or counting, it can judge neither guilt nor innocence.

Only an omniscient and omnipotent being would be able to count each of the individuals who together comprise the immeasurable multitude. Amnesty would therefore be what law gives when it is compelled to confront its constitutive limit. It is what law that is founded on the possibility of measure gives when, faced with the immeasurable, it must give up on judgment yet, for the sake of continuity, must remain in force anyway. Amnesty is a limit of law where law applies in no longer applying.

Indecisionism

The point of rereading *The Sickness Unto Death* is not simply to conclude that Kierkegaard was a royalist or a Christian fundamentalist *avant la lettre*.[87] Nor is it merely to confirm that Schmitt's decisionism is inseparable both from a certain tradition of mediaeval Christian political theology and from a particular reading of Kierkegaard. Rather, what we find by rereading *Political Theology* and *Homo Sacer I* alongside *The Sickness Unto Death* is that the state of emergency is neither the only nor the most illustrative example of the sovereign exception. Far from it: Anti-Climacus's analogy, which measures amnesty unfavorably against forgiveness, exposes an angle of the sovereign exception that an exclusive focus on the state of emergency ultimately only obscures. Yet what would it mean to suggest that amnesty, understood here as a democratic iteration of the divine power of forgiveness, is a more illustrative example of the state of exception than the state of emergency? On the one hand, it would imply a basic genealogical argument, namely, that Schmitt derives the problematic for his theorization of the sovereign exception from Anti-Climacus's dialectical exposition of forgiveness. When Schmitt notes that the Christian Trinity protects itself from *stasis* better than does the Greek concept of the One, he shows that he has read Anti-Climacus closely.[88] It would not be difficult to situate this argument in the history of modern political philosophy more generally, not least because of the way the right of grace has traditionally exemplified sovereignty.[89] Yet on the other hand, this same suggestion would indicate the point at which Schmitt's *own* appropriation of the concept of the exception from Kierkegaard becomes *indecisive*. In *Political Theology*, Schmitt claims that "[t]he exception in jurisprudence is analogous to the miracle [*Wunder*] in theology."[90] Strikingly, however,

Schmitt then suspends this same claim, admitting that "a detailed presentation of the meaning of the concept of the miracle in this context [namely, with reference to the limits of the modern constitutional state] will have to be left to another time."[91] This admission is more than merely neutral methodological chatter. In it, Schmitt states nothing less than his inability to carry through with the application of *Political Theology*'s own thesis. Even though he has committed himself to proving that "all significant concepts of the modern theory of the state are secularized theological concepts," Schmitt here defers the application of that thesis to *Political Theology*'s own central concept: the sovereign exception. Despite the fact that *Political Theology* presents itself as an elaboration of this single concept, it nevertheless does not— or cannot—apply its political theological thesis to that concept.[92] At the center of Schmitt's text we thus find a nonapplication of *the one rule it seeks to apply* to *the one concept it seeks to explain*.

How should we understand this nonapplication? A clue may be found in the work of Kierkegaard, to whom Schmitt turns to illustrate the concept of the exception in *Political Theology*'s opening chapter. For Kierkegaard, the miracle is an encounter with nonknowledge that precipitates the leap of faith.[93] The leap, in turn, consists of the decisiveness with which the disciple is moved from the aesthetic to the ethical sphere; in his leap, the disciple concretely becomes the exception he already was potentially in his pure, objectless inwardness.[94] Before Schmitt analogized the exception in jurisprudence to the miracle in theology, Kierkegaard had thus already posited the miracle as the precondition for the disciple's ethical decision to reveal himself as exception. Writing under the pseudonym Johannes Climacus, Kierkegaard argued in *Philosophical Fragments* that the essential content of the miracle [*Under*] is that, in it, the eternal breaks into the continuity of history, or that the "eternal condition is given in time."[95] This break precipitates the leap when it evokes anew history's potential to not-be, which subsists alongside all of history's actualized possibilities as their enabling condition.[96] To realize that a timeless potential to not-be has always already accompanied each of history's turns is also to realize that even though those turns' shape and course may now be unchangeable, they were nevertheless not at any point necessary.[97] And to release one's understanding of unchangeable deeds from the grip of necessity is, in turn, to restore the potential of time in a single decisive instant.[98] Climacus's miracle is Paul's *parousia*. Absolved of history, we enter into the fullness of time for the first time; the scales fall from our eyes. The miracle precipitates the "birth within a birth" that, according to Climacus, is faith.[99] This miracle reveals itself even and especially in Johannes Climacus's own discourse. In order for Climacus's rhetoric to be consistent with the logic of its dialectic—in order for his discourse on the miracle to express the eternal within time—Johannes Climacus, who signs the preface to his text with only his initials, must abandon any claim to be the owner and author of his discourse.[100] Instead, Climacus claims, as he must, his very discourse is a miracle.[101]

How might this indicate an indecision on Schmitt's part? On the one hand, were Schmitt to follow through with his thesis, and explain how the miracle is the theological counterpart of the exception, he would be obliged to carry through with the logic of Johannes Climacus's dialectic, and his thesis would reproduce the error Anti-Climacus attributes to Johannes Climacus: it would abolish the distance between God and man through the thesis of the contemporaneity of the eternal and the temporal. Yet as soon as the exception is understood in this manner, the thesis of an undivided sovereign power would no longer be defensible. Whereas Schmitt turns to the exception in order to formulate a jurisprudence opposed to the "immanence philosophy" that "draws God into the world and permits law and the state to emanate from the immanence of the objective," the ultimate lesson of the doctrine of the miracle is that, as Adorno puts it, "the image of man is identical with that of the 'exception.'"[102] Taken to the extreme, in other words, the doctrine of the miracle would abolish any possibility of singularizing the exception: not only would the exception define the essence of humanity per se, as Adorno argues, but anyone who followed the doctrine of the miracle to its logical conclusion would have to claim, with Johannes Climacus, that no discourse *on* the miracle could also avoid being a discourse *of* the miracle—that is to say, a discourse in which the infinite is revealed in the disciple's own language, expropriating him of his very name.

Thus, *on the other hand*, Schmitt cannot carry through with his own thesis that the exception in jurisprudence is analogous to the miracle in theology.

Despite the fact that the miracle's introduction of timelessness into time satisfies a key condition for the mystic fiction of the King's Two Bodies, and thus provides an otherwise suitable ground for a political theological doctrine of sovereignty, were Schmitt to apply his own thesis to the example of the miracle, he would not only find his own name thrown into question (along with everything the concept of name implies for Schmitt); he would also undermine the strongest point of his intervention against monism, immanentism, and the liberal democratic principle of the separation of powers. For under political conditions where every individual is already defined as an exception, it would become more difficult, though by no means impossible, to sustain the argument that there will be, in any given state, only a single, undivided power capable of deciding the exception. Complete immanence of the exception would divide, distribute, and neutralize it, turning it into the very rule against which Schmitt first sought to define it. Before the exception became the rule, as Agamben says of late modernity, the idea that individuals naturally seek to exempt themselves from law was less a counterargument to the normal rule of law than its *raison d'être*.[103] But where normal political and legal order is already understood to consist of nothing more than a set of natural exceptions, its constitutive outside could no longer be defined with reference to an exception (which would, on the contrary, remain just one among many expressions of that order's normal functioning). The exception to an entire order of exceptions could only be a general principle of equality, which would already necessarily participate implicitly in any order defined on the basis of its shared exceptionality, but which would also have to be excluded from that same order as a potential that threatens, or promises, to turn it inside out.

The miracle thus places Schmitt in an odd position. Like the Grand Inquisitor conjured by Dostoyevsky's Ivan Karamazov, Schmitt will draw on the doctrine of the miracle only insofar as it allows him to ground the immanent transcendence of the sovereign.[104] Far from thinking the miracle as a borderline concept, Schmitt will thus permit an exception to its application to the political, lest that application abolish the very indivisibility he seeks to establish by theorizing the sovereign exception in the first place. He thus withdraws his thesis from the one problem to which it was designed to apply. But even as Schmitt remains consistent with his thesis *on* the exception by making *an* exception *for* the exception, his emphasis on decision thereby re verts to indecision. Because taking Johannes Climacus's doctrine of the miracle to the extreme would mean giving up the ghost of Anti-Climacus's opposition to immanentism, Schmitt encounters in his logic the "either/or" he so liberally makes a part of his rhetoric. Rather than choose either Climacus or Anti-Climacus, on the one hand, or confront their undecidability, on the other, he relies on a pragmatic methodological directive that allows him to defer decision and undecidability alike. Faced with the theological dissolution of political sovereignty implicit in the analogy of exception to miracle, Schmitt backs off the problem altogether, settling for the security of the middle road. Compromise in theory turns out to have been necessary to justify the practice of dictatorship.

Ignoscenza

Schmitt's indecision returns in the way Agamben frames his approach to the question of sovereign exception in *Homo Sacer I*. In the text's opening pages, Agamben argues that there exists a "blind spot" or "vanishing point" in Foucault's argument regarding the individualizing and totalizing powers of the state. To begin rethinking Foucault's argument, Agamben turns to the concept of *servitude volontaire*, and inquires into the point where "the voluntary servitude of individuals comes into contact with objective power."[105] *Homo Sacer I* explicates this point of contact by tracing the threshold of individualizing and totalizing powers in the experiences of the concentration camps, refugees, Nazi medicine, and euthanasia, as well as upon works of legal, political, and philosophical thought. But by rereading *Homo Sacer I* alongside *The Sickness Unto Death*, it becomes apparent that the point of departure from which Agamben begins rereading Foucault is itself structured by a blind-spot. Agamben opens *Homo Sacer I* by joining Foucault's late 1970s studies of governmentality to Arendt's writings on concentration camps, and by rethinking Arendt's discussions of totalitarian power alongside Foucault's inquiries into biopower.[106] But in so doing, Agamben sets aside not only Foucault's vaguely Schmittian suggestion that the state's totalizing and individualizing powers are genealogically derived from techniques of "pastoral power" originally developed in Christian institutions, but also, more importantly, the discussions of spontaneity, grace, and the miracle that connect Arendt's *Origins of Totalitarianism* with her inquiry into unpredictability, forgiveness, and the miracle in *The Human Condition*.[107]

Indeed, Agamben's claim that "Arendt establishes no connection between her research in *The Human Condition* and the penetrating analyses she had previously devoted to totalitarian power" does not so much reveal an ostensible inconsistency in Arendt's thought as it does confirm Agamben's inheritance of Schmitt's inability to think through the implications of his own analogy between sovereign exception and miracle.[108] When Agamben argues, in *Homo Sacer I*, that the state's totalizing and individualizing powers touch in the sovereign exception, he turns to the example of the state of emergency to illustrate his argument.[109] But, as Agamben later argues, the very concept of the example is, in Cantorian set theory, that which so explicitly exhibits its belonging to a given set that it excludes itself from that same set: the example is not inside but beside the set it defines.[110] By this logic, the state of emergency would also have to exclude itself from the set it defines in order to serve as an example of the sovereign exception in a strict sense. No doubt this is why Agamben argues that the epoch of late modern biopolitics is characterized by the way the exception has become the rule and the state of emergency the norm. Yet if there were a truly exemplary example of the sovereign exception—an example that would exhibit its own exteriority from the set whose belonging it defines—that example would have to be an exception even to the logic implicit in its own modification of the noun "exception" by the adjective "sovereign": an example that fully exhibited or delimited the exception would have to exempt itself even from the grammar by which the general adjective subsumes the particular noun under its rule.[111] But whereas the exemplary example of the sovereign exception would thereby need to be capable of opening an exception even and especially to sovereignty itself, there is no state of emergency that does not depend for the force of its declaration and enactment on an undivided institution of sovereign power. The example of the state of emergency is thus not merely an unexceptional example of the sovereign exception; it also lodges a blind-spot in our understanding of the exception. By arresting the logic of exemplarity before it has a chance to divide the exception from the sovereignty whose paradigm it defines, the example of the state of emergency functions to preserve the idea of the indivisibility of sovereign power, which is to say, the sharpest point of Schmitt's polemic against the separation of powers in constitutional democracy.

Agamben's internal exclusion of a more exemplary example of the sovereign exception runs like an archipelago through his work. In *The Idea of Prose*, and later in *The Coming Community*, Agamben mentions mercy in his discussions of the unbaptized children who, according to Saint Thomas, could neither be afflicted with painful punishment for their sin (since its commission was not their fault and since they do not know what they lack) nor absolved of it (since they are still bearers of original sin), but only abandoned to a condition of limbo where they remain forgotten by God.[112] Agamben's interest in this condition consists in the fact that, as a form of punishment which is privative rather than afflictive, the abandonment that establishes it also paradoxically opens the possibility for a certain experience of happiness, justice, and peace. Precisely because limbo marks the withdrawal of divine justice, it gives rise to an ability to live what Agamben calls "simply human life."[113] As distinct from the despair described by Kierkegaard or the bad conscience traced by Nietzsche, the life lived in limbo is neutral in relation to the Christian economy of salvation.[114] Because that economy frames purely human potentiality as originary guilt or sin, the being who remains neutral to it also remains without relation to the fundamental substance in which law grounds its reference.[115] To live in limbo is to become capable of beatifically ignoring divine forgetfulness itself. Without being compelled to experience life as a debt owed to a power beyond life, those who live in limbo become capable of what Agamben calls "the only ethical experience," namely, being one's own possibility or potentiality.[116]

With *Homo Sacer I*, Agamben's account of abandonment undergoes a small displacement. To clarify what he understands by the term "ban," Agamben notes that "in Romance languages, to be 'banned' originally means both to be 'at the mercy of' and 'at one's own will, freely,' to be 'excluded,' and also 'open to all, free.'"[117] Abandonment here no longer describes a neutral relation either to wrath or to mercy. It is rather, as Agamben remarks in his reading of Heidegger, characterized by a certain "absolution."[118] It would then seem that being at the mercy of is a constitutive part of what it means to be banned. But how? In *Homo Sacer I*, Agamben argues that the essence of law, as ban, is to withdraw itself, to maintain itself in its own privation, and to apply in no longer applying.[119] Agamben's notion of ban thus resembles Nietzsche's definition of mercy as "the name justice [*der Gerechtigkeit*] gives to its own self-preservation through self-cancellation."[120] In Nietzsche's account, the absolution of debt or guilt through mercy [*Gnade*] also marks a threshold of irreversible subjectivation. Indebted now not merely for a calculable debt but also for the cancellation of all debts, the debtor promises to repay a debt that has become infinite. Law subjects by absolving animal life, in advance, of a *Schuld* the canceled yet preserved form of which then serves as the *a priori* substrate in which law grounds its reference.[121] Understood in Nietzsche's sense, mercy would then seem to describe an operation where, to use Agamben's terms, law captures life in a relation of ban. Its conversion of finite into infinite debt would operate on precisely the threshold between temporal and timeless embodiment that has traditionally grounded the political theological doctrine of sovereignty. Mercy, the sublation of law, would seem to qualify as an exemplary ban.

Homo Sacer I, like Agamben's earlier work, takes up the question of what it means to live in purgatorial limbo. Though the lives in question Agamben considers are now those of refugees, Agamben's concern is still with the problem of what forms of ethics and life can emerge at the limit where law fails to inscribe life in itself and itself in life.[122] But whereas in *The Idea of Prose* and *The Coming Community* Agamben could continue to treat abandonment as the condition in which human beings are finally able to appropriate impotentiality as their own innermost power, the unforeseen problem he claims to have encountered in *Homo Sacer I*—the concept of the sacredness of life—seems to have required him to alter the concept of ignorance on which his earlier account of abandonment rested.[123] For though ignorance of divine forgetfulness may excuse unbaptized children from participating in the Christian economy of guilt and sin, ignorance of the law does not excuse *homo sacer* from being at the mercy of the sovereign power that abandons it to camps.[124] Under conditions where sovereign power comes into its own by positing the substance of life in a sacred guilt from which it also withdraws the application of law, it would seem that there could no longer be neutrality toward mercy.[125] Given the way mercy captures life in and through the nonapplication of law to *Schuld*, it would seem, on the contrary, that mercy would have to emerge as a fundamental problem for any political ontological inquiry into the sovereign ban. Yet, despite this, none of Agamben's scattered mentions of forgiveness and its institutional iterations in *Homo Sacer I* and *III* achieve the rigor, coherence, or elegance of the other philosophical concepts he develops in those texts.

Agamben addresses this pronounced silence in *The Open: Man and Animal*. His main concern in the text is to show how the anthropological machine (the *dispositif* of philosophical and colonial anthropology) rests on a category of the "human" it can concretely determine only by repeatedly defining what is not animal.[126] At the core of humanism Agamben thus finds an empty space or caesura which is certainly not animal (humanism will insist upon this point) but which is not clearly and distinctly human either (since humanism merely presupposes the essence of the human without attempting to name it). This undecidable space, which constantly calls for decisions on the essence of the human, is the same space in which Agamben earlier located the emergence of naked life. It demarcates that on which the sovereign exception decides whenever it decides the exception.[127] In these terms, even Heidegger's definition of the human as a being capable of Eckhartian "releasement" or "letting be" [*Gelassenheit*] would be predicated on an internal exclusion of the animal, which Heidegger defines as a being incapable of letting be.[128] The problem posed by *Homo Sacer I*—namely, how to think through a "politics freed from any relation of ban"—thus becomes, in *The Open*, a question of how to idle or render inoperative the anthropological machine.

It is at this crucial point in his inquiry that Agamben returns to the idea of the completely abandoned life which is paradoxically blessed because of its capacity for ignorance. Yet whereas in *The Idea of Prose* Agamben defined this ignorance through its obliviousness to both wrath and mercy, he now refines it by asking why the etymology of the Latin *ignoscere* is not "not to know" but rather "to forgive."[129] To describe the verb form of the non-knowledge in which ignorance merges with forgiveness, Agamben proposes a neologism, *ignoscenza*.[130] Since it is almost unprecedented for Agamben to invent a new term, we should linger over the appearance of this one. Why does Agamben here invent a term rather than once again renew the meaning of an existing term from Hebrew, Greek, Latin, or German? And why does this invention appear at this precise point in his inquiry? On the one hand,

Agamben's ontology requires him to find a way to render *ignoscere* intelligible in something like a middle voice, since he would otherwise be compelled to articulate the auto-affective passivity that interests him in an outmoded grammar that would require him to emphasize either the term's active sense (ignoring) or its passive sense (ignorance). But perhaps the more fundamental reason Agamben must find a way for forgiveness to merge with ignorance at this point in his inquiry is that, left to its own devices, *ignoscere* remains unable to cut the knot of the sovereign ban. Under conditions where abandonment is not merely divine forgetfulness but "being at the mercy of"—or, more to the point, where abandoned life is sacred even if unbaptized—Agamben's ethics obliges him to come up with a way to appropriate not only forgetfulness but also forgiveness as a purely immanent, nonsovereign possibility. His ontological formula for unbanned forgiveness, "letting be outside of being," accomplishes precisely this: it introduces a novel form of forgiveness as a nonsovereign mode of nonrelation. Yet even though his genealogical inquiry into the concept of life thereby returns to the onto-theological problem Climacus posed under the name "miracle," the political ontological inquiry into sovereign power that concluded by calling for that genealogy remains limited to the example of the state of emergency. With this, the unthought that governs Agamben's inquiry begins to emerge in outline. In order for Agamben to have revealed the good to consist in the self-grasping of evil (which is his own requirement for nonsovereign ethics), he would have been obliged to come up with forms of unbanned politics by thinking them on the same plane of immanence with the sovereign ban itself.[131] But the account of sovereign power Agamben offers in *Homo Sacer I* presupposes that the exemplar of the sovereign exception is the state of emergency, and hence forecloses on the line of inquiry that would have thought sovereignty through the exemplarity of forgiveness and its iterations. When, despite this point of departure, not only Agamben's genealogy of posthistorical life but also his study of Pauline messianism then lead him to pose questions explicitly related to forgiveness, he finds himself called upon to think through a problem the articulation of which his ethics demands yet which his initial inquiry into sovereign power precludes.[132] His neologism is both a sign of this predicament and a metatheoretical response to it. Without recapitulating his earlier remarks on ignorance in and as *ignoscenza*, Agamben would not have been able to think forgiveness on the same plane as the sovereign ban, and would have remained unable to break with the relation of ban in the manner he understands to be ethical. By inventing a term that permits him to articulate forgiveness indiscernibly with ignorance, Agamben reintroduces within the limits of his inquiry the problem *Homo Sacer I* foreclosed upon by collapsing exception and emergency. If the miracle designates the problematic in relation to which Schmitt's decisionism becomes indecisive, it also names the example of sovereign power Agamben thinks only by gracefully ignoring.

Servitude Volontaire

The internal exclusion of forgiveness in Agamben's inquiry requires us to rethink his thesis on *servitude volontaire*. For Agamben, originary *Schuld* is part of the operation by which sovereign power captures life in its ban. The theological analogue of originary *Schuld* is sin. The voluntary servitude that emerges in relation to sin is what Kierkegaard calls *Hengivenhed*, which Howard and Edna Hong translate alternately as "devotedness," "givingness," and "devotion."[133] Devotion is the self's capacity to lose its life to the world in order to win its life after death; in the giving up of the self, the freedom of the self is gained.[134] If the devoted self is to escape the paradox of the potentiation of sins, it must find itself at and as the extreme point of impotence, at the limit where the self is impotent even to become impotent. Only at this desperate limit does the self find itself free directly before God; only at this limit does the self find itself unable to be free of despair. Devotion thus entails a claim to a freedom [*Frihed*] of a very particular kind. The task of the self, according to Kierkegaard, is to become itself in freedom, but freedom can only be achieved through a precise dialectic of possibility and necessity.[135] Too much possibility leads to the unfreedom of fantasy and the imagination; too much necessity leads to the unfreedom of determinism or fatalism.[136] In both cases, not only freedom but also the self is lost. When the self lacks necessity, it loses itself in what Kierkegaard calls the "abyss" [*Afgrunden*] of possibility.[137] When "everything is possible," the self loses itself because it ultimately reflects upon itself as a mere possibility, that is, as a mere element of fantasy or imagination.[138] Without necessity, it is impossible for the self to find in itself the power [*Kraft*] to submit to the "limitations" [*Graendse*] in one's life, and the self becomes "unreal."[139] When the self lacks possibility, on the other hand, it loses itself in necessity. If "everything is possible" drowns the self in possibility, "everything is necessary" suffocates the self with necessity. Possibility is like breathing: respiration is the mode of repetition proper to freedom.[140]

But as surely as inhale follows from exhale, inspiration follows from desperation. The breathing that *is* possibility only becomes possible when there is *no* possibility, that is to say, when the self encounters the extreme limit of its life. Only at the threshold where the self is suffocating for lack of possibility, or drowning for lack of necessity, where the self cannot help itself and resigns itself to death—only at this abject limit of life, where the body begins to resemble the spiritless corpse it already is potentially, can the self grasp concretely rather than abstractly that "for God everything is possible," and thus find itself directly before God, free of despair, having become grounded transparently in the power that constituted it.[141] "What is decisive [*Afgjørende*] is that with God everything is possible," Kierkegaard argues, and then adds:

> but the critical decision [*Afgjørelsen*] does not come until a person is brought to his extremity, when, humanly speaking, there is no possibility. Then the question is whether he will believe that for God everything is possible, that is, whether he will believe. But this is the very formula for losing the understanding; to believe is indeed to lose the understanding in order to gain God.[142]

We can imagine how Arendt might have read these passages. Kierkegaard's strange conjunction of dialectical rigor, extreme exposure, and decisionism is surely not far from the totalitarian ambition to construct castles of merciless logical consistency on the clearing of the isolated, lonely self.[143] We can also see why Agamben would refer to Kierkegaard to define the extreme situation characteristic of the state of exception.[144] For Kierkegaard, it is only at the extreme limit of life, at the threshold where the possibility of not living has become concretely possible in life itself, that life can be given up to forgiveness. The condition of possibility for all possibility, whether virtual or actual, is for Kierkegaard the experience of impossibility that precipitates the leap. When Jean-Luc Nancy suggests that abandonment is not merely a matter of withdrawal, desertion, or neglect, but a withdrawal that simultaneously "opens a profusion of possibilities," he writes within a Kierkegaardian problematic that Heidegger, like Schmitt, only augmented.[145] The withdrawal of law in abandon is a withdrawal of precisely the character of necessity that, according to Kant, no law can lack.[146] Abandonment induces abjection by drowning subjects in possibility.

How does this help us rethink Agamben's account of *servitude volontaire*? In her 1977 text *Aparté: Conceptions and Deaths of Søren Kierkegaard*, Sylviane Agacinski draws out the relations between the theological concept of abandon, the doctrine of grace, and the configuration of *servitude volontaire* within Christendom's heterosexual matrix. Agacinski suggests that Kierkegaard's writings on repetition tacitly respond to the question of "detachment" in the work of Meister Eckhart—which, she notes, circles around a teaching of abandonment.

> All that [i.e., Kierkegaard's arguments regarding repetition, recollection, and love] can also be found in the treatises of Meister Echkart. Detachment, the dialectic of detachment: another name for repetition. Especially: "Of True Obedience," "Of the Utility of Abandonment to be Practiced Inwardly and Outwardly," "Of Detachment and the Possession of God." Abandon (yourself), detach (yourself), give in, give up . . . at the moment of absolute detachment, God will infuse you and you will possess him.
>
> *A ban don(ation)*: "to give up one's claim on, to desist from holding back . . ."[147]

Agacinski, a careful reader of Derrida, here brings into play the aporia of the gift (*le don*), which Derrida considered in his seminar of 1977–78, as well as in his later seminars on pardon and perjury. Agacinski's spacing and rewriting of "abandon" as "a ban don(ation)" suggests that abandonment is not enacted, declared, willed, or even decided, but is rather donated or given. It follows from this that the ban is not, as one reading of Agacinski might suggest, an exchange ("give in, give up, and in return God will give the gift that keeps on giving: eternal life"). Rather, the ban gives the condition of possibility for devotion. It gives the gift of giving up (or, in what amounts to the same thing, the impotence that the self is impotent to achieve by itself). In Kierkegaard's writings on repetition, which, as Agacinski notes, distinguish repetition sharply from "mere" physical reproduction, not just anyone is in a position to receive this gift. Only the Christian woman, as exemplified by Mary Magdalene, is capable of abandon. The "feminine nature," Agacinski cites Kierkegaard writing in *The Sickness Unto Death*, "is devotedness, abandon, and it is unfeminine if it is not that."[148]

> "True woman, the only one who is any good, is the one who is herself only by not being herself; a woman who is happy without devotion, that is, without giving herself, no matter what she gives it, is altogether unfeminine." Her suffering, her particular despair, is not to realize her loss, it is to be deprived of that to which she wants to abandon herself. If a man abandons himself, it is never *properly speaking* (this term does not apply to him), if he happens to abandon himself, "his self remains behind as a sober awareness of devotion . . ."
>
> When a woman realizes the full extent of her nature, of her abandon, she becomes a model of Christian living—this is Mary Magdalene.[149]

Man cannot abandon himself; or rather, he can do so only improperly. Woman, on the other hand, is for Kierkegaard "weakness itself." But, in Christian doctrine, this weakness is a form of strength. The Christian virtue of weakness is modeled or exemplified by Mary Magdalene because "Mary Magdalene alone is complete frailty, complete submission; she is the 'total impotence' required for forgiveness. She weeps, she is silent. She has understood or believed that the forgiveness of Christ, as God or man, is obtained only by not seeking to obtain it. A doctrine of grace."[150] Only woman, as exemplified by Mary Magdalene, can receive the gift of abandon, that is to say, the gift of impotence in the absence of which forgiveness cannot be truly given. For this reason, Agacinski explains, Kierkegaard will consider "feminine abandon" an "enviable position."[151] Yet at the same time, woman, who because of her nature can abandon herself naturally, cannot, for this same reason, decide on the extreme act of renunciation, which Agacinski calls the "true religious castration."[152] Because abandon is one of woman's natural potentialities, abandon is a given only for her and yet, for that very reason, cannot be chosen by her at all. Apart from the example of Magdalene, who is excluded from belonging to the very gender for which she is an example, woman, for Kierkegaard, is as incapable of authentic religiosity as she is, for Dostoyevsky's Mitya, incapable of forgiveness.[153] The antithesis of grace and nature here reappears as a doctrine of sex difference. The feminine abandon exemplified by Magdalene remains, for Kierkegaard, a specifically feminine potential that is available only for man.[154] The knight of faith leaps by internally excluding woman.

In the reading of Dostoyevsky Julia Kristeva outlines in her 1987 *Black Sun*, forgiveness is uncoupled from this kind of male supremacy, but still depends for its intelligibility on an idealized concept of sex difference. For Kristeva, forgiveness is not only central to modern aesthetics, as beauty's necessary condition, but is also a sublimation capable of adequately treating abjection.[155] The act of naming and composing that Kristeva takes to be the generative core of art, as well as forgiveness's most powerful aesthetic effect, is, in her account, predicated on a reconciliation of the affect connected to the mourned mother with the symbolic as founded in paternal law.[156] Forgiving is here form-giving *poesis*, productivity in the fullest sense, where productivity turns out to be indistinct from the kinship relations of heterosexual reproduction. A similar dynamic emerges in the study of Arendt that Kristeva offers in the first book of her *Le Génie Féminin* trilogy. In the final section of that text, Kristeva comments on Arendt's theorization of the faculties of forgiveness and promise, tracing the way Arendt posits the conditions of possibility for a nonsovereign political community. Kristeva closes her commentary by showing how both faculties are ultimately designed to preserve what Arendt calls the "fact of natality."[157] Calling this the "miracle of rebirth," Kristeva presents "the full experience of natality" as the source for a reconciliation of life and politics with thought.[158] Like forgiveness in *Black Sun*, natality is here the pure generativity of unconditioned *poesis*, as exemplified by birth. Natality is capable of giving rise to a nonsovereign political community because it is constituting power itself.

The problem with Kristeva's account is not merely that it treats "birth" and "rebirth" as synonyms, thereby ignoring Arendt's distinction between the two, but also that its own poetic account of the miracle mystifies what Arendt calls the riddle of political foundation. Kristeva renders the fact of natality in precisely the "pseudo-religious language" Arendt critiques in Enlightenment thinkers, who were unable to resist turning to religion "when they had to deal with the problem of foundation."[159] When Arendt calls natality the "miracle of being," she has a very specific concept of miracle in mind.[160] For Kant, who takes up the problem from Spinoza, the miracle names an event the appearance of which is unintelligible on the basis of natural laws of cause and effect.[161] In "The Contest of the Faculties," Kant applies this criterion to dispel the mendacious illusion that the absolute monarch could somehow be limited by laws which emanate from the people, thus already implying the analogy Schmitt would later fail to elucidate.[162] For Arendt, who rereads Kant on this point, the foundation of a juridical-political order is similarly situated: insofar as the new can be reduced to a law of cause and effect or to a temporal succession, the new is by definition not the new.[163] On the face of it, then, Arendt would seem to be in agreement with Schmitt. Legal order, for each, would seem to originate in and through the revelation of a necessarily inexplicable miracle. Yet whereas Schmitt's indecision in relation to Kierkegaard forces him to give up his attempt to turn Kant's analogy against itself, Arendt's account of the foundation of law brings to bear on that analogy precisely the perplexities Johannes Climacus attaches to the concept of the miracle in *Philosophical Fragments*. Writing in 1946, Arendt argued that modern philosophy has taken all of its new concepts from Kierkegaard, naming "contingency" as one such concept.[164] Thirteen years earlier, she had already explained the function of "contingency" in Kierkegaard's thought. "Chance is what is outside the self, which draws into itself through this outsideness the entire obligation of the transcendent, of that which is willed by God alone. In being taken with absolute seriousness, a seriousness that is identical with absolute logic, the contingent becomes the last locus in which God himself speaks, however distant he may be."[165] Arendt returned to the problem of contingency in her 1974–75 New School lectures, where she took up the question of foundation for the last time in her life. After discussing "abandonment" and "letting be" in Heidegger, Arendt turned to the problem of contingency, arguing thrice that contingency is the price a thinker must pay for the gift of freedom.[166] Even though contingency entails a certain incalculability, irreducibility, randomness, and possibility for error that renders it unthinkable for traditional philosophy, the freedom it enables is nevertheless not predicated on either a love of fate or a new religion.[167] Rather, contingency entails a mode of understanding all its own, a mode distinct from knowledge of cause and effect or temporal succession. Because freedom is a matter of "being able to do what could also be left undone," Arendt argues, any capacity for action will necessarily be accompanied by an understanding that "whatever would be done now could just as well have been left undone."[168] In order for an act to come into being

as a free act, it is obliged to carry with it the remnant of its own potential to
not-be. "Contingency" is the name that Arendt gives to this potential to not-
be.[169] If an act were not contingent, if it were not just as possible to act as to
not act, then action will not have been action at all. It will have been mere
necessity (in relation to which, as Kant says, there can be no beginning).
Only insofar as action embraces its own contingency, its own potential to
not-be, can action fully embrace its own potential for freedom. Contingency
here ceases to operate as a theological category, as the placeholder for the
voice of God. It emerges instead as the pivotal concept of Arendt's political
ontological account of the capacity to begin. When Arendt goes on to argue
that the capacity to begin is inexplicable in Aristotelian categories of potentiality and actuality, we may then read her argument alongside Climacus's
claim that there is an "error" in the Aristotelian account of potentiality.[170] In
the traditional interpretation of the Aristotelian account of entelechy, the
actualization of potential is equivalent to potential's exhaustion, and the potential to not-be is obliterated. A sovereign act, as Agamben observes, would
in this sense be an act that completely removes the potential to not-be that
enables it: no potential to not-be would remain after a fully actualized act.
When Arendt argues that freedom requires the possibility of being able to do
what could also have been left undone, she suggests, in effect, that freedom
cannot persist in the absence of the potential to not-be. If a sovereign act is
indeed one that exhausts the potential to not-be, then Arendt would consider it to be by definition opposed to freedom.

Political thought is implicated in this same dynamic. Against Kierkegaard's formulation of concrete religious freedom gained through the loss of
abstract understanding, Arendt understands political thought to be a constitutive part of freedom's political reality. When political thought renders
done deeds intelligible not merely as unchangeable or irreversible but also as
inevitable or necessary, it purges the contingency that enabled those deeds in
the first place.[171] It gives up on the political ontological principle that such
deeds, while unchangeable and irreversible, could just as well not have been.
Done deeds consequently acquire the character of necessity; they take on the
status of laws that govern subsequent thought and action.[172] In order for
"coming into being" (Climacus) or the "capacity for the new" (Arendt) to

remain possible, political thought is therefore obliged to remain in touch with the remainder—the potential to not-be, the contingency—that precedes, enables, and ultimately exceeds even possibility itself.

"Natality" is Arendt's name for this potential to not-be, this contingency that cannot be collapsed into the acts it enables. She calls natality a "miracle" not because she discerns in it some mysterious or religious content, but because, in a formal sense, the miracle is that which breaks with the laws of cause and effect that, on their own terms, can offer no resistance to the natural necessities of decline and disaster.[173] In its ontological incommensurability with any concept of law, even that of constitutional positive law, natality certainly does then bear a superficial resemblance to the sovereign exception.[174] But natality is also, as we have seen, ontologically incommensurable with sovereignty's very principle. Whereas Schmitt's account of the sovereign exception remains a compromise between his attraction to Climacus's concept of the miracle and his sympathy for Anti-Climacus's attack on constitutional democracy, Arendt's account of natality takes Climacus to the extreme, stripping the miracle down to its basic political ontological elements in the process. For Arendt, "miracle" is merely a name for the occluded form in which the faculty of freedom survives under political conditions where political action remains determined by the necessities of sovereignty, security, and health. Under such conditions, political acts appear miraculous only because their recuperative contingency appears to arrive from a source exterior to humanity.[175] Far from serving as the theological analogue to the sovereign exception or as some modern renewal of Hesiodic legend, Arendt's account of natality demystifies the miraculous by tracing its contingency back to its entirely immanent origin: free political action's potential to not-be.[176] Far from being a mystic fiction of pure generativity, natality is the pivotal principle of a political theory designed to dissolve the immanent transcendence of sovereign power altogether.[177]

Arendt's commitment to immanentism is perhaps clearest in her 1944 essay on Kafka, which she wrote while editing Kafka's diaries for Schocken Books and while finishing the manuscript she then called *The Elements of Shame: Anti-Semitism—Imperialism—Racism* (which she would later publish as *The Origins of Totalitarianism*).[178] In that essay, Arendt argues that "[t]he

outstanding feature of K. in *The Castle* is that he is interested only in univer-
sals, in those things to which all men have a natural right."[179] As a result, Arendt suggests, the meaning of K.'s oft-misinterpreted strangeness becomes
more intelligible:

> [H]e is the only normal and healthy human being in a world where everything
> human and normal, love and work and fellowship, has been wrested out of man's
> hands to become a gift endowed from without—or, as Kafka puts it, from above.
> Whether as fate, as blessing or as curse, it is something mysterious, something
> which man may receive or be denied, but never can create. Accordingly, K.'s aspi-
> ration, far from being commonplace and obvious is, in fact, exceptional and
> scandalous.[180]

Arendt's point is not merely that where the exception has become the norm,
the norm also becomes an exception. Her reading of Kafka also marks her
opposition to the rhetoric and logic of Anti-Climacus. At a moment when
literary historians had already started to institutionalize Kafka as a Kierkegaardian, Arendt finds in *The Castle* a staunch defense of everything Anti-
Climacus attacks. Arendt's counterintuitive reading of K. as an advocate of
human rights (which only appears to contradict her critique of human rights
in *Origins*) underscores the very form of Kafka's storytelling: his humor.
Kafka's contribution, says Arendt, is that he permits his reader to laugh at
"the human possibility of erring."[181] Whereas totalitarian societies treat error,
that potential immanent in all action, as a crime against what Arendt calls
"omnicompetence," Kafka's humor "permits man to prove his essential freedom through a kind of serene superiority to his own failures."[182] In this, Arendt's Kafka turns Kierkegaard's Anti-Climacus on his head. Let us recall
that, to illustrate the absurdity of defiance, Anti-Climacus closes Part I of *The
Sickness Unto Death* with the allegory of an error in a text that somehow suddenly becomes self-conscious of its own existence.

> Figuratively speaking, it is as if an error slipped into an author's writing and the
> error became conscious of itself as an error—perhaps it actually was not a mis-
> take but in a much higher sense an essential part of the whole production—and
> now this error wants to mutiny against the author, out of hatred against him,
> forbidding him to correct it and in maniacal defiance saying to him: No, I refuse
> to be erased; I will stand as a witness against you, a witness that you are a second-
> rate author.[183]

Because Kierkegaard's name appears on the title page of *The Sickness Unto Death* as the text's editor, this allegory silently implicates Kierkegaard within Anti-Climacus's categories. Regardless of whether the author did or did not commit the error in question, it would fall to the editor to take responsibility for the fact that the error has now taken on a life of its own. This figure can serve as an allegory for Anti-Climacus's entire attack on immanentism: regardless of how a human self-consciousness managed to appear in the work of God the author in the first place, it is now the work's editor who must account for the error's continued defiant existence. The Christian subject comes into being as an editor called upon to answer for the error whereby an essential errancy has become conscious of itself as a necessity. Nothing could be further from, or closer to, Kafka's patience with the potential for erring; nothing could better exemplify Kafka's exposure of his contemporaries' misguided pride in necessity as such.[184] Kafka reveals Kierkegaard's limit to consist not so much in the fact that Kierkegaard thinks life in terms of error as in the way Kierkegaard thinks error itself: as self-consciousness that is rageful to the extent it remains unselfconscious about its superfluity for life. Adorno is not wrong to select this allegory as the point in Kierkegaard's *oeuvre* most able to dialectically reverse its doctrine of despair and sacrifice into an emancipation of hope.[185] Voluntary servitude begins where natality ends.

"Everything is Possible"

> Commentaries in the history of philosophy should represent a kind of slow motion, a congelation or immobilization of the text: *not only* of the text to which they relate, *but also* of the text in which they are inserted—so that they have a double existence and a corresponding ideal: the pure repetition of the former text and the present text *in one another*.
>
> —Gilles Deleuze, 1968

Part of the urgency of Agamben's inquiry derives from his argument that sovereign power is the source of democracy's complicity with its declared enemy, totalitarianism. Insofar as modern democracies subscribe to the logic of the sovereign exception (and fail to prevent its corollary, the abandonment of naked life), Nazism and Fascism will stubbornly remain as political possibilities.[186] It may seem strange to suggest that forgiveness and its iterations exemplify these possibilities, but this is exactly the implication of Arendt's tacit rereading of *The Sickness Unto Death* in the closing pages of Part III of *Origins of Totalitarianism*. "Everything is possible," which Arendt argues is the "central assumption" and "fundamental belief" of totalitarian power, is also, as we have seen, Kierkegaard's formula for the power of forgiveness that belongs to God alone.[187] Arendt's catachrestic reiteration of Kierkegaard should not be confused with Dostoyevsky's account of the nineteenth-century nihilism espoused by Raskolnikov and Ivan Karamazov, in which "everything is permitted."[188] Whereas Raskolnikov and Karamazov imagine the possibility of murder in situations where morality has been suspended, Arendt considers political and legal conditions that have nullified even the category of criminality itself.[189] In its attempt to actualize the belief that "everything is possible," totalitarianism unknowingly stumbles across a constitutive limit of law.

> [I]n their effort to prove that everything is possible, totalitarian regimes have discovered without knowing it that there are crimes which men can neither punish nor forgive. When the impossible was made possible it became the unpunishable, unforgivable absolute evil which could no longer be understood and explained by the evil motives of self-interest, greed, covetousness, resentment, lust for power, and cowardice; and which therefore anger could not revenge, love could not endure, friendship could not forgive.[190]

Here, as elsewhere, Arendt's argument implies an intricate political ontology. As Levinas suggests, a world in which everything is possible would be equivalent to one in which "nothing is impossible."[191] But to understand potentiality in a strict sense, as Arendt does, is to see that, under conditions where the impossible has been made possible, and where, consequently, nothing is impossible, the very possibility of possibility becomes exhausted too. Since there can be no possibility without a relation to the impossible, the political conditions under which "everything is possible" are paradoxically also political conditions that establish the reign of absolute necessity.[192] Under such conditions, as Kafka shows, law remains in force but loses its significance. Both the potential for punishment and the potential to not punish—mercy—are extinguished in what Levinas calls "suffocation in the impossibility of the possible."[193]

That Arendt is here engaged in a rereading of Kierkegaard becomes clearer when she turns not to the *Muselmann* but to Lazarus to clarify her argument that to survive the camps was to return from the "living dead."[194] The parable of Lazarus has a specific meaning for Kierkegaard. In a text written under his own name two years before the publication of *The Sickness Unto Death*, Kierkegaard cited the parable of Lazarus in order to illustrate the relation between "mercy" and "mercilessness."[195] Kierkegaard suggests that, although the rich man has it "richly enough in his power" to show mercy to the leprous Lazarus, he does not, and, as such, shows "inhuman unmercifulness."[196] When Arendt invokes Lazarus's return from the dead in *Origins*, and when Kierkegaard meditates on the same miracle in the opening of *The Sickness Unto Death*, the name "Lazarus" cannot be separated from the apocryphal indeterminacy that collapses the biblical Lazarus of Mark with the Lazarus of Luke.[197] The name signifies more than merely the survival of death or the occupation of an intermediate space between life and death. "Lazarus" also names the helplessness of a subject "at the mercy of," which is to say, the *homo sacer* exposed to unceremonial death.[198]

By remaining attentive to Arendt's rereading of Kierkegaard here, we gain a sharper understanding of the impasse around which the closing chapter of *Origins* circles. On the one hand, when Arendt summarizes totalitarian power not by returning to Goebbel's definition of politics as "the art of making what seems impossible possible," but instead by catachrestically reiterating Kierkegaard's "everything is possible," she would seem to be suggesting that the impossibility of forgiveness for the camps derives from the implication of its principle in their existence. As scandalous as this suggestion is, it nevertheless exposes a sobering political truth. Certainly, under political conditions where certain forms of life are apprehended as originarily guilty or sinful in and because of their very being, the old sovereign power to mercifully let live acquires a new, biopolitical coefficient.[199] But if forgiveness does not survive after everything has been made possible, it is more fundamentally because the potential to not forgive has been lost in the flood too. Part of the camps' criminality is that the sheer scale of the perpetrators' crimes itself threatens to exempt them from law's judgment. "Where all are guilty, nobody in the last analysis can be judged," Arendt warned in her January 1945 critique of the concept of collective German guilt.[200] Where judgment becomes impossible, so too does punishability. By a tortuous route, immunity acquires the attribute of necessity. Forgiveness, which requires unpredictability as one of its conditions of possibility, consequently ceases to exist. Mercilessness turns out to be not only cause but also effect of general *anomie*.

But, on the other hand, in order not to invite the return of that same mercilessness in her own thinking, Arendt is also unable to not forgive forgiveness. Writing explicitly against the law of noncontradiction whose application by totalitarian power she twice calls specifically "merciless," Arendt concludes *Origins* with a set of subtly anomalous repetitions.[201] At the same time she seems to let forgiveness perish by rendering its formula indistinct from the fundamental belief that produced the death camps, her antidote to totalitarianism is nonetheless a life of the mind founded on what she twice calls the "saving grace" of companionable solitude.[202] Likewise, even though she twice calls the camps a manifestation of hell on earth, Arendt argues that the camps nevertheless cannot reproduce the only tolerable aspect of the concept of Hell: "the Last Judgment, the idea of an absolute standard of justice combined with the infinite possibility of grace."[203] Forgiveness and its iterations thus define *both* the formula of the omnipotence totalitarian power aspires to actualize *and* the grace of which its merciless actualization of that formula remains incapable. The repetitions in the closing pages of *Origins* take forgiveness's iterability to the extreme: opening with forgiveness's unforgivability (its implication in a world in which "everything is possible"), Arendt concludes by introducing the possibility of forgiving forgiveness (by embracing its iteration in the "saving grace" of thought).

What's curious about these repetitions is the way they prepare for the unexpected turn that is the conclusion of *Origins*. *Origins*, which George Kateb fittingly calls a book on "that which immeasurably intensifies despair," somehow finds a way to conclude by affirming natality and the capacity to begin.[204] The necessity and even possibility of this turn are hardly self-evident. Is it mere Pollyannaish wish fulfillment or banally redemptive thinking, as Arendt's critics would have it? Or is it the mark of a careful and deliberate mode of political thought, one that poses to itself the same questions it brings to bear on the problems that concern it, one that resists what it comprehends? Consider that in her discussion of imperialism in *Origins*, introducing a problem to which she would return throughout her work, Arendt remarks that man "has not been granted the gift of undoing."[205] This inability to undo is what Arendt would later call the predicament of irreversibility: "being unable to undo what one has done though one did not, and could not, have known what he is doing."[206] In *The Human Condition*, Arendt would show how the faculty of forgiveness can permit an escape from this predicament.[207] But early in *Origins* Arendt had already started to formulate a response to irreversibility, and it was not forgiveness. In *Origins* Arendt argued that it was only a certain capacity for telling, which she called "legend," that, as she put it, let man become "master of what he had not done and capable of dealing with what he could not undo."[208] By belatedly recounting historical facts and events in a measure appropriate to what Arendt deemed the human condition, legends enabled man to claim responsibility for a history he did not create. Though these legends temper historical reality with the truth of narrative invention, they do not aim at any kind of universal explanation and thus remain distinct from ideology as Arendt defines it. Arendt's brief and by no means uncritical discussion of legends in *Origins* seems to provide a response to the common critique of *Origins* (namely, that its narration errs and strays from the historical facts).[209] *Origins*, on this read, would itself be a legend designed to offer the modern political subject a way to begin responding to the shame of modernity itself. Arendt's remark that the story of Nazism "*in itself* can yield nothing but sorrow and despair" suggests that *Origins* is perhaps even designed to constitute shame as an enduring problem for political thought.[210]

Yet while it would certainly then be possible to approach *Origins* as a work of testimony, particularly in the sense Derrida has given to the term,[211] even this would risk misunderstanding the mode of telling *Origins* already immanently is. We receive a sense of this mode from Arendt's discussion of forgiveness in *The Human Condition*. Commenting on a passage in Luke, Arendt notes a subtle but critical question of translation.

> It is important to keep in mind that the three key words of the text—*aphienai*, *metanoein*, and *hamartanein*—carry certain connotations even in New Testament Greek which the translations fail to render fully. The original meaning of *aphienai* is "dismiss" and "release" rather than "forgive"; *metanoein* means "change of mind" and—since it serves also to render the Hebrew *shuv*—"return," "trace back one's steps," rather than "repentance" with its psychological emotional overtones; what is required is: change your mind and "sin no more," which is almost the opposite of doing penance. *Hamartanein*, finally, is indeed very well rendered by

"trespassing" in so far as it means rather "to miss," "fail and go astray," rather than "to sin[.]" The verse which I quote in the standard translation could also be rendered as follows: "And if he trespass against thee ... and ... turn again to thee, saying, *I changed my mind*; thou shalt *release* him."[212]

To begin to grasp the implications of Arendt's retranslation of *metanoein* as "change of mind," we must first recall that "change of mind" was already the phrase she drew upon in *Origins* to define the faculty of thought itself: "the human capacity to think is the capacity to change one's mind."[213] Yet if the potential for *nous* (thought) is the same as the potential for *metanoein* (change of mind), and if the latter is a condition of possibility for *aphienai* (dismissal or release), then what we call "forgiveness" could not emerge without a prior potential for thought. This would clarify why Arendt later locates radical evil in the inability to think.[214] If thought is the capacity to change one's mind, and if *aphienai* presupposes this capacity, then an inability to think will entail not merely utter logical consistency but also an incapacity for forgiveness, and thoughtlessness will entail precisely the mercilessness Arendt attributes to the deductive consistency of totalitarian ideology in *Origins*. This would also clarify why Arendt's opposition to the latter brings her to claim, in her Gifford Lectures, that "thinking is like Penelope's web; it undoes every morning what it has finished the night before."[215] Rethought as *shuv*, thinking would be rooted in the very same capacity to undo Arendt emphasized in her 1958 discussion of forgiveness.[216]

But this raises another question. How can the capacity to change one's mind (*metanoein*) be the same as the capacity for thought itself (*nous*)? Assuming *metanoein* is predicated on the *nous* it modifies, it would seem that defining the capacity for *nous* as the capacity for *metanoein* would knot thought into tautology. The capacity for thought would apparently presuppose itself: no capacity for thought (*metanoein*) without prior capacity for thought (*nous*). A vertiginous circle would thus define the thinking of thought itself. The very delicate problem of how to begin thinking would become particularly perplexing. For if thought can come into being only insofar as it is already underway, then under what conditions would it be able to begin in the first place?

Arendt takes up this problem in her Gifford lectures, arguing that philosophical thought has been imagined through the metaphor of a circle ever since Aristotle defined philosophical thought as *noesis noeseos* (a thinking of thinking). Quoting Aristotle, Arendt suggests that thought's "inherent law, which only a god can tolerate forever, man merely now and then, is 'unceasing motion, which is motion in a circle.'"[217] In a text that opens by asking whether thinking itself could provide an antidote to the radical evil of thoughtlessness, Arendt's quotation of Aristotle has a striking political implication. It suggests that thought's inherent law is commensurable with what, in *Origins*, she called "totalitarian lawfulness."[218] For to define the inherent law of thought as "unceasing motion" is to put thought's dynamic on the same plane as the totalitarianism for which "all laws have become laws of movement."[219] Yet isn't an understanding of precisely this commensurability part of the political thought Arendt wanted to teach when she argued that radical evil inheres not in stupidity, but in an inability to think?[220] If so, then to think thought in the metaphor of a circle would not only be to succumb to what Arendt, in 1973, called a "singularly empty" thought of thought. It would also be to think thought thoughtlessly, to thoughtlessly maintain the inhuman in the image of thought professional philosophy so carefully preserves.[221]

To understand the way Arendt escapes from this circle, let us first note that the Greek μετά does not, as we might expect, designate transcendence. In the genitive and dative cases, "meta" is a preposition that refers to that which is "among," "in the midst of," "between," or "in common." In the accusative, it indicates that which "comes after," either in the hostile sense of "pursuit," the hierarchical sense of "rank" or "worth," or the temporal sense of "sequence" or "succession." As a prefix, "meta-" refers most often to a "change" of some kind, but it can also carry its other meanings, which is why "*metanoein*" can equally be translated "after-thought."[222] But if Arendt does not follow Hegel in defining thought as after-thought, this is not simply because "after-thought" implies mere regret, absent-mindedness, or thought without consequence.[223] It is because the way Arendt thinks thought is *itself* predicated on a rethinking of Kierkegaard's opposition to Hegel on the question of the self-relation constitutive of the self. For Kierkegaard, in whose thought Arendt locates "the birth of the self," the self is a self-relating relation that rests transparently in the transcendent power that constituted it.[224] Implicit in this definition, according to Adorno, is that the self raises itself to the status of creator in the same gesture that it reduces itself to the eternally circular movement of creaturely life.[225] The counterpart to Kierkegaard's attack on the monist reduction of God to animal life is thus Kierkegaard's affirmation of a subject in which, as Agamben would say, *zoe* is the bearer of sovereign power. Arendt, who, like Adorno, clearly understood eternal recurrence as the temporality proper to *zoe*, is critical of the very idea of a sovereignty that would be immanent to naked life. The totalitarianism in which the human species as such becomes the bearer of laws of almost divine natural necessity is, in Arendt's account, precisely immanent transcendence.[226] Arendt's argument that only a god could endure the ceaseless motion of thought thus implies that human thought would begin only where eternally recurrent movement came to a stop.[227] To "stop and think" would not then describe a humanist cliché; it would indicate an experience of impassability akin to *stasis* that would paradoxically also be the only way to heal the fracture between *zoe* and *bios.*[228] As distinct from the Kierkegaardian subject, Arendt's thought would not catch its breath by coming to rest transparently in the transcendent power that constituted it. *Nous* would become *metanoein*—thought could be defined as a change of mind—because the faculty of thought, like any other faculty, would come into being only in relation to its own potential to not-be, its contingency. But because thought's potential to not-be is, in Arendt's account, the condition of possibility for radical evil, the potential to not-be constitutive of the faculty of thinking would be the same inability to think that, for Arendt, is the very source of inhumanity itself.[229] K.'s statement in *The Castle*—"those who are ignorant [*dem Unwissenden*] naturally consider everything possible"—suggests nothing less.[230] Because thought can only come into being in relation to its own inability to think, the capacity to begin thinking would thus emerge in relation to thought's own potential for radical evil and inhumanity itself. For Arendt, the subject comes into its own not by resting transparently in the transcendent power that constituted it, but by stumbling across the scandal of its own immanent potential to not think. Only when an encounter with thoughtlessness gives thought pause would thought get the chance to return to the potential to not-be that endows it with its capacity to begin. Only by remaining open to encounters with its own potential for thoughtlessness, without also having anything to do with that thoughtlessness, could thought bring itself into being as thought by changing its mind.

Like the leap in Kierkegaard, or Deleuze's "thought which is born in thought," the relation Arendt establishes between *metanoein* and *nous* would then be a coming into existence of that which is already in existence.[231] Neither circle nor renaissance, it would be a redoubling of a *dynamis* prior to the substance of the subject. In this political ontology, the concept of contingency no longer possesses, as it did for Kierkegaard, the status of a theological placeholder. Rather than finding the guarantee of its forgiven individuality in the ground of sin, the thinking subject's nonrelation to its own thoughtlessness is the constitutive principle for what Arendt calls the "two-in-one" of thought's relation to itself in "con-science" or the "silent dialogue" between it and itself.[232] Thought constitutes itself as a self-relation, a "two-in-one," by remaining open to its potential to not think. Arendt's "life of the mind" does not, therefore, describe the full living presence of a mind possessed of its own innately generative constituting power.[233] Only by thinking through the nonrelation thought must maintain with thoughtlessness in order to come into existence as thought was Arendt able to think thought as a form of life free from the totalitarian belief that "everything is possible."

The name Arendt gives to this form is "friendship," the same friendship that, as she wrote in *Origins*, is unable to forgive totalitarianism's crimes. Though it is Arendt's name for the principle of conscience's relation to itself, the companionable solitude of friendship is as unrelated to the psychoanalytic concept of the moralizing superego as her account of thought's constitutive encounter with thoughtlessness is incommensurable with the psychoanalytic explanation of trauma. Friendship is simply the principle through which the thinking subject becomes able to live with itself, which is to say, to live in relation to its own potential to not think. Understood in this manner, "living with oneself" means that "the self that we all are must take care not to do anything that would make it impossible for the two-in-one to be friends."[234] The significance of this "taking care" becomes clearer when Arendt remarks that living with oneself has no political valence "unless special emergencies arise. That while I am alive I must be able to live with myself is a

consideration that does not come up politically except in 'boundary situations.'"[235] Such situations, which are none other than states of emergency, severely test the principle of friendship. Arendt seems to suggest that when exceptional situations force *zoe* to present itself as a desperate necessity, they
also present the paradoxical possibility of surviving without also living with
oneself. Since friendship is the mode of the self's self-relation insofar as it is
able to live with itself, the moment that self-preservation becomes the self's
constitutive principle, the self is longer itself; the self-preserving self is its
own worst enemy. Since the life of the mind is indiscernible from its plurality, there can be no living or thinking that would not be living and thinking
among, in the midst of, or in common with this plurality. Friendship implies
an immanence of the singular and the plural—a basic immeasurability, a
constitutive division—that rules out in advance the possibility of a life relating to itself as an exception.[236] When friendship is, in spite of everything, lost,
stripped, suspended, or extinguished, only the arrival of *aphienai* from elsewhere would be able to return thought to its immanence; only *aphienai*
would be able to return the political to thought. *Aphienai* would then be the
capacity to release the subject from the shame of being compelled to live *zoe*
as its unerring law. Giving back to the subject its constitutive principle,
aphienai would reproduce in the subject a possibility for living and thinking,
despite its reversion to exception.

Beginning and the End

Perhaps it is now clearer why, unlike Schmitt and even Agamben, Arendt
scandalously lets the power to forgive appear as the exemplar of totalitarian
power. Not despite but *because of* this exemplarity is Arendt able to think
through the way forgiveness excludes itself from the very set it defines. Precisely Arendt's capacity to think forgiveness as exemplary of totalitarianism's
aspiration to omnipotence *also* permits her to think forgiveness in its immanence as a power of the life of the mind and as a nonsovereign political relation.[237] An intricate political ontology is at work here as well. As we have
seen, forgiveness enables a dismissal of the irreversible effects of done deeds
that would otherwise become laws unto themselves.[238] It is a mode of natality
because it returns to action the capacity to begin which action, left open to

its own immanent errancy, will necessarily exhaust. *Aphienai* thus has nothing to do with form-giving *poesis*. It is rather the materialization, as potential to not-be, of the potential to not-be that remains always anterior to action. It is, for this same reason, distinct from pure or unconditioned action. Since there is no forgiveness that is not also a *re*action and an *un*doing, and yet, since forgiveness is "the only reaction that does not merely re-act but acts anew and unexpectedly, unconstrained by the act that provokes it," it materializes the capacity to begin in a counterintuitive way.[239] It repeats, in a no longer Kierkegaardian sense, the capacity to begin. Despite the fact that, according to Kant, beginning and repetition are opposed, and quite contrary to Kierkegaard's opposition of birth to repetition, Arendt finds in the redoubling of action's potential to not-be a way to achieve precisely the break with the laws of causality, that, according to Kant, is the necessary condition for any beginning. *Aphienai* can be *both* new beginning *and* repetition because it is the *return to* as well as the *release of* the contingency that enables and remains after any given act. The paradox implicit in Arendt's account of forgiveness is that forgiveness is powerless to begin on its own (since it cannot begin without reacting to or undoing a prior act) and yet precisely that powerlessness leaves it more ontologically proximate to the constitutive principle of the capacity to begin than even action itself. Contingent on a done deed that could have been left undone—indeed, that "ought not to have happened"—forgiveness's own capacity to begin is not unconditional.[240] But because forgiveness is able to release action's immanent errancy from its tendency to acquire the form of law, forgiveness has the capability to return to action the contingency action literally cannot do without. Though the encounter that provokes forgiveness is far from unconditional, forgiveness is that which lets the unconditional capacity to begin come into being.

Does the closing chapter of *Origins* bear witness to a dynamic of this sort? Certainly, that chapter does not allow Arendt to escape the impasse in which she finds herself. On the contrary, it redoubles the terms that constitute that impasse. By its close, *Origins* arrives at a threshold where the impossibility of forgiveness *itself* calls into being the limits absent in totalitarianism's "everything is possible." Everything is not possible: forgiving totalitarianism's crimes is not possible. Yet it is the impossibility of forgiveness that opens up the limit lacking in totalitarianism. It is not forgiveness but the impossibility of forgiveness that, pushing back the limits of the possible, begins to undo totalitarianism. This redoubling ultimately recoils on and alters even the concept of forgiveness itself. After its encounter with its potential to not-be, the word "forgiveness" no longer expresses what it used to express: it no longer names the sufficient principle for totalitarian omnipotence. The terms with which Arendt closes *Origins* are definitely proximate to the terms she would later draw upon to theorize the faculty of forgiveness. But whatever permitted *Origins* to close in the way it did was not forgiveness. It could only have been a withdrawal of law Arendt's telling had already changed from a sovereign power into the power to change one's mind. Left unactualized, the potential to not forgive forgiveness yielded an unexpected effect: it restored the possibility for political thought. Arendt was able to let the text on shame close so unpredictably because her writing could not, and could only, undo the despair it narrated. Written in the midst of ongoing thoughtlessness, the substance of *Origins* is the impossibility of return.

Notes

I thank Joshua Barkan, Helen Kinsella, Gregg Lambert, and David Peña for their comments on drafts of this essay.

1. See Giorgio Agamben, *Homo Sacer I: Sovereign Power and Naked Life*, trans. Daniel Heller-Roazen (Stanford: Stanford University Press, 1998), 15–17.

2. Ibid., 15.

3. Ibid. See also Giorgio Agamben, *Potentialities: Collected Essays in Philosophy*, ed. and trans. D. Heller-Roazen (Stanford: Stanford University Press, 1999), 161.

4. See G. W. F. Hegel, *Science of Logic*, trans. A. V. Miller (New York: Humanity Books, 1999), 126–27, 107. Hegel's discussion of the relations between the notions of "determination," "limit," "constitution," and "alteration" cannot be limited to the *Science of Logic*. The status of these notions is not only logical and ontological, but also political. See, for example, *The Philosophy of Right*, trans. T. M. Knox (Oxford: Oxford University Press, 1952), 291 (Addition to §298); *The Phenomenology of Spirit*, trans. A. V. Miller (Oxford: Oxford University Press, 1977), 96–97. For an argument regarding the political character of the ontological categories of potentiality and actuality, see Agamben, *Homo Sacer I*, 44; Giorgio Agamben, *Homo Sacer III: Remnants of Auschwitz; The Witness and the Archive*, trans. D. Heller-Roazen (New York: Zone Books, 2000), 146–47; Giorgio Agamben, *The Open: Man and Animal*, trans. K. Attell (Stanford: Stanford University Press, 2004), 79.

5. Agamben, *Potentialities*, 161, 170.

6. Carl Schmitt, *Political Theology: Four Chapters on the Concept of Sovereignty*, trans. G. Schwab (Cambridge: MIT Press, 1988), 38. In the opening chapter of *Political Theology*, Schmitt writes, "the exception is to be understood to refer to a general concept in the theory of state, and not merely to a construct applied to any emergency decree or state of siege." He repeats the same distinction later: "not every extraordinary measure, not every police emergency measure or emergency decree is necessarily an exception. What characterizes an exception is principally unlimited authority, which means the suspension of the entire existing order. In such a situation it is clear that the state remains, whereas law recedes." When Schmitt praises Bodin's reference to the state of emergency, he does so not because he finds it especially illustrative of the sovereign exception, but only because it "reduced his [Bodin's] analysis of the relationships between prince and estates to a simple either/or." See Schmitt, *Political Theology*, 5, 8, 12. See also Jacques Derrida, *On Cosmopolitanism and Forgiveness*, trans. S. Critchley and R. Kearney (London: Routledge, 2001), 42; Jacques Derrida, "To Forgive: The Unforgivable and the Imprescriptable," trans. E. Rottenberg, in *Questioning God*, ed. J. D. Caputo, M. Dooley, and M. J. Scanlon (Indianapolis: Indiana University Press, 2001), 43; Alain Badiou, *Saint Paul: The Foundation of Universalism*, trans. R. Brassier and A. Toscano (Stanford: Stanford University Press, 2003), 70; Slavoj Žižek, "From Politics to Biopolitics . . . and Back," *South Atlantic Quarterly* 103, no. 2/3 (Spring/Summer 2004): 504.

7. On the relation of forgiveness to the sovereign right of grace, see Hannah Arendt, *The Human Condition* (Chicago: University of Chicago Press, 1958), 239; Ernst Kantorowicz, "*Deus per naturam, deus per gratiam*: A Note on Mediaeval Political Theology," *Selected Studies* (New York: J. J. Augustin Publisher, 1965), 123, 126, 135. On the necessity of distinguishing between these concepts, see Derrida, *On Cosmopolitanism and Forgiveness*, 42.

8. Hannah Arendt, "Understanding and Politics," in *Essays in Understanding, 1930–1954*, ed. J. Kohn (New York: Harcourt, Brace & Co., 1994), 308. For Agamben's account of philosophy's implication in the absolution of violence, see *Language and Death: The Place of Negativity*, trans. K. Pinkus (Minneapolis: University of Minnesota Press, 1991), 106.

9. Adorno argues that the opening passages of *The Sickness Unto Death* contain the "founding passages of existential philosophy." *Kierkegaard: Construction of the Aesthetic*, trans. R. Hullot-Kentor (Minneapolis: University of Minnesota Press, 1989), 58, cf. 68. However, Adorno goes on to say, existentialism is based on a misreading of these same passages (72, 78). The problem Kierkegaard sets for himself in this text, Adorno argues, is not "the meaning of the being of existence," as existentialism presumes, but the paradox of a specific kind of power, the power to found re-

ality itself (107). As Agamben notes in *Homo Sacer I*, Schmitt turns to Kierkegaard in order to define the concept of decision he sets forth in his *Political Theology* (16). On the necessity of reading Schmitt alongside Kierkegaard, see also Karl Löwith, "The Occasional Decisionism of Carl Schmitt," trans. G. Steiner, in *Martin Heidegger and European Nihilism*, ed. R. Wolin (New York: Columbia University Press, 1995), 141; Slavoj Žižek, "Carl Schmitt in the Age of Post-Politics," in *The Challenge of Carl Schmitt*, ed. Chantal Mouffe (New York: Verso Books, 1999), 19, 21; Jacques Derrida, *Politics of Friendship,* trans. G. Collins (New York: Verso, 1997), 69, 219.

10. Accordingly, this essay will swerve from the kind of commentaries on *The Sickness Unto Death* that can be found in *International Kierkegaard Commentary, Volume 19: The Sickness Unto Death*, ed. Robert Perkins (Macon, GA: Mercer University Press, 1987) and *Kierkegaard Studies* 2, ed. N. J. Cappelørn and H. Deuser (Berlin: De Gruyter, 1997).

11. Georges Burdeau, quoted in Agamben, *Homo Sacer I*, 39.

12. Agamben, *Homo Sacer I*, 42.

13. Ibid., 40.

14. Ibid.

15. Ibid., 39.

16. Ibid., 40.

17. Ibid., 41.

18. Ibid.

19. Ibid., 41. See also Hannah Arendt, *On Revolution* (New York: Viking Press, 1963), 161–63.

20. See G. W. F. Hegel, *Introduction to the Lectures on the History of Philosophy,* trans. T. M. Knox and A. V. Miller (Oxford: Clarendon Press, 1985), 71–73. See also Agamben, *Homo Sacer I*, 45; Agamben, *Potentialities*, 182; Theodor Adorno, *Metaphysics: Concept and Problems,* trans. E. Jephcott, and ed. R. Tiedemann (Stanford: Stanford University Press, 2000), 37, 49, 52, 62–64.

21. Agamben, *Homo Sacer I*, 45.

22. Ibid., 46.

23. Ibid. See also Agamben, *Potentialities*, 183–84.

24. Ibid., 48.

25. See Søren Kierkegaard, *The Sickness Unto Death: A Christian Psychological Exposition for Upbuilding and Awakening*, ed. and trans. H. V. Hong and E. H. Hong (Princeton: Princeton University Press, 1980), 14, 30, 49, 82, 131. Vincent McCarthy is right to emphasize that the "power" in question in *The Sickness Unto Death* is "Constituting Power." See "'Psychological Fragments': Kierkegaard's Religious Psychology," in *Kierkegaard's Truth: The Disclosure of the Self*, ed. J. H. Smith (New Haven: Yale University Press, 1981), 280.

26. Agamben, *Homo Sacer I*, 44, see also 59.

27. See Jon Stewart, "Kierkegaard's Phenomenology of Despair in *The Sickness Unto Death*," in *Kierkegaard Studies* 2, ed. N. J. Cappelørn and H. Deuser (Berlin: Walter de Gruyter, 1997), 133–34, 136–38.

28. See, for example, G. W. F. Hegel, *Philosophy of Mind, Being Part Three of The Encyclopædia of the Philosophical Sciences (1830)*, trans. W. Wallace (Oxford: Oxford University Press, 1971), §382.

2930. See, generally, Hegel, *Phenomenology*, 79–103 ("Force and the Understanding"). See also G. W. F. Hegel, *Logic, Being Part One of the Encyclopædia of the Philosophical Sciences (1830)*, trans. W. Wallace (Oxford: Oxford University Press, 1975), 82, 85.

30. See Søren Kierkegaard, *Philosophical Fragments; Johannes Climacus*, ed. and trans. Howard V. Hong and Edna H. Hong (Princeton: Princeton University Press, 1985), 166–72.

31. See Kierkegaard, *The Sickness Unto Death*, 13. Not coincidentally, Alexander García Düttmann describes Agamben's concept of the "remainder" in much the same terms. "The notion of a remainder in Agamben designates the relation of the relation, the fact *that* the relation relates. Here, it is not a matter of relating to something, but of *being* a relation, of entering the relation and touching its factuality, its *that*-it-relates." To break with the logic of sovereignty, in Düttmann's cogent summary, "one must maintain oneself in the relating of the relation." See Alexander García Düttmann, "Never Before, Always Already: Notes on Agamben and the Category of Relation," *Angelaki* 6, no. 3 (December 2001): 5, emphasis in original.

32. *The Sickness Unto Death* correlates the distinction between infinitude [*Uendelighed*] and finitude [*Endelighed*] with the Greek concepts of ἄπειον and πέραξ, which the Hongs, in turn, translate as "the unlimited" and "the limited." See *The Sickness Unto Death*, 35.

33. *The Sickness Unto Death* outlines no fewer than four modes and four aspects of despair. Many disciplined commentaries on *The Sickness Unto Death* compute, in detail, the algebra enabled by these categories. I depart from this style of commentary, concurring instead with Alastair Hannay's argument that "Kierkegaard's *main* claim [is] that the fundamental form that despair takes—that is, the way in which despair manifests itself, the behavior we should call despair in the most basic sense— is that of aiming at, or willingly accepting, specifications of selfhood that do *not* have the form of a selfhood established by God." "Basic Despair in *The Sickness Unto Death*," *Kierkegaard Studies* 1, ed. N. J. Cappelørn and H. Deuser (Berlin: De Gruyter, 1996), 18, emphasis in original.

34. See Kierkegaard, *The Sickness Unto Death*, 8–9, 17. As is the case with "anxiety" in *The Concept of Anxiety*, which suggests that "the more profound the anxiety,

the more profound the culture," the ability to despair in *The Sickness Unto Death* functions as an ontological criterion for cultural rank. See *The Concept of Anxiety: A Simple, Psychologically Orienting Deliberation on the Dogmatic Issue of Hereditary Sin*, ed. and trans. Reidar Thomte and A. B. Anderson (Princeton: Princeton University Press, 1980), 42; cf. Adorno, *Kierkegaard*, 32–33.

35. See Kierkegaard, *The Sickness Unto Death*, 6, 21. See also Thomas Pepper, "Prepositions of Death: Kierkegaard's *The Sickness Unto Death* read with Marguerite Duras's '*La Maladie de la mort*'," in *Kierkegaard Studies Yearbook* 2, ed. N. J. Cappelørn and H. Deuser (Berlin: de Gruyter, 1997), 98–99.

36. See Kierkegaard, *The Sickness Unto Death*, 6.

37. Ibid., 14.

38. See Agamben, *Homo Sacer I*, 44.

39. Kierkegaard, *The Sickness Unto Death*, 108–9, 18.

40. See Gustav Aulén, *Christus Victor: An Historical Study of the Three Main Types of the Idea of Atonement*, trans. A. G. Hebert (New York: Macmillan, 1951), 90–91, 147.

41. See, for example, Hegel, *Phenomenology*, 91–94.

42. See Louis Mackey, *Kierkegaard: A Kind of Poet* (Philadelphia: University of Pennsylvania Press, 1971), 247–48.

43. See Richard Lanham, *A Handlist of Rhetorical Terms*, 2nd ed. (Berkeley: University of California Press, 1991), 36. Kenneth Burke has noted the centrality of *gradatio* in the Pauline Epistles. See "On Catharsis, or Resolution," *Kenyon Review* 21, no. 3 (1959): 365; "Catharsis—Second View," *Centennial Review of Arts and Sciences* 5 (1961): 124.

44. See, variously, Hannah Arendt, *The Life of the Mind*, Volume II (New York: Harcourt, Brace & Jovanovich, 1978), 65, 70; Adorno, *Kierkegaard*, 111–13; Aulén, *Christus Victor*, 157.

45. See Lanham, *A Handlist of Rhetorical Terms*, 32.

46. Defiance, according to Kierkegaard, is the specifically masculine genre of despair. See *The Sickness Unto Death*, 49, 67.

47. Kierkegaard, *Concluding Unscientific Postscript*, 343, quoted in Mackey, *Kierkegaard*, 245.

48. See Ernst Kantorowicz, "*Deus per naturam, deus per gratiam*," 123; Ernst Kantorowicz, *The King's Two Bodies: A Study in Medieval Political Theology* (Princeton: Princeton University Press, 1957), 47.

49. See Kantorowicz, "*Deus per naturam, deus per gratiam*," 125, 130–37; Kantorowicz, *The King's Two Bodies*, 87.

50. See Kantorowicz, "*Deus per naturam, deus per gratiam*," 123, 126, 129, 135; Kantorowicz, "The Sovereignty of the Artist: A Note on Legal Maxims and Renais-

sance Theories of Art," in *Selected Studies* (New York: J. J. Augustin Publisher, 1965), 364–65. See also Arlette Lebigre, "Pardon, Grâce, Amnistie: Deux Mille Ans D'Arbitraire," *L'Histoire* 143 (April 1991): 86-7; Peter Brown, "Vers la Naissance du Purgatoire: Amnistie et pénitence dans le christianisme occidental de l'Antiquité tardive au Haut Moyen Age," *Annales: Histoire, Sciences Sociales* 6 (November/December 1997): 1250-51.

51. See Mackey, *Kierkegaard*, 248, cf. 257. See also Jacques Derrida, *The Gift of Death*, trans. D. Wills (Chicago: University of Chicago Press, 1995), 58.

52. See Michel Foucault, "What Is an Author?" in *Language, Counter-Memory, Practice: Selected Essays and Interviews*, trans. D. Bouchard (Ithaca: Cornell University Press, 1977), 122, 124.

53. See Adorno, *Kierkegaard*, 12.

55. See Löwith, "The Occasional Decisionism of Carl Schmitt," 142.

55. By reading *The Sickness Unto Death* from this angle, I have in mind not only Adorno's approach but also Kierkegaard's own journal entry of May 13, 1848, which suggests that in *The Sickness Unto Death* the order of the rhetorical exceeds that of the dialectical. See H. Hong and E. Hong, "Historical Introduction," in *The Sickness Unto Death*, xiv.

56. Schmitt, *Political Theology*, 49–52, 66.

57. See Carl Schmitt, *Political Romanticism*, trans. Guy Oakes (Cambridge: MIT Press, 2001), 3, 117, 159; Carl Schmitt, *The Concept of the Political*, trans. George Schwab (Chicago: University of Chicago Press, 1996), 64–65, 72; Schmitt, *Political Theology*, 53–54.

58. See Carl Schmitt, *The Crisis of Parliamentary Democracy*, trans. Ellen Kennedy (Cambridge: MIT Press, 1988), 36.

59. See Mackey, *Kierkegaard*, 1–84.

60. See Schmitt, *Political Theology*, 36. See also Schmitt, *Concept of the Political*, 42.

61. Schmitt, *Concept of the Political*, 39, 43–45; Adorno, *Kierkegaard*, 107; cf. Derrida, *Politics*, 113–33.

62. Kierkegaard, *The Sickness Unto Death*, 67–74.

63. To name the error of the "merely negative" (unchristian) concept of sin characteristic of "defiance," Kierkegaard turns to the Latinate *constituere*. "So here it is again, this view that sin is merely a negation, which like stolen goods can never be legitimized—a negation, a powerless attempt to constitute oneself [*at constituere sig*], which, however, undergoing all the torment of powerlessness in despairing defiance, it is incapable of doing" (105–6). See also, on this point, Hannah Arendt, *Love and Saint Augustine*, ed. J. V. Scott and J. C. Stark (Chicago: University of Chicago Press, 1996), 87–88.

64. Kierkegaard, *The Sickness Unto Death*, 110.

65. Ibid., 113.

66. Ibid., 115.

67. To the sin of defiance Kierkegaard gives the name "offense"; to "offence" Kierkegaard correlates the Jews of the New Testament (the Hongs note Matthew 9:2–3 and Mark 2:7). Spiritless pagans, on the other hand, do not even possess the capacity to be offended by the idea that one's sins could be forgiven.

68. Sylviane Agacinski, *Aparté: Conceptions and Deaths of Søren Kierkegaard*, trans. K. Newmark (Gainesville: Florida University Press, 1988), 169.

69. See Kierkegaard, *Concept of Anxiety*, 37.

70. Kierkegaard, *The Sickness Unto Death*, 118.

71. Aristotle, *Politics,* Book III:11, 1281a: 40–43.

72. See *Homo Sacer I*, 1, 87. In her 1999 lectures on Arendt, Julia Kristeva drew on Arendt's treatment of *zoe* in order to offer an immanent critique of Arendt's thinking on the body. *Zoe*, which Kristeva glosses as "the degree zero of the human and a primary expression of biological life," is, according to Kristeva, exemplified by "women and slaves." *Hannah Arendt: Life Is a Narrative*, trans. Frank Collins (Toronto: University of Toronto Press, 2001), 62. In the passage of the *Politics* to which Kierkegaard refers, for instance, Aristotle poses as a question the relation between the bodies of brutes and the bodies of men. See *Politics,* Book III, 11, 1281b:15–20.

73. See Kierkegaard, *Philosophical Fragments*, 41.

74. Kierkegaard, *The Sickness Unto Death*, 118.

75. Ibid.

76. Adorno attributes Kierkegaard's struggle against the category of the historical to the events of 1848 (35, cf., 48). Yet precisely because of this struggle, Adorno suggests, a certain correspondence emerges between Kierkegaard's metaphors of reification and Marx's historical materialist theories of the same (39). For his part, Löwith locates the intellectual historical relation between Marx and Kierkegaard ("these two great opponents of Hegel's philosophy of absolute knowledge") in their theories of "decision" (157). Löwith's critique of Schmitt is that he misreads Marx and Kierkegaard to find in their work a concept of decision for decision's own sake, a decision grounded in nothing more than decisiveness itself, whereas, according to Löwith, both Marx and Kierkegaard measured their concepts of decision against a higher court of appeal (the social or God) (158). In the course of this argument, Löwith touches on but does not inquire into another red thread that binds the three theorists. Both *The Sickness Unto Death* (written in 1848) and *The 18th Brumaire of Louis Bonaparte* (written about 1848) are texts concerned with the dialectical exposition of a "miracle" (cf. *Sickness Unto Death* [7, 39] and *18th Brumaire* [13, 20, 53, 124, 133]). Meanwhile, as I discuss below, in *Political Theology* (a text that names 1848 as the

year that *pouvoir constituant*, rather than royalism, became the dominant form of power [51]), Schmitt takes up remarks he made in *Die Diktatur* to argue that the miracle is the theological category that corresponds to the political category of the sovereign exception.

77. Kierkegaard, *The Sickness Unto Death*, 120.

78. Ibid., 121.

79. Ernst Bloch, *Natural Law and Human Dignity*, trans. D. J. Schmidt (Cambridge: MIT Press, 1986): 25–27, 31, 36–44.

80. Kierkegaard, *The Sickness Unto Death*, 122.

81. Ibid., 122–23, translation modified. The Hongs translate *"lade Stratten fare"* into "punishment has to be abandoned." I prefer Lowrie's formulation ("punishment cannot be applied") not merely because it does not add "abandon" where the term is not mentioned, but because it cuts to the quick of the logic of "abandon," where "the rule applies to the exception in no longer applying, in withdrawing from it" (*Homo Sacer I*, 18).

82. The text of the amnesty is reproduced in its entirety in *The Making of Italy, 1796–1870*, ed. D. Smith (New York: Walker & Co., 1968), 116–17. Significantly, even though the amnesty refers to itself as an act of forgiveness, its concluding clause sets forth a condition that undermines the unconditionality implied by that self-reference. As Luigi Salvatorelli notes, the text "spoke of 'forgiveness' and ended with a threat to be carried out in case the pope's hopes in the effects of this forgiveness should prove vain." *The Risorgimento: Thought and Action*, trans. M. Domani (New York: Harper & Row, 1970), 112.

83. See, generally, Edgar Holt, *The Making of Italy, 1815–1870* (New York: Atheneum, 1971), 119–75.

84. See Nicole Loraux, *The Divided City: Memory and Forgetting in Athens*, trans. C. Pache (New York: Zone Books, 2002), 15 (but cf. 148), 42–43, 241.

85. On *hamartia*, see Jean-Pierre Vernant, *Myth and Tragedy in Ancient Greece*, trans. J. Lloyd (New York: Zone Books, 1990), 62, 5. On judgment, see Agamben, *Homo Sacer III*, 18–19.

86. Kierkegaard, *The Sickness Unto Death*, 123, translation modified. The Hongs translate *"opgiver"* as "to abandon." Lowrie's translation of *"opgiver"* as "to give up" is not only more in line with the Benjaminian injunction to translate literally but also prevents the collapse of a number of distinct Danish phrases and terms (*lade Stratten fare, opgiver, Hengivenhed*) into the single Latinate, "abandon."

87. For an intimation of the latter, see Arendt, "Søren Kierkegaard," in *Essays in Understanding*, ed. J. Kohn (New York: Harcourt, Brace & Co., 1994), 47.

88. See, on this point, Derrida, *Politics of Friendship*, 108–9.

89. Hannah Arendt argues that "it is characteristic of all of Existenz philosophy,

that by 'existential' it fundamentally understands what Kierkegaard had presented in the category of the Exception." "What Is Existenz Philosophy?" *Partisan Review* 13, no. 1 (1946): 44. When seeking to find a determining ground to define the single person who may be excepted from the coercive laws of the commonwealth, Kant enters into a set of deductions based on the meaning of the word "gracious." "If we try to find a definite meaning for the word *gracious* [*gnädig*], as distinct from kind, beneficent, protective etc., we see that it can be attributed only to a person to whom no *coercive rights* apply [and whom Kant had already called the "exception"]. Thus only the head of the *state's government*, who enacts and distributes all benefits that are possible within the public laws (for the *sovereign* who provides them is, as it were, invisible, and is not an agent but the personified law itself), can be given the title of *gracious lord* [*gnädigen herr*] for he is the only individual to whom coercive rights do not apply." In *The Metaphysics of Morals*, Kant even suggests that the right to grant clemency [*Begnadigungsrecht*] is "the only one which deserves to be called a right of majesty." For his part, Hegel argues that "[t]he right to pardon [*Begnadigungsrecht*] criminals proceeds from the sovereignty of the monarch, since it is this alone which is empowered to realize the spirit's power to make undone what has been done and to destroy a crime by forgiving and forgetting it." Significantly, instead of the more juridical "*Tat*" ("deed"), Hegel here uses "*das Geschehene*," which signifies an "event" or "happening." Translated more literally, Hegel's description of the spirit's power "to make undone what has been done" ("*das Geschehene ungeschehen zu machen*") would read, "to make the happened unhappened." It would thus need to be reread alongside the *Critique of Judgment*, in the first footnote of which Kant uses exactly the same phrase to give an example of a desire aimed at something impossible (Guyer and Matthews translate "*das Geschehene ungeschehen zu machen*" with "to make what has happened not have happened" instead of following Meredith's "to undo the past"). See Immanuel Kant, *Critique of the Power of Judgment*, trans. P. Guyer and E. Matthews (Cambridge: Cambridge University Press, 2000), 65, cf. 32. See also Immanuel Kant, "On the Common Saying: 'This May Be True in Theory, but It Does Not Apply in Practice,'" in *Political Writings*, ed. and int. Hans Reiss, trans. H. B. Nisbet, 2nd ed. (Cambridge: Cambridge University Press, 1991), 77, emphasis in original; Kant, *The Metaphysics of Morals*, 109; Hegel, *The Philosophy of Right*, 186.

90. Schmitt, *Political Theology*, 36.

91. Ibid., 37.

92. Ibid., 8.

93. See Adorno, *Kierkegaard*, 98–99.

94. Ibid., 103–5.

95. Søren Kierkegaard, *Philosophical Fragments*, trans. D. Swenson (Princeton:

Princeton University Press, 1936), 53. The Hongs translate *"Under," "Vidunderet,"* and *"Forundring"* as "wonder." See Kierkegaard, *Philosophical Fragments,* ed. and trans. H. and E. Hong, 36, 65, 145.

96. See Kierkegaard, *Philosophical Fragments,* ed. and trans. H. and E. Hong, 86.

97. Ibid., 76–85.

98. Ibid., 18.

99. Ibid., 97.

100. Ibid., 21–22, 53–54.

101. Ibid., 36.

102. Schmitt, *Political Theology,* 50; Adorno, *Kierkegaard,* 104.

103. Cf. Immanuel Kant, "Idea for a Universal History with a Cosmopolitan Purpose" and "Perpetual Peace: A Philosophical Sketch," in *Political Writings,* ed. and int. Hans Reiss, trans. H. B. Nisbet, 2nd ed. (Cambridge: Cambridge University Press, 1991), 46, 112–13.

104. See Fyodor Dostoyevsky, *The Brothers Karamazov,* trans. A. MacAndrew (New York: Bantam Books, 1981), 307, 309.

105. Agamben, *Homo Sacer I,* 6.

106. Ibid., 4.

107. See Michel Foucault, "The Subject and Power," in *Michel Foucault: Beyond Structuralism and Hermeneutics,* 2nd ed. (Chicago: University of Chicago Press, 1983), 213; Hannah Arendt, *The Origins of Totalitarianism* (New York: Harcourt Brace Jovanovich, 1973), 246, 447, 456, 469, 476; *The Human Condition,* 178, 236–47. Leon Botstein relies heavily on the category of the miracle in his 1978 response to Martin Jay. See Martin Jay and Leon Botstein, "Hannah Arendt: Opposing Views," *Partisan Review* 45, no. 3 (1978): 369, 371, 375, 376.

108. Agamben, *Homo Sacer I,* 4; Agamben, *Homo Sacer III,* 15, 51; Giorgio Agamben, *State of Exception,* trans. K. Attell (Chicago: University of Chicago Press, 2005), 56.

109. Agamben, *Homo Sacer I,* 12. See also Ulrich Raulff, "An Interview with Giorgio Agamben," *German Law Journal* 5, no. 5 (May 2004): 609.

110. Ibid., 21–22.

111. See Hegel, *Logic (1830),* 33.

112. Giorgio Agamben, *The Idea of Prose,* trans. M. Sullivan and S. Whitsitt (Albany: SUNY University Press, 1995), 77–78; Giorgio Agamben, *The Coming Community,* trans. M. Hardt (Minneapolis: University of Minnesota Press, 1993), 5–7.

113. See Agamben, *Idea of Prose,* 79–82, and *Coming Community,* 7.

114. See Agamben, *Coming Community,* 6. See also Agamben, *The Open,* 19, 21, 90.

115. See Agamben, *Coming Community,* 44–45, and *Homo Sacer I,* 26–27.

116. See Agamben, *Coming Community*, 45.

117. Agamben, *Homo Sacer I*, 29.

118. Ibid., 61. Cf. Giorgio Agamben, *Potentialities*, 124, and *Language and Death*, 101.

119. Ibid., 28.

120. Friedrich Nietzsche, *On the Genealogy of Morals*, trans. Walter Kaufmann (New York: Vintage Books, 1967), 73.

121. Ibid., 91–92. See also Gilles Deleuze, "To Have Done With Judgment," *Essays Critical and Clinical*, trans. D. Smith and M. A. Greco (Minneapolis: University of Minnesota Press, 1997), 12–17.

122. Agamben, *Means Without Ends*, 21, and *Homo Sacer I*, 128.

123. Agamben, *Homo Sacer I*, 12.

124. Ibid., 27.

125. Ibid., 65–66, 109–10.

126. Agamben, *The Open*, 75.

127. Ibid., 37–38.

128. Ibid., 58, 62, 91. See also Jacques Derrida, *Of Spirit*, trans. G. Bennington and R. Bowlby (Chicago: University of Chicago Press, 1989), 52–53, 119n3.

129. Agamben, *The Open*, 91.

130. Kevin Attell's footnote on *ignoscenza* suggests that, "[i]n addition to meaning 'not knowing,' the word would ... also carry the sense of 'forgiveness' or 'pardon,' and might best be understood as a sort of 'forgetful forgiveness.'" Agamben, *The Open*, 98n3.

131. Agamben, *Coming Community*, 13–15.

132. On messianic time as a recapitulation of the past that enables one to "finally take leave of the past," see Giorgio Agamben, "The Time that Is Left," *Epoché* 7, no. 1 (Fall 2002): 10. See also Agamben, *State of Exception*, 85, cf. 25, and note 118 above.

133. See Kierkegaard, *The Sickness Unto Death*, 49–50.

134. Ibid., 50, 67.

135. Ibid., 29.

136. Ibid., 29–42.

137. Ibid., 36.

138. Ibid., 30–31.

139. Ibid., 36.

140. Ibid., 38–39; cf. Søren Kierkegaard, *Either/Or, Part II*, trans. H. and E. Hong (Princeton: Princeton University Press, 1987), 24, 53.

141. On the corpse as a limit of life, see Julia Kristeva, *Powers of Horror: An Essay on Abjection*, trans. L. Roudiez (New York: Columbia University Press, 1982), 3. See also Agamben, *Homo Sacer III*, 48.

142. Kierkegaard, *The Sickness Unto Death*, 38. In his reading of Kierkegaard's 1846 "At a Graveside," Geoffrey Hale notes the significance of the Danish "*Af-gjørende*" for Kierkegaard's account of the concept of decision. "Death's decision is decisive, and this is the only word (*ord*) that describes this decision; there is no other. Kierkegaard must take 'death's decision' literally. It literally does (*gjører*) away (*af*) with everything, puts an end to everything, and brings everything to a halt." *Kierkegaard and the Ends of Language* (Minneapolis: University of Minnesota Press, 2002), 88.

143. Arendt, "Søren Kierkegaard," 48. See also Arendt, *Origins*, 471–76.

144. Agamben, *Homo Sacer III*, 48.

145. Quoted in Agamben, *Homo Sacer I*, 37.

146. On law and the form of the necessary, see Immanuel Kant, *Critique of Practical Reason*, trans. H. W. Cassirer (Milwaukee: Marquette University Press, 1998), 19ff.

147. Agacinski, *Aparté*, 143.

148. Kierkegaard, *The Sickness Unto Death*, 50.

149. Agacinski, *Aparté*, 167, emphasis in original.

150. Ibid., 169.

151. Ibid., 171. Even as Kierkegaard raises questions of sexual difference at every turn in his writings, he also suspends those questions with studied indifference. This indifference, which Agacinski, reading *The Sickness Unto Death*, calls "sovereign," does not reverse or displace sexual difference (173; *The Sickness Unto Death*, 50), but merely neutralizes it in a way that pushes the hierarchy of sex to "the limit of its violence" (173).

152. Agacinski, *Aparté*, 169.

153. Dostoyevsky, *The Brothers Karamazov*, 714–15.

154. For a discussion of a similar schema in *Fear and Trembling*, see Thomas Pepper, "Abraham: Who Could Possibly Understand Him?" *Kierkegaard Studies* 1, ed. N. J. Cappelørn and H. Deuser (Berlin: De Gruyter, 1996), 238.

155. See Julia Kristeva, *Black Sun: Depression and Melancholia*, trans. L. Roudiez (New York: Columbia University Press, 1987), 190, 206.

156. Ibid., 207, 214, cf. 23.

157. Julia Kristeva, *Hannah Arendt*, trans. Ross Guberman (New York: Columbia University Press, 2001), 239.

158. But cf. Mary Dietz, "The Arendt Question in Feminism," in *Turning Operations: Feminism, Arendt, and Politics* (New York: Routledge, 2002), 119–40, esp. 127–29.

159. Arendt, *The Life of the Mind*, Volume II, 208, 211–15.

160. Arendt, *Origins*, 469.

161. For Kant, what matters in defining the word "*Wunder*" is "only to know

what they are for us, i.e. for our practical employment of reason." He thus defines miracles as "events in the world, the causes and effects of which are absolutely unknown to us and so must remain." "Religion within the Boundaries of Mere Reason," in *Religion within the Boundaries of Mere Reason and Other Writings*, trans. A. Wood and G. Di Giovanni (Cambridge: Cambridge University Press, 1998), 100; cf. Baruch Spinoza, "Of Miracles," in *A Theologico-Political Treatise*, trans. R. H. M. Elwes (New York: Dover, 1951), 81–97.

162. Cf. Immanuel Kant, "Contest of the Faculties" and "Perpetual Peace," in *Political Writings*, ed. and int. Hans Reiss, trans. H. B. Nisbet, 2nd ed. (Cambridge: Cambridge University Press, 1991), 186–87, 108.

163. See Hannah Arendt, "What Is Freedom?" *Between Past and Future: Six Exercises in Political Thought* (New York: Viking Press, 1961), 168–69; Arendt, *The Life of the Mind*, Volume II, 20, 27, 29, 210; Immanuel Kant, *Critique of Pure Reason*, trans. N. Smith (New York: St. Martin's Press, 1965), 464–79.

164. Arendt, "What Is Existenz Philosophy?," 45.

165. Arendt, "Søren Kierkegaard," 48.

166. Arendt, *The Life of the Mind*, Volume II, 174, 195, 196, 198. See also Arendt, "What Is Existenz Philosophy?" 36.

167. See Arendt, "What Is Existenz Philosophy?" 45; Arendt, *The Life of the Mind*, Volume II, 198.

168. Arendt, *The Life of the Mind*, Volume II, 198, 207.

169. Agamben, *Homo Sacer III*, 145–48.

170. Arendt, *The Life of the Mind*, Volume II, 207, 30; Kierkegaard, *Philosophical Fragments*, ed. and trans. H. and E. Hong, 74–75; Agamben, *Potentialities*, 183.

171. See Kierkegaard, *Philosophical Fragments*, ed. and trans. H. and E. Hong, 76–78; Arendt, *The Human Condition*, 246.

172. Such as when guilt over an act or inactivity becomes the premise for ideological deductive logic. See Arendt, *Origins*, 473.

173. Arendt, "Franz Kafka: A Revaluation," in *Essays in Understanding*, ed. J. Kohn (New York: Harcourt, Brace & Co., 1994), 74; Arendt, "What Is Freedom?" 170.

174. Arendt, *Origins*, 465.

175. Arendt, *The Human Condition*, 236, 246.

176. Ibid., 246–47.

177. See Arendt, "What Is Freedom?," 150, 155, 164–65, 169–71; Arendt, *The Human Condition*, 234.

178. Elizabeth Young-Bruehl, *Hannah Arendt, For Love of the World* (New Haven: Yale University Press, 1982), 200.

179. Arendt, "Franz Kafka," 72.

180. Ibid., 73.

181. Ibid., 75. See also Agamben, *Homo Sacer III*, 134; Agamben, *Potentialities*, 220–21

182. Ibid., 78.

183. Kierkegaard, *The Sickness Unto Death*, 74.

184. See Arendt, *Origins*, 246. See also Arendt, "Kafka: A Revaluation," 70, 71, 74.

185. See Adorno, *Kierkegaard*, 133; cf. Theodor Adorno, *Minima Moralia: Reflections from Damaged Life*, trans. E. Jephcott (New York: Verso Books, 1974), 121.

186. See Agamben, *Homo Sacer I*, 10.

187. See Arendt, *Origins*, 427, 437, 440, 459.

188. See Dostoyevsky, *The Brothers Karamazov*, 317. See also Fyodor Dostoyevsky, *Crime and Punishment*, trans. D. McDuff (New York: Penguin Books, 1991), 328.

189. See Arendt, *Origins*, 440–41.

190. Ibid., 459. See also *The Life of the Mind*, Volume II, 184; Adorno, *Minima Moralia*, 55–56.

191. Emmanuel Levinas, *Totality and Infinity*, trans. A Lingis (Pittsburgh: Duquesne University Press, 1969), 55.

192. Agamben, *Homo Sacer III*, 147.

193. Levinas, *Totality and Infinity*, 57. See also Agamben, *Homo Sacer III*, 77.

194. Arendt, *Origins*, 441.

195. Søren Kierkegaard, "Mercifulness, a Work of Love, Even if It Can Give Nothing and Is Capable of Doing Nothing," in *Works of Love: Some Christian Reflections in the Form of Discourses*, trans. E. Hong and H. Hong (Princeton: Princeton University Press, 1995), 323–24.

196. Kierkegaard derives from this parable two lessons: "one can be merciful without being able to do the slightest" and that "being able to be merciful is a much greater perfection than to be able to do something" (323). Here, as in *The Sickness Unto Death*, Kierkegaard finds an exception to the normal rule of entelechy: the potential to not-do is, in the case of mercy, superior to the potential to do.

197. Kierkegaard, *The Sickness Unto Death*, 7–8.

198. Thus, for example, Foucault will turn to the parable of Lazarus to show how the leper is not driven off "before first being inscribed within a sacred circle." "Abandonment is for him a salvation," Foucault will then go on to argue. See Michel Foucault, *Madness and Civilization: A History of Insanity in the Age of Reason*, trans. R. Howard (New York: Random House, 1965), 6.

199. "The deepest cause of the Nazi destruction of Jews (and Gypsies)," writes George Kateb, "was the conviction that the people put to death were being punished for the worst possible *sin*, not crime. The worst possible sin, Protestantism seems to have taught Europe (and social Darwinism and Marxist materialism echoed it) was not behavioral but ontological, with the sinners deserving damnation all the more

because they were not responsible. They could not be responsible, after all, for who they were." *Hannah Arendt: Politics, Conscience, Evil* (Totowa, NJ: Rowman & Allanheld, 1984), 81, emphasis in original. Derrida addresses the same question in his analysis of Vladimir Jankélévitch's remark that "A Jew does not have the right to be, existing is his sin." His account then takes up the problem I have already touched upon above: the concept of the subject the substance of which derives from an originary guilt or debt. See Derrida, "To Forgive: The Unforgivable and the Imprescriptable," 43. See also Max Horkheimer and Theodor Adorno, *Dialectic of Enlightenment: Philosophical Fragments,* ed. G. S. Noerr, trans. E. Jephcott (Stanford: Stanford University Press, 2002), 144.

200. Hannah Arendt, "Organized Guilt and Universal Responsibility," in *Essays in Understanding,* ed. J. Kohn (New York: Harcourt, Brace & Co., 1994), 126.

201. Arendt, *Origins,* 471, 478, cf. 469–70.

202. Ibid., 476.

203. Ibid., 445, 447. See also Agamben, *Means Without Ends,* 135.

204. Kateb, *Hannah Arendt,* 52.

205. Arendt, *Origins,* 208.

206. Arendt, *Human Condition,* 237; *Life of the Mind,* Volume II, 30.

207. Arendt, *Human Condition,* 237.

208. Arendt, *Origins,* 208.

209. See Young-Bruehl, *For Love of the World,* 251.

210. Arendt, "The Image of Hell," in *Essays in Understanding* ed. J. Kohn (New York: Harcourt, Brace & Co., 1994), 200; cf. Agamben, *The Idea of Prose,* 85.

211. See Derrida, *Politics of Friendship,* 32; Jacques Derrida, *Monolingualism of the Other; or, The Prosthesis of Origin,* trans. P. Mensah (Stanford: Stanford University Press, 1998), 20; Jacques Derrida, *Demeure: Fiction and Testimony,* trans. E. Rottenberg (Stanford: Stanford University Press, 2000), 75.

212. Arendt, *The Human Condition,* 240n78, ellipses and emphasis in original.

213. Arendt, *Origins,* 430.

214. Arendt, *The Life of the Mind,* Volume I, 4.

215. Ibid., 88.

216. Arendt, *The Human Condition,* 238.

217. Ibid., 123–24.

218. Ibid., 5; Arendt, *Origins,* 461.

219. Arendt, *Origins,* 463.

220. Arendt, *The Life of the Mind,* Volume I, 4, 13, 191. See also Hannah Arendt, "Thinking and Moral Consideration," *Social Research* 38, no. 3 (Autumn 1971): 417.

221. Arendt, *The Life of the Mind,* Volume I, 124.

222. See H. G. Liddell and R. Scott, *Greek-English Lexicon* (Oxford: Oxford Uni-

versity Press, 1987), 500–501. Cf. Martin Heidegger, "What is Metaphysics?" in *Basic Writings,* ed. D. F. Krell (San Francisco: Harper and Rove, 1977), 108–9.

223. Cf. Hegel, *Logic (1830),* 4, with Arendt, *Life of the Mind,* Volume I, 190–91.

224. Arendt, "What Is Existenz Philosophy?," 42.

225. Adorno, *Kierkegaard,* 81–82.

226. Arendt, *Origins,* 462; Arendt, "What Is Authority?," 99–100.

227. Arendt, *The Life of the Mind,* Volume I, 4, 6. See also Agamben, *Potentialities,* 301 n42.

228. See Arendt, *Life of the Mind,* Volume I, 173, 178, 191. See also Agamben, *Means Without Ends,* 11.

229. See, in this connection, Agamben, *Coming Community,* 37; Agamben, *Potentialities,* 181.

230. Franz Kafka, *The Castle,* trans. M. Harman (New York: Schocken Books, 1998), 56.

231. See Kierkegaard, *Philosophical Fragments,* 76; Gilles Deleuze, *Difference and Repetition,* trans. P. Patton (New York: Columbia University Press, 1995), 167; Arendt, *The Life of the Mind,* Volume I, 123–24.

232. Arendt, *The Life of the Mind,* Volume I, 5–6.

233. See Hegel, *Philosophy of Mind,* 14.

234. Arendt, *The Life of the Mind,* Volume I, 191.

235. Ibid., 192.

236. Ibid. See also Agamben, *Means Without Ends,* 10–11; cf. Derrida, *Politics of Friendship,* 215–16, 223–24, 231.

237. See Arendt, *The Human Condition,* 234–36.

238. Ibid., 246.

239. Ibid., 241.

240. Arendt, "What Remains? The Language Remains," *Essays in Understanding,* ed. J. Kohn (New York: Harcourt, Brace & Co., 1994), 14.

Index

In this index an "f" after a number indicates a separate reference on the next page, and an "ff" indicates separate references on the next two pages. A continuous discussion over two or more pages is indicated by a span of page numbers, e.g., "57–59."